D0700865

Reflections on Community Studies

Reflections on Community Studies

Arthur J. Vidich
Associate Professor of Sociology
and Anthropology, Graduate Faculty,
New School for Social Research

Joseph Bensman
Associate Professor of Sociology,
City College of New York

Maurice R. Stein
Associate Professor of Sociology,
Brandeis University

HARPER TORCHBOOKS
Harper & Row, Publishers
New York, Evanston, San Francisco, London

This book was originally published by John Wiley and Sons, Inc. and is here reprinted by arrangement.

First HARPER TORCHBOOK edition published 1971

STANDARD BOOK NUMBER: 06-131591-5

*To Robert E. Park, Robert S. and Helen M. Lynd,
and W. Lloyd Warner, gratefully*

Preface

This book concerns the methodology of the community study, if by methodology we understand something more than the mechanics of research. The mood which these essays establish is the personal quality of community studies, that is, the intimate connection between the investigator, his methods of investigation, his results, and his own future intellectual development. No one has yet been able to present a formal methodology for the optimum or proper method for the scientific study of the community. This is necessarily so because there is no way to disentangle the research method from the investigator himself.

Anyone who studies a community is as much changed by his work, even while in the midst of it, as the community he studies. During the research and his personal experience of it, the investigator is led into interests and problems that were initially outside the scope of his imagination, so that only with the passage of time does his own work inevitably become fairly sharply defined.

To the extent that the community sociologist responds to his own personal experience, he develops the techniques, methods, and theories necessary to comprehending his particular data. Community sociology at its best always relies on this kind of creative response, so that the great studies, even when the critic might feel they are inadequate or misdirected, always have the quality of individuality, integrity, and discovery. By the same token, nothing in the tradition of community studies points in the direction of a general, ahistorical, all-encompassing theory of society. The complexity of history combined with the particularity of its investigators mitigates against a grand scheme. Intimate contact with the world and its inhabitants usually imposes a certain modesty on the investigator.

Anthropologists constantly use the community study as a standard technique of field research. Those hardy investigators of the primitive and tribal world confront distant and unknown societies whose alien ways of life they have to communicate to their Western readers. Theirs is a straightforward but real problem: how to present an authentic, living portrait of a society. They have no self-consciousness about the community study as a "method" of investigation or any doubts as to its usefulness and validity. For them, social reality thrusts itself forward and demands that a way be found for reducing it to words without unduly offending its integrity as they see it. As a result of their endeavors, the anthropologists have produced a rich library of community studies.

The anthropological style of investigation was first applied to the study of an American community when the Lynds went to Muncie, Indiana, in the early 1920's. The Lynds originally were not academic anthropologists or sociologists, but they had a keen eye and an ear for life in the concrete and, most important, a capacity for detaching themselves from the beliefs and values of the local residents. Because they were able to assume the attitude of the outsider (like the anthropologist, who, however, achieves this attitude much easier because he *is* an alien outsider), the Lynds' study of *Middletown* and their later study of *Middletown in Transition* still stand as important case histories in the description and analysis of American society.

Shortly after the publication of *Middletown in Transition*, W. Lloyd Warner, then recently returned from his study of the Australian aborigines, went to Newburyport to conduct a study of its aborigines by the same techniques he had found so useful among the Murngin. From Warner's experience it is clear that his study of Yankee City has been much more than an application of anthropological methods to the study of a modern community. In Warner we have an example of how the investigator's personal research experience influences his image of the city, of sociology, of modern society, and of himself. It has probably come as a surprise to Warner himself that he should have come back to the basic problems concerning the symbolic coordination of society, which he posed in his Murngin study, in his latest book on Yankee City, *The Living and the Dead*. The link between *The Murngin* and *The Living and the Dead* is Warner's special intellectual problem, but it is also the fundamental problem of the symbolic integration of society, and herein we find the connection between Warner's problem, which he has been driven to solve, and a generic problem, which all students of society have faced. A reading of these two books makes social theory itself come alive because the relationship between theory, theorist, and reality is visible.

It is clear, however, that Warner's encounter with Yankee City involved more than an anthropological study of a tribal community. Newburyport did not quite fit the tribal model. Class structure, labor, the corporation, and the ethnic group did not lend themselves to the ethnographic treatment. Before long Warner found himself embroiled in most of the central issues and problems of modern industrial society, and it is a credit to his intellectual integrity that he faced these problems and made them his own. Because he responded to his reality, we now have a unique and unequaled portrait of an American city which no amount of general theory could ever produce.

But to complete the picture, it was not possible for Warner to ignore the press of his data. Yankee City opened up issues that went far beyond the community, and before long Warner found himself engaged in an examination of the fundamental institutions of American society. *Democracy in Jonesville* and *The Corporation in the Emergent American Society* find Warner grappling with issues central to the fundamental structure of Western institutions. Clearly we have here an example of an investigator whose personal experience is inextricably intertwined with the discovery of the world. Surely a method of investigation which can carry a researcher from *The Murngin* in aboriginal Australia to *The Living and the Dead* in Newburyport is worthy of further examination.

Since the Lynds and Warner, hundreds of studies of communities have been conducted and written. By themselves these studies do not necessarily add up to a description of the "total" society. In fact, any unfriendly critic can easily point to the lack of theoretical accumulation in the total product produced by the community sociologists, but intramural criticism, especially by sociologists who would like to solve all the problems of life in a single theory, is much less important than detailed efforts aimed at capturing the evolving and disappearing reality as it presents itself to the individualistic observers who try to capture it. Community sociologists have certainly not presented an integrated portrait of the world, but this has not been their objective. They have tried, at best, to capture some segment of an elusive reality which would be true to the world of the observed as seen by the particular perspective of the observer. Insofar as the community sociologist is true to his task, his method of investigation remains as a major method in the social sciences.

Critics have pointed out the "weaknesses" of the community study method as a scientific mode of investigation. They have noted that the community portrait usually rests on the observations of a single person, that the procedures of observation are not systematized, that there is no guarantee that another investigator would produce similar results, that the values of the observer cannot be disentangled from his data, and, finally, that there is never any way of knowing if the work is scientifically valid.

But no matter how continuously and intensively the critics have attacked the community studies and their methods, no sooner has the attack been made than there appears another series of frequently independent and unrelated studies which confound the critics. *Middletown, The Yankee City Series, Street Corner Society, Caste and Class in a Southern Town, Deep South, Crestwood Heights, Small Town in Mass Society, The Eclipse of Community, The Living and the Dead,* each has reopened the problems of community inquiry along new and unexpected lines. Moreover, in more recent years the community study method has been applied to mental institutions, prisons, hospitals, schools, and almost all other forms of total institutions characteristic of a bureaucratic world. The capacity for the community study to survive and to illuminate contemporary society may well be intrinsic to its scope, its methods, and its problems.

Over the past thirty or forty years sociology and anthropology have seen the growth of a wide range of highly complex methods and techniques of research as well as a continuous expansion, proliferation, and reformulation of its concepts and basic theories. All of the methodological specialization and complexity of apparatus developed in the interest of creating a scientific anthropology and sociology have given the proponents of these methods a point of departure for denigrating the scientific validity of community studies. After all, statistical methods, computer technology, model building, cross-cultural uniformities, empirical replications, linguistic constructs, theory construction, and so forth, are terms whose scientific tone arises from linguistic habit. Thus the proponents of rigorous method and systematic theory have not found it difficult to pronounce the community study "perhaps acceptable as a branch of humanistic studies, but certainly not to be taken seriously as social science."

The increased specialization of social science under its newer methodologies has led to a continuous narrowing of the specific problem to which any specific study is addressed. One result of this has been any number of highly specialized, technically perfected studies which, however, are characterized by a paucity of concepts, theories, and interpretations capable of presenting any image of the larger society being studied. The development of abstract concepts, complex indices, and statistical devices in the more "scientific" methodologies, and the use of highly "structured" research "instruments" has left the analysts using these instruments in the position of having little direct knowledge of the social world they are supposed to survey. Thus the analyst who uses these instruments is unable to present an image of social behavior as it appears in its "natural setting," because he is not in a position to observe behavior as it is experienced and acted out by the participants described in his study. As a result, as abstract social science progresses, the image of reality which it purports to describe is increasingly lost.

The survival of the community study perhaps can be explained precisely because it has not absorbed too completely the major techniques of the more "advanced" social sciences. Though more recent studies of the community have tended to focus their attention on selected problems rather than attempts to describe the whole community, they have always shown, no matter how imperfectly, the interrelationship between the various segments of community life. As a result the "totality" has neither been neglected nor shattered into unrelated segments. Community researchers have been "functionalists" in the symphonic sense of that term whether they have bothered to use the rhetoric of functionalism or not. As a consequence of the unwillingness of most community researchers to forsake direct observation and direct reporting of the community life, we still have coherent images of the community and social life which are unattainable by other methodologies.

The point may be emphasized by postulating what would result if all research were conducted by questionnaires, surveys, checklists, and the other modern technologies. These devices, which essentially allow the investigator to accumulate a relatively narrow dimension of experience from a large number of persons, produce a collective portrait of responses to an item. Theoretically a sufficient accumulation of such responses, when "recombined," should add up to a total portrait of reality. In actual fact, however, the reality is not reconstitutable because it was from the very beginning a reality evoked in response to the research instrument.

In spite of the grandiose elaboration of research methodologies and abstract theories, it appears that the ear and the eye are still important instruments for gathering data, and that the brain is not always an inefficient mechanism for analyzing them. Because these ancient instruments are still effective, sociologists of all methodological persuasions as well as laymen have come to rely on the community study as a source for their over-all images of society. They use these studies for building their substantive theories of society, and they use them as reference points in doing other research and for their commentaries on the society at large. This dependence has led to a remarkable success for the community research which goes far beyond what might be expected in relation to the number and cost of the studies of communities available to us.

The preceding comments have been based on the assumption that the methodology of community study has been less formalized and less abstract than is true of sociological research in general. It must be recognized, however, that individual community researchers have employed different degrees of methodological formalization in their work, and not all agree as to the amount, kind, or direction such formalization should take. It has been typical of these researchers that they use whatever methods that will enable them to reach a solution to their problem.

Community researchers have been particularly conscious that everything they do in the field, the preparation for entering the field, the process of analyzing data, the intellectual conversations with other students, and the reporting of the study itself are all the methodology of the study, and it is in this sense that we have asked our contributors to conceive of the problem of methodology.

Moreover, almost all students of the community have engaged in other types of research and have employed other research methods, so that the community studies themselves have been methodologically eclectic. The use of diverse techniques has further served as a continuous reminder of the limits of any one method or technique. As a consequence of the quality of their field experience, community researchers have always been uncommitted to any specific method and highly conscious of the relations between their methods, their problems, and their results.

In their writings the community sociologists have displayed a degree of methodological self-consciousness that is unique in the social sciences. This self-consciousness is nowhere better illustrated than in William Foote Whyte's essay "On the Evolution of Street Corner Society," where for the first time we have a full-length description of the relation between a study and the biography, psychology, and intellectual development of its author. We have reprinted his essay in this symposium because it represents such a deeply insightful analysis of the research process. It is because the community sociologists have been methodologically self-conscious and sophisticated that we have undertaken this book.

All the contributors to this volume either have engaged in community research or have been serious students of the community studies. Each has had the experience of confronting a wide range of intractable data. We have asked the contributors to report their reflections of the methodology on which their work rests. However, we have not attempted to prescribe too closely the direction these commentaries should take, since we felt that their direction should be determined by the researcher's own experiences. Instead, in asking our contributors for their reflections on their experiences, we merely indicated an interest in the following problems:

1. The relationship between the community study and the other research work the investigator has conducted.

2. The relationship between the methods of community study and the other methods the investigator has employed.

3. The community research as related to the investigator's emerging consciousness of problems not anticipated in the original plans of the study.

4. The community study as a means of studying problems which have a theoretical focus independent of both the community study method and the particular community studied.

5. The adequacy of alternative theoretical frameworks in the study of the community.

6. Changes and revisions in basic methodology which the investigator might have made in the light of later experience and reflection.

7. The response of the community to the research process and to the publication of the study.

8. Ethical problems involved in the relationship of the researcher with the community.

9. The organization and financing of community research as it is related to the selection of research problems and the collection and treatment of research data.

10. Changes over time in the theoretical focus of community studies and the development of a tradition of community studies.

11. The image of American society emerging from the community study.

12. Problems and issues involved in doing community studies in places other than the United States.

It will be clear that our contributors have addressed themselves to these themes in relation to the specific problems and field situations they confronted in their research. In keeping with the spirit of his original work, each contributor has responded to our suggested themes only insofar as his data and his personal scientific interests were amenable to them. As a result of this procedure, the essays are at once both a series of statements on community study methods and a continuation of the work originally engaged in by the author himself. Therefore, the essays deepen the original studies which are now part of the established literature of community studies and may be read in conjunction with the substantive reports out of which they have grown, and they illustrate a range of methodological issues which have not been treated by the formal discourses on social science methodology.

In undertaking this project, it was not our intention to "solve" any of the methodological problems of the social sciences. Our intention has been just the reverse. If we have been able to show that methodology is always a function of the particular problems under investigation and that each investigator must always confront the methodological problems forced on him by his experience, we will consider this enterprise successful. The problem to which we hope we have contributed a solution, then, is the problem of continuing to keep the issue of methodology an open issue which never has a solution independent of particular substantive problems and investigators.

ARTHUR J. VIDICH
JOSEPH BENSMAN
MAURICE R. STEIN

June 1964

Contents

Part One

The Community Sociologist Discovers the World

1

The Slum: On the Evolution

of Street Corner Society

William F. Whyte

In the years since completing *Street Corner Society,* I have several times sought to teach students the research methods needed for field studies of communities or organizations. Like other instructors in this field, I have been severely handicapped by the paucity of reading matter that I can assign to students.

There are now many good published studies of communities or organizations, but generally the published report gives little attention to the actual process whereby the research was carried out. There have also been some useful statements on methods of research, but, with a few exceptions, they place the discussion entirely on a logical-intellectual basis. They fail to note that the researcher, like his informants, is a social animal. He has a role to play, and he has his own personality needs that must be met in some degree if he is to function successfully. Where the researcher operates out of a university, just going into the field for a few hours at a time, he can keep his personal social life separate from field activity. His problem of role is not quite so complicated. If, on the other hand, the researcher is living for an extended period in the community he is studying, his personal life is inextricably mixed with his research. A real explanation, then, of how the research was done necessarily involves a rather personal account of how the researcher lived during the period of study.

This account of living in the community may help also to explain the process of analysis of the data. The ideas that we have in research are only in part a logical product growing out of a careful weighing of evidence. We do not generally think problems through in a straight line. Often we have the experience of being immersed in a mass of confusing data. We study the data carefully, bringing all our powers of logical analysis to bear upon them. We come up with an idea or two. But still the data do not fall in any coherent pattern. Then we go on living with the data—and with the people—until perhaps some chance occurrence casts a totally different light upon the data, and we begin to see a pattern that we have not seen before. This pattern is not purely an artistic creation. Once we think we see it, we must reexamine our notes and perhaps set out to gather new data in order to determine whether the pattern adequately represents the life we are observing or is simply a product of our imagination. Logic, then, plays an important part. But I am convinced that the actual evolution of research ideas does not take place in accord with the formal statements we read on research methods. The ideas grow up in part out of our immersion in the data and out of the whole process of living. Since so much of this process of analysis proceeds on the unconscious level, I am sure that we can never present a full account of it. However, an account of the way the research was done may help to explain how the pattern of *Street Corner Society* gradually emerged.

I am not suggesting that my approach to *Street Corner Society* should be followed by other researchers. To some extent my approach must be unique to myself, to the particular situation, and to the state of knowledge existing when I began research. On the other hand, there must be some common elements of the field research process. Only as we accumulate a series of accounts of how research was actually done will we be able to go beyond the logical-intellectual picture and learn to describe the actual research process. What follows, then, is simply one contribution toward that end.

Personal Background

I come from a very consistent upper-middle-class background. One grandfather was a doctor; the other, a superintendent of schools. My father was a college professor. My upbringing, therefore, was very far removed from the life I have described in Cornerville.

As Swarthmore College I had two strong interests: economics (mixed with social reform) and writing. In college I wrote a number of short stories and one-act plays. During the summer after college I made an attempt at a novel. This writing was valuable to me largely in what it taught me about myself. Several of the stories appeared in the college literary magazine, and one was accepted for publication (but never published) in *Story* magazine. Three of the one-act plays were produced at Swarthmore in the annual one-act playwriting contest. Not a bad start for someone who had hopes, as I did then, for a writing career. But yet I felt uneasy and dissatisfied. The plays and stories were all fictionalized accounts of events and situations I had experienced or observed myself. When I attempted to go beyond my experience and tackle a novel on a political theme, the result was a complete bust. Even as I wrote the concluding chapters, I realized that the manuscript was worthless. I finished it, I suppose, just so that I could say to myself that I had written a novel.

Now I had read the often-given advice to young writers that they should write out of their own experience, so I had no reason to be ashamed of this limitation. On the other hand, it was when I reflected upon my experience that I became uneasy and dissatisfied. My home life had been very happy and intellectually stimulating—but without adventure. I had never had to struggle over anything. I knew lots of nice people, but almost all of them came from good, solid middle-class backgrounds like my own. In college, of course, I was associating with middle-class students and middle-class professors. I knew nothing about the slums (or the gold coast for that matter). I knew nothing about life in the factories, fields, or mines—except what I had gotten out of books. So I came to feel that I was a pretty dull fellow. At times this sense of dullness became so oppressive that I simply could not think of any stories to write. I began to feel that, if I were really going to write anything worthwhile, I would somehow have to get beyond the narrow social borders of my existence up to that time.

My interest in economics and social reform also led in the direction of *Street Corner Society*. One of my most vivid college memories is of a day spent with a group of students in visiting the slums of Philadelphia. I remember it not only for the images of dilapidated buildings and crowded people but also for the sense of embarrassment I felt as a tourist in the district. I had the common young man's urge to do good to these people, and yet I knew then that the situation was so far beyond anything I could realistically attempt at the time that I felt like an insincere dabbler even to be there. I began to think sometimes about going back to such a district and really learning to know the people and the conditions of their lives.

My social reform urges came out in other forms on the campus. In my sophomore year I was one of a group of fifteen men who resigned from their fraternities amid a good deal of fanfare. This was an exciting time on the campus, and some of the solid fraternity men were fearful lest the structure would crumble under their feet. They should not have worried. Fraternities went right along without us. In my senior year I became involved in another effort at campus reform. This time we were aiming at nothing less than a reorganization of the whole social life of the campus. The movement got off to a promising start but then quickly petered out.

These abortive reform efforts had one great value to me. I saw that reform was not so easy. I recognized that I had made a number of mistakes. I also came to the realization that some of the people who had fought against me the hardest were really pretty nice fellows. I did not conclude from this that they were right and I was wrong, but I came to recognize how little I really knew about the forces that move people to action. Out of my own reflections about the failures of my campus reform efforts grew a keener interest in understanding other people.

There was also a book that I had read, which weighed most heavily with me at this time. It was the *Autobiography of Lincoln Steffens*. I got my hands on it during the year I spent in Germany between high school and college. In my efforts to master German, this was the only thing written in English that I read for some time, so perhaps it weighed more heavily with me than it otherwise would. In any case I was fascinated by it and read it through several times. Steffens had begun as a reformer, and he never abandoned this urge to change things. Yet he had such an unending curiosity about the world around him that he became more and more interested in discovering how society actually functioned. He demonstrated that a man of a background similar to my own could step out of his own usual walks of life and gain an intimate knowledge of individuals and groups whose activities and beliefs were far different from his own. So you could actually get these "corrupt politicians" to talk to you. This I needed to know. It helped me sometimes when I had the feeling that the people I was interviewing would much rather have me get out of there altogether.

Finding Cornerville

When I was graduated from Swarthmore in 1936, I received a fellowship from the Society of Fellows at Harvard. This provided me with a unique sort of opportunity—three years of support for any line of research I wished to pursue. The only restriction was that I was not allowed to accumulate credits toward a Ph.D. degree.

I am grateful now for this restriction. If I had been allowed to work for the Ph.D., I suppose I should have felt that I must take advantage of the time and the opportunity. With this avenue cut off, I was forced to do what I wanted to do, regardless of academic credits.

I began with a vague idea that I wanted to study a slum district. Eastern City provided several possible choices. In the early weeks of my Harvard fellowship I spent some of my time talking up and down the streets of the various slum districts of Eastern City and talking with people in social agencies about these districts.

I made my choice on very unscientific grounds: Cornerville best fitted my picture of what a slum district should look like. Somehow I had developed a picture of run-down three- to five-story buildings crowded in together. The dilapidated wooden-frame buildings of some other parts of the city did not look quite genuine to me. To be sure, Cornerville did have one characteristic that recommended it on a little more objective basis. It had more people per acre living in it than any other section of the city. If a slum meant overcrowding, this was certainly it.

Planning the Study

As soon as I had found my slum district, I set about planning my study. It was not enough for me at the time to plan for myself alone. I had begun reading in the sociological literature and thinking along the lines of the Lynds' *Middletown*. Gradually I came to think of myself as a sociologist or a social anthropologist instead of an economist. I found that, while slums had been given much attention in the sociological literature, there existed no real community study of such a district. So I set out to organize a community study for Cornerville. This was clearly a big job. My early outline of the study pointed to special researches in the history of the district, in economics (living standards, housing, marketing, distribution, and employment), politics (the structure of the political organization and its relation to the rackets and the police), patterns of education and recreation, the church, public health, and—of all things—social attitudes. Obviously, this was more than a one-man job, so I designed it for about ten men.

With this project statement in hand I approached L. J. Henderson, an eminent biochemist who was secretary of the Society of Fellows.

We spent an hour together, and I came away with my plans very much in a state of flux. As I wrote to a friend at this time:

Henderson poured cold water on the mammoth beginning, told me that I should not cast such grandiose plans when I had done hardly any work in the field myself. It would be much sounder to get in the field and try to build up a staff slowly as I went along. If I should get a ten-man project going by fall, the responsibility for the direction and co-ordination of it would inevitably fall upon me, since I would have started it. How could I direct ten people in a field that was unfamiliar to me? Henderson said that, if I did manage to get a ten-man project going, it would be the ruination of me, he thought. Now, the way he put all this it sounded quite sensible and reasonable.

This last sentence must have been written after I had had time to recover from the interview, because I remember it as being a crushing experience. I suppose good advice is just as hard to take as poor advice, and yet in a very short time I realized that Henderson was right, and I abandoned the grandiose plan I had made. Since people who offer painful but good advice so seldom get any thanks for it, I shall always be glad that I went to see Henderson again shortly before his death and told him that I had come to feel that he had been absolutely right.

While I abandoned the ten-man project, I was reluctant to come down to earth altogether. It seemed to me that, in view of the magnitude of the task I was undertaking, I must have at least one collaborator, and I began to cast about for means of getting a college friend of mine to join me in the field. There followed through the winter of 1936–1937 several revisions of my outline of the community study and numerous interviews with Harvard professors who might help me to get the necessary backing.

As I read over these various research outlines, it seems to me that the most impressive thing about them is their remoteness from the actual study I carried on. As I went along, the outlines became gradually more sociological, so that I wound up this phase planning to devote major emphasis to a sort of sociometric study of the friend-ship patterns of people. I would start with one family and ask them who their friends were and who the people were that they were more or less hostile to. Then I would go to these friends and get the list of their friends and learn in the process something of their activities together. In this way I was to chart the social structure of at least some of the community. Even this, of course, I did not do, for I came to find that you could examine social structure directly through observing people in action.

When, a year later in the fall of 1937, John Howard, also a Harvard junior fellow, changed his field from physical chemistry to sociology,

I invited him to join me in the Cornerville study. We worked together for two years, with Howard particularly concentrating on one of the churches and its Holy Name Society. The discussions between us helped immensely in clarifying my ideas. But only a few months after I had begun Cornerville field work, I had completely abandoned the thought of building up a Cornerville staff. I suppose that I found Cornerville life so interesting and rewarding that I no longer felt a need to think in large-scale terms.

Although I was completely at sea in planning the study, at least I had valuable help in developing the field research methods which were eventually to lead to a study plan as well as to the data here reported.

It is hard to realize now how rapid has been the development of sociological and anthropological studies of communities and organizations since 1936, when I began my work in Cornerville. At that time nothing had yet been published on W. Lloyd Warner's "Yankee City" study. I had read the Lynds' *Middletown* and Carolyn Ware's *Greenwich Village* with interest and profit, and yet I began to realize, more and more as I went along, that I was not making a community study along those lines. Much of the other sociological literature then available tended to look upon communities in terms of social problems so that the community as an organized social system simply did not exist.

I spent my first summer following the launching of the study in reading some of the writings of Durkheim and Pareto's *The Mind and Society* (for a seminar with L. J. Henderson, which I was to take in the fall of 1937). I had a feeling that these writings were helpful but still only in a general way. Then I began reading in the social anthropological literature, beginning with Malinowski, and this seemed closer to what I wanted to do even though the researchers were studying primitive tribes and I was in the middle of a great city district.

If there was then little to guide me in the literature, I needed that much more urgently to have the help of people more skilled and experienced than I in the work I was undertaking. Here I was extraordinarily fortunate in meeting Conrad M. Arensberg at the very outset of my Harvard appointment. He also was a junior fellow, so that we naturally saw much of each other. After having worked for some months with W. Lloyd Warner in the Yankee City study, he had gone with Solon Kimball to make a study of a small community in Ireland. When I met him he had just returned from this field trip and was beginning to write up his data. With Eliot Chapple, he was also in the process of working out a new approach to the analysis of social organization. The two men had been casting about together for ways of establishing such social research on a more scientific basis. Going over the Yankee City data and the Irish study, also, they had set up five different theoretical schemes. One after the other each of the first four schemes fell to the ground under their own searching criticism or under the prods of Henderson or Elton Mayo or others whom they consulted. At last they began to develop a theory of interaction. They felt that, whatever else might be subjective in social research, one could establish objectively the pattern of interaction among people: how often A contacts B, how long they spend together, who originates action when A, B, and C are together, and so on. Careful observation of such interpersonal events might then provide reliable data upon the social organization of a community. At least this was the assumption. Since the theory grew out of research already done, it was natural that these previous studies did not contain as much of the quantitative data as the theory would have required. So it seemed that I might be one of the first to take the theory out into the field.

Arensberg and I had endless discussions of the theory, and in some of these Eliot Chapple participated. At first it seemed very confusing to me—I am not sure I have it all clear yet—but I had a growing feeling that here was something solid that I could build upon.

Arensberg also worked with me on field research methods, emphasizing the importance of observing people in action and getting down a detailed report of actual behavior completely divorced from moral judgments. In my second semester at Harvard, I took a course given by Arensberg and Chapple concerning social anthropological community studies. While this was helpful, I owed much more to the long personal conversations I had with Arensberg throughout the Cornerville research, particularly in its early stages.

In the fall of 1937 I took a small seminar with Elton Mayo. This involved particularly readings from the works of Pierre Janet, and it included also some practice in interviewing psychoneurotics in an Eastern City hospital. This experience was too brief to carry me beyond the amateur stage, but it was helpful in developing my interviewing methods.

L. J. Henderson provided a less specific but nevertheless pervasive influence in the development of my methods and theories. As chairman of the Society of Fellows, he presided over our Monday-night dinners like a patriarch in his own household. Even though the group included A. Lawrence Lowell, Alfred North Whitehead, John Livingston Lowes, Samuel Eliot Morrison, and Arthur Darby Nock, it was Henderson who was easily the most imposing figure for the junior fellows. He seemed particularly to enjoy baiting the young social scientists. He took me on at my first Monday-night dinner and undertook to show me that all my ideas about society were based upon softheaded sentimentality. While I often resented Henderson's sharp criticisms, I was all the more determined to make my field research stand up against anything he could say.

First Efforts

When I began my work, I had had no training in sociology or anthropology. I thought of myself as an economist and naturally looked first toward the matters that we had taken up in economics courses, such as economics of slum housing. At the time I was sitting in on a course in slums and housing in the Sociology Department at Harvard. As a term project I took on a study of one block in Cornerville. To legitimize this effort, I got in touch with a private agency that concerned itself in housing matters and offered to turn over to them the results of my survey. With that backing, I began knocking on doors, looking into flats, and talking to the tenants about the living conditions. This brought me into contact with Cornerville people, but it would be hard now to devise a more inappropriate way of beginning a study such as I was eventually to make. I felt ill at ease at this intrusion, and I am sure so did the people. I wound up the block study as rapidly as I could and wrote it off as a total loss as far as gaining a real entry into the district.

Shortly thereafter I made another false start—if so tentative an effort may even be called a start. At the time I was completely baffled at the problem of finding my way into the district. Cornerville was right before me and yet so far away. I could walk freely up and down its streets, and I had even made my way into some of the flats, and yet I was still a stranger in a world completely unknown to me.

At this time I met a young economics instructor at Harvard who impressed me with his self-assurance and his knowledge of Eastern City. He had once been attached to a settlement house, and he talked glibly about his associations with the tough young men and women of the district. He also described how he would occasionally drop in on some drinking place in the area and strike up an acquaintance with a girl, buy her a drink, and then encourage her to tell him her life story. He claimed that the women so encountered were appreciative of this opportunity and that it involved no further obligation.

This approach seemed at least as plausible as anything I had been able to think of. I resolved to try it out. I picked on the Regal Hotel, which was on the edge of Cornerville. With some trepidation I climbed the stairs to the bar and entertainment area and looked around. There I encountered a situation for which my adviser had not prepared me. There were women present all right, but none of them was alone. Some were there in couples, and there were two or three pairs of women together. I pondered this situation briefly. I had little confidence in my skill at picking up one female, and it seemed inadvisable to tackle two at the same time. Still, I was determined not to admit defeat without a struggle. I looked around me again and now noticed a threesome: one man and two women. It occurred to me that here was a maldistribution of females which I might be able to rectify. I approached the group and opened with something like this: "Pardon me. Would you mind if I joined you?" There was a moment of silence while the man stared at me. He then offered to throw me downstairs. I assured him that this would not be necessary and demonstrated as much by walking right out of there without any assistance.

I subsequently learned that hardly anyone from Cornerville ever went into the Regal Hotel. If my efforts there had been crowned with success, they would no doubt have led somewhere but certainly not to Cornerville.

For my next effort I sought out the local settlement houses. They were open to the public. You could walk right into them, and—though I would not have phrased it this way at the time—they were manned by middle-class people like myself. I realized even then that to study Cornerville I would have to go well beyond the settlement house, but perhaps the social workers could help me to get started.

As I look back on it now, the settlement house also seems a very unpromising place from which to begin such a study. If I had it to do over again, I would probably make my first approach through a local politician or perhaps through the Catholic church, although I am not myself Catholic. John Howard, who worked with me later, made his entry very successfully through the church, and he, too, was not a Catholic—although his wife was.

However that may be, the settlement house proved the right place for me at this time, for it was here that I met Doc. I had talked to a number of the social workers about my plans and hopes to get

acquainted with the people and study the district. They listened
with varying degrees of interest. If they had suggestions to make,
I have forgotten them now except for one. Somehow, in spite of the
vagueness of my own explanations, the head of girls' work in the
Norton Street House understood what I needed. She began describing Doc to me. He was, she said, a very intelligent and talented
person who had at one time been fairly active in the house but had
dropped out, so that he hardly ever came in any more. Perhaps he
could understand what I wanted, and he must have the contacts that
I needed. She said she frequently encountered him as she walked
to and from the house and sometimes stopped to chat with him. If
I wished, she would make an appointment for me to see him in the
house one evening. This at last seemed right. I jumped at the
chance. As I came into the district that evening, it was with a feeling
that here I had my big chance to get started. Somehow Doc must
accept me and be willing to work with me.

In a sense, my study began on the evening of February 4, 1937,
when the social worker called me in to meet Doc. She showed us
into her office and then left so that we could talk. Doc waited quietly
for me to begin, as he sank down into a chair. I found him a man
of medium height and spare build. His hair was a light brown,
quite a contrast to the more typical black Italian hair. It was thinning
around the temples. His cheeks were sunken. His eyes were a light
blue and seemed to have a penetrating gaze.

I began by asking him if the social worker had told him about
what I was trying to do.

"No, she just told me that you wanted to meet me and that I should
like to meet you."

Then I went into a long explanation which, unfortunately, I omitted
from my notes. As I remember it, I said that I had been interested
in congested city districts in my college study but had felt very
remote from them. I hoped to study the problems in such a district.
I felt I could do very little as an outsider. Only if I could get to
know the people and learn their problems first hand would I be able
to gain the understanding I needed.

Doc heard me out without any change of expression, so that I had
no way of predicting his reaction. When I was finished, he asked:
"Do you want to see the high life or the low life?"

"I want to see all that I can. I want to get as complete a picture
of the community as possible."

"Well, any nights you want to see anything, I'll take you around.
I can take you to the joints—gambling joints—I can take you around

to the street corners. Just remember that you're my friend. That's all they need to know. I know these places, and, if I tell them that you're my friend, nobody will bother you. You just tell me what you want to see, and we'll arrange it."

The proposal was so perfect that I was at a loss for a moment as to how to respond to it. We talked a while longer, as I sought to get some pointers as to how I should behave in his company. He warned me that I might have to take the risk of getting arrested in a raid on a gambling joint but added that this was not serious. I only had to give a false name and then would get bailed out by the man that ran the place, paying only a five-dollar fine. I agreed to take this chance. I asked him whether I should gamble with the others in the gambling joints. He said it was unnecessary and, for a greenhorn like myself, very inadvisable.

At last I was able to express my appreciation. "You know, the first steps of getting to know a community are the hardest. I could see things going with you that I wouldn't see for years otherwise."

"That's right. You tell me what you want to see, and we'll arrange it. When you want some information, I'll ask for it, and you listen. When you want to find out their philosophy of life, I'll start an argument and get it for you. If there's something else you want to get, I'll stage an act for you. Not a scrap, you know, but just tell me what you want, and I'll get it for you."

"That's swell. I couldn't ask for anything better. Now I'm going to try to fit in all right, but, if at any time you see I'm getting off on the wrong foot, I want you to tell me about it."

"Now we're being too dramatic. You won't have any trouble. You come in as my friend. When you come in like that, at first everybody will treat you with respect. You can take a lot of liberties, and nobody will kick. After a while when they get to know you they will treat you like anybody else—you know, they say familiarity breeds contempt. But you'll never have any trouble. There's just one thing to watch out for. Don't spring [treat] people. Don't be too free with your money."

"You mean they'll think I'm a sucker?"

"Yes, and you don't want to buy your way in."

We talked a little about how and when we might get together. Then he asked me a question. "You want to write something about this?"

"Yes, eventually."

"Do you want to change things?"

"Well—yes. I don't see how anybody could come down here where it is so crowded, people haven't got any money or any work to do, and not want to have some things changed. But I think a fellow should do the thing he is best fitted for. I don't want to be a reformer, and I'm not cut out to be a politician. I just want to understand these things as best I can and write them up, and if that has any influence. . . ."

"I think you can change things that way. Mostly that is the way things are changed, by writing about them."

That was our beginning. At the time I found it hard to believe that I could move in as easily as Doc had said with his sponsorship. But that indeed was the way it turned out.

While I was taking my first steps with Doc, I was also finding a place to live in Cornerville. My fellowship provided a very comfortable bedroom, living room, and bath at Harvard. I had been attempting to commute from these quarters to my Cornerville study. Technically that was possible, but socially I became more and more convinced that it was impossible. I realized that I would always be a stranger to the community if I did not live there. Then, also, I found myself having difficulty putting in the time that I knew was required to establish close relations in Cornerville. Life in Cornerville did not proceed on the basis of formal appointments. To meet people, to get to know them, to fit into their activities, required spending time with them—a lot of time day after day. Commuting to Cornerville, you might come in on a particular afternoon and evening only to discover that the people you intended to see did not happen to be around at the time. Or, even if you did see them, you might find the time passing entirely uneventfully. You might just be standing around with people whose only occupation was talking or walking about to try to keep themselves from being bored.

On several afternoons and evenings at Harvard, I found myself considering a trip to Cornerville and then rationalizing my way out of it. How did I know I would find the people whom I meant to see? Even if I did so, how could I be sure that I would learn anything today? Instead of going off on a wild-goose chase to Cornerville, I could profitably spend my time reading books and articles to fill in my woeful ignorance of sociology and social anthropology. Then, too, I had to admit that I felt more comfortable among these familiar surroundings than I did wandering around Cornerville and spending time with people in whose presence I felt distinctly uncomfortable at first.

When I found myself rationalizing in this way, I realized that I would have to make the break. Only if I lived in Cornerville would

I ever be able to understand it and be accepted by it. Finding a place, however, was not easy. In such an overcrowded district a spare room was practically nonexistent. I might have been able to take a room in the Norton Street Settlement House, but I realized that I must do better than this if possible.

I got my best lead from the editor of a weekly English-language newspaper published for the Italian-American colony. I had talked to him before about my study and had found him sympathetic. Now I came to ask him for help in finding a room. He directed me to the Martinis, a family which operated a small restaurant. I went there for lunch and later consulted the son of the family. He was sympathetic but said that they had no place for any additional person. Still, I liked the place and enjoyed the food. I came back several times just to eat. On one occasion I met the editor, and he invited me to his table. At first he asked me some searching questions about my study: what I was after, what my connection with Harvard was, what they had expected to get out of this, and so on. After I had answered him in a manner that I unfortunately failed to record in my notes, he told me that he was satisfied and, in fact, had already spoken in my behalf to people who were suspicious that I might be coming in to "criticize our people."

We discussed my rooming problem again. I mentioned the possibility of living at the Norton Street House. He nodded but added: "It would be much better if you could be in a family. You would pick up the language much quicker, and you would get to know the people. But you want a nice family, an educated family. You don't want to get in with any low types. You want a real good family."

At this he turned to the son of the family with whom I had spoken and asked: "Can't you make some place for Mr. Whyte in the house here?"

Al Martini paused a moment and then said: "Maybe we can fix it up. I'll talk to Mama again."

So he did talk to Mama again, and they did find a place. In fact, he turned over to me his own room and moved in to share a double bed with the son of the cook. I protested mildly at this imposition, but everything had been decided—except for the money. They did not know what to charge me, and I did not know what to offer. Finally, after some fencing, I offered fifteen dollars a month, and they settled for twelve.

The room was simple but adequate to my purposes. It was not heated, but, when I began to type my notes there, I got myself a small oil-burner. There was no bathtub in the house, but I had to go out to Harvard now and then anyway, so I used the facilities of the great university (the room of my friend, Henry Guerlac) for an occasional tub or shower.

Physically, the place was livable, and it provided me with more than just a physical base. I had been with the Martinis for only a week when I discovered that I was much more than a roomer to them. I had been taking many of my meals in the restaurant and sometimes stopping in to chat with the family before I went to bed at night. Then one afternoon I was out at Harvard and found myself coming down with a bad cold. Since I still had my Harvard room, it seemed the sensible thing to do to stay overnight there. I did not think to tell the Martinis of my plan.

The next day when I was back in the restaurant for lunch, Al Martini greeted me warmly and then said that they had all been worried when I did not come home the night before. Mama had stayed up until two o'clock waiting for me. As I was just a young stranger in the city, she could visualize all sorts of things happening to me. Al told me that Mama had come to look upon me as one of the family. I was free to come and go as I pleased, but she wouldn't worry so much if she knew of my plans.

I was very touched by this plea and resolved thereafter to be as good a son as I could to the Martinis.

At first I communicated with Mama and Papa primarily in smiles and gestures. Papa knew no English at all, and Mama's knowledge was limited to one sentence which she would use when some of the young boys on the street were making noise below her window when she was trying to get her afternoon nap. She would then poke her head out of the window and shout: "Goddam-sonumabitcha! Geroutahere!"

Some weeks earlier, in anticipation of moving into the district, I had begun working on the Italian language myself with the aid of a Linguaphone. One morning now Papa Martini came by when I was talking to the phonograph record. He listened for a few moments in the hall trying to make sense out of this peculiar conversation. Then he burst in upon me with fascinated exclamations. We sat down together while I demonstrated the machine and the method to him. After that he delighted in working with me, and I called him my language professor. In a short time we reached a stage where I could carry on simple conversations, and, thanks to the Linguaphone and Papa Martini, the Italian that came out apparently sounded authentic. He liked to try to pass me off to his friends as *paesano mio*—a man from his own home town in Italy. When I was careful to keep my remarks within the limits of my vocabulary, I could sometimes pass as an immigrant from the village of Viareggio in the province of Tuscany.

Since my research developed so that I was concentrating almost exclusively upon the younger, English-speaking generation, my knowledge of Italian proved unnecessary for research purposes. Nevertheless, I feel certain that it was important in establishing my social position in Cornerville—even with that younger generation. There were schoolteachers and social workers who had worked in Cornerville for as much as twenty years and yet had made no effort to learn Italian. My effort to learn the language probably did more to establish the sincerity of my interest in the people than anything I could have told them of myself and my work. How could a researcher be planning to "criticize our people" if he went to the lengths of learning the language? With language comes understanding, and surely it is easier to criticize people if you do not understand them.

My days with the Martinis would pass in this manner. I would get up in the morning around nine o'clock and go out to breakfast. Al Martini told me I could have breakfast in the restaurant, but, for all my desire to fit in, I never could take their breakfast of coffee with milk and a crust of bread.

After breakfast, I returned to my room and spent the rest of the morning, or most of it, typing up my notes regarding the previous day's events. I had lunch in the restaurant and then set out for the street corner. Usually I was back for dinner in the restaurant and then out again for the evening.

Usually I came home again between eleven and twelve o'clock, at a time when the restaurant was empty except perhaps for a few family friends. Then I might join Papa in the kitchen to talk as I helped him dry the dishes, or pull up a chair into a family conversation around one of the tables next to the kitchen. There I had a glass of wine to sip, and I could sit back and mostly listen but occasionally try out my growing Italian on them.

The pattern was different on Sunday, when the restaurant was closed at two o'clock, and Al's two brothers and his sister and the wives, husband, and children would come in for a big Sunday dinner. They insisted that I eat with them at this time and as a member of the family, not paying for my meal. It was always more than I could eat, but it was delicious, and I washed it down with two tumblers of Zinfandel wine. Whatever strain there had been in my work in the preceding week would pass away now as I ate and drank and then went to my room for an afternoon nap of an hour or two that brought me back completely refreshed and ready to set forth again for the corners of Cornerville.

Though I made several useful contacts in the restaurant or through the family, it was not for this that the Martinis were important to me. There is a strain to doing such field work. The strain is greatest when you are a stranger and are constantly wondering whether people are going to accept you. But, much as you enjoy your work, as long as you are observing and interviewing, you have a role to play, and you are not completely relaxed. It was a wonderful feeling at the end of a day's work to be able to come home to relax and enjoy myself with the family. Probably it would have been impossible for me to carry on such a concentrated study of Cornerville if I had not had such a home from which to go out and to which I might return.

Beginning with Doc

I can still remember my first outing with Doc. We met one evening at the Norton Street House and set out from there to a gambling place a couple of blocks away. I followed Doc anxiously down the long, dark hallway at the back of a tenement building. I was not worried about the possibility of a police raid. I was thinking about how I would fit in and be accepted. The door opened into a small kitchen almost bare of furnishings and with the paint peeling off the walls. As soon as we went in the door, I took off my hat and began looking around for a place to hang it. There was no place. I looked around, and here I learned my first lesson in participant observation in Cornerville: Don't take off your hat in the house—at least not when you are among men. It may be permissible, but certainly not required, to take your hat off when women are around.

Doc introduced me as "my friend Bill" to Chichi, who ran the place, and to Chichi's friends and customers. I stayed there with Doc part of the time in the kitchen, where several men would sit around and talk, and part of the time in the other room watching the crap game.

There was talk about gambling, horse races, sex, and other matters. Mostly I just listened and tried to act friendly and interested. We had wine and coffee with anisette in it, with the fellows chipping in to pay for the refreshments. (Doc would not let me pay my share on this first occasion.) As Doc had predicted, no one asked me about myself, but he told me later that, when I went to the toilet, there was an excited burst of conversation in Italian and that he had to assure them that I was not a G-man. He said he told them flatly that I was a friend of his, and they agreed to let it go at that.

We went several more times together to Chichi's gambling joint, and then the time came when I dared to go in alone. When I was greeted in a natural and friendly manner, I felt that I was now beginning to find a place for myself in Cornerville.

When Doc did not go off to the gambling joint, he spent his time hanging around Norton Street, and I began hanging with him. At first, Norton Street meant only a place to wait until I could go somewhere else. Gradually, as I got to know the men better, I found myself becoming one of the Norton Street gang.

Then the Italian Community Club was formed in the Norton Street Settlement, and Doc was invited to be a member. Doc maneuvered to get me into the club, and I was glad to join, as I could see that it represented something distinctly different from the corner gangs I was meeting.

As I began to meet the men of Cornerville, I also met a few of the girls. One girl I took to a church dance. The next morning the fellows on the street corner were asking me: "How's your steady girl?" This brought me up short. I learned that going to the girl's house was something that you just did not do unless you hoped to marry her. Fortunately, the girl and her family knew that I did not know the local customs, so they did not assume that I was thus committed. However, this was a useful warning. After this time, even though I found some Cornerville girls exceedingly attractive, I never went out with them except on a group basis, and I did not make any more home visits either.

As I went along, I found that life in Cornerville was not nearly so interesting and pleasant for the girls as it was for the men. A young man had complete freedom to wander and hang around. The girls could not hang on street corners. They had to divide their time between their own homes, the homes of girl friends and relatives, and a job, if they had one. Many of them had a dream that went like this: some young man, from outside of Cornerville, with a little money, a good job, and a good education would come and woo them and take them out of the district. I could hardly afford to fill this role.

Training in Participant Observation

The spring of 1937 provided me with an intensive course in participant observation. I was learning how to conduct myself, and I learned from various groups but particularly from the Nortons.

As I began hanging about Cornerville, I found that I needed an explanation for myself and for my study. As long as I was with Doc and vouched for by him, no one asked me who I was or what I was doing. When I circulated in other groups or even among the Nortons without him, it was obvious that they were curious about me.

I began with a rather elaborate explanation. I was studying the social history of Cornerville—but I had a new angle. Instead of working from the past up to the present, I was seeking to get a thorough knowledge of present conditions and then work from present to past. I was quite pleased with this explanation at the time, but nobody else seemed to care for it. I gave the explanation on only two occasions, and each time, when I had finished, there was an awkward silence. No one, myself included, knew what to say.

While this explanation had at least the virtue of covering everything that I might eventually want to do in the district, it was apparently too involved to mean anything to Cornerville people.

I soon found that people were developing their own explanation about me: I was writing a book about Cornerville. This might seem entirely too vague an explanation, and yet it sufficed. I found that my acceptance in the district depended on the personal relationships I developed far more than upon any explanations I might give. Whether it was a good thing to write a book about Cornerville depended entirely on people's opinions of me personally. If I was all right, then my project was all right; if I was no good, then no amount of explanation could convince them that the book was a good idea.

Of course people did not satisfy their curiosity about me simply by questions that they addressed to me directly. They turned to Doc, for example, and asked him about me. Doc then answered the questions and provided any reassurance that was needed.

I learned early in my Cornerville period the crucial importance of having the support of the key individuals in any groups or organizations I was studying. Instead of trying to explain myself to everyone, I found I was providing far more information about myself and my study to leaders such as Doc than I volunteered to the average corner boy. I always tried to give the impression that I was willing and eager to tell just as much about my study as anyone wished to know, but it was only with group leaders that I made a particular effort to provide really full information.

My relationship with Doc changed rapidly in this early Cornerville period. At first he was simply a key informant—and also my sponsor. As we spent more time together, I ceased to treat him as a passive informant. I discussed with him quite frankly what I was trying to do, what problems were puzzling me, and so on. Much of our time was spent in this discussion of ideas and observations, so that Doc became, in a very real sense, a collaborator in the research.

This full awareness of the nature of my study stimulated Doc to look for and point out to me the sorts of observations that I was interested in. Often when I picked him up at the flat where he lived with his sister and brother-in-law, he said to me: "Bill, you should have been around last night. You would have been interested in this." And then he would go on to tell me what had happened. Such accounts were always interesting and relevant to my study.

Doc found this experience of working with me interesting and enjoyable, and yet the relationship had its drawbacks. He once commented: "You've slowed me up plenty since you've been down here. Now, when I do something, I have to think what Bill Whyte would want to know about it and how I can explain it. Before, I used to do things by instinct."

However, Doc did not seem to consider this a serious handicap. Actually, without any training he was such a perceptive observer that it only needed a little stimulus to help him to make explicit much of the dynamics of the social organization of Cornerville. Some of the interpretations I have made are his more than mine, although it is now impossible to disentangle them.

While I worked more closely with Doc than with any other individual, I always sought out the leader in whatever group I was studying. I wanted not only sponsorship from him but also more active collaboration with the study. Since these leaders had the sort of position in the community that enabled them to observe much better than the followers what was going on and since they were in general more skillful observers than the followers, I found that I had much to learn from a more active collaboration with them.

In my interviewing methods I had been instructed not to argue with people or pass moral judgments upon them. This fell in with my own inclinations. I was glad to accept the people and to be accepted by them. However, this attitude did not come out so much in interviewing, for I did little formal interviewing. I sought to show this interested acceptance of the people and the community in my everyday participation.

I learned to take part in the street corner discussions on baseball and sex. This required no special training, since the topics seemed to be matters of almost universal interest. I was not able to participate so actively in discussions of horse racing. I did begin to follow the races in a rather general and amateur way. I am sure it would have paid me to devote more study to the *Morning Telegraph* and other racing sheets, but my knowledge of baseball at least insured that I would not be left out of the street corner conversations.

While I avoided expressing opinions on sensitive topics, I found that arguing on some matters was simply part of the social pattern and that one could hardly participate without joining in the argument. I often found myself involved in heated but good-natured arguments about the relative merits of certain major-league ball players and managers. Whenever a girl or a group of girls would walk down the street, the fellows on the corner would make mental notes and later would discuss their evaluations of the females. These evaluations would run largely in terms of shape, and here I was glad to argue that Mary had a better "build" than Anna, or vice versa. Of course, if any of the men on the corner happened to be personally attached to Mary or Anna, no searching comments would be made, and I, too, would avoid this topic.

Sometimes I wondered whether just hanging on the street corner was an active enough process to be dignified by the term "research." Perhaps I should be asking these men questions. However, one has to learn when to question and when not to question as well as what questions to ask.

I learned this lesson one night in the early months when I was with Doc in Chichi's gambling joint. A man from another part of the city was regaling us with a tale of the organization of gambling activity. I had been told that he had once been a very big gambling operator, and he talked knowingly about many interesting matters. He did most of the talking, but the others asked questions and threw in comments, so at length I began to feel that I must say something in order to be part of the group. I said: "I suppose the cops were all paid off?"

The gambler's jaw dropped. He glared at me. Then he denied vehemently that any policemen had been paid off and immediately switched the conversation to another subject. For the rest of that evening I felt very uncomfortable.

The next day Doc explained the lesson of the previous evening. "Go easy on that 'who,' 'what,' 'why,' 'when,' 'where' stuff, Bill. You ask those questions, and people will clam up on you. If people accept you, you can just hang around, and you'll learn the answers in the long run without even having to ask the questions."

I found that this was true. As I sat and listened, I learned the answers to questions that I would not even have had the sense to ask if I had been getting my information solely on an interviewing basis. I did not abandon questioning altogether, of course. I simply learned to judge the sensitiveness of the question and my relationship to the people so that I only asked a question in a sensitive area when I was sure that my relationship to the people involved was very solid.

When I had established my position on the street corner, the data simply came to me without very active efforts on my part. It was only now and then, when I was concerned with a particular problem and felt I needed more information from a certain individual, that I would seek an opportunity to get the man alone and carry on a more formal interview.

At first I concentrated upon fitting into Cornerville, but a little later I had to face the question of how far I was to immerse myself in the life of the district. I bumped into that problem one evening as I was walking down the street with the Nortons. Trying to enter into the spirit of the small talk, I cut loose with a string of obscenities and profanity. The walk came to a momentary halt as they all stopped to look at me in surprise. Doc shook his head and said: "Bill, you're not supposed to talk like that. That doesn't sound like you."

I tried to explain that I was only using terms that were common on the street corner. Doc insisted, however, that I was different and that they wanted me to be that way.

This lesson went far beyond the use of obscenity and profanity. I learned that people did not expect me to be just like them; in fact, they were interested and pleased to find me different, just so long as I took a friendly interest in them. Therefore, I abandoned my efforts at complete immersion. My behavior was nevertheless affected by street corner life. When John Howard first came down from Harvard to join me in the Cornerville study, he noticed at once that I talked in Cornerville in a manner far different from that which I used at Harvard. This was not a matter of the use of profanity or obscenity, nor did I affect the use of ungrammatical expressions. I talked in the way that seemed natural to me, but what was natural in Cornerville was different from what was natural at Harvard. In Cornerville, I found myself putting much more animation into my speech, dropping terminal g's, and using gestures much more actively. (There was also, of course, the difference in the vocabulary that I used. When I was most deeply involved in Cornerville, I found myself rather tongue-tied in my visits to Harvard. I simply could not keep up with the discussions of international relations, of the nature of science, and so on, in which I had once been more or less at home.)

As I became accepted by the Nortons and by several other groups,

I tried to make myself pleasant enough so that people would be glad to have me around. And, at the same time, I tried to avoid influencing the group, because I wanted to study the situation as unaffected by my presence as possible. Thus, throughout my Cornerville stay, I avoided accepting office or leadership positions in any of the groups with a single exception. At one time I was nominated as secretary of the Italian Community Club. My first impulse was to decline the nomination, but then I reflected that the secretary's job is normally considered simply a matter of dirty work—writing the minutes and handling the correspondence. I accepted and found that I could write a very full account of the progress of the meeting as it went on under the pretext of keeping notes for the minutes.

While I sought to avoid influencing individuals or groups, I tried to be helpful in the way a friend is expected to help in Cornerville. When one of the boys had to go downtown on an errand and wanted company, I went along with him. When somebody was trying to get a job and had to write a letter about himself, I helped him to compose it, and so on. This sort of behavior presented no problem, but, when it came to the matter of handling money, it was not at all clear just how I should behave. Of course, I sought to spend money on my friends just as they did on me. But what about lending money? It is expected in such a district that a man will help out his friends whenever he can, and often the help needed is financial. I lent money on several occasions, but I always felt uneasy about it. Naturally, a man appreciates it at the time you lend him the money, but how does he feel later when the time has come to pay, and he is not able to do so? Perhaps he is embarrassed and tries to avoid your company. On such occasions I tried to reassure the individual and tell him that I knew he did not have it just then and that I was not worried about it. Or I even told him to forget about the debt altogether. But that did not wipe it off the books; the uneasiness remained. I learned that it is possible to do a favor for a friend and cause a strain in the relationship in the process.

I know no easy solution to this problem. I am sure there will be times when the researcher would be extremely ill advised to refuse to make a personal loan. On the other hand, I am convinced that, whatever his financial resources, he should not look for opportunities to lend money and should avoid doing so whenever he gracefully can.

If the researcher is trying to fit into more than one group, his field work becomes more complicated. There may be times when the groups come into conflict with each other, and he will be expected to take a stand. There was a time in the spring of 1937 when the boys arranged a bowling match between the Nortons and the Italian Community Club. Doc bowled for the Nortons, of course. Fortunately, my bowling at this time had not advanced to a point where I was in demand for either team, and I was able to sit on the sidelines. From there I tried to applaud impartially the good shots of both teams, although I am afraid it was evident that I was getting more enthusiasm into my cheers for the Nortons.

When I was with members of the Italian Community Club, I did not feel at all called upon to defend the corner boys against disparaging remarks. However, there was one awkward occasion when I was with the corner boys and one of the college boys stopped to talk with me. In the course of the discussion he said: "Bill, these fellows wouldn't understand what I mean, but I am sure that you understand my point." There I thought I had to say something. I told him that he greatly underestimated the boys and that college men were not the only smart ones.

While the remark fitted in with my natural inclinations, I am sure it was justified from a strictly practical standpoint. My answer did not shake the feelings of superiority of the college boy, nor did it disrupt our personal relationship. On the other hand, as soon as he left, it became evident how deeply the corner boys felt about his statement. They spent some time giving explosive expressions to their opinion of him, and then they told me that I was different and that they appreciated it and that I knew much more than this fellow and yet I did not show it.

My first spring in Cornerville served to establish for me a firm position in the life of the district. I had only been there several weeks when Doc said to me: "You're just as much of a fixture around this street corner as that lamppost." Perhaps the greatest event signalizing my acceptance on Norton Street was the baseball game that Mike Giovanni organized against the group of Norton Street boys in their late teens. It was the old men who had won glorious victories in the past against the rising youngsters. Mike assigned me to a regular position on the team, not a key position perhaps (I was stationed in right field), but at least I was there. When it was my turn to bat in the last half of the ninth inning, the score was tied, there were two outs, and the bases were loaded. As I reached down to pick up my bat, I heard some of the fellows suggesting to Mike that he ought to put in a pinch-hitter. Mike answered them in a loud voice that must have been meant for me: "No, I've got confidence in Bill Whyte. He'll come through in the clutch." So, with Mike's confidence to buck me up, I went up there, missed two swings, and then banged a hard grounder through the hole between second and short. At least that is where they told me it went. I was so busy getting down to first base that I did not know afterward whether I had reached there on an error or a base hit.

That night, when we went down for coffee, Danny presented me with a ring for being a regular fellow and a pretty good ball player. I was particularly impressed by the ring, for it had been made by hand. Danny had started with a clear amber die discarded from his crap game and over long hours had used his lighted cigarette to burn a hole through it and to round the corners so that it came out a heart shape on top. I assured the fellows that I would always treasure the ring.

Perhaps I should add that my game-winning base hit made the score 18–17, so it is evident that I was not the only one who had been hitting the ball. Still, it was a wonderful feeling to come through when they were counting on me, and it made me feel still more that I belonged on Norton Street.

As I gathered my early research data, I had to decide how I was to organize the written notes. In the very early stage of exploration, I simply put all the notes, in chronological order, in a single folder. As I was to go on to study a number of different groups and problems, it was obvious that this was no solution at all.

I had to subdivide the notes. There seemed to be two main possibilities. I could organize the notes topically, with folders for politics, rackets, the church, the family, and so on. Or I could organize the notes in terms of the groups on which they were based, which would mean having folders on the Nortons, the Italian Community Club, and so on. Without really thinking the problem through, I began filing material on the group basis, reasoning that I could later redivide it on a topical basis when I had a better knowledge of what the relevant topics should be.

As the material in the folders piled up, I came to realize that the organization of notes by social groups fitted in with the way in which my study was developing. For example, we have a college-boy member of the Italian Community Club saying: "These racketeers give our district a bad name. They should really be cleaned out of here." And we have a member of the Nortons saying: "These racketeers are really all right. When you need help, they'll give it to you. The legitimate businessman—he won't even give you the time of day." Should these quotes be filed under "Racketeers, attitudes toward"? If so, they would only show that there are conflicting attitudes toward racketeers in Cornerville. Only a questionnaire (which is hardly feasible for such a topic) would show the distribution of attitudes in the district. Furthermore, how important would it be to know how many people felt one way or another on this topic? It seemed to me of much greater scientific interest to be able to relate the attitude to the *group* in which the individual participated. This shows why two individuals could be expected to have quite different attitudes on a given topic.

As time went on, even the notes in one folder grew beyond the point where my memory would allow me to locate any given item rapidly. Then I devised a rudimentary indexing system: a page in three columns containing, for each interview or observation report, the date, the person or people interviewed or observed, and a brief summary of the interview or observation record. Such an index would cover from three to eight pages. When it came time to review the notes or to write from them, a five- to ten-minute perusal of the index was enough to give me a reasonably full picture of what I had and of where any given item could be located.

Venture into Politics

July and August, 1937, I spent away from Cornerville with my parents. Perhaps I was just too accustomed to the family summer vacation to remain in Cornerville, but at least I rationalized that I needed some time to get away and do some reading and get some perspective upon my study. The perspective was not easy to come by at that time. I still did not see the connecting link between a broad study of the life of the community and intensive studies of groups.

I came back feeling that I must somehow broaden my study. That might have meant dropping my contacts with the Nortons and the Italian Community Club in order to participate more heavily in other areas. Perhaps that would have been the logical decision in terms of the way I saw my Cornerville study at the time. Fortunately, I did not act that way. The club took only one evening a week, so there was no great pressure to drop that. The Nortons took much more time, and yet it meant something important to me to have a corner and a group where I was at home in Cornerville. At the time I did not clearly see that there was much more to a study of a group than an examination of its activities and personal relationships at a particular point in time. Only as I began to see changes in these groups did I realize how extremely important it is to observe a group over an extended period of time.

While I wandered along with the Nortons and the Italian Community Club more or less by a process of inertia, I decided I should expand the study by getting a broader and deeper view of the political life of the community. Street corner activities and politics in Cornerville were inextricably intertwined. There were several political organizations seeking to build up rival candidates. I felt that I could best gain an inside view of politics if I aligned myself actively with one political organization, yet I was afraid this might so label me that I would have difficulty with my study afterward in relation to people who were against this particular politician.

The problem solved itself for me. In the fall of 1937 there was a mayoralty contest. An Irish politician who had formerly been mayor and governor of the state was running again. Among the good Yankees, Murphy's name was the personification of corruption. However, in Cornerville, he had a reputation for being a friend of the poor man and of the Italian people. Most of the Cornerville politicians were for him, and he was expected to carry the district by a tremendous majority. I therefore decided that it would be a good thing for my study if I could get my start in politics working for this man. (Among my Harvard associates, this new political allegiance led to some raised eyebrows, but I rationalized that a complete novice could hardly be of any influence in securing the election of the notorious politician.)

In order to enlist in the campaign, I had to have some sort of local connection. I found this with George Ravello, state senator representing our ward and two others. At the restaurant where I lived, I met Paul Ferrante, who was Ravello's secretary and also a friend of the Martini family. Ferrante's services to Ravello were entirely on a volunteer basis. Paul was unemployed at the time and was working for the politician in hopes that he would some day get a political job out of it.

After a little preliminary discussion, I enlisted as the unpaid secretary of the unpaid secretary of the state senator for the duration of the mayoralty campaign. When that election was over, I reenlisted, for there was a special election for a vacant seat in Congress, and George Ravello was running for that office. Fortunately for my study, all the other Cornerville politicians were at least officially for Ravello, since he was running against several Irishmen. I therefore felt that I could be active in his campaign without creating barriers for myself anywhere else in the district.

As a campaign worker for the state senator, I was a complete anomaly. Most workers in such campaigns can at least claim to be able to deliver substantial numbers of votes; I could not pledge anything but my own. It was hard for the organization to get used to this. On one occasion, George Ravello gave me a ride up to the State House, in the course of which he wanted to know when I was going to deliver him the endorsement of the Italian Community Club. This was quite a touchy topic within the club at the time. On the one hand, all the members were interested in seeing an Italian-American advance to higher office, and yet they were embarrassed by being identified with George Ravello. The language he used in public was hardly refined, and he had gained publicity that had embarrassed the young men on several occasions. There was, for example, the time when a woman was testifying against a bill introduced into the senate by Ravello. Ravello got angry in the midst of the hearing and threatened to throw the good woman off the wharf and into the harbor if she ever set foot in his district. On another occasion the newspapers carried a picture of Ravello with a black eye, which he had received in a fight with a member of the State Parole Board.

I explained to Ravello that it was against the policy of the club to endorse candidates for any public office. While this happened to be true, it was hardly a satisfactory explanation to the Senator. Still, he did not press the matter further, perhaps recognizing that the support of the Italian Community Club did not count for very much anyway.

Not being able to deliver votes, I sought to make myself useful by running errands and doing various odd jobs, such as nailing up Ravello posters in various parts of the district.

I am sure no one thought I was any real help to the Senator's campaign, but neither did I appear to be doing any harm, so I was allowed to hang around in the quarters which served as a combination political office and funeral parlor.

I found this one of the more unpleasant places to hang around, because I never was able to gain complete scientific detachment regarding funeral parlors. One of my most vivid and unpleasant memories of Cornerville stems from this period. One of the Senator's constituents had died. The stairs to his flat being too narrow to accommodate the casket, the deceased was laid out for friends and family in the back room of the funeral parlor. Unfortunately, he was laid out in two pieces, since he had had his leg amputated shortly before his death. The rest of his body had been embalmed, but I was told that there was no way of embalming a detached leg. The gangrenous leg gave off a most sickening odor. While family and friends came in to pay their last respects, we political workers sat in the front part of the office trying to keep our attention on politics. Now and then Paul Ferrante went about the room spraying perfume. The combination of perfume with the gangrenous stench was hardly an improvement. I stayed at my post through the day but finished up a trifle nauseated.

Since the politicians did not know what to do with my services and yet were willing to have me hang around, I found that I could develop my own job description. Before one of the meetings of the political workers, I suggested to Carrie Ravello—the candidate's wife and the real brains of the family—that I serve as secretary for such meetings. I then took notes while the meeting proceeded and typed her out a summary for later use. (The invention of carbon paper enabled me to retain my own copy of all the records.)

Actually, it was of no importance for the organization to have such a record. Although they were officially considered meetings to discuss political strategy and tactics, they were only pep rallies for the second string of political powers supporting Ravello. I never did get in on the top-level political discussions where the real decisions were made. However, my note taking at these political meetings did give me a fully documented record of one area of activity. From here I went on to the large-scale political rally, where I sought to record on the spot the speeches and other activities of the leading Ravello supporters.

When election day came, I voted as the polls opened and then reported for duty at the candidate's headquarters. There I found I had been assigned to work with Ravello's secretary in another ward. I spent the first part of election day outside of Cornerville following Ferrante around and being of no real use to myself or to the organization. I did not worry about my contribution, because I was getting a growing impression that a lot of what passed under the name of political activity was simply a waste of time. On election-day morning we stopped in to chat with a number of friends of Paul Ferrante and had a drink or a cup of coffee here and there. Then we drove around to offer voters transportation to the polls, which in such a crowded district would be just around the corner. We made about thirty stops and took one voter to the polls, and she said she had been going to walk down in five minutes anyway. The others were either not home or told us they were going to walk down later.

At two o'clock I asked if it would be all right for me to leave and return to my ward. This was readily granted, so I was able to spend the rest of the day in Cornerville.

When I got home, I began hearing alarming reports from the home ward of the Irish politician who was Ravello's chief rival. He was said to have a fleet of taxicabs cruising about his ward so that each of his repeaters would be able to vote in every precinct of the ward. It became clear that, if we did not steal the election ourselves, this low character would steal it from us.

Around five o'clock one of the senator's chief lieutenants rushed up to a group of us who were hanging on the corner across the street from my home polling place. He told us that Joseph Maloney's section of our ward was wide open for repeaters, that the cars were ready to transport them, and that all he needed were a few men to get to work. At the moment the organization was handicapped by a shortage of manpower to accomplish this important task. The senator's lieutenant did not ask for volunteers; he simply directed us to get into the cars to go to the polling places where the work could be done. I hesitated a moment, but I did not refuse.

Before the polls had closed that night, I had voted three more times for George Ravello—really not much of a feat, since another novice who had started off at the same time as I managed to produce nine votes in the same period of time. Two of my votes were cast in Joseph Maloney's end of the ward; the third was registered in my home polling place.

I was standing on the corner when one of the politician's henchmen came up to me with the voting list to ask me to go in. I explained that this was my home polling place and that I had already voted under my own name. When they learned that this had been when the polls opened, they told me that I had nothing to worry about and that a new shift was now on duty. They had the name of Frank Petrillo picked out for me. They told me that Petrillo was a Sicilian fisherman who was out to sea on election day, so we were exercising his democratic rights for him. I looked at the voting list to discover that Petrillo was forty-five years old and stood five feet nine. Since I was twenty-three and six feet three, this seemed implausible to me, and I raised a question. I was assured that this made no difference at all, since the people inside the polling place were Joe Maloney's people. I was not completely reassured by this, but, nevertheless, I got in line to wait my new turn in the rush of the hour before the polls closed.

I gave my name, and the woman at the gate checked me in, I

picked up my ballot, went back to the booth, and marked it for George Ravello. As I was about to put the ballot into the box, this woman looked me over and asked me how old I was. Suddenly the ridiculousness of my masquerade struck home to me. I knew I was supposed to say forty-five, but I could not voice such an absurd lie. Instead, I compromised on twenty-nine. She asked how tall I was, and again I compromised, giving the figure as six feet. They had me all right, but still the questioning went on. The woman asked me how I spelled my name. In the excitement I spelled it wrong. The other woman checker now came over and asked me about my sisters. I thought I had recalled seeing the names of some female Petrillos on the list, and, in any case, if I invented names that did not appear, they could be names of women who were not registered. I said, "Yes, I have two sisters." She asked their names. I said, "Celia and Florence."

She leered at me and asked, "What about this Marie Petrillo?"

I took a deep breath and said, "She's my cousin."

They said they would have to challenge my vote. They called for the warden in charge of the polling place.

I had a minute to wait before he stepped forward, and that was plenty of time to mull over my future. I could see before my eyes large headlines on the front pages of Eastern City's tabloids—HARVARD FELLOW ARRESTED FOR REPEATING. Why wouldn't they play it up? Indeed, this was an ideal man-bites-dog newspaper story. In that moment I resolved that at least I would not mention my connection with Harvard or my Cornerville study when I was arrested.

The warden now stepped up, said he would have to challenge my vote, and asked me to write my name on the back of the ballot. I went over to the booth. But, by this time, I was so nervous that I forgot what my first name was supposed to be and put down "Paul." The warden took my ballot and looked at the back of it. He had me swear that this was my name and that I had not voted before. I did so. I went through the gate. He told me to stop. As I looked over the crowd coming in, I thought of trying to run for it, but I did not break away. I came back. He looked at the book of registered voters. He turned back to the booth, and for a moment his back was to me. Then I saw him scratch out the name I had written on the back of the ballot. He put the ballot into the box, and it registered with a ring of the bell. He told me I could go out, and I did, trying to walk in a calm and leisurely manner.

When I was out on the street, I told the politician's lieutenant that my vote had been challenged. "Well, what do you care? We didn't lose anything by it." Then I told him that the vote had finally gone through. "Well, so much the better. Listen, what could they have done to you? If the cops had taken you in, they wouldn't hold you. We would fix you up."

I did not eat well that night. Curiously enough, I did not feel nearly so guilty over what I had done until I had thought that I was going to be arrested. Up to that point I had just gone numbly along. After supper I went out to look up Tony Cardio of the Italian Community Club. As I had walked into his home precinct to repeat, I encountered him coming out of the polling place. As we passed, he grinned at me and said: "They're working you pretty hard today, aren't they?" I immediately jumped to the conclusion that he must know that I was going in to repeat. Now I felt that I must see him as soon as possible to explain in the best way that I could what I had been doing and why. Fortunately for me, Tony was not home that night. As my anxiety subsided, I recognized that, simply because I knew my own guilt, it did not necessarily follow that everybody else and Tony knew what I had done. I confirmed this indirectly when I had a conversation with Tony later about the election. He raised no question concerning my voting activities.

That was my performance on election day. What did I gain from it? I had seen through firsthand personal experience how repeating was accomplished. But this was really of very little value, for I had been observing these activities at quite close range before, and I could have had all the data without taking any risk. Actually, I learned nothing of research value from the experience, and I took a chance of jeopardizing my whole study. While I escaped arrest, these things are not always fixed as firmly as the politician's henchman think they are. A year later, when I was out of town at election time, somebody was actually arrested for voting in *my* name.

Even apart from the risk of arrest, I faced other possible losses. While repeating was fairly common in our ward, there were only relatively few people who engaged in it, and they were generally looked down upon as the fellows who did the dirty work. Had the word got around about me, my own standing in the district would have suffered considerable damage. So far as I know, my repeating never did become known beyond some of the key people in Ravello's organization. Most of my repeating had been done outside of Cornerville, and my Norton Street friends did not vote in the same precinct where I put in my second Cornerville vote. I had not been observed by anyone whose opinion could damage me. Furthermore,

I was just plain lucky that I did not reveal myself to Tony Cardio; in fact, I was lucky at every point.

The experience posed problems that transcended expediency. I had been brought up as a respectable, law-abiding, middle-class citizen. When I discovered that I was a repeater, I found my conscience giving me serious trouble. This was not like the picture of myself that I had been trying to build up. I could not laugh it off simply as a necessary part of the field work. I knew that it was not necessary; at the point where I began to repeat, I could have refused. There were others who did refuse to do it. I had simply got myself involved in the swing of the campaign and let myself be carried along. I had to learn that, in order to be accepted by the people in a district, you do not have to do everything just as they do it. In fact, in a district where there are different groupings with different standards of behavior, it may be a matter of very serious consequence to conform to the standards of one particular group.

I also had to learn that the field worker cannot afford to think only of learning to live with others in the field. He has to continue living with himself. If the participant observer finds himself engaging in behavior that he has learned to think of as immoral, then he is likely to begin to wonder what sort of a person he is after all. Unless the field worker can carry with him a reasonably consistent picture of himself, he is likely to run into difficulties.

Back on Norton Street

When the campaign was over, I went back to Norton Street, I did not sever my ties with the Ravello organization altogether. For this there were two reasons: I wanted to maintain my connections for possible further research in politics; but then also I did not want them to think of me as just another of those "phonies" who made a fuss over the politician when he seemed to have a chance to win and abandoned him when he lost. Still, I had no strong personal tie to hold me to the organization. Carrie Ravello I liked and respected; the Senator puzzled and interested me, but I never felt that I got to know him. His one-time secretary just dropped out of sight for a while after the election—still owing me ten dollars. The others did not really matter to me personally. And, as I review my notes today, even their names have little meaning.

As I became more active once again on Norton Street, the local world began to look different. The world I was observing was in a process of change. I saw some of the members of the Italian Community Club establishing contacts with the upper world of Yankee control as I followed them to All-American Night at the Women's Republican Club. I saw the stresses and strains within the Nortons growing out of contacts with the Aphrodite Club and the Italian Community Club. I watched Doc, completely without scientific detachment, as he prepared for his doomed effort to run for public office.

Then in April 1938, one Saturday night I stumbled upon one of my most exciting research experiences in Cornerville. It was the night when the Nortons were to bowl for the prize money; the biggest bowling night of the whole season. I recall standing on the corner with the boys while they discussed the coming contest. I listened to Doc, Mike, and Danny making their predictions as to the order in which the men would finish. At first, this made no particular impression upon me, as my own unexpressed predictions were exactly along the same lines. Then, as the men joked and argued, I suddenly began to question and take a new look at the whole situation. I was convinced that Doc, Mike, and Danny were basically correct in their predictions, and yet why should the scores approximate the structure of the gang? Were these top men simply better natural athletes than the rest? That made no sense, for here was Frank Bonnelli, who was a good enough athlete to win the promise of a tryout with a major-league baseball team. Why should not Frank outdo us all at the bowling alley? Then I remembered the baseball game we had had a year earlier against the younger crowd on Norton Street. I could see the man who was by common consent the best baseball player of us all striking out with long, graceful swings and letting the grounders bounce through his legs. And then I remembered that neither I nor anyone else seemed to have been surprised at Frank's performance in this game. Even Frank himself was not surprised, as he explained: "I can't seem to play ball when I'm playing with fellows I know like that bunch."

I went down to the alleys that night fascinated and just a bit awed by what I was about to witness. Here was the social structure in action right on the bowling alleys. It held the individual members in their places—and I along with them. I did not stop to reason then that, as a close friend of Doc, Danny, and Mike, I held a position close to the top of the gang and therefore should be expected to excel on this great occasion. I simply felt myself buoyed up by the situation. I felt my friends were for me, had confidence in me, wanted me to bowl well. As my turn came and I stepped up to bowl, I felt supremely confident that I was going to hit the pins that

I was aiming at. I have never felt quite that way before—or since. Here at the bowling alley I was experiencing subjectively the impact of the group structure upon the individual. It was a strange feeling, as if something larger than myself was controlling the ball as I went through my swing and released it toward the pins.

When it was all over, I looked at the scores of all the other men. I was still somewhat bemused by my own experience, and now I was excited to discover that the men had actually finished in the predicted order with only two exceptions that could readily be explained in terms of the group structure.

As I later thought over the bowling-alley contest, two things stood out in my mind. In the first place, I was convinced that now I had something important: the relationship between individual performance and group structure, even though at this time I still did not see how such observation would fit in with the over-all pattern of the Cornerville study. I believed then (and still believe now) that this sort of relationship may be observed in other group activities everywhere. As an avid baseball fan, I had often been puzzled by the records of some athletes who seemed to be able to hit and throw and field with superb technical qualifications and yet were unable to make the major-league teams. I had also been puzzled by cases where men who had played well at one time suddenly failed badly, whereas other men seemed to make tremendous improvements that could not be explained simply on the basis of increasing experience. I suspect that a systematic study of the social structure of a baseball team, for example, will explain some of these otherwise mysterious phenomena. The other point that impressed me involved field research methods. Here I had the scores of the men on that final night at the bowling alleys. This one set of figures was certainly important, for it represented the performance of the men in the event that they all looked upon as the climax of the year. However, this same group had been bowling every Saturday night for many months, and some of the members had bowled on other nights in between. It would have been a ridiculously simple task for me to have kept a record for every string bowled by every man on every Saturday night of that season and on such other evenings as I bowled with the men. This would have produced a set of statistics that would have been the envy of some of my highly quantitative friends. I kept no record of these scores, because at this time I saw no point to it. I had been looking upon Saturday night at the bowling alleys as simply recreation for myself and my friends. I found myself enjoying the bowling so much that now and then I felt a bit guilty about neglecting my research. I was bowling with the men in order to establish a social position that would enable me to interview them and observe important things. But what were these important things? Only after I passed up this statistical gold mine did I suddenly realize that the behavior of the men in the regular bowling-alley sessions was the perfect example of what I should be observing. Instead of bowling in order to be able to observe something else, I should have been bowling in order to observe bowling. I learned then that the day-to-day routine activities of these men constituted the basic data of my study.

Replanning the Research

The late spring and summer of 1938 brought some important changes into my research.

On May 28, I was married to Kathleen King, and three weeks later we returned to Cornerville together. Kathleen had visited me at the restaurant and had met some of my friends. Even as a married man, I did not want to move out of the district, and Kathleen, fortunately, was eager to move in. This presented problems, because, while we were not asking for everything, we did hope to find an apartment with a toilet and bathtub inside it. We looked at various gloomy possibilities until at last we found a building that was being remodeled on Shelby Street. Some of my Norton Street friends warned us against the neighborhood, saying that the place was full of Sicilians who were a very cut-throat crowd. Still, the apartment had the bathtub and toilet and was clean and relatively airy. It had no central heating, but we could be reasonably comfortable with the kitchen stove.

Now that we were two, we could enter into new types of social activities, and Kathleen could learn to know some of the women as I had become acquainted with the men. However, these new directions of social activity were something for the future. My problem now was to find where I was and where I was going. This was a period of stocktaking.

In describing my Cornerville study, I have often said I was eighteen months in the field before I knew where my research was going. In a sense this is literally true. I began with the general idea of making a community study. I felt that I had to establish myself as a participant observer in order to make such a study. In the early months in Cornerville I went through the process that sociologist Robert Johnson has described in his own field work. I began as a nonparticipating observer. As I became accepted into the community, I found myself becoming almost a nonobserving participant. I got the feel of life in Cornerville, but that meant that I got to take for granted the same things that my Cornerville friends took for granted. I was immersed in it, but I could as yet make little sense out of it. I had a feeling that I was doing something important, but I had yet to explain to myself what it was.

Fortunately, at this point I faced a very practical problem. My three-year fellowship would run out in the summer of 1939. The fellowship could be renewed for a period up to three years. Applications for renewal were due in the early spring of 1939.

I was enjoying Cornerville, and I felt that I was getting somewhere, yet at the same time I felt that I needed at least three more years. I realized that so far I had little to show for the time I had spent. When I submitted my application for renewal, I must also submit some evidence that I had acquitted myself well in the first three-year period. I would have to write something. I had several months in which to do the writing, but the task at first appalled me. I sat down to ask myself what it was in Cornerville upon which I had reasonably good data. Was there anything ready to be written up? I pondered this and talked it over with Kathleen and with John Howard, who was working with me in the district.

Still thinking in terms of a community study, I recognized that I knew very little about family life in Cornerville, and my data were very thin upon the church, although John Howard was beginning to work on this area. I had been living with the restaurant family in a room that overlooked the corner where T. S., the most prominent Cornerville racketeer, sometimes was seen with his followers. I had looked down upon the group many times from my window, and yet I had never met the men. Racketeering was of obvious importance in the district, yet all I knew about it was the gossip I picked up from men who were only a little closer to it than I. I had much more information regarding political life and organization, but even here I felt that there were so many gaps that I could not yet put the pieces together.

If these larger areas were yet to be filled in, what on earth did I have to present? As I thumbed through the various folders, it was obvious that the Norton and Community Club folders were fatter than the rest. If I knew anything about Cornerville, I must know it about the Nortons and the Italian Community Club. Perhaps, if

I wrote up these two stories, I would begin to see some pattern in what I was doing in Cornerville.

As I wrote the case studies of the Nortons and of the Italian Community, a pattern for my research gradually emerged in my mind.

I realized at last that I was not writing a community study in the usual sense of that term. The reader who examines *Middletown* will note that it is written about people in general in that community. Individuals or groups do not figure in the story except as they illustrate the points that the authors are making (the sequel, *Middletown in Transition*, presents one exception to this description with a chapter on the leading family of the community). The reader will further note that *Middletown* is organized in terms of such topics as getting a living, making a home, training the young, and using leisure.

The Lynds accomplished admirably the task they set out to accomplish. I simply came to realize that my task was different. I was dealing with particular individuals and with particular groups.

I realized also that there was another difference that I had stumbled upon. I had assumed that a sociological study should present a description and analysis of a community at one particular point in time, supported of course by some historical background. I now came to realize that *time* itself was one of the key elements in my study. I was observing, describing, and analyzing groups as they evolved and changed through time. It seemed to me that I could explain much more effectively the behavior of men when I observed them over time than would have been the case if I had got them at one point in time. In other words, I was taking a moving picture instead of a still photograph.

But, if this was a study of particular individuals and there were more than twenty thousand people in the district, how could I say anything significant about Cornerville on this individual and group basis? I came to realize that I could only do so if I saw individuals and groups in terms of their positions in the social structure. I also must assume that, whatever the individual and group differences were, there were basic similarities to be found. Thus I would not have to study every corner gang in order to make meaningful statements about corner gangs in Cornerville. A study of one corner gang was not enough, to be sure, but, if an examination of several more showed up the uniformities that I expected to find, then this part of the task became manageable.

On the Italian Community Club, I felt that I needed no additional data. There were few enough college men in Cornerville at the time, so that this one group represented a large sample of people in this category. It also seemed to me that they represented significant points in the social structure and in the social mobility process. There would certainly be others like them coming along after they had left the district, even as the Sunset Dramatic Club had gone before them. Furthermore, examination of their activities showed up important links with Republican politics and with the settlement house.

I now began to see the connection between my political study and the case study of the corner gang. The politician did not seek to influence separate individuals in Cornerville; consciously or unconsciously he sought out group leaders. So it was men like Doc who were the connecting links between their groups and the larger political organization. I could now begin writing my study by examining particular groups in detail, and then I could go on to relate them to the larger structures of the community. With this pattern in mind, I came to realize that I had much more data on politics than I had thought.

There were still important gaps in my study. My knowledge of the role of the church in the community was fragmentary, and this I hoped to fill in. I had done no systematic work upon the family. On the one hand, it seemed inconceivable that one could write a study of Cornerville without discussing the family; yet, at the same time, I was at a loss as to how to proceed in tying family studies into the organization of the book as it was emerging in my mind. I must confess also that for quite unscientific reasons I have always found politics, rackets, and gangs more interesting than the basic unit of human society.

The gap that worried me most was in the area of the rackets and the police. I had a general knowledge of how the rackets functioned, but nothing to compare with the detailed interpersonal data I had upon the corner gang. As my book was evolving, it seemed to me that this was the gap that simply must be filled, although at the time I had no idea how I would get the inside picture that was necessary.

I finished the writing of my first two case studies and submitted them in support of my application for a renewal of the fellowship. Some weeks later I received my answer. The fellowship had been renewed for one year instead of the three for which I had been hoping. At first, I was bitterly disappointed. As I was just beginning to get my bearings, I did not see how it would be possible to finish an adequate study in the eighteen months that then remained.

I am now inclined to believe that this one year cut-off was a very good thing for me and my research. In a sense, the study of a community or an organization has no logical end point. The more you learn, the more you see that there is to learn. If I had had three years instead of one, my study would have taken longer to complete. Perhaps it might have been a better study. On the other hand, when I knew I had just eighteen months to go, I had to settle down and think through my plans more thoroughly and push ahead with the research and writing much more purposefully.

Again the Corner Gang

The most important steps I took in broadening my study of street corner gangs grew out of Doc's recreation center project, although at first I had some other interests in mind. It began with one of my periodic efforts to get Doc a job. When I heard that the Cornerville House had finally been successful in getting its grant to open three store-front recreation centers, I sought to persuade Mr. Smith, the director, to man them with local men who, like Doc, were leaders in their groups. I found that he had planned to man them with social workers trained in group work. When I realized that it was hopeless to get him to select three local men, I tried to urge at least Doc upon him. I could see that Mr. Smith was tempted by the idea and afraid of it at the same time. When I brought Doc in to meet him, I found that I lost ground instead of gaining it, for, as Doc told me later, he had got a dizzy spell there in the settlement-house office, and he had been in no condition to make a favorable personal impression. If Doc and I had figured out correctly the underlying causes for his dizzy spells, then a steady job and the money that would enable him to resume his customary pattern of social activity would cure these neurotic symptoms. On the other hand, I could hardly explain this to Mr. Smith. I was afraid that it appeared that I was simply trying to do a favor for a friend. As my last effort in this direction, I turned over to Mr. Smith a copy of my case study of the Nortons—and asked him please to keep it confidential, since I was not ready to publish.

This made the difference. Mr. Smith agreed to hire Doc.

As the preliminary activities of setting up the recreation centers got under way, I began to worry about my confident predictions of Doc's success. In the preliminary meetings to discuss plans for the centers, Doc was passive and apparently apathetic. Nevertheless, almost from the moment that Doc's center opened, it became apparent that it was to be a success.

On one of my early visits to Doc's center, he introduced me to Sam Franco, who was to play a far more important part in my study than brief mentions of him in the book indicate. Doc met Sam the night his center opened. Sam's gang was hanging around outside of the center looking the place over. Sam came in as the emissary of his group—a move which immediately identified him as the leader to Doc. The two men discussed the center briefly, and then Sam went out and brought his gang in. By the second night of the center, Sam had become Doc's lieutenant in its administration. Doc knew a few people in this part of the district, but Sam knew everybody.

Doc knew that I was trying to extend my corner gang study, and he suggested that Sam might be the man to help me. Doc had already learned that Sam had been keeping a scrapbook with newspaper accounts of Cornerville activities and some personal material on his own group.

I invited Sam and his scrapbook up to our apartment. There I learned that Sam had got started on his scrapbook after an experience on a National Youth Administration Project, where he had been working for a man who was writing a study of the problems of youth in this region. The scrapbook was completely miscellaneous and undirected, but it did have one part that particularly interested me. Sam had a section for his own gang with one page for each member. At the top of the page was a line drawing (from memory) of the individual, and then he wrote in such points as age, address, education, job, and ambition. (Usually he had written "none" opposite the heading "ambition.")

My task was now to persuade Sam that, while it was fine to look upon these men as individuals, it was even better to look upon them in terms of their relations with each other. I had only begun my explanation when Sam got the point and accepted it with enthusiasm. Of course, this was the sort of thing he knew; he had so taken it for granted that it had not occurred to him how important it might be. From this point on until the end of my study Sam Franco was my research assistant. I even managed to get Harvard to pay a hundred dollars for his services.

We began with an analysis of Sam's own gang, the Millers. We also looked at other gangs that came into Doc's recreation center. Here we had the great advantage of having two sharp observers checking each other on the same groups. I was reassured to find that they were in complete agreement on the top-leadership structure of every gang—with one exception. This one exception did trouble me until the explanation presented itself.

I had spent part of one afternoon listening to Doc and Sam argue over the leadership of one gang. Doc claimed that Carl was the man; Sam argued that it was Tommy. Each man presented incidents that he had observed in support of his point of view. The following morning Sam rushed up to my house with this bulletin: "You know what happened last night? Carl and Tommy nearly had it out. They got into a big argument, and now the gang is split into two parts with some of them going with Carl and the rest going with Tommy." So their conflicting views turned out to be an accurate representation of what was taking place in the gang.

As I worked on these other gang studies, I assumed that I had finished my research on the Nortons. Still, I kept in close touch with Doc, and, just for recreation, I continued to bowl with the remnants of the Nortons on some Saturday nights.

With my attention directed elsewhere, I failed to see what was happening among the Nortons right before my eyes. I knew Long John was not bowling as he had in previous years, and I also knew that he was not as close to Doc, Danny, and Mike as he had been. I had noticed that, when Long John was on Norton Street, the followers badgered him more aggressively than they ever had before. I must have assumed some connection among these phenomena, and yet I did not make much of the situation until Doc came to me and told me of Long John's psychological difficulties.

It was as if this information set off a flash bulb in my head. Suddenly all the pieces of the puzzle fell together. The previous season, I had stumbled upon the relationship between position in the group and performance at the bowling alleys. I now saw the three-way connection between group position, performance, and mental health. And not only for Long John. Doc's dizzy spells seemed to have precisely the same explanation.

We could put it more generally in this way. The individual becomes accustomed to a certain pattern of interaction. If this pattern is subject to a drastic change, then the individual can be expected to experience mental-health difficulties. That is a very crude statement. Much further research would be needed before we could determine the degree of change necessary, the possibilities of compensating with interactions in other social areas, and so on. But here at least was one way of tying together human relations and psychological adjustment.

Furthermore, here was an opportunity to experiment in therapy. If my diagnosis was correct, then the line of treatment was clear: reestablish something like Long John's preexisting pattern of interaction, and the neurotic symptoms should disappear. This was the first real opportunity to test my conclusions on group structure. I embraced it with real enthusiasm.

Convinced as I was of the outcome that should follow, I must confess that I was somewhat awestruck when, under Doc's skilfully executed therapy program, Long John not only lost his neurotic symptoms but also closed out the season by winning the prize money in the final bowling contest. Of course, this victory was not necessary to establish the soundness of the diagnosis. It would have been enough for Long John to have reestablished himself *among* the top bowlers. His five-dollar prize was just a nice bonus for interaction theory.

Studying Racketeering

My meeting with Tony Cataldo, the prominent Cornerville racketeer, came about almost by chance. I dropped in one afternoon at the restaurant where I had first lived in Cornerville. Ed Martini, Al's older brother, was there at the time. He was grumbling about a pair of banquet tickets he had had to buy from a local policeman. He said that his wife did not want to go to banquets; perhaps I might like to accompany him.

I asked what the occasion was. He told me that the banquet was in honor of the son of the local police lieutenant. The young man had just passed his bar examinations and was starting out on his legal career. I thought a moment. It was perfectly obvious what sorts of people would be present at the banquet: mainly policemen, politicians, and racketeers. I decided that this might be an opportunity for me.

At the banquet hall, Ed and I took up our position in the lounge outside the men's room. Here we encountered Tony Cataldo and one of his employees, Rico Deleo. It turned out that Ed Martini knew Tony slightly and that Rico lived right across the street from me. Rico asked what I was doing, and I said something about writing a book on Cornerville. Tony said he had seen me around taking photographs of the *feste* that had been staged on Shelby Street the previous summer. This proved to be a fortunate association in his mind, since I could talk quite freely about what I had been trying to learn of the *feste*—which were actually just a minor interest in the research.

The four of us went up to a banquet table together, where we had to wait more than an hour for our food. We munched on olives and celery and sympathized with one another over the poor service. After the dinner we stepped downstairs and bowled three strings together. By this time Tony was quite friendly and invited me to stop in at his store any time.

I paid several visits to the back room of the store from which Tony operated some of his business. A week after we had met, Tony invited Kathleen and me to dinner at his home. His wife, an attractive young girl, told us later that he had spoken of us as a Harvard professor and a commercial artist. She was very upset that he gave her only one day's notice for the dinner when she felt she needed at least a week to prepare for such important personages. The food was nevertheless quite elaborate, and each course seemed like a whole meal. After dinner Tony drove us out to meet some of his relatives in one of the suburbs. Then we all went bowling together.

We had dinner twice at their home, and they came to ours twice. On each occasion, apart from the small talk, the research pattern was similar. We talked some about the *feste*, about the club life of the *paesani* from the old country, and about such things which Tony associated with my study. Then I gradually eased him into a discussion of his business. The discussion seemed to move naturally in this direction. It was just like a friend asking a legitimate business-man about the progress he was making and the problems he was meeting. Tony seemed glad to unburden himself.

I now felt optimistic about my future in racketeering. We seemed to be getting along very well with the Cataldos, and I was ready to follow Tony into the new field. However, after the first exchanges of sociability, Tony seemed to lose interest in us.

I was puzzled by this sudden cooling off. I am not sure I have the full explanation, but I think there were at least two parts of it.

In the first place, Tony ran into a business crisis at about this time. Some men broke into his horse room one afternoon, held it up, and took all the money from the customers and from Tony. In order to maintain good relations with his customers, Tony had to reimburse them for the robbery, so that afternoon was doubly costly. It was also most frustrating, because, as the men were making their getaway, Tony could look out of the window and see them running right beneath him. He had a clear shot at them, yet he could not shoot, because he knew that a shooting would close down gambling in Cornerville like nothing else. As long as these things were done quietly, the "heat" was not so likely to be on.

This might have accounted for an interruption in our social life together but hardly for a complete cessation. It seems to me that the other factor was a problem in social status and mobility. At first Tony had built me up to his wife—and probably to friends and relatives also—as a Harvard professor. Both the Cataldos were highly status conscious. They did not allow their young son to play with the local riffraff. They explained that they only lived in the district because it was necessary for business reasons and that they still hoped to move out. When we were their guests, they introduced us to their friends and relatives who lived in more fashionable parts of the city.

On the other hand, when the Cataldos came to our house for dinner they just met with us and nobody else. Furthermore, Tony was now seeing me associating with the men on Shelby Street who were distinctly small fry to him. At first he had thought that his contact with me was something important; now, perhaps, he considered it insignificant.

To some extent I was aware of this risk and thought of the possibility of having Harvard friends in to dinner with the Cataldos. I had been keeping the two worlds apart. One Harvard friend, a symbolic logician, had once asked me to introduce him to a crap game. He explained that he had figured out mathematically how to win in a crap game. I explained that my crap-shooting friends had reached the same mathematical conclusion by their rule-of-thumb method, and I begged off from this adventure. On another occasion, we had the wife of one of my Harvard associates visiting us when one of the local men dropped in. Sizing up his new audience, he began regaling her with accounts of famous murders that had taken place in Cornerville in recent years. She listened with eyes wide open. At the end of one particularly hair-raising story she asked, "Who killed him?"

Our Cornerville friend shook his head and said: "Lady! Lady! Around here you don't ask them things."

That incident did us no damage, for the man knew us well enough to take it all as a joke. Still, I was hesitant about mixing Harvard and Cornerville. I did not worry about what Cornerville would do to Harvard, but I did worry lest some Harvard friend would unintentionally make a blunder that would make things awkward for me or would act in such a way as to make the local people ill at ease. For that reason I kept the two worlds separate, but that meant that Tony could not improve his social standing through associating with us.

When it became evident that I was at a dead end with Tony, I cast about for other avenues leading to a study of racketeering. Two possibilities seemed open. Tony had an older brother who worked for him. I reasoned that, since the two men were brothers and worked so closely together, Henry would know almost as much about racket developments as Tony. I already had seen something of Henry, and I set about building the relationship further. This went along smoothly with visits back and forth from house to house as well as conversations in the back room of the store. (This indicates that Tony did not drop us out of suspicion, for in that case he could have seen to it that we did not take up with his brother.)

This led to a good deal of discussion of Tony's racket organization, which was exceedingly valuable to me. Still, I had an uneasy feeling that I was not getting what I needed. I was not yet ready to give up the possibility of getting close to Tony and of observing him in action. I understood that he was a member of the Cornerville Social and Athletic Club, which was located right across the street from our apartment. I joined the club then in order to renew my pursuit of Tony Cataldo.

At first I was disappointed in the fruits of my decision. While officially a member, Tony was rarely in the clubroom. In a few weeks it became evident that I was not going to cement relations with him in this area. What next? I considered dropping out of the club. Perhaps I would have done so if there had been other research openings then demanding my attention. Since I had planned to concentrate upon the role of the racketeer and had no other plans at the time, I rationalized that I should stay with the club. I did not record the reasons for my decision at the time. Perhaps I had a hunch that interesting things would break here. Or perhaps I was just lucky.

At least I recognized that the club presented some new angles in research. It was far larger than any corner gang I had studied. Here was an opportunity to carry further the observational methods I had used on the Nortons.

When I wrote my first draft of this present statement, I described how I developed these new methods to a point where I had systematic knowledge of the structure of the club *before* the election crisis. In other words, when Tony entered and sought to manipulate the club, I already had a full picture of the structure he was attempting to manipulate. I must now admit, following a review of my notes, that this is a retrospective falsification. What I first wrote was what I *should* have done. Actually, I began my systematic observations of the club several weeks before the election. When the crisis arrived, I had only an impressionistic picture of group structure. The notes I had then justified no systematic conclusions.

There were two factors that propelled me into more systematic efforts at charting the organizational structure. In the first place, when I began spending time in the club, I also began looking around for *the* leader. Naturally, I did not find *him*. If Tony was not around much, then somebody must take over in his absence. The club had a president, but he was just an indecisive nice guy who obviously did not amount to much. Of course, I did not find *the* leader because the club consisted of two factions with two leaders and—just to make matters more confusing for me—Carlo Tedesco, the leader of one faction, was not even a member of the club when I began my observations. Since I was completely confused in my crude efforts to map the structure, it followed that I must get at the data more systematically.

Then the political crisis underlined the necessity of pushing ahead with such observations. I had to learn more about the structure that Tony was seeking to manipulate.

Here I had a more complicated task than any I had faced before. The club had fifty members. Fortunately, only about thirty of them were frequent attenders, so that I could concentrate on that smaller number, but even that number presented a formidable problem.

I felt I would have to develop more formal and systematic procedures than I had used when I had been hanging on a street corner with a much smaller group of men. I began with positional map-making. Assuming that the men who associated together most closely socially would also be those who lined up together on the same side when decisions were to be made, I set about making a record of the groupings I observed each evening in the club. To some extent I could do this from the front window of our apartment. I simply adjusted the venetian blind so that I was hidden from view and so that I could look down and into the store-front club. Unfortunately, however, our flat was two flights up, and the angle of vision was such that I could not see past the middle of the clubroom. To get the full picture, I had to go across the street and be with the men.

When evening activities were going full blast, I looked around the room to see which people were talking together, playing cards together, or otherwise interacting. I counted the number of men in the room, so as to know how many I would have to account for. Since I was familiar with the main physical objects of the clubroom, it was not difficult to get a mental picture of the men in relation to tables, chairs, couches, radio, and so on. When individuals moved about or when there was some interaction between these groupings, I sought to retain that in mind. In the course of an evening, there might be a general reshuffling of positions, I was not able to remember every movement, but I tried to observe with which members the movements began. And when another spatial arrangement developed, I went through the same mental process as I had with the first.

I managed to make a few notes on trips to the men's room, but most of the mapping was done from memory after I had gone home. At first, I went home once or twice for mapmaking during the evening, but, with practice, I got so that I could retain at least two positional arrangements in memory and could do all of my notes at the end of the evening.

I found this an extremely rewarding method, which well compensated me for the boring routines of endless mapping. As I piled up these maps, it became evident just what the major social groupings were and what people fluctuated between the two factions of the club. As issues arose within the club, I could predict who would stand where.

In the course of my observations I recorded 106 groupings. Upon inspecting the data, I divided the club tentatively into the two factions I thought I was observing. Then, when I reexamined the data, I found that only 40, or 37.7 per cent, of the groupings observed contained members of both factions. I found further that only 10 out of these 40 groupings contained two or more members of each faction. The other 30 were cases where a single individual of the other faction joined in the card game or conversation. I then divided the groupings into two columns, placing in one column those which were predominantly of one faction and in the other column those which were predominantly of the other faction. Then I underlined in red those names which did not "belong" in the column where I found them. Out of a total of 462 names, 75, or approximately 16 per cent, were underlined in red. Of course, we would not expect a pure separation of two cliques in any club, but the figures, crude as they were, seemed to demonstrate that the two factions were real entities which would be important in understanding any decisions made by the club.

This observation of groupings did not, in itself, point out the influential people in the club. For that purpose I tried to pay particular attention to events in which an individual originated activity for one or more others—where a proposal, suggestion, or request was followed by a positive response. Over a period of six months, in my notes I tabulated every observed incident where A had originated activity for B. The result of this for pair events (events involving only two people) was entirely negative. While I might have the impression that, in the relationship between A and B, B was definitely the subordinate individual, the tabulation might show that

B originated for A approximately as much as A for B. However, when I tabulated the set events (those involving three or more people), the hierarchical structure of the organization clearly emerged.

As this phase of the research proceeded, I saw more clearly how to relate together the large racket organization and the street corner gang or club. In fact, the study of the role of Tony Cataldo in this setting provided the necessary link, and the observational methods here described provided the data for the analysis of this linkage.

While I was working up these research methods, I committed a serious blunder. It happened during the political crisis. Tony had been trying to persuade the club to invite his candidate in to address us, although nearly all the members were disposed to support Fiumara. At this crucial point I participated actively, saying that, while we were all for Fiumara, I thought it was a good idea to hear what other politicians had to say. The vote was taken shortly after I spoke, and it went for Tony against Carlo. That led to the rally for Mike Kelly in our clubroom and to the most serious dissension within the club.

Here I violated a cardinal rule of participant observation. I sought actively to influence events. In a close and confused contest such as this, it is quite likely that my endorsement of Tony's position was a decisive factor. Why did I so intervene?

At the time I was still hoping to reestablish close relations with Tony Cataldo, and I wanted to make some move that would build in that direction. So I sought to do the impossible: to take a stand which would not antagonize Carlo and his boys but would be appreciated by Tony. It was a foolish and misguided attempt. I did antagonize Carlo, and he forgave me only on the assumption that I was ignorant of the situation in which I was acting. Ignorance being preferable to treachery, I accepted this excuse.

Ironically enough, my effort to win favor with Tony was a complete failure. Before the political crisis, he had hardly known Carlo and had not recognized his leadership position in the club. When Carlo opposed him so vigorously and effectively, Tony immediately recognized Carlo's position and made every effort to establish closer relations with him. As I had taken a position on his side in the crisis, Tony needed to make no efforts to establish closer relations with me.

I did not have to speak in this situation at all. If I had spoken against Tony, it seems likely that this would have done more to reestablish our close relations than what I actually did.

As I thought over this event later, I came to the conclusion that my action had not only been unwise from a practical research standpoint;

it had also been a violation of professional ethics. It is not fair to the people who accept the participant observer for him to seek to manipulate them to their possible disadvantage simply in order to seek to strengthen his social position in one area of participation. Furthermore, while the researcher may consciously and explicitly engage in influencing action with the full knowledge of the people with whom he is participating, it is certainly a highly questionable procedure for the researcher to establish his social position on the assumption that he is not seeking to lead anyone anywhere and then suddenly throw his weight to one side in a conflict situation.

Marching on City Hall

I suppose no one goes to live in a slum district for three and a half years unless he is concerned about the problems facing the people there. In that case it is difficult to remain solely a passive observer. One time I gave in to the urge to do something. I tried to tell myself that I was simply testing out some of the things I had learned about the structure of corner gangs, but I knew really that this was not the main purpose.

In all my time in Cornerville I had heard again and again about how the district was forgotten by the politicians, how no improvements were ever made, how the politicians just tried to get themselves and their friends ahead. I heard a good deal about the sporadic garbage collections, but perhaps the bitterest complaint concerned the public bathhouse, where in the summer of 1939 as well as in several earlier summers there was no hot water available. In a district where only 12 per cent of the flats had bathtubs, this was a matter of serious moment.

People complained to each other about these matters, but apparently it did no good to try to work through the local politicians, who were primarily concerned about doing favors for friends and potential friends. If you could not go through the local politicians, why not go direct to the mayor—and on a mass basis? If, as I assumed, the corner gang leaders were able to mobilize their gangs for action in various directions, then it should be possible through working with a small number of individuals to organize a large demonstration.

I talked this over with Sam Franco, who was enthusiastic and ready to act at once. He promised me the support of his section of Cornerville. For the Norton Street area I called on Doc. For the area around George Ravello's headquarters, I picked one of the local leaders. With my new acquaintances on Shelby Street, I was able to cover that end of the district.

Then began the complicated task of organizing the various groups, bringing them together, and getting them ready to march at the same time. And who was going to lead this demonstration? Since I was the connecting link among most of these corner gang leaders and since I had begun the organizing activity, I was the logical man to take over. But I was not then prepared to depart so far from my observer's role. I agreed with the others that I would serve on the organizing committee, but we would have to have a different chairman. I proposed Doc, and all the others agreed to this. But, as I talked with Doc, I found that, while he was happy to go along with us, he was not prepared to accept the leadership responsibility. I then proposed Mike Giovanni, and he too was acceptable to the small group with whom I was working in preparing the demonstration. Mike said that he would conduct a public meeting in Cornerville in getting people together for the march, but he thought that the chairman from that point on should be elected by the representatives of the different corners who were there assembled. We agreed on this.

But then we had a misunderstanding as to the composition of this public meeting. San Franco brought just several representatives from his end of the district, while a large part of the Shelby section marched en masse down to the meeting. Thus, when there were nominations for chairman, a man from Shelby Street who had previously taken no part in the planning was nominated and elected. Sam Franco's friends were considerably annoyed by this, for they felt they could have elected one of their candidates if they had simply brought their boys along. Sam and several of the other men also suspected our chairman's motives. They were convinced that he would try to turn the demonstration to his personal advantage, and I had to concede that there was a good possibility of this. From this point on, part of the efforts of our committee were to hem in the chairman so that he would have no opportunity to go off on his own tangent.

In this election meeting we had been misled by our own conception of democratic processes. It makes sense to elect a chairman only from a regularly constituted group or constituency. In this case the election had turned out quite fortuitously because of the overrepresentation of Shelby Street.

We next had difficulty with the date on which we were to march.

It had been set about a week from the election meeting, but now the men on Shelby Street were telling me that their people were all steamed up and wanted to march much sooner. I consulted Sam Franco and one or two other members of the committee but was not able to get all the committee together. In spite of this, I told them that maybe we should move the march up a couple of days. We then scheduled a meeting of the full committee to take place the night before the march. When the committee began assembling, it became evident that some of them were annoyed that they had been bypassed, and I realized that I had made a serious blunder. Fortunately, at this point one of the local politicians came in and tried to argue against the march. This was a great morale booster. Instead of arguing with each other as to how we had been handling the plan, we got all our aggressions off against the politician.

The next morning we assembled in the playground in front of the bathhouse. We had had mimeographed handbills distributed through the neighborhood the day before; the newspapers had been notified. We had our committee ready to lead the march, and we had the playground pretty well filled. Some of the older generation were there lining the sides of the playground. I assumed they would be marching with us, but, significantly enough, they did not. We should have realized that, if we wanted to get the older generation, we had to work through their leadership too. As the march got under way, young boys from all over the district thronged in among us carrying their home-made banners. And so we set off for city hall right through the center of the business district. We had the satisfaction of stopping traffic all along the route, but it was not for long, since the parade moved very fast. We had made the mistake of having all our committee up in front, and it seemed that everybody behind us was trying to get to the front, so that we leaders were almost stampeded. And some of the women pushing baby carriages were unable to keep up.

We had no opposition from the police, who were only concerned with an orderly demonstration as we assembled in the courtyard below the city hall. Then the ten committee members went up to see the mayor, while the rest of the marchers sang "God Bless America" and other songs to the accompaniment of an improvised band. We had known that the mayor was out of town, but our demonstration could not wait, so we talked to the acting mayor. He got our names and a list of our grievances, treating us seriously and respectfully. As our committee members began to speak, I heard Sam saying behind

me in a low voice: "Get out of here, you cheap racketeer." I turned
to see the local politician, Angelo Fiumara, elbowing his way in.
Fiumara stood his ground and spoke up at the first opportunity:
"I would like to add my voice to the protest as a private citizen. . . ."
Sam interrupted, calling out: "He's got nuttin' to do with us. He's
just trying to chisel in." Mike Giovanni reiterated Sam's remarks,
and the acting mayor ruled that he would not hear Fiumara at that
time. While the speaking was going on, I distributed a prepared
statement to the reporters. At the end of our session the acting
mayor promised that all our protests would be seriously considered
and that any possible action would be taken.

We then marched to the bathhouse playground, where we told
our followers what had taken place in the mayor's office. Here again,
Angelo Fiumara tried to address the crowd, and we elbowed him out.
The next day's newspapers carried big stories with pictures of our
demonstration. We were given credit for having three hundred to
fifteen hundred marchers with us in the various papers. The fellows
happily accepted the figure of fifteen hundred, but I suspect three
hundred was closer to the truth. The day after the demonstration,
engineers were examining the boilers in the bathhouse, and in less
than a week we had hot water. The street-cleaning and the garbage
collections also seemed to be pepped up, for at least a short time.
For all the mistakes we had made, it was evident that the demonstration had brought results. But now the problem was: What next?
We had got an organization together, and we had staged a demonstration. Somehow, we must keep Cornerville working together.

In this effort we were completely unsuccessful. Several committee
meetings petered out without any agreements on concerted action.
I think there were several difficulties here. In the first place, the
committee members were not accustomed to meeting together or
working together personally. There was nothing to bring them
together except the formal business of the meeting. Their ties were
on their various street corners. In the second place, we had started
off with such a sensational performance that anything else would be
anticlimax. It seemed hard to get up enthusiasm for any activity
that would be dwarfed beside our protest march.

I came to realize that any over-all street corner organization would
have to be built around some sort of continuing activity. The softball
league developed the following spring and met this need to some
extent. In fact, I worked with the same men in setting up the league,
so in a sense the march on city hall did have continuing consequences,
though they fell far short of our fond hopes.

Farewell to Cornerville

Through the spring and summer of 1940, most of my time was spent in writing the first draft of *Street Corner Society*. I already had the case studies of the Nortons and the Italian Community Club. I followed these with three manuscripts which I then called "Politics and the Social Structure," "The Racketeer in the Cornerville S. and A. Club," and "The Social Structure of Racketeering."

As I wrote, I showed the various parts to Doc and went over them with him in detail. His criticisms were invaluable in my revision. At times, when I was dealing with him and his gang, he would smile and say: "This will embarrass me, but this is the way it was, so go ahead with it."

When I left Cornerville in midsummer of 1940, the Cornerville S. and A. Club had a farewell beer party for me. We sang "God Bless America" three times and the "Beer Barrel Polka" six times. I have moved around many times in my life, and yet I have never felt so much as though I were leaving home. The only thing that was missing was a farewell from the Nortons, and that was impossible, for the Nortons were no more by this time.

Cornerville Revisited

Compared to the anthropologist who studies a primitive tribe in a remote part of the world, the student of a modern American community faces distinctly different problems. In the first place, he is dealing with a literate people. It is certain that some of these people, and perhaps many of them, will read his research report. If he disguises the name of the district as I have done, many outsiders apparently will not discover where the study was actually located. I am still surprised to encounter people who locate Cornerville some hundreds of miles from its actual locale. The people in the district, of course, know it is about them, and even the changed names do not disguise the individuals for them. They remember the researcher and know the people with whom he associated and know enough about the various groups to place the individuals with little chance of error.

In such a situation the researcher carries a heavy responsibility. He would like his book to be of some help to the people in the district; at least, he wants to take steps to minimize the chances of it doing any harm, fully recognizing the possibility that certain individuals may suffer through the publication.

I cannot write a sequel entitled "Cornerville in Transition," for my visits back to the district have been infrequent and of short duration. However, I can provide a little information on what has happened to some of the chief people in the book in the intervening years and as to what effect, if any, the book has had on them and the district.

It took Doc a long time to find a secure place upon the economic ladder. He had no steady job until the war boom got well under way. Then at last he caught on and was doing very well until the postwar cutback came. People were then laid off according to their seniority, and Doc was out of work once more.

At last he did get a job in an electronics plant. At the time of my last visit (December 1953) I found that he had worked his way up to a position as assistant supervisor in the production planning department of the factory. Such a department is a nerve center for the factory, for it handles the scheduling of the orders through every department of the plant.

Doc has achieved some success in attaining this position, but he tends to minimize his accomplishments. He explains, "On the technical side, I stink. The only place I really shine is where I have to go around and talk the foreman into running a new order ahead of the one he was planning to run. I can do that without getting him upset." So Doc is applying some of the social skill he displayed in Cornerville in this new factory world. However, he is working in an industry of very advanced technical development, so that his lack of knowledge in this field will probably set a ceiling upon his advancement.

Doc got married shortly after he got his first steady job in World War II. His wife was an attractive Cornerville girl, a very intelligent and able person who had developed a small clothing store of her own.

I had one visit with Doc about five years after the book was published. Doc's reaction at the time seemed a combination of pride and embarrassment.

I asked Doc for the reaction of the members of his own gang. He said that Mike (to whom I had sent a copy) had seemed to like the book. Danny's only comment was: "Jesus, you're really a hell of a guy. If I was a dame, I'd marry you." The other members of the gang? So far as Doc knew, they had never read it. The question had come up all right. One night on the corner, one of the fellows said to Doc: "Say, I hear Bill Whyte's book is out. Maybe we should go up to the library and read it." Doc steered them off.

"No, you wouldn't be interested, just a lot of big words. That's for the professors."

On another occasion, Doc was talking to the editor of the English-language weekly newspaper dealing with the Italian colony. The editor was thinking of publishing an article about the book. Doc discouraged him, and no such notice appeared.

I assume that in his quiet way Doc did everything he could to discourage the local reading of the book for the possible embarrassment it might cause a number of individuals, including himself. For example, it could hardly be pleasant reading for the low-ranking members of the Nortons to see it pointed out how low they ranked and what sort of difficulties they got into. Therefore, I have every sympathy with Doc's efforts in limiting the circulation of the book.

Mike Giovanni moved on from Cornerville to become a labor-union leader. It began with a job in a rapidly expanding war industry. Mike had no sooner been hired than he began looking around to organize a union. Shortly after this, he was fired. He took his case to the appropriate government agency, charging that he was fired for union activities. The company was ordered to put Mike back to work. He wrote me that, when he reappeared on the job, the situation seemed to change suddenly and dramatically. The other workers had thought they had seen the last of him. Now that he showed what could be done, they began signing up. For some months Mike was at the plant gate for half an hour before the shift came on and half an hour after his shift went home, distributing pledge cards. And he personally signed up fifteen hundred members. When the union was recognized, Mike became its vice-president. He also wrote a weekly column in the union paper under the heading of "Mr. CIO." The column was written in a colorful style and must have commanded a good deal of attention in the local.

At the next union election, Mike ran for president. He wrote me that his opponent was a man who had had very little to do with organizing the union. But he was a popular fellow—and he was an Irishman. Mike lost. Shortly after this time, the company began large-scale layoffs following the end of the war. Without a union office, Mike's seniority did not protect him, and he dropped out of his job.

All I know about Danny is that he finally got married to the pious girl who had always loved him in spite of his gambling and other activities. At last reports he is still working in Spong's horse room.

George and Carrie Ravello have been out of politics for a long time, but George has a fancy new funeral parlor.

What has happened to Chick Morelli? I was particularly anxious to answer that question, and yet I hesitated to go out for the answer.

I debated the question with myself. I finally decided that Chick could be the individual whom I had hurt. I must find out what the book had done to him.

I telephoned Chick to ask if I could see him. At first he missed my name, but then he replied quite cordially. Still I was wondering what would happen when we sat down to talk.

I found that he had moved out of Cornerville, but, paradoxically enough, he still lived in the same ward inside the city. Doc, the old corner boy, had moved to the suburbs, and Chick, the man who was on his way up, had stayed in the center of the city.

Chick introduced me to his wife, an attractive and pleasant girl, who neither came from Cornerville nor was of Italian extraction. We sat in the living room of an apartment that, with its furniture, books, curtains, and so on, looked distinctly middle class. For a few minutes we skirted about the subject that we all knew we were going to discuss. Then I asked Chick to tell me frankly his reactions to my book.

Chick began by saying that there were just two main criticisms as far as he was concerned. In the first place, he said that he did not think I distinguished his own way of speaking sufficiently from that of the corner boys when I quoted him. "You made me talk too rough, just like a gangster."

I expressed surprise at this, and here his wife joined in with the comment that she thought that I had made Chick look like a snob. Chick agreed that he had got that picture too. His wife pulled the book down from the shelf and reread the passage where I quote Doc on the occasion of a political meeting in which Chick is on and off the stage seven times in order to take the tickets that he is going to sell for the candidate. They both laughed at this, and Chick commented that he would never do a thing like that any more. She said that Chick had told her before they got married that he had once had a book written about him. But she added that he didn't give her the book to read until after they had been married.

Chick laughed at this, and then he went on to his second criticism. "Bill, everything you described about what we did is true all right, but you should have pointed out that we were just young then. That was a stage that we were going through. I've changed a lot since that time."

Chick expressed concern over the reactions of other people to my book. "You know, after the book was out a while, I ran into Doc, and he was really upset about it. He said to me, 'Can you imagine that! After all I did for Bill Whyte, the things he put in the book about me. You know that thing about when I said you would step on the neck of your best friend just to get ahead. Well, now, maybe I said that, but I didn't really mean it. I was just sore at the time.'"

Chick seemed really concerned about what the book had done to my relationship with Doc. I did not tell him that Doc had read every page of the original manuscript, nor did I give my interpretation that Doc was simply going around repairing his fences after some of these intimate reactions had been exposed.

Chick assured me that he was not the hard character that the book seemed to make him. "Really, I'm a soft touch." And he gave me instances where he had helped out his friends at no advantage to himself.

As I was getting ready to leave, I asked Chick if he had anything more to say about the book.

"Well, I wonder if you couldn't have been more constructive, Bill. You think publishing something like this really does any good?"

I asked what he meant. Then he mentioned my pointing out (as he had told me himself) that he had difficulty with his *th* sound. I had also discussed the commotion the fellows sometimes caused in the theaters, the fact that they sometimes went to dances without ties, and so on—all points that make Cornerville look like a rather uncouth district. (I am unable to locate any references in the book to commotion in the theaters or men at dances without ties.)

"The trouble is, Bill, you caught the people with their hair down. It's a true picture, yes; but people feel it's a little too personal."

As he walked with me to the subway station, we got to talking about his political career. I had been quite astounded to hear that he had missed being elected to the Board of Aldermen by a scant three votes. The Chick Morelli whom I had known never could have come so close. Without expressing my surprise, I tried to get him to talk about this.

"You know, the funny thing is, Bill, I didn't get many votes from Cornerville. The people that you grow up with, it seems, are jealous of anybody that is getting ahead. Where I got my support was right around here where I live now. I know these fellows on the street corner, and I really fit with them."

As if to demonstrate for me, he nodded and waved cordially at several corner groups as we walked by. In a later visit to Cornerville, I learned that Chick Morelli had at last been elected to office.

Chick left me with a good deal to think over. In the first place, it is hard to describe the sense of relief I felt after seeing him. Although it must have hurt him at the time to read the book, he had been able to take it in stride, and he was now even able to laugh at himself in that earlier period. As I discussed these things later with Doc, I began to wonder whether the book might perhaps even have helped Chick. It was Doc who presented this theory. He argued that not many people have an opportunity to see themselves as other people see them. Perhaps the reading of the book enabled Chick to get valuable perspective on himself and even enabled him to change his behavior. Certainly, Doc argued, Chick had changed a good deal. He was still working hard to get ahead, but he seemed no longer the self-centered, insensitive person that he had earlier appeared to be. Chick certainly had to change in order to have any hopes of getting ahead in Democratic politics—and somehow, for reasons that I cannot now explain, Chick had decided that his future lay with the Democrats rather than with the Republicans, in whose direction he seemed to be moving as I left Cornerville. So, at least, the book had not hurt Chick, and it seemed just possible that it had helped him.

I was also pleased to find that basically Chick accepted the book. This, of course, pleased me as a writer, but it also spoke well of Chick. I suspect that the man who can accept such a portrait of himself is also the man who can change the behavior described.

Chick's objections to the book seemed quite interesting to me. As to the way I had quoted him in the book, I felt on very firm ground. He did talk differently from the corner boys, but not quite as differently as he had imagined. If a quotation from him contained an ungrammatical expression or some typical corner-boy phrase, I am reasonably sure that that part of it is authentic. I was so sensitive to the differences between Chick and the corner boys that I would have been unlikely to imagine any expressions that made them appear more alike. The criticism seemed to say more about Chick's status and aspirations than it did about my research methods.

Perhaps, indeed, I should have pointed out that Chick and his friends were young and were just going through a stage of development. But youth, in itself, does not seem to be a full explanation. These men were not adolescents; they were at least in their mid-twenties. I think that the important fact is that they had not yet secured any firm foothold in society. They were young men who had left home and had not yet arrived anywhere. I am inclined to agree that this is an important factor in explaining the aggressiveness, the self-centeredness, and so on, that appear in Chick and some of his friends at that period. Later on, when Chick had found something of a place for himself, he could relax and be more concerned with other people. Is this just a phenomenon of social mobility out of the slums and into middle-class status? As I think back upon my own career, I can recall with a trace of embarrassment some of the things that I said and did in the early stages when I was struggling to gain a good foothold on the academic ladder. It is easy to be modest and unassuming once you have achieved a fairly secure position and won a certain amount of recognition.

I had no quarrel with Chick's point that I had caught people with their hair down, and yet I could sympathize with the people who felt that way. If you are going to be interviewed for the newspaper, you put on your good suit and your best tie, make sure that the kitchen dishes are cleaned up, and in general take all the steps you associate with making a public appearance. You appear before the public in the role that you would like to play before the public. You cannot do this with a social researcher who comes in and lives with you. I do not see any way of getting around this difficulty. I suppose there must always be aspects of our reports that will give a certain amount of embarrassment to the people we have been studying. At least I was reassured to find that the reaction in this case had not been nearly so serious as I had feared.

While we can only speculate about the impact of the book upon Doc and Chick and many others, there is one man upon whom it has had a profound effect—and I was not always sure that the effect would be constructive. Working with me made Sam Franco, who had only a high-school education, want to be a human-relations research man.

When the war broke out, Sam enlisted in the Marine Corps. I wrote to him around the time that *Street Corner Society* was to be published, asking whether I should send a copy to him. He wrote to say that his unit was about to be shipped overseas, that where he was going he would be able to carry nothing extra, and that I should send the book to his wife in Cornerville. Some months later I again heard from him. He had fought through three island landings. On the third, his closest friend in the service was killed beside him, and he was knocked unconscious by the concussion. He came to on a hospital ship heading back to San Diego. His first letter to me from the hospital seemed somewhat discouraged and disorganized, as is natural for a man who has gone through such experiences. A week later he wrote me again, full of enthusiasm. He had called for his wife to send the book as soon as he had returned to this country, and now he had read it. He wanted me to know that he believed in the book, and he believed in this sort of work. He was going back to Cornerville to carry on himself.

He even enrolled in a correspondence course in sociology, but this he abandoned after a while. He wrote me that somehow it did not seem the sort of thing that he and I had been doing in Cornerville.

After returning to Eastern City, he got himself a very good job with a firm that handled window decorations for department stores, and he was making money on the side with floats for parades and various odd jobs in the artistic line. Still, he had not abandoned the idea that he wanted to do social research. He even worked at it in the Marine Corps Reserve, where he was first a corporal and then a sergeant. (He had been offered a chance to go to OCS during his basic training but had turned it down.) The reserve unit had one evening of training each week, and after each session Sam would pound out a record of what had taken place on his typewriter. He not only observed; he also experimented on the informal group structure. He picked out a task that would call for four or five men. He picked out one individual and told him to get three or four others of his own choosing and then do the job. Then Sam observed which individuals the man chose and how effectively the job was done. He picked out men whom he considered followers in the informal structure, and observed the inefficiencies and incoordinations that developed as they sought to get the group working with them. He also picked out individuals he had tabbed as leaders and observed the marked contrast in the effectiveness of the performance. Of course, the freedom that he gave the individual to pick his own work associates helped Sam to delineate the natural groupings.

Sam went through this process, obsessed with the idea that even the Marine Corps (for which he had the typical Marine Corps loyalty) could be a much more effective organization if officers and noncoms had a better understanding of informal group structures.

As best I could, operating from a great distance, I tried to get Sam the help that he needed. First, George Homans took an interest in his field work and got him in touch with a Marine Corps officer who was then attached to Harvard. On his own, Sam managed to interest his superior officers of the Marine Corps Reserve in his group observations.

Sam wrote that he was quite prepared to drop his decorating job and reenlist in the Marine Corps if he could have some assurance that he would be able to pursue the sort of human-relations research upon which he was embarked. We found, however, that the Marine Corps had no provision for any such activity. There were some people within the Corps who thought so well of Sam and his ideas that they even sought to get a special classification set up for him, but that was too much to expect. So Sam continued researching on his own, torn between his job and the work he wanted to do.

The Korean War changed all this. We visited Sam and his family several weeks after the outbreak of hostilities. At the time he had already received his call to go back into the service, and he was a very discouraged and disgruntled man. There was, of course, the question of survival. When a Marine goes into battle, he told me, he does not expect to come through it alive. In fact, his whole training conditions him to accepting death on the battlefield. If, by some remarkable good fortune, he does escape, he feels that he has more than used up his chances of survival. If he should go into combat again, death would be an absolute certainty. And now he had a family to think of, and he had got used to peacetime pursuits. He and the other men in his reserve unit would go back when they were called, of course, but they all felt that they had done as much as should be asked of them.

There was something more than physical survival at stake. For years Sam had been struggling to do research on human relations. Perhaps it was a foolish and vain hope, but he hated to give it up. And going back to combat duty certainly meant giving it up.

I said it was too bad that Sam was in the Marine Corps, for that was the one branch of the services that presented the very least opportunity to develop the work in which he was interested. If he were in the Air Force or in the Navy or even in the Army, there might be some chance of his fitting into a research program. It was then that he told me that there was some chance of being assigned to "detached duty," that, as a Marine, he could be assigned to one of the other services if a special request came through and was accepted by the Marine Corps. Without any real hope of success, I told him I would work on this.

I wrote to a man I knew who was in charge of a research program in the Air Force. I gave a full account of Sam's work with me and of what I thought he could do—if he were working under professional supervision. I got back a noncommittal letter indicating that something might possibly be done. A few weeks later, to my surprise, I learned that the wheels were actually turning. The research unit of the Air Force had made an official request that Sam Franco be assigned to it. The papers were on their way up the line in the Air Force, and strong recommendations for Sam from his superior officers in the Marine Corps were also going up through channels.

At last I heard that the request had been turned down, and this looked final, even though Sam told me that there was one loophole remaining. Meanwhile, Sam was back in training and awaiting shipment overseas. Toward the end of December 1950, he called me long distance. "Bill, it's just like in the movies. Yesterday I received my orders to ship out for Korea, and today the papers came through for the assignment with the Air Force."

Sam has been with the Air Force for about three years now, for the first two on detached duty and finally as an Air Force master sergeant as the result of a transfer that had to be approved by the commanding generals of both the Marine Corps and the Air Force. So, at last, he has been able to get into research full time. He has been operating in an atmosphere where questionnaires are the accepted method and where the professional research men readily admit that they cannot utilize Sam as he should be utilized. Nevertheless, he has been out on several brief organizational studies and has shown that he can get data that are generally unavailable to the civilians with the research unit. How far he can go, no one can yet say, but he is in the field where he wants to be and is working at writing up his observations on discipline and leadership in military organizations.

So the story has a happy ending—so far. But it was only by an extraordinary chance that Sam was able to pursue the work that he wanted to do. Had the chance not come, his association with me might simply have served to frustrate him with ambitions that he could never expect to gratify.

How widely has the book been read in Eastern City and in Cornerville in particular? Here I had one of my great surprises at the very outset. The publisher sent review copies to the major newspapers in the largest cities in the country. I did not expect to get very many such newspaper reviews, but I assumed at least that the book would get some attention in the Eastern City papers. I was sure that no one who was really familiar with the life of the city could read the book without knowing he was reading of his own city or without identifying the particular section of it. This local angle would naturally bring the book a good deal more attention. What effect this would have—other than selling copies—I did not stop to imagine.

Curiously enough, while the book did receive full-column reviews in several large metropolitan newspapers, not a single one of the Eastern City dailies gave it any attention whatsoever. Just why this was, I am still unable to conjecture. The nearest I got to a local review was one which appeared in the nearest major city, but there the reviewer shrewdly guessed that the locale of my study had been in a city a thousand miles away.

Even without newspaper fanfare, the book naturally attracted some attention in Cornerville. Kathleen's book jacket (a street corner scene) was posted on the bulletin board for "recent books of interest" in the Cornerville branch library for at least five years after publication. It proved popular enough, so that the library had to buy a second copy, and then someone did me the compliment of stealing a copy. Sam Franco, however, reports after a visit with a member of the local library staff: "When she told me that the book was very popular, I said that it did not tie in with what I had found out. When I mentioned your book, most of them knew of it. When I pinpointed them into telling me something about the book, they would in all cases tell me they had never read it. . . . Still, it is my strong opinion that your book was intensively read by the settlement houses, social workers, and all those involved in your book." Even here, we must have our reservations, for, according to Doc, most of the Nortons had not read the book.

I seem to be looked upon by the social workers, at Norton Street at least, as a man who turned against his own people. One of my informants passed on this reaction from the settlement, after talking with one of the social workers. He said that they felt that "they had taken you in good faith, but you gave them the business. He went on to say that you only gave one side of the story in order to make sensational reading, that you were immature, that your 'sophomoric attitude' hurt them. I asked him to explain how the book hurt them. He didn't know what to say and then said that the book didn't really hurt them but that many social workers and all the people at Harvard read the book, and that's what he said was 'hurting.'"

What has been happening to social work in Cornerville? Today the Cornerville House has two full-time workers of Italian extraction (but not from Cornerville) on its staff. The Norton Street House has a full-time man, born and reared in Cornerville, on its staff for work with young boys. I believe that all three of these people have had college educations and professional training beyond that.

On my latest visit to Cornerville I had a long talk with Mr. Kendall, who was head of boys' work in the period of my study and is now head of the Cornerville House.

He began by recognizing that the settlements do not generally reach the corner boys with whom I was dealing. However, he said that some people questioned whether this group should be reached by a settlement. The parents like to look upon the settlement as a place where their children are in a wholesome environment. If the typical corner group were taken in, its very presence might drive out those whom the settlements have been successful in reaching.

I acknowledged this possibility, but further discussion brought out an interesting contradiction within the experience of Mr. Kendall and his Cornerville House. In the late stages of World War II, Kendall became concerned that the house gymnasium was getting very little use. He hired a returning war hero and corner-boy leader to do "outside work" in organizing a basketball league. Within several weeks he had organized *forty-two* teams into several basketball leagues. In the succeeding months the house was seething with basketball excitement, and everyone seems now to look back upon this period as one of the highpoints in the history of the house. Mr. Kendall mentioned no cases of groups dropping out because various roughnecks were using the gym. (After this one season the emergency funds that had made the position possible were no longer available, and the very successful organizer was not retained on the staff.)

There was also a dancing class that brought in first a few and then large numbers of adolescent girls and boys. The boys, from all I could learn, seemed to be authentic corner boys. At first there was some horseplay, but the teacher, a very capable Italian-American woman, soon got things organized in real ball-room style.

Apparently a settlement house can take in a broader range of groups than may be commonly supposed—given always the limitation that a corner gang wants a meeting place for every night of the week and that no settlement can provide such space.

What are the prospects for hiring local men who have not had college or social-work training? The answer seems to be: Not very good. The heads of the institutions who would make such appointments are under pressure to move in quite a different direction. The schools of social work have for years been trying to get social work recognized as a profession. How can it become a profession if the young man who got his basic training on the street corner is accepted? The standards must be raised. That means a college degree *and* an M.A. in social work.

No one is threatened that his funds will be cut off if he hires other than M.A.'s in social work. But the head worker is asked how many people on his staff have this degree, and he hears references to other institutions which are not "measuring up." Upon inquiry, he learns that the institutions that are not "measuring up" are those which persist in hiring people who do not have their social-work M.A.'s.

A similar pressure affects even the summer camping activities. No one can require that all the counselors be social-work M.A.'s, but it seems to be desirable that they be *college boys*. The agency that evaluates summer camps circulates a questionnaire which asks how many college boys and how many noncollege boys are to serve as counselors. It is evident what the right answer is on this point. On this question, the better the settlement-house camp, the fewer local men it will have as counselors. (Of course, there will be a few local college men available, but the pressure toward hiring college men will inevitably lead the institution to look outside the district.)

So there seems to be little chance that future corner-boy leaders will play a greater role in organizing settlement-house activities. Perhaps it is only through reaching social-work students that *Street Corner Society* could have any impact upon social work.

Reflections on Field Research

As I carried through the Cornerville study, I was also learning how to do field research. I learned from the mistakes I made. The most important of these I have described fully. I learned from the successes that I had, but these were less spectacular and more difficult to describe. It may therefore be worthwhile to try to summarize the main characteristics of the research.

Of course, I am not claiming that there is a one best way to do field research. The methods used should depend upon the nature of the field situation and of the research problem. I am simply trying to fit together the findings of the study and the methods required to arrive at such findings.

In the first place, the study took a long time. This was due in part to the fact that I had had no previous field experience and very little educational background that was directly relevant to my problem. But that was not all. It took a long time because the parts of the study that interest me most depended upon an intimate familiarity with people and situations. Furthermore, I learned to understand a group only through observing how it changed *through time*.

This familiarity gave rise to the basic ideas in this book. I did not develop these ideas by any strictly logical process. They dawned on me out of what I was seeing, hearing, doing—and feeling. They grew out of an effort to organize a confusing welter of experience.

I had to balance familiarity with detachment, or else no insights would have come. There were fallow periods when I seemed to be just marking time. Whenever life flowed so smoothly that I was taking it for granted, I had to try to get outside of my participating self and struggle again to explain the things that seemed obvious.

This explains why my research plans underwent such drastic changes in the course of the study. I was on an exploration into unknown territory. Worse than unknown, indeed, because the then existing literature on slum districts was highly misleading. It would have been impossible to map out at the beginning the sort of study I eventually found myself doing.

This is not an argument against initial planning of research. If his study grows out of a body of soundly executed research, then the student can and should plan much more rigorously than I did. But, even so, I suspect that he will miss important data unless he is flexible enough to modify his plans as he goes along. The apparent "tangent" often turns out to be the main line of future research.

Street Corner Society is about particular people and situations and events. I wanted to write about Cornerville. I found that I could not write about Cornerville in general without discarding most of the data I had upon individuals and groups. It was a long time before I realized that I could explain Cornerville better through telling the stories of those individuals and groups than I could in any other way.

Instead of studying the general characteristics of classes of people, I was looking at Doc, Chick, Tony Cataldo, George Ravello, and others. Instead of getting a cross-sectional picture of the community at a particular point in time, I was dealing with a time sequence of interpersonal events.

Although I could not cover all Cornerville, I was building up the structure and functioning of the community through intensive examination of some of its parts—*in action*. I was relating the parts together through observing events between groups and between group leaders and the members of the larger institutional structures (of politics and the rackets). I was seeking to build a sociology based upon observed interpersonal events. That, to me, is the chief methodological and theoretical meaning of *Street Corner Society*.

2

French Canada: The Natural

History of a Research Project

Everett C. Hughes

The French Canada project, part of which was reported in *French Canada in Transition,* was not "designed," but rather was a growth of some twenty-five years. One might even speak of it as a social movement, for eventually many people were drawn into it. This essay was originally prepared as a memorandum describing the natural history of that movement for a conference which Robert Lamb organized for the purpose of assessing our knowledge and methods of study—not just of French Canada, but of other societies as well. My aim at that conference was to set a starting point for discussion of the several orders of social phenomena to which the sessions were devoted: the individual, small groups, institutions, and communities. Then, as now, I considered the French Canada studies as part of the study of the evolution of Canadian society, always related to the historical period in which they were conducted.

The Beginnings

In the late 1920's, Carl A. Dawson began to study the process of settlement of the frontier as seen in the growth and changes of a number of communities in the western provinces of Canada. Some of these communities were experiments in settling British urban workers on the land; many were created by people of Continental European origin; others were settled by sects seeking on the distant prairie a haven where they could practice a peculiar faith in peace

Author's Note: This paper was presented at the annual meeting of the Society for Applied Anthropology, summer 1952. A similar version of this chapter appeared in *Anthropologica,* N.S. Vol. V, No. 2, 1963; reprinted here by permission. *French Canada in Transition* was published by the University of Chicago Press, 1943. A paperback edition appeared in 1963.

and prosperity. Dawson had thus chosen as his own one of Canada's great problems.

He had just begun this work when I joined him in the still new department of sociology, where we two made up the staff, at McGill University. I had had no previous interest in Canadian problems and little knowledge of the country. In the several months between my appointment and my departure from Chicago for Montreal, I read a good deal about the French Canadians, of whom I knew a large number lived in Montreal. I decided to study the French Canadians simply because their presence seemed the most interesting fact about Montreal and that region. By so slight a joining of circumstances, I picked Canada's other great problem: the mutual adjustment of the two major ethnic groups. My choice complemented Dawson's. A few years later the Rockefeller Foundation granted funds to McGill University for social research. A committee decided to spend it on study of unemployment, a pressing problem of that time. Dawson and I insisted that an understanding of unemployment required an understanding of the basic pattern of employment in Canada, and that pattern was clearly ethnic. Our plan was not highly regarded by most of the committee, but, since we had a plan and kept at it, eventually more of the money was spent on our studies than on others. Among our studies were monographs on various ethnic elements, including the British immigrants, in Canadian cities as well as on the land; eventually, I got some students subsidized to study the division of labor between French and English in a number of industries on the plea that this too was necessary to an understanding of unemployment.

From graduate school to Montreal I took two conceptions of a people such as the French Canadians: (1) they were an immigrant group in the course of being assimilated, and (2) they were a national minority.

In the United States, sociologists had devoted much of their effort to a study of European immigrants who had come to America more recently than they had. From simple talk of loyalty and Americanization, some of the sociologists had gone on to seek a more general set of concepts for describing the changes that took place when diverse peoples met in the same community. Park adapted the socialization cycle of Simmel to this problem; contact was followed successively by conflict, accommodation, and assimilation. Application of these concepts to the contact of peoples rested on the assumption that one people was more ephemeral than the other, that one would disappear into the other. Although other Canadians knew well that the French Canadians were not an immigrant people but a "charter member" group, I felt that they generally thought that the French would, and ought eventually, to disappear; that the English Canadian group would and ought to outlast the French Canadians as an ethnic entity. A few studies appeared now and again on the number of French who spoke English or who otherwise appeared to be abandoning their culture. Without going into why I think the measurement of change of individual cultural traits is a false way to study the relations between ethnic groups, I will simply say that for some reason I did not accept this model of the assimilation cycle and resisted the desire of some of my students to proceed with studies on that model.

The second conception was of the French Canadians as a territorial national minority, such as one finds in Europe where a political boundary is altered, leaving some people in the wrong country. The people thus marooned may then seek to have the boundary changed so that their citizenship and ethnic identity will again correspond; or, if a whole people has been deprived of sovereignty, they may seek to found a new and separate state. The French Canadians were made into a people and a minority in precisely this way; but there was no movement among them to join France, and there appeared to be no major or persistent movement to seek political separation from Canada. They did show minority behavior in their insistence on a certain autonomy and in their constant resistance to alleged encroachment on their rights. I found the national minority model of use, but as I read the voluminous literature, it appeared to me that political objectives as such were relatively unimportant to French Canadians. The most constant plaint was that French Canadians got less than their fair share of good positions, wealth, and power in the economic and political institutions. Their great battle cry, along with cultural autonomy, was *parity*—a share in all positions commensurate with their proportion of the population. Parity, however, implied not separation but integration into a larger whole. I find in my notes that I quite early came to the idea of studying just what the place of French and English was in the larger whole of which both were part, and especially of discovering the ethnic division of labor (or of economic function), both in its major outlines and in its subtleties.

Studying the Ethnic Division of Labor

In following this lead, I read a good deal on the establishment of industries in Quebec, which led me to the labor movement. The Catholic Church had tried early to keep the French labor of Quebec out of unions, especially out of unions that were religiously "neutral." A few good studies had been done on the movement to organize Catholic labor syndicates; these led me to a literature—of which I had known nothing—on the various attempts to establish a separate Catholic labor movement in various parts of Europe. A good deal of this literature dealt with the German Rhineland, where Protestant entrepreneurs from outside the region had brought heavy industry to utilize local resources and had mobilized local Catholic peasants as their labor force. Protestant labor leaders had followed the entrepreneurs to organize the local labor, exactly as in Quebec. As I followed this case, I saw more clearly the model of the region or community industrialized by outsiders, cultural aliens. The local region furnished labor, raw materials, or power, or all three. The newcomers furnished capital, enterprise, and technical knowledge. In the course of development, the native nonindustrial middle or upper class, or both, found many of its functions usurped by the alien industrial leadership. In fact, the community had two sets of leaders, one traditional and "spiritual," the other new, secular, and technological. The strain between the two caused many repercussions in politics and in local institutions. To rise in the new order required new skills; but the educational institutions were geared to produce those qualities and skills valued in the preindustrial regime. To retool the schools and universities quickly for the new order would have required even more cultural aliens. Similar dilemmas occurred in other institutions: trade and labor organizations, local government, religious organizations, charities, and even families and cliques.

It appeared to me there were essentially two kinds of industrial communities or regions: (1) those in which by some social and economic chemistry local people themselves initiated the great changes of industrialization, eventually drawing a supply of labor from outside (a situation to which the assimilation cycle concept may be applied with some reason); and (2) those to which industry is brought by outsiders who exploit local labor and who undertake as many social changes as they think necessary for their purposes, within the limits of their power as counterbalanced by that of the local society. England and New England are of the first kind; the Rhineland and French Canada are of the second. Since the agents of social change in the Rhine country differed from the native people in religion but not in language, it seemed promising to examine this region to better sort out the aspects caused by ethnic difference from those caused by the industrial invasion and differences of religion. I did, in fact, spend more than a year in Germany digging up the story of industrialization there and trying out with data of the German occupational and religious censuses various schemes of tabulation which I might use in analyzing the division of labor between French, English, and others in Canada. The study of the Rhine case did indeed fix in my mind more clearly the model of a whole region undergoing that series of changes known as industrialization, with one ethnic element being the active, enterprising agent of change, and the other having to adjust itself, reluctantly, to these changes.

When I returned from the German excursion, I started a few students on the ethnic division of labor in Montreal. William Roy went to a number of industrial concerns and obtained data which he worked into tables showing the proportions of French and English among employees of different kinds and ranks. From these tables we gleaned several characteristic patterns. In heavy machine industries, a solid core of old-country British skilled workmen apparently could keep the French out of apprenticeships. In industries with mass production, utilizing semiskilled operators, the working force was almost completely French. Fiduciary functions were apparently kept closely in English hands, including the faithful pensioners so often kept on as night watchmen. If there was need for extensive contact with the public, especially the little people of the city and region, the French got their chance.

Stuart Jamieson worked on the professions and found that not only were there marked differences in choice of profession among French, English, and Jewish, but that in the same profession each of the groups tended to practice in a certain way. The professionals of each group performed not only the peculiar services wanted by their own peoples but also some special part of the professional services of the larger system of which all were part. Thus French and Jewish lawyers tended to practice in small firms, whereas a great majority of the English lawyers were gathered into a few large firms. A leading figure in each large firm was a member of the boards of a group of powerful corporations. Each such English firm had, however, one or two French members, apparently to act as liaison with French people and to plead before French judges. It thus became clear to me that it was much too simple to say merely that the French preferred certain occupations and the English preferred others, and that the English discriminated against French in appointing people to positions of authority in industry (although these things were doubtless true). One had to regard the whole as a system in which interaction of the two peoples had brought about a division of function that was, in some points, quite subtle.

Rural Communities as Gauges of Change

During this time, I had some conversations with my close friend and associate, Robert Redfield, who had a crew working on a series of communities in Yucatan. He hoped to learn something of the change from what he called folk culture to urban civilization by studying simultaneously a series of communities, each of which was assumed to represent a point in this kind of change. It seemed to me that if we were to understand fully what was happening in metropolitan Montreal, we had to find a base line from which to gauge changes in French Canadian culture and institutions. I began to think of a series of community studies with a village with no English people in or near it at one end, and with Montreal, where about one-fifth of all French Canadians live, at the other. Each community was to be picked for some special combination of the forces that might be at work on French Canadian institutions and mentality.

At the same time, Horace Miner, an enterprising graduate student of anthropology at the University of Chicago, obtained a field fellowship to study the base-line rural community. After much searching of statistics and maps, the community of St. Denis de Kamouraska was picked as being likely to show traditional French Canadian institutions operating in full force. It was remote but not backwoodsy or poor. This turned out to be an excellent choice, for it became clear that many of the traditional customs and practices depended on prosperity. A daughter of the house could not be kept at home spinning and weaving on her own loom with wool and flax from the family farm unless the family land was plentiful and fertile. Farmers on poor, hilly, and back-country farms had to go out to work in lumber camps, and their daughters had to go to towns to work. Thus the common phenomenon of proud preservation of traditions by a prosperous peasantry after they are lost by the agricultural laboring class. Miner's work has been published and is well known.[1] A couple of years ago he returned to the community for a few weeks and published some notes in the *American Journal of Sociology* on change since his first study.

It was our intention to study a series of rural communities, at various distances from the cities and from English people, with varying terrain and soil. The notion was that each kind of situation would tend to produce its own pattern of functional connections with the larger industrial and urban world outside. Léon Gérin, a French Canadian sociologist who studied under LePlay, had done a series

[1] Horace M. Miner, *St. Denis: A French-Canadian Parish*, Chicago: University of Chicago Press, 1939.

of studies of rural communities some forty years earlier, and Raoul Blanchard, the French geographer, had given a basic description of the soil and terrain, modes of agriculture, and movements of populations. We used these works to make tentative choices of kinds of communities to be studied. Some rather superficial studies of new northern settlements have been made since then, but no detailed studies to determine the flow of people and goods from country to city and from farm to industry, or the flow of fashion and other changes from city to country.

The middle term of the series was to be a small industrial city, many of which were located in the province of Quebec. We worked over government and business statistics with great care before choosing the first town, which my wife and I were to study ourselves. In the north and on the mountainous fringes of Quebec are towns with pulp mills, company towns where various nonferrous ores are mined, and a few where colossal power developments have brought aluminum smelters far out into the backwoods of yesterday. In some of these the industry created the town. Some are seasonal; some hire men only, and so on. Since we wanted to see what effect the newer industry had on French Canadian institutions, we chose to start with a community in which all these institutions had been in existence well before industry came, in which there were local French families of a wide variety of occupations and of a typical range of social classes, and in which consequently there were French Canadians accustomed to the roles of political and economic leadership. The problem was not defined primarily in terms of English and industrial influence on, let us say, the language spoken by people, but in terms of the operating social structure. Again, as in the case of Miner's work, this study has been published.

The Plan of the Book

The foreword and first chapter of the book contain some of the material I have enlarged upon in this essay. Next we described briefly the rural family and parish, for these are the cradle of the industrial labor force of the cities, and they are the institutions that undergo change under the influence of industry and the English. After considering the larger series of industrial towns and cities, we dealt with our chosen community. To understand the industrial town of today, it seemed to me that we had to know its past, the rise and decline of enterprises, institutions, and families through more than a century. With this setting in mind, we took up the division of labor, in and outside industry. In industry we were able to describe fairly exactly, I think, the division of labor, and to account for the details of it. Subsequent studies in other industries and cities have revealed very little deviation from these patterns.

In the section on nonindustrial occupations, we attempted to set up a scheme for analyzing what will happen in an interethnic community to those service and business enterprises that are subject to daily small choices of customers and clients, rather than to the major policy choices of executives. It seemed to me that we could posit that there are some services and goods wanted by both ethnic elements in identical form, whereas others are wanted by one more than by the other. Further, we can suppose that there are some things that people insist on getting from people of their own kind, whereas they are relatively indifferent about the hands from which they get other things.

From there we considered institutions, distinguishing those areas of life in which there is but one set of going concerns (institutions) operated by and for both elements of the population, and noting the changes brought about in them by industrialization, and the part played in them by French and English. Business, sports, and government showed but a single set of institutions. In religion and education there was almost complete separation of the two ethnic elements, but it turned out that the English as well as the French schools and churches had been profoundly affected by the new people of industry. The Catholic parishes and their auxiliary institutions showed great modification to suit industrial and urban conditions.

In the later chapters we presented the less formal aspect of things; or perhaps I should say the livelier side, for the French have a rich ceremonial calendar: informal social contacts, public gatherings, amusements, and fashions. The book closes with reference to Montreal, the metropolis. It was our aim to continue with studies in Montreal, but I left Canada at this point.

There are some bad lacunae in the study and in the book. Although we presented some data concerning cliques in the chapter on social contacts and had a good deal more in our field notes, we did not adequately analyze the operation of small and informal groups in the town and in the industries. I am reasonably sure that there were no interethnic small groups to speak of in the industries, but we should have obtained the data on small groups and informal understandings and controls. Our knowledge of informal organization of industry was confined to the upper levels of the hierarchy.

The analysis of the more intimate life of the masses of the people of the town is sketchy. The story of the working-class family—the internal stresses and strains of such a family newly come from farm to town and factory—is only touched upon. We did not get adequate case material on this point. In fact, what the family as a going concern is in Cantonville, what crises it meets in its ongoing life, we did not find out. M. Jean-Charles Falardeau of Université Laval studied the families of a large working-class parish in Quebec City. He has published material on the contingencies and life cycle of urban French Canadian families. We still do not have adequate knowledge of the changes in consumption patterns of individuals and families of the various classes of urban French Canadians. Such knowledge is necessary to an understanding of family objectives and of conflict between the family and its individual members.

The Structure of the French Canadian Personality

Just before I left Montreal I began talking with a psychiatrist who was analyzing some young people of the sophisticated classes of French Canadians. Although he had some rather ready clichés about them, he was really interested in learning the structure of French Canadian personalities. I had run into a number of restless, uneasy French young men who knew that they had been trained for a world that was passing, and that they had not the nerve to break away from their protective families far enough to start over and take the ego risks of a new kind of learning and a new kind of career. The contingency of being bred a gentleman a little too late had trapped them. This aspect of the industrialization of the region—the personality problems, the psychological risks—has not been studied. The most recent information I have shows that the French graduates of the French Canadian engineering schools still tend to seek the cover of semibureaucratic jobs. Whether they do it before or after a rebuff or two in industry, before or after a minor failure, I do not know. But the whole structure should be studied: the family, the church-controlled educational system, and so on, as they operate to produce people geared to certain patterns of risk and security, with certain balances with respect to reaching out and traveling far as against digging in and staying near home, with certain capacities for aggressive interaction and for tolerating criticism. And it should be studied by some combination of observing and analyzing personal careers with use of the devices now available for delving into the dreams and nightmares of people. The question may be this: Will the

French Canadian middle-class personality ever gear into the inter-actional systems of industrial line organizations; or will they skirt the edges, catching a slight hold only in certain liaison or staff positions which they hold precisely because they are French? In that case it might be that if French Canadians do rise in the line organization of industry they may be people of some new class created by industry itself. The story of the individual in French Canada, of the forming of his personality, and of his meeting the new big world as a series of career crises demanding fateful decisions on his part, has not been told either in my study or in any other.

Other Areas for Study

The program for studying a whole series of industrial communities was not carried through. The great recent development in Quebec has been that of new towns around new industries in the far north. In such towns there is no established French middle class, no set of local businesses and institutions, around them is no established *habitant*, or farm-owning class. It might be argued that we should have studied a north-country boom town in the first place, but I still think it served our purpose better to start with a town in which the French Canadian institutions and a French Canadian society were in full operation before English people brought industry. Yet the whole region will not be understood until someone analyzes what kinds of social and political structure grow up where the new English-managed industry builds a town with French labor, but with no counterbalancing French social élite except the clergy.

Even on the rural front, the full variety of typical communities has not been studied. Aileen Ross of McGill University has done one good study of the social processes of ethnic succession on the frontier between French and English in the eastern townships of Quebec.

The third kind of community in my study was to be metropolitan—Montreal. I had started there, and most of the work done by the few students I attracted (they were just beginning to flock my way when I left) was centered there. I carried some of the material to Chicago with me, and with the aid of a research assistant I brought along—Margaret McDonald—a couple of articles were published on the ethnic division of labor. A few students came along and carried out small bits of work that fitted into the general scheme.

The plan was to work out the whole scheme of division of labor with as much detail and subtlety as we could. It had already become clear that the Jewish people had to be drawn into the scheme. The fact that the English and French are so clearly marked off from each other and that they have so many separate institutions made the Jews and Jewish institutions more visible than in many communities; they are a kind of third term in the local system. We also planned to watch changes in the larger institutional systems (philanthropy, education, etc.) of the French world in Montreal, and to see what kinds of connections might grow up between French and English institutions as the city grew.

My hypothesis concerning charitable institutions, for instance, was that the French would adopt the English institutional forms—raising money by city-wide campaigns, distribution of money and services by professional social workers, and so on—but that the French Catholics and English Protestants would continue to maintain fully separate systems of going concerns in this field. The English Protestant institutions are those developed to replace, under urban and industrial conditions, the earlier parochial charitable institutions. It seemed almost inevitable that the French, finding their own parochial institutions inadequate to the new conditions, would follow the only available model. Aileen Ross has studied further the English philanthropic structure, but I do not believe anyone is studying the further adaptation of the French. I do know that the French and English are sharing some of the faculty of their schools of social work.

Some parts of the study as originally conceived were pursued by Prof. Oswald Hall and his students. They also studied hospitals and one of the students, M. Jacques Brazeau, did a penetrating study of the career contingencies of French Canadian physicians. Hall's group and some others have studied the inner organization of industries that have personnel of the two ethnic groups. (Incidentally, a little observation in a large company in Montreal suggested that the reason all their dietitians had nervous breakdowns a few months after being hired was simply that progressive English dietitians were hired to feed French Canadian *pères de famille*. Think of a compulsive English-speaking Protestant spinster dietitian trying to feed a bunch of hearty peasoupers.) They also studied the induction of French and English recruits into the Canadian Army, with emphasis on small-group formation as a factor in adjustment. But there is not quite, I think, a persistent effort to build out the model of study of Montreal that we had conceived.

But a most interesting and unforeseen thing has happened. I had early concluded that the future of French Canada lay very much in the great national headquarters city of Montreal, and that Quebec City, the older and more purely French headquarters of French Canada, would have a minor role in the new industrial society.

I visited there occasionally because it was picturesque and because I wanted statistics from provincial bureaus, but I did not take Quebec City seriously.

No sooner had I resettled in Chicago than I began, in one way or another, to meet people from Quebec City. Eventually, I was invited there for a semester as visiting professor at the Université Laval (I had never been invited in any way to the Université de Montreal, although I had tried to make contacts there). Laval had established a very lively faculty of social sciences. I found there an active group of people engaged in a variety of movements of a "take the bull by the horns" spirit with respect to the industrialization of Quebec. A "metropolicentric" Montrealer, I knew almost nothing of the people or the movements in Quebec. Since then my contacts have been with the young social scientists of this faculty, nearly all of whom are continuing work on the economic and social changes accompanying industrialization of the province. I certainly did not create this group, nor did I design their research. Yet I have been a part of the movement of which they are also part, and the general design worked out in course of my study has been, in general, followed out in their work. What interests me much more than the influence of this model on their work or on anyone's work is an incidental implication of some importance for applied social scientists. At a certain point in the history of Quebec, an outsider came there under circumstances that made it a most intriguing and natural thing to start study of the bi-ethnic community and region, and to turn that study toward the changes wrought by industrialization. I, the outsider, for a long time got little or no interest from English students of the region. The first to work with me on the problem was a New England boy born of French Canadian parents; he looked at the whole project with interest but from a slight distance. The next was a Western Canadian who looked on the whole world from a slight distance. This combination kept the work going for some time. Perhaps it was inevitable that, if the work was to be continued, it should be done by the French Canadians themselves, the people most affected by the changes. What good is a research design that does not include some reference to those who will execute it?

BIBLIOGRAPHY

Blanchard, Raoul. "Etudes canadiennes, 2e série. I. La Région du Fleuve St. Laurent entre Quebec et Montreal," *Revue de Géographie alpine*, XXIV (1936), 1–189.

Blanchard, Raoul. "Etudes canadiennes, 2e série. II. Les Cantons de l'Est," *ibid.*, XXV (1937), 1–210.

——. "Etudes canadiennes, 2e série. III. Les Laurentides," *ibid.*, XXVI (1938), 1–183.

——. *L'est du Canada français.* 2 vols. Montreal, 1935.

Brazeau, Jacques. "The French-Canadian Doctor in Montreal." Unpublished M.A. thesis, McGill University, 1951.

Dawson, Carl A. *The Settlement of the Peace River Country.* Toronto: Macmillan Company of Canada, Ltd., 1934.

——. *Group Settlement.* Toronto: Macmillan Company of Canada, Ltd., 1936.

Hughes, Everett C. "The French-English Margin in Canada," *American Journal of Sociology,* XXXIX (July 1933), 1–11.

——. "The Industrial Revolution and the Catholic Movement in Germany," *Social Forces,* XIV (December 1935), 286–292.

——. "Industry and the Rural System in Quebec," *Canadian Journal of Economics and Political Science,* IV (August 1938), 341–349.

——, with Margaret L. McDonald. "French and English in the Economic Structure of Montreal," *Canadian Journal of Economics and Political Science,* VII (November 1941), 493–505.

——. *Programme de Recherches Sociales pour le Quebec.* Université Laval, 1943, p. 41.

——. "The Study of Ethnic Relations," *Dalhousie Review* (Halifax), XXVII (January 1948), 477–482.

——. "Queries Concerning Industry and Society Growing Out of Study of Ethnic Relations in Industry," *American Sociological Review,* XIV (April 1949), 211–220.

Jamieson, Stuart M. "French and English in the Institutional Structure of Montreal." M.A. thesis, McGill University, 1938.

Laval University. *Symposium: The Social Impact of Industrialization in the Province of Quebec.* Laval University, 1952.

   Falardeau, Jean C. "Changes in Community Organization, Group Attitudes and Collective Behavior."

   Faucher, Albert, and Maurice Lamontagne. "Industrial Development."

   Hughes, Everett C. "Synthesis and General Evaluation."

   Keyfitz, Nathan. "Population Changes and Trends."

   Lemelin, Charles. "Agricultural Development."

   Lortie, Léon. "Changes in the Educational System."

   Perrault, Jacques. "Social Movements and Juridical Changes."

   Tremblay, Maurice. "The New Schools of Thought."

   Wade, H. Mason. "Political Evolution."

Reynolds, Lloyd G. *British Immigrant in Canada.* Toronto: Oxford Press, 1935.

Ross, Aileen D. "The French and English Social Elites of Montreal." Unpublished M.A. thesis, University of Chicago, 1941.

——. "Ethnic Relations and Social Structure." Unpublished Ph.D. thesis, University of Chicago, 1950.

Roy, William H. "The French-English Division of Labor in Quebec." Unpublished M.A. thesis, University of Chicago, 1941.

3

The Mental Hospital:
The Research Person
in the Disturbed Ward

Morris S. Schwartz

More than a decade has elapsed since I left the mental hospital which served as my research site [1] for some five years, and which provided the data that resulted in the publication of *The Mental Hospital*.[2] In reviewing the field notes taken while I was there, I am struck by the clarity and vividness with which I am able to recall the persons and events described. The sharpness and immediacy of the imagery evoked and the "hereness" of the memories and thoughts stimulated attest to the deep and lasting impression this experience had for me. Thus my reflections on the problems and processes faced and generated by an investigator in a mental hospital draw upon sources that are now from ten to fifteen years old. Nevertheless, I believe that the issues and dilemmas I confronted, the experiences I had, and the problems I pose have a contemporary relevance to investigators working in the mental hospital or in other institutions whose purpose is the improvement of human welfare.

[1] This research was supported by a grant (MH-06822) from the National Institute of Mental Health.
[2] The hospital studied housed approximately 75 patients, most of whom were diagnosed as schizophrenic. The major treatment used was psychoanalytically oriented intensive psychotherapy and each patient saw an individual therapist 3–5 times a week. The entire medical staff was in training or already had received their psychoanalytic training. Thus the doctors ranged in status from residents in training to psychoanalysts who were on the training faculty of the Washington Psychoanalytic Institute. The ward that became the focal point of our investigation ordinarily contained 14–15 women patients with 2–6 nurses and attendants and a few student nurses on one shift. It was referred to as the "disturbed ward."

My discussion will concern primarily the relationship between the investigator and the process of the investigation, and the investigated. I shall depict aspects (f my internal life and the impact the environment and the patients had on me. I shall describe how I confronted myself, faced my task, and discovered my role. I shall relive some of the situations that developed between myself and patients and staff.

As a consequence of my first few days in the mental hospital, a set of questions emerged, at first only on the periphery of my awareness, as a fleeting irritant that promised to return. Subsequently, these questions became of central concern in the initial stages of my field work. These questions were:

Who was doing the observing? Why was I there? What stance should I take? Where shall I look, and what shall I look for? With what am I looking? How shall I describe what I see?

Ordinarily all these questions are not brought into central focus together. When he does face them, an investigator usually has a ready-made answer supplied by his discipline, his preference, his cultural tradition, and his training. Complications or uncertainties that arise in the answers may be ignored or compromised. It seems to me that these questions are basic to any research enterprise that examines human beings in interaction with each other, and that they must be asked honestly, and honestly and directly answered before or while the central research problem is engaged. Confronting these questions is just as much a part of the "real work" of research as describing the social phenomena that is its central focus.

In addition, a set of ruminations were stimulated in me that led me beyond the immediate confines of the research. I wondered about the implications of understanding these particular subjects and this particular context for an understanding of the human condition. It seemed to me that these unfortunate human beings that carry the label "mental patient," persons who have been made into an inferior and deformed caricature of what they might have been, might have more to teach us about ourselves than we could learn from each other. Their existence, their orientations, and their mode of relating to the world posed a number of questions for me:

What is the nature of reality, and how does one penetrate it? What is relevant and useful knowledge about human behavior? What is the relation of knowledge to wisdom in living? How can we judge or evaluate wise (mature, or mentally healthy) behavior?

It seemed to me that the answers to these questions might more easily be sought in the living situation of psychotic persons and in the contrast of this situation with our more ordinary life circumstances.

I shall touch briefly on these issues, believing it is worthwhile to expose them, for often the secondary or peripheral questions may turn out to be more important than the original research questions.

Initiation

My initial period at the hospital was one of disorientation, shock, and disequilibration. It lasted for about three or four weeks and was highlighted by my need and attempt to find firm ground upon which to stand and to reconstitute an integrated "self" with which to operate.

Although I had previously done some research in mental hospitals, I was utterly unprepared for the impact of the hospital and especially the ward. The intensity of emotion expressed, the incomprehensible behavior of patients, the unreality of the context (the locked doors and closed world), the psychoanalytic language and interpretations that always "looked behind" the apparent and surface transaction and gave it an "odd twist," the eerie silence of apathy and the penetrating shrieks of a disturbed patient in a panic, all combined to produce a form of culture shock. In addition, my own fears and insecurities about interacting with these strange people, about the direction and success of the research enterprise, and about my personal capacity to cope contributed to a disequilibrium of self and to my disorientation as observer.

Life on the ward appeared at first as a continuous flow of confused transactions, eruptions of intense feelings, unpredictable behaviors, and obscure processes caught in some primitive mold with a contemporary façade. I simply could not sort it out. I did not know where to look, what to concentrate on, how to make some order out of the chaos. At this point I had not as yet acquired the confidence that the fog would lift in time, that directions for ordering and organizing myself and the research would emerge, and that I would develop some perspective on the situation. I felt that the experience was so complex, intense, confused, and disorienting that perhaps I should give up. But I did not, perhaps out of stubbornness—once you start a venture like this you simply do not quit—or refusal to take the easy way out.

All seemed fluid, impossible to encompass, or stabilize. Patients moved from one mood to the next and contradictory behaviors appeared almost simultaneously. Staff moved busily and intently about, making feeble attempts to keep things under control; order seemed continually on the verge of collapse. The life process proceeded in a raw emotional state with patients in disarray, shouting and cursing without apparent provocation, sitting gloomily or glaring hostilely, responding with too much closeness or too much distance, attacking or avoiding, or grimly preoccupied with their own fantasies and hallucinations. When I turned from the patients and tried to look at the ward as a whole, it appeared to me as an instance of entropy being fought fiercely by the staff, with disorder slowly winning out.

Because of my internal confusion, I could not develop a clear image of the people surrounding me. They seemed variable and vague. It was difficult to pinpoint them as personalities, not because of any defect in them but because it was difficult for me to focus long enough, to look deeply enough, or to see clearly enough through my own anxiety. When I managed to pursue my concern about grasping the "ward as a whole," I realized that as soon as I began dividing up the ebb and flow of events into categories or breaking processes down into smaller units that the product became pallid when compared to the experienced reality. For the segments somehow did not represent the whole, nor did they together retain the quality of the phenomena in process. In addition, the flow of life in the ward was such an intensely human experience that theories and conceptions of social organization or interpersonal relations did not seem particularly relevant or important. What is more, they were then incapable of sustaining me as a self or as a role performer. In a sense these analytic categories barely clung to me, rather than serving as a support for me to hang onto. I was captured by the experienced moment of human tragedy and by the poignancy of the human condition as lived out by these helpless and seemingly hopeless human beings. The penetrating humanness of the situation immobilized or obliterated my observer role. It suspended and kept as insignificant the research work to be done. It seemed more important to be with, feel with, experience deeply and understand the meaning of the patient's situation in a direct, emotional, intuitive way than to devise categories, delineate processes, dissect, and interpret, conceptualize, and generalize. After a while I became accommodated to the tragic frame of the patient's life and kept it as background rather than as foreground to my research. Later I learned about the dangers of "identifying with the patient," of losing one's self in fascination with the pathological, of becoming overinvolved. But for the moment my experience on the ward was the world, and my immediate tasks were to assimilate this world, to disentangle my identity and find my role, and to relate this ward world to this "person that I was."

At the beginning my personal defenses were severely jolted. Thus the question arises: if my professional apparatus (that is, my role as researcher) and my conceptual tools for grasping and formulating the phenomena about me were severely tried and were not quite adequate in sustaining me, then what did? The answer, in part, is my personal psychoanalysis.[3] Although later it contributed to the erosion of my defenses, fortunately there was a time differential, and at this point the therapeutic situation was supportive and sustaining for me. In part I was sustained by my curiosity, my fascination with this strange, tragic, and touching world, and the apprehended possibilities of being "opened up" in many directions and perhaps seeing with eyes and perspectives as yet unfamiliar to me. And finally, I maintained active and continuing discussions with my collaborator, Dr. Alfred H. Stanton. Although these discussions focused on the intellectual or research problems I was encountering rather than on my emotional state, they were supportive because I felt that I was not completely alone in grappling with some of these problems.

I proceeded in something of a daze for the first few weeks. I talked with patients and staff. I gathered a great deal of information. I formed relationships. I asked questions. It was not yet quite real, not clearly focused. My objective was clear: I wanted to gather the others' perception of the research, to find out from them what they thought I was doing or what I should be trying to do. I first explained to them in general terms that I wanted to study interaction on the ward in particular and the hospital as a social organization in general. I vaguely hoped that finding out about the hospital and its internal workings would in some way contribute to facilitating patient welfare. My collaborator and I believed that a patient's progress was related to the nature of the social organization of the hospital. The precise nature of this relationship was not clear to us but its importance as a problem was.

Of course, such explanations were not satisfactory to clinically oriented people who had immediate emergencies to deal with. They were not satisfactory to me, either. I continued to hope that, by hearing their expectations of the research, their definition of possible foci, and their delineation of my role, I might thereby discover for myself who I was, what my role might be, how I might proceed with

[3] As a condition for taking the position as sociological investigator in the mental hospital, I was asked to undertake "a training analysis." I was no less eager than my advisors who would have me do so.

my work, and what I should look for. Thus I vainly hoped—vain because the hospital staff had no previous experience with this kind of research enterprise and was as much in the dark as I was—that I might transfer the others' definition of my role into a self-definition. Of course, this defining process also went on with my collaborator, who was similarly trying to work out a role definition with and for me. This dilemma was particularly acute in my situation because there were no role models available. Although a few social scientists had done research in mental hospitals previously, their intentions and goals were sufficiently different from mine, and their reports sufficiently lacking in precise information, to make emulation either inadvisable or impossible. Thus I found it necessary to discover and fashion my own role and through it, in collaboration with my colleague, to formulate a useful research endeavor.

My conversations and explanations created a great deal of suspicion among both patients and staff. The patients objected to being observed, to being used as guinea pigs, to being reported. Both patients and staff were concerned about what kind of an informer I would be and for whom. The doctors half seriously and half jokingly saw me as attempting to be something like "an analyst of the analysts." Of course, there was curiosity about what I might find out, encouragement for the enterprise, but initially there was only a minimal acceptance of me and the project by patients and by the nursing and psychiatric staff. Whatever personal or interpersonal factors may have played a part in the psychiatric staff's reservations about me and my role, their professional training and ideology also worked in that direction. They were committed to the psychodynamic point of view, which was seen as sufficient unto itself for their task of helping patients. The intrusion of another discipline with its only vaguely understood usefulness, with its possibilities for disrupting the established ways, served minimally as a source of irritation and maximally as a threat and disruption to their basic assumptions and procedures. To some extent the prestige of having the research at the hospital, and the general commitment to the investigation by the persons in authority served to counteract the suspicion and rejection. In addition, the status and prestige of my collaborator, his involvement in the project, and the fact that he was the psychiatric administrator of the ward we were studying served to mitigate some of the hostility toward me and my role in the project.

I endured this stage of initiation for approximately one month, at the end of which I had reached a tacit agreement with the staff.

They would scrutinize me, but they would suspend judgment until their information and evaluation had crystallized into definite form.

In Transition: Self-equilibrium

In the transition stage (between the first and sixth month of the project) I was absorbing and assimilating the shock of initiation. During this time I gradually established some equilibrium of self, a role delineation, working answers to those troublesome questions asked earlier, and a beginning specification of the research problems that would preoccupy me.

As the initial impact wore off, my confusion began to lift. I was able to differentiate events more clearly, and the persons who were previously dimly perceived figures now came more sharply into focus, assuming clear and identifiable personalities with distinctive rhythms and characteristics. As I developed some detachment from myself and the situation, I was able to focus on persons and processes in an orderly fashion. As confusion, chaos, and anxiety diminished, I was able to turn my gaze outward a little more easily and persistently.

One of the discriminations I began to make was between anxiety that had an internal source, that is, distress that originated from thoughts, memories, and conflicts generated in my analytic sessions or as a consequence of my current emotional life, and anxiety that was provoked from the outside and communicated to me by upset patients or a disturbed ward. Although it became much easier to distinguish between these two sources of anxiety, there were many instances when its origins were obscure and it was difficult to distinguish between the "outside" and "inside." This was especially true when both were acting reciprocally to reinforce each other. Whatever the source of the anxiety, I had to, and eventually did, learn how to handle these waves of debilitating affect. I did this by recognizing some of the prodromal signs, by identifying and anticipating the experience of anxiety, by persisting despite the discomfort, by recognizing that anxiety was not indefinite and interminable and would diminish or disappear, and by discussing it analytically. But as a precondition for discovering and identifying order in the external environment, I began to manage my own internal disorder which was stimulated and represented by the anxiety I experienced.

The currents of affect—especially patient upsets and panics—in the institution, the terror and dread experienced and expressed there, were phenomena that were difficult to ignore or forget. I remained highly sensitive to the moods and nuances of the ward, and because the emotions therein were intense and conspicuously displayed, I experienced a recurrent emotional drain. I also continued to respond with feelings of loneliness, futility, confusion, and helplessness, parallel to or as a response to those so frequently manifested by patients. But at this time these responses were not so disequilibrating as before. As I became more secure in my person and role, I could absorb the emotional cross currents. As I was able to delineate specific problems for research as well as record and organize my observations, the dis-ease in the context and in myself became peripheral rather than central in my operation. In addition, a range of emotions were evoked in me in the "ordinary" course of being in the ward and relating to patients on a person-to-person basis: pity, sympathy, anger, tenderness, fear, puzzlement, despair, hope, and shock. These too had to be grappled with and managed.

One of the important accommodations I had to make was to recognize and abide by certain critical values and norms held by the institution's staff. One of these values required that persons interacting with patients manifest "sensitivity to the patient." The expectation was that the patient would be accorded respect and not demeaned in any way; that one should become aware of the patient's peculiar sensitivities and respond so as to minimize the possibility of upsetting him or in some way injuring his self-esteem. There was a generalized feeling and attitude that these patients, having suffered much anguish, were still vulnerable to the impact of others and were so finely attuned to negative attitudes of others and in such delicate balance that an insensitive other might "rub raw flesh" and easily provoke a disturbance in them.

Although the norm of being sensitive to the patient was not necessarily adhered to universally and at all times, it was a dominant theme in the institution and was one of the standards by which I was judged. Thus, in the transition stage, there was considerable scrutiny of my behavior to see if I would make a misstep. Sometimes a nurse would accuse me of having upset a patient, either because of my presence, because I said the wrong thing, acted inappropriately, or tried to relate to a patient whom I should have left alone. Or I was accused of talking to one patient and not to another, thus making one feel jealous and neglected. At times these criticisms had some basis in fact and became a source of concern to me. At other times it seemed that the staff was searching for some concrete basis for rejecting me, or for evidence that my presence was disruptive and that the research should be abandoned. These accusations and forms of scapegoating also had a source beyond myself and the project. In relating with patients as part of their daily routines, anger, frustration, and dissatisfaction were inevitably provoked in the nursing staff—feelings that were ordinarily "bottled up" in them. They could not officially "take it out on the patient," nor could they "explode at the doctors." As an outsider I served as a convenient target. Since I had no power in the institution and since in some way I threatened all staff members, using me as a focus of hostility provided them with a release at the same time that it facilitated their solidarity.

Another norm, related to the one just discussed, was that personnel should avoid responding to the patient in kind if he manifested assaultive, abusive, or demeaning behavior. Thus staff members were expected to restrain both their verbal and physical behavior. But more than restraint was called for. One also was expected to be therapeutic in handling the patient. Thus one continually faced the possibility and the experience that a patient would violate crucial conventions such as trying to kill himself, injuring others, or urinating on the floor. These actions might be disconcerting, threatening, anxiety provoking, or saddening, but one was supposed to respond so that the patient would not feel guilty, hurt, or in any way lowered in his self-esteem. Thus my responses had three orientations: they had to be acceptable to the patient, deemed appropriate by the staff, and satisfactory to me.

Although it was impossible to know whether one's responses were indeed therapeutic, much of the staff's energy and thought was devoted to thinking about how to avoid being untherapeutic. Being subjected to these standards made me cautious and inhibited my spontaneity. I trod very carefully, tried to avoid missteps and upsetting the delicate equilibrium in which the patient was presumed to exist. It was only later on that I relaxed sufficiently and came to trust my verbal and other responses so that I could be spontaneous with patients. At this earlier time, I watched myself to ensure that I did not perpetrate gross violations. By and large, I managed to avoid upsetting patients, but some distress on their part was inevitable during the time that I was not fully integrated into the ward.

A value almost universally accepted and acted upon that played a dominant role in the institution was the interpretative-analytic mode. In part this meant that small details of interaction were used as signs or indicators of larger and more important meanings. These indicators were used as clues to the unconscious motivations or to the presumed deeper reality that underlay the surface upon which people operated. Thus the apparent, conventional, and the easily understood were discounted or dismissed as unimportant, and there was a constant search for the hidden, the obscure, or the unknown thought or wish. Some of this probing for hidden meanings struck me as a kind of a game in which greater and greater efforts were being made to find more and more complex psychodynamic explanations of a person's behavior. Also present was the threat of uncovering something very touchy or a vital area that would best be left unexposed. Thus I felt that my motives, statements, and activities, like everyone else's, were under scrutiny and that frequently my self-esteem was being assaulted. As an outsider who was trying to come to terms with this, I had the feeling of being observed and discussed by a number of persons, only one of whom was being paid for this activity. However, I was fascinated by this analytic-interpretive mode. It appealed to me in a number of ways. I was eager to learn about it and learn how to use it for whatever personal benefit might accrue from it. Facility with it would make it easier for me to become an "insider" in the institution. If I could accommodate myself to it and familiarize myself with it, I might not be so vulnerable to the attacks of others who used it against me. The frankness that was part of this mode of relating was new and refreshing and appeared as a welcome relief from the hypocrisies to which we are ordinarily subjected.

I have alluded to the fact that the ward was constituted by three separate, stratified, but interrelated worlds: patients, nursing staff, and doctors. I had to accommodate to each and all of them, and vice versa.

The patients, lowest in the hierarchy, intrigued me most, and it was with them that I had the deepest emotional involvement. During the transition period, some patients were quite hostile toward me, frequently protesting that they did not want to be observed. They attacked me verbally and sometimes physically. At first I reacted with concern, guilt, resentment, and the wish to disappear from the scene. But I quickly learned the institutional norm that made it easier to handle these assaults: these attacks were irrational manifestations of the patient's illness; the patient could not help or control what he was doing; and the attacks were not directed toward me personally but probably represented some distortion from the past. After my initial recoil I could react to subsequent attacks, in which I was despised, cursed, or in other ways demeaned, with "she's not really angry at me." I came to see these assaults as an occupational hazard. Nonetheless, regardless of the explanation and rationale given for the patients' resentment or hostility, I felt that to some degree they had a right to be suspicious and resentful. For, basically, they were concerned with whether I would respect them. Was I going to regard them as fellow human beings or as objects of a research study, that is, as categories to be classified or as anonymous persons who mattered only because of the data they would produce for me? No amount of verbal reassurance on this score satisfied them. It only was after participating in the ongoing ward life and continuing to relate to them on a human level that the attacks decreased, and I was accepted as a regular, ordinary, and unexceptional ward participant. In effect, it was after I accepted them in some ways as ordinary and unexceptional—just like any other human being—that they accepted me and my role on the ward. Involved here was the reciprocal discovery of our common humaneness, achieved in the course of being together for many months. I achieved this by relating with patients on a person-to-person basis and not "hiding behind" my role as observer, by involving myself with them at the "simply human level," by exposing "who" I was, and by establishing grounds for mutual respect in our daily contacts. It is natural and inevitable that such personal-human involvement will occur with patients if one is not afraid of it and permits it to take its course. In my case, establishing the person-to-person relationship with patients (and also with nursing staff) was a precondition for stabilizing my role as investigator.

In addition to being an irritant and target for attack in the early months of the project, I also was a center of attraction. I became a source of interest and curiosity, a reference point, and the embodiment of something "new and different going on in the ward." I was continuously asked questions about the specific purposes of the project. There also was much concern about the confidentiality of what I was doing, about how much information would get to the outside, and whether I could really be trusted to "understand" or be sympathetic.

Eventually, I came to have friendly relations with many patients, casual relations with some, and distant relations with a few. They attracted and interested me in many ways—not only as persons but as provokers of important questions. Two questions stood out as I came to know patients better. One concerned the nature of reality and the other the nature of will. Reality is usually defined by the sane, and by definition patients in the hospital are not in "tune with" or do not have an adequate "grasp on" reality. Often what was real for the patient was labeled as hallucination, delusion, or distortion by the staff. These particular experiences were classified as psychotic and thereby excluded from the "realm of reality." The identification of these experiences as constructions not actually present or existent facilitated an easy generalization on the part of the staff: that the patient's other expressions, designations, and evaluations were similarly invalid or unreal. It was important that such a generalization be resisted. For it seemed to me that many patients were identifying a central reality in contemporary life that needs continuous exposure. They were protesting what human beings do to, and make of, each other. By allusion, direct statement, and physical withdrawal they were decrying the omnipresent reality of hypocrisy, cruelty, lack of compassion, and destructiveness in our interpersonal relations. At times their accusations about the kind of world we sane people had made were harsh and bitter; at other times they were poignant and plaintive. But whatever form these identifications took, I could not escape asking questions about the accuracy of their appraisal and interpretation of this social reality. To what degree did they have a clearer grasp of reality in this realm than those of us who are sane? Were they right in general and only wrong in detail? By painting a totally black picture without shadings of light and dark and blanketing all social relations, were they overemphasizing a reality that we tend to ignore or deny? Under the promptings of such thoughts I concluded that the best I could do was to conceive of any situation as presenting multiple realities, all of which had some validity, any one of which was difficult to establish as superior or more compelling.

In a similar fashion I was led to ponder the nature of will and determinism. The patient's illness was defined in part by the fact that there were "things he couldn't stop doing" and other "things that he couldn't do." He was not able to change his behavior just "by willing it." On the other hand there were many things that were "under his control" and that he could will, direct, and accomplish. In the hospital the patient's (and anyone else's) limitations of will power were explained by a theory of psychic determinism. Yet the degree to which one was "in control," the circumstances under which control varied, the basis for variations in the types of processes that were controllable, and the reasons for a successful compared with an unsuccessful "exercise of will" with similar events were still unclear, and predictability was difficult in specific situations.

The nursing staff, the middle strata in this hospital world, constituted my most constant interacting partners. A good deal of my time on the ward was spent talking with them, observing them, or being observed by them. At first there was an uneasy relationship between us since they were not sure they could trust me, but they gradually became accustomed to my presence; we warmed to each other and my absences were remarked upon and noted with some regret. I came to be a customary and expected part of their daily routine, and I had my most comfortable and persistent relations with them. They came to trust me and as far as I know had no occasion to feel that this trust had been misplaced. In addition, after the first few months, they were an excellent source of data, speaking freely about patients, themselves, their activities, thoughts, and feelings.

The nursing staff had an opportunity to see me in interaction with patients and saw how I approached them and what my attitudes were. They saw me both as a person and in various aspects of my role and noted how my concerns, norms, and values in regard to patients were similar to theirs. On the other hand, since most of the psychiatrists spent little time on the ward I was focusing on, they had a much more restricted view of my role. They only experienced segmental aspects of my role performance, becoming aware of it either by hearsay, direct report, or brief encounters. Thus the staff participants in the hospital had differential access to my role by virtue of the different positions they occupied and had different kinds of data from which to form an opinion of my activity.

My relations with the medical staff were the most problematic. It seemed to me that they did not quite know how to assimilate me and my role. Although they eventually accepted the project, the tension between us was never quite eliminated. They did not often volunteer important or intimate information to me, giving it instead to my collaborator. I always was something of an outsider to them and tended to be kept at a distance from their "center of things." They had their own community to which I was only partially admitted. They had their own set of values and ideologies revolving around the importance of the unconscious and the psychoanalytic mode as a way of life. They saw as the important reality the seething inner world that was the source of human behavior. All else was epiphenomena: social structures, social processes, institutional ideology, and role were mere abstractions obscuring hidden motives and serving as defense mechanisms against recognitions of the vital reality. Thus we started from different premises and points of view and came to different conclusions about where to look and how to conceptualize human process. Even when I surrendered the sociological perspective for the intrapsychic, interpersonal one—and I did so for a time—it did not result in my coming any closer to them. Throughout the project a feeling of reciprocal threat in my relations with some of the psychiatric staff persisted in some form. On the one hand, they threatened me with their superior power and status, with their importance in permitting the project to proceed, and with their powerful tools for throwing doubt on my motives, exposing my sensitive and vulnerable spots, and provoking my anxiety. On the other hand, I threatened them with my observations and interpretations of their behavior and its effects upon patients and eventually with a competing procedural mode and conceptual framework for achieving the therapeutic objectives they valued.

Lest I leave the wrong impression, let me hasten to add that my participation with the psychiatric staff, both in the hospital and out, formally and informally, was active and full. In the hospital I was accorded many of the privileges they had: to eat at the doctors' table, to attend clinical staff conferences, to listen in to their conversations about patients and discuss patients with them. Outside of the hospital we attended each other's parties and socialized quite freely, and I formed close friendships with a number of them. I was invited to take psychoanalytic training at the Washington School of Psychiatry alongside them, attending clinical seminars as well as theoretical courses. I was asked to teach sociology at the Washington School and interested a few of the psychiatrists in the discipline. At a later date I was asked to teach at Washington Psychoanalytic Institute.

Although in many senses I was an "insider" in both a professional and personal way, the difference between myself and the psychiatrists was clear and persistent: I could not join the community of psychoanalysts which meant that I was relegated to an inferior status and could not be accepted as a professional equal. On the personal level I probably contributed to the tension between us by manifesting (especially after my initial enchantment with psychoanalysis as a panacea diminished) either overtly or covertly my critical attitudes toward their view of psychoanalysis [4] as an answer to all human problems, toward their restrictedness and rigidities in understanding human behavior, and toward their ideological commitment to psychoanalysis as if it were a religion rather than one attempt to understand the workings of human beings. In addition, at a later date I probably contributed to the difficulties between us by manifesting skepticism about the efficacy, wisdom, or appropriateness of their psychotherapeutic modes and framework in many situations.

Working with these very sick, difficult, and slow-changing patients in an intensive way, year after year, requires a certain amount of grandiosity, faith and hope, and belief in one's approach and assump-

4 I mean here depth psychology and not necessarily Freudian psychodynamics.

tions. Under these circumstances, anyone who threatens this faith, throws doubt on the assumptions, or unmasks the discrepancy between ideology and practice, will inevitably become a target for hostility and rejection.

Despite the difficulties and tensions that characterized our relations, I arrived at an accommodation with the psychiatric staff that included mutual respect and a constructive working relationship. I respected them for their devotion to patients, for their hard work and the difficulties they were willing to endure, for their insights and the remarkable results they sometimes achieved with very sick and seemingly hopeless patients. They, in turn, recognized that I also was concerned about patients, was trusted by them, and was skillful in relating with them. At times my contributions were felt to be useful for their purposes, and they facilitated my research task by contributing to my exploration of specific problems on the ward or in the institution. Despite reservations of certain members of the psychiatric staff about me or my work, I was not in any way hindered in carrying out the project.

In Transition: Role Delineation

While I was trying to define a role for myself, patients and staff quite independently were allocating functions to me—functions that often were not acceptable to me. I have already indicated that both patients and staff cast me in the role of spy; the patients saw me as an informer who might be conveying information to the public. Somehow they confused the fact that the research funds came from the U. S. Public Health Service with the fact that we would make public revelations and reports about their activities. Some nursing personnel felt that I might convey information to the medical staff and the persons in authority—especially on the way they handled patients and on their role performance. The medical staff saw me not so much as an informer but as a more advantaged observer who might detect their shortcomings. This meant that I had to inspire in each of these groups a sense of trust and confidence that I would not injure them in the ways they feared. Such a trusting relationship could only emerge out of the day-to-day interaction during the six months of this transition period. During this time they found that their fears were not justified and that I was, in fact, trustworthy. Thus one of my functions—to make sure that the observations I made were kept in confidence—was established in part as my own role definition and in part in response to, and as a reaction against, the others' definition of me. But during this transition period I had to sustain the discomfort of being distrusted and suspected. Added to this was a self-generated, nagging doubt about my right to invade patients' privacy and observe them without their permission. Patients had been informed but their consent had not been solicited about participating in the project. It was assumed that they were in no condition to make a decision about this matter, and we, as researchers, did not ask their permission to study them.

For a while the nursing staff tried to dilute or eliminate my observer role by trying to use me as a ward employee. Since they could always use another "set of hands" or "pair of eyes," I was often asked to "watch the hall" or to watch a patient. A number of these requests were made under stress, when a nurse was having a particularly difficult time "keeping things under control." It was natural for them to call on me when I was available and apparently had a great deal of free time. Other requests were "testing operations"—attempts on their part to see whether they could get me to abandon my observer role and to adopt a service function. I was able to refuse these requests without jeopardizing my position with the patients or staff. In general I did not participate in restraining patients, but in some emergency situations I did help when asked to do so. But I made it clear in each instance that it was an exception to my general policy. However, I took a more active role in informing personnel when a patient might be endangering himself or someone else. There were a number of instances in which I did not "pitch in" and later had some misgivings about it—for example, when my participation might have prevented a patient from escaping. Or conversely there were occasions when I did "help out" and subsequently found that my assistance was superfluous. Fortunately, I did not have to make these decisions around life and death matters such as attempted suicide or destructive assault.

I also was placed in the position of scapegoat on the ward and became a focus of some hostility because my presence was presumed to be disturbing the ward equilibrium and particular patients. However, this attitude subsided by the end of the transition period when it became obvious that such was not the case.

Toward the end of the transition stage a few patients and nurses cast me in the role of confidant and counselor. They gave a number of reasons for this. Some patients felt they could talk to me because I was not paid to listen to them, as was the staff. They objected strenuously to, as they put it, the "paid friendships" offered by the staff. Since I was not in the formal role of therapist, "a paid listener," some patients felt they could talk to me more freely than they would to a therapist. Their negativism made them reluctant to do this with someone "who was supposed to help by talking with them." However, these patients were exceptions to the general and active use of the therapists. Some staff felt that since I had no "ax to grind," I would be neutral and unbiased about the information they gave me, especially about those transactions in which they were personally involved.

In attempting to carve out a set of functions and delineate an appropriate role for myself, a number of problems became manifest. Under the impact of my immersion in the psychodynamic perspective, and in conjunction with my internal reorganization after the initial disorganization, I had almost unnoticed lost my identity as a sociologist. So potent was the attraction of psychoanalysis, so persuasive was the context in which I operated, and so separated was I from other sociologists that I did not know to which discipline I was committed. This meant that I was confused about the focus I should have, the frame of reference I ought to use, and the mode of analysis that might be most fruitful. I eventually resolved this dilemma by committing myself to learning the psychoanalytic discipline in order to enhance my understanding of specific persons and their behavior, and by recognizing that a social psychological and sociological perspective was the most appropriate one for the task I had undertaken in the hospital. However, the problem of how best to join the psychodynamic and sociological perspectives is still with me.

Another set of problems in role definition related to the boundaries set by the institution, by patients, by staff, and by myself. I have already indicated that patients would not permit me to relate to them as objects—nor did I wish to do so. And this also was true of the staff. They would not let me "play" a role or hide behind the role of neutral, distant observer. I had to expose myself as a human being before I was accepted as a sociologist. Also I had to develop a set of functions that would permit me to "get the job done," to be comfortable in the role, and have it provide me with sufficient self-esteem and security to maintain my personal integrity. Thus I had to fit the others' expectations of me and my role with my expectations and performance. This required that I achieve some balance between activity and passivity. By and large I tried to be inconspicuous on the ward, avoided becoming the center of attention if possible and withheld my opinions, evaluations, suggestions, and judgments. Although at times I had strong feelings in regard to issues that arose, I restrained myself from giving overt expression to these feelings. Thus I learned that, although I felt deeply and reacted intensely covertly, I could do so without obvious overt manifestations of my internal emotional state. I adopted this passive mode because I felt that it would be most productive for the research and because it suited my personal needs at the time. I was uncertain about the effects of my more active participation. I wanted to proceed cautiously to avoid disrupting the ordinary flow of events. At the beginning of the project I was somewhat frozen in this inactive mode, but gradually I relaxed and became less passive, with greater freedom and flexibility in my responses. But the impulse to help directly by suggestion or action was a force that I had to contend with constantly. I could contain this impulse more easily when I was convinced that the study we were doing could be used directly in the interest of patients.

During this transition stage a good deal of my energy was consumed in clarifying my role, developing some stability in it, and accommodating it to the other persons and roles in the institution. Another attempt at role clarification revolved around the degree to which I would participate as an "insider and outsider" in the hospital. I shall describe in a later section my attempt to maintain an interstitial position. At this point I should like to indicate only that I felt strongly the need to be involved and thus get at what appeared to me to be important and meaningful phenomena, while at the same time I wanted to be objective so that my distortions and emotional involvement did not lead me to observe what was not there. I thought that by combining and balancing my insider and outsider position, and by trying to make adjustments and readjustments between the two, I might maximize my participation for research purposes.

Some of my effort was directed toward discovering the best fit between my observer role and the roles of others around me. Since the psychotherapeutic hour was considered the most important vehicle for achieving patient improvement, I had to limit my activity in relation to it. Thus there was no free and open observation of the patient with the doctor "in the hours." Insofar as these hours took place openly on the ward, as they sometimes did, I could observe them. Ward routines were not to be interfered with for the purposes of the research nor was any risk (as interpreted by the staff) to be taken with the patients for research purposes. Thus I had to be quite clear about staff expectations and their hierarchy of values in order to weave my role into the fabric of staff duties and functions.

In Transition: Finding Answers

At the end of the transition period I arrived at some tentative answers to the central questions I had posed—questions that were stimulated by my initial disequilibrium and answers that I pursued during my attempts to discover, define, and establish my role and person in the hospital. The weakening of my personal defenses, the widespread psychoanalytic probing in the institution, the general questioning of assumptions and conventions by the staff, and the confrontation with patients who represented a radically different set of values and orientation toward the world, all forced a number of appraisals and reappraisals about myself as observer and participant in relation to the observed.

Who Was Observing Whom?

When I first asked myself this question, my anxiety was so high I was not able to focus on the answer. As I lived with, handled, identified the sources, and analyzed the anxiety, it decreased in frequency and intensity. I could then proceed to answer the question and formulate a rational response without too much disruption by anxiety.

During the first weeks of the project it became clear to me that I could not look upon the hospital participants as objects of investigation, a view that we are taught to strive for; that it would not suffice to identify myself only as a sociologist with a specific training and problem to investigate. Such a role delineation would ignore the importance of relating as a person to other persons rather than as an observer to objects. Thus, early in the project, I recognized that I had to relate to others in the hospital as one human being (called researcher) to another (where he was more unfortunate he was called patient; where he was less unfortunate he was called staff member). However, it took some weeks before the full impact of this recognition and its implications penetrated my everyday working relations and before I could use this insight effectively in my work. Thus the "I" that was doing the observing, encountering the other and being engaged and observed by the other was first a personal one, and only secondarily a role performer. The human person had to precede the role person before I could accept myself, or be accepted, in the role of sociologist. When I accepted the patients' (and staff's) and my own common humanity, when I felt that our similarities were greater than our differences and that these similarities were more important in the human condition than were the differences, I could then confidently differentiate myself from the observed into the special role of observer-investigator.

Why Was I There?

It is easy to justify one's presence in the name of science, understanding, and the discovery of new knowledge. But these may not be, and were not, meaningful terms for the persons being observed. Each patient with her private anguish could not care less for my public quest for information and enlightenment. Each prisoner confined by the inner turmoil and dark workings of his un-understood inner world, hemmed in by the narrow space and closed doors of the all-too-real outer world, could not be very sympathetic to my desire to explore freely. Their suffering made me feel that I could only justify my presence if my work was of direct help to them, not just helpful in the byways and possible applications of pure science (if such application would indeed some day be made). This indirect usefulness was too remote and too long in coming to quiet present doubts and suspend the present need for justification. For as I faced this patient or that, I had to justify to myself as well as to them my right to intrude, to look, and to probe without their permission. I increasingly felt it most important to find an authentic and justifiable rationale for my presence. This I found in my awakening desire to help alleviate their condition through the research, to make the research relevant to patients' needs. Thus I felt that my compassion for patients had to be articulated with the project and that the project should be used in their service. For me the research was sanctioned by its usefulness, and its value as an independent enterprise divorced from its usefulness was secondary. I then realized that I was committed to sociopsychological knowledge and conceptualization not for its own sake, but in the interest of patient welfare. I could not see the patients as means to my research ends, but the research as means to their ends.

As I became more accepted and comfortable on the ward, I found that I was also justifying my presence on the simply human level. My relations with some patients and staff were genuine experiences for both of us, and these relations and experiences had an independent value and existence apart from the research.

Finally, I was there because of my desire to find out about the irrational in human behavior. I was also there because of my commitment to the field of social psychology, because of my interest in and sympathy for the underdog, and because of my need and desire to persist in a difficult situation that had many pregnant possibilities for discovery. In addition to being there to produce the kind of knowledge that would be therapeutically relevant to other unfortunate persons similarly situated, I hoped that the publication of such knowledge would enable me to make a career for myself.

What Stance Should I Take?

As a consequence of my initial disorientation, I at first searched for a situation that would provide personal security and a social position that would afford an opportunity and vantage point from which I might observe, gather data, and experience the flow of events without being captured by them. A number of choices were open to me. I could try to immerse myself and become deeply involved in the life of the nursing staff and to a lesser extent in the life of the medical staff. Such an identification would, I hoped, enable me to see events from their point of view. Or I could follow my deepest sympathies and try to get close to patient life and thereby get a glimpse of their deviant view of the world. In each instance I was making the identification for the purpose of seeing events from the perspective of the other. But I discovered that involvement in and identification with the other, when it became excessive, was "overinvolvement" (and each instance has to be evaluated on its own) and acted as a hindrance rather than as a help in viewing phenomena from the perspective of the other. In addition, too much closeness to patients became highly disturbing and thus an interference in observation. Therefore, my problem was to filter through myself as observer the experiences, thoughts, and feelings of the other in order to see the world from their orientation, not simply to identify fully and completely with the observed. I held as my goal the narrowing of the gap between my interpretation and the actuality of their subjective outlook and experience.

Although I could not avoid intrusion of my own experience and frame of reference, I felt controlled immersion in and identification with the life and view of the other was indispensable for assimilating the other's experience and for gathering significant data. This intrusion took form in two ways. On the one hand I experienced the same events as patients and staff and had an independent reaction, which at times was different and at other times the same as theirs. By virtue of the differences in personality and social position we maintained in the hospital, it was inevitable that these differences would occur. If I wanted to describe or explain their outlook, I had to account for, reconcile, or correct these differences. However, I did not merely naively experience phenomena; I also interpreted, conceptualized, formulated, and filtered these phenomena in accordance with, and through, my sociopsychological frame of reference and the analytic and moral purposes of the research.

In view of the complexities implicit in my stance, my solutions were far from satisfactory. I tried to differentiate, compare, absorb, merge, and balance the various experiences, outlooks, and interpretations by developing an insider-outsider position both actually and imaginatively. When I was "on the scene" I was involved emotionally and experientially, either directly or indirectly, in the immediate situation. I lived it as it occurred to me and as I was caught up in it at a pressing moment. In reviewing the situation I tried to detach myself from it and to see it from the other participants' point of view. In contemplation I tried to hold in abeyance my own involvement, to identify the other's experience, and play the various experiences into each other and then to organize and extract patterns of interaction.

In a similar fashion I was "in" each of the groupings in the hospital —patients, nurses, and doctors—but not "of" them. I spent long hours talking with them, participating with them in their recreation, and living with them as closely as one can without formally being in their social position. I participated as an "insider" while maintaining some detachment as I reflected on the interaction in the immediate situation. But I also spent many hours distant from their daily concerns: trying to analyze what they did and felt and to objectify their experiences (and mine) in order that they might be identified, explained, and interrelated. I tried to arouse the affect and the impact experiences on the ward had for me.

Thus I was involved yet detached while encountering the research subjects and detached yet involved while engaged in retrospective rumination.

The foregoing discussion may leave the impression that my problems in finding a stance and style of work and their resolution were worked out in a calculated and deliberate way and that my intentions to maintain the balance between the outsider and insider role were uniformly successful. This was far from true. It was only gropingly that I discovered this position and only with difficulty was I able to maintain it. The transitions from insider to outsider and back again were not always easy to make, and the insights and understandings afforded by these roles not easy to come by. In addition, my decision to adopt this interstitial position was not exclusively a rational role decision. I sought it because it suited my personal style and then saw that it was acceptable to the institution and could be productive to the research. By establishing a situation in which I was engaged, but outside, distant yet in the situation, I established person and role boundaries that were comfortable for me. I could maintain my personal integrity while I was simultaneously deeply involved in the hospital world with the opportunity to observe events that were felt to be meaningful for all participants.

Where Should I Look and What Should I Look For?

The processing of events, the intense happenings, the fleeting nature of some events and the recurring nature of others, the profusion of expression and impression led me to wonder how I could identify, absorb, and conceptualize the phenomena that came tumbling out in rapid unpredictability. With such a large number and variety of emotions, experiences, impressions, and thoughts, the problem became one of exclusion. How could I exclude what was extraneous and irrelevant? What criteria should I use for determining what was important and relative? How could I make the connections between events that were significant for what I was trying to discover and order these connections in a coherent way?

I first made the individual patient my point of reference: his inner dynamics as well as his outward behavior. The patient's attraction was magnetic, his plight desperate, and his needs insistent and ever present. In addition, I was deeply involved with and captivated by the depth psychological point of view and what it had to offer for understanding human behavior. I maintained a fascination with and a feeling of mystery about the origins, meanings, and interconnections of patients' thoughts, feelings, values, and behavior. Of equal impact and significance, however, were the recurrence of patient difficulty and disturbance on the ward. I became increasingly aware that institutional and ward operations frequently moved away from their professed goals and often social situations were untherapeutic for patients. The cumulative and recurrent effects of these untherapeutic situations, as well as my awareness of the simple sociological principle that individual behavior is in some way related to the social context in which it appears, focused my attention and concern on the relation between disturbed individual behavior and the social situation. Thus I moved back and forth in my observations between individual behavior and affect and the patterning of the social context. I tried to look at each level in its separateness and interdependence in terms of the immediate situation and in short-range historical perspective. Moreover, this double focus became even more refined so that we focused on pathological manifestations of the patient's behavior as these were directly relatable to specifiable social situations and to the transactional modes that might interrupt or alter them.

Thus I was able to combine my sociopsychological interests and knowledge-seeking needs with my social action concerns and thereby be relieved of the discomfort that stemmed from the question: "Of what use will my knowledge be?" On one hand, this solution permitted me to try to understand individual patients and social structure and to formulate hypotheses about the relation between the two. On the other hand, it opened the possibilities of planning changes for the patient's benefit on the basis of some knowledge and understanding about the kinds of situations that occasion beneficial or untherapeutic effects. In addition, I felt that attempts at intervention and their observed effects might contribute some validation or invalidation of our sociopsychological hypotheses.

How Shall I Describe What I See?

At first I tried to apply a variety of analytic tools that I brought with me from the academy. I soon found that these were useful but inadequate. For example, when I tried to explain ward transactions with their intensity, subtlety, strangeness, complexity, and variability in terms of role behavior, I found this concept insufficient to the task. It did not catch, it appeared to me, the most significant characteristics that I was experiencing. I felt that the barrenness of standard concepts had to be supplemented if I was to portray the rich nature of the phenomena manifested by others. Thus I added to my sociopsychological conceptual tools those of interpersonal psychiatry and to a structural view an emphasis on process. I also concluded that if I was to capture the emotional tones and unconscious patterning of events in addition to the overt behavior, I would need more than formal tools. I would have to depend also on my intuition and on the recognition of the feelings and fantasies stimulated in me and on my unconscious motivations and perceptions as experienced in the immediate situation. Because patients' inner life (as well as staff's) was so obscure and complex, as was its relation to overt behavior, it seemed that one possible way of approaching it was indirectly—in terms of its impact on me. Examining this impact and its stimulation of feeling within me might then give me some clues about the source and nature of the patient's subjective life.

The problem became how to discriminate and identify, absorb and assimilate, and to use the subtle and not quite tangible phenomena in the research task; how to exercise the array of formal and informal conceptual tools and processes to make the covert overt, the intangible

tangible, the unarticulated communicable, and the vague and imprecise sharp and clear.

Thus I concluded that my description and analysis of the phenomena under observation would have to be both subtle and complex, would have to be based, in part, on intuitive, nonverbal approaches, that it would have to be viewed from a multiplicity of perspectives, and that it would have to emphasize process if I were to render an accurate account, make a useful interpretation, and indicate the implications for social change and its contribution to patient welfare.

By the end of the transition period, the project had a focus that meshed with that of the institution and my role was well delineated. I entered a new phase in my relation to patients and staff in the conduct of the project when I followed the "charge nurse" in an attempt to record the various tasks she performed during the day and the amount of time she spent at different activities.

Working Through

In the working-through phase of the project—from the sixth month to the end of the project three and a half years later—I settled down for the long haul. Problems of role delineation and self-maintenance were now peripheral, whereas the delineation and investigation of specific research problems became central. The time and location study of the charge nurse, during which I recorded notes in the presence of others, marked the transition from the preparatory phase to the "working through" phase of the project. After this event the investigation was formally articulated with ward operations—that is, it existed alongside and in conjunction with ward activities without interfering or being too conspicuous—and it was more fully accepted by patients who were relieved to know that staff as well as patients were being studied.

Although my acclimatization to the hospital and its inmates made it easier to work more effectively, I soon realized that such "adjustment" was not pure gain. For in becoming accustomed to the "crazy situation" and the deviant ways of acting and thinking, in taking the situation for granted, I was losing a certain freshness of perception and response, losing a clear vision and contrast of life "inside" and "out," and losing the incisive sharpness and impact of events and experiences that comes from being an observant stranger. The peculiarities of patient and staff behavior, the open talk, the air of tension and disorder, the piercing quality of patient disturbance—all assumed a degree of ordinariness because I experienced them as not quite so exceptional and because I had come to act and think in part in the institutionally established framework. I felt that I had lost something of significance in becoming more "a part of the place." This is not to say that I no longer was an outsider. To some extent I was. But the repeated and prolonged experience of being inside no longer permitted a purely fresh, naive perception; the institution and its subparts to some degree had become part of me, and to that degree I had lost detachment and distance from it and the originality of perception that stems therefrom.

However, such acclimatization did not mean that I reacted emotionally in a matter of fact way to patient disturbance and suffering. On the contrary, I still empathized greatly with them and was extremely uneasy when collective disturbances broke out, but I found that I could handle my own distress more easily and did not "take it home with me." In retrospect it seems to me anxiety and distress on the part of the observer is a fair price to pay for continuing sensitivity to the patient's inner state and existential condition.

Before I continue with the description of the working-through phase, it might be well to discuss my relations with other sources and resources in the research. I have not emphasized sufficiently the central role of my collaborator, Dr. Stanton. All decisions about procedure and policy were made jointly although he was formally the project's principal investigator. I was free to pursue the problems I considered significant in ways that suited me and that I thought would prove fruitful. In evolving specific research plans, strains were inevitable and did in fact occur. We had problems in acclimating ourselves to each other's frame of reference, and there were, of course, personal tensions stemming from our personality differences. But these were overshadowed by our persistence in collaborating on a particular problem, our agreement on the types of problems that merited investigation, and by a coming together of our perspectives. We did not have much difficulty in selecting the language with which to discuss our data and findings, in discussing our observations, and in recording notes. He was especially important in facilitating my role and acceptance in the hospital and opening up channels of information and possibilities for investigation. Whatever stress resulted from our relationship was neither long-lasting nor unamenable to remedy. Thus, while I discuss these experiences and actions as my own, it should be remembered that Dr. Stanton was a constant other, fully and actively involved with me in the conduct of the investigation, in determining its course, analyzing data, and preparing the publication of our findings.

Another source of support and discussion, although on just a one-hour-a-week basis, was my meetings with two senior psychiatrists on the staff of the hospital. With each and both I discussed the conduct of the research, the problems I was interested in and why, and my reactions to various occurrences in the hospital. I received from them a view a little different from my own and a set of interpretations that helped me maintain some perspective on my involvement in the hospital situation. I was enabled to take a longer term view toward events and toward my emotional reactions to these events. I feel that such outside consultants, who are sensitive to interpersonal involvements and difficulties, can play a valuable role in keeping an investigator disentangled from his own biases and blind spots.

However, I did not enlist such outside consultation from social scientists. With one exception I somehow felt that I wanted to "work my role and personal problems out" alone. This I now feel was an error. The stimulation, viewpoints, and suggestions that I could have obtained from other social scientists probably would have facilitated my task and provided some of the disciplinary and relationship support that would have eased my personal strain. The one exception to my isolation from social scientists was my wife, then my fiancée. She spent two summers working on the project and was in continuing contact with it, through me, for its duration. And as a consequence she supplied personal and role support throughout all phases of the research.

Finally, another source of support was my psychoanalyst. The requirement that I undertake an examination of my own inner dynamics was made on the assumption that a prerequisite for understanding the psychotic, neurotic, and normal selves of research subjects was an understanding of one's inner dynamics and manifestations of similar or parallel psychological processes. This experience not only afforded me insight and understanding but gave me security in dealing with patients.

If an observer followed my activity in the hospital, and particularly the ward, he would have seen me occupied with the following activities. Most of the time I sat quietly in a corner of the ward taking notes in a little black notebook. Patients and staff often approached me, at which time I ceased taking notes and carried on conversation with them. However, the note taking was no great source of concern nor was it interfered with. At other times I walked around the ward initiating greetings and conversations with patients and staff. I spent some time in the combination kitchen-nurse's station (where no patient entered, except by accident or in violation of the rule), discussing with the staff current ward events or problems and their own reactions and thoughts about these events. At this stage my relations were easy and comfortable with patients and staff in the ward. I was rarely attacked verbally and never attacked physically by patients during this period. They, as well as staff members, became accustomed to my presence and indicated their acceptance when they told me they had "missed me" when I was away for a few days.

At this time I settled into an intensive relationship with the disturbed ward and a more or less peripheral relationship with the rest of the hospital which I looked upon as background and context for the transactions occurring on the ward. My relations with ward staff were a mixture of formal and informal activity—carrying on casual conversations or asking specific and directed questions. My relations with patients were mostly informal. Rarely did I interview them in a structured way, although in the course of my informal conversations, where appropriate, I asked questions that were of interest to me at the time. However, I did not pursue questions when I felt they might interfere with our informal relations. When I investigated a specific problem, I relied primarily on systematic observation rather than interviewing. And, in general, I spent long periods of time on the ward, trying to observe events over time, and to draw the connections between events, experiences, and relationships.

The products of these observations, conversations, and relations were, of course, the gradual and increasing delineation of specific problems to be studied. The first of these we focused on was patient excitement.[5] Because it was conspicuous, troublesome, and recurrent, it presented itself with some impact on our awareness. We thus became interested in the social conditions under which a patient became excited and the conditions under which it disappeared. By accepting this kind of a problem as valid and important, we were saying in effect that we would make ward problems research problems; that the research focus would stem from specific problematic situations, rather than from theoretical concerns or from formulations deriving from our conceptual or research interests in the field of social psychology. In pursuing this problem we discovered that we would

[5] A. H. Stanton and M. S. Schwartz, "The Management of a Type of Institutional Participation in Mental Illness," *Psychiatry* XII (1949), 12–26; and A. H. Stanton and M. S. Schwartz, "Observations on Dissociation as Social Participation," *Psychiatry*, XII (1949), 339–354.

have to emphasize staff-staff interactions as well as patient-patient and patient-staff transactions. In addition, this initial problem set the pattern of focus and analysis for problems that we subsequently delineated and pursued: patient incontinence [6] and patient requests.[7] In time we cast these concrete problems into a larger frame, seeing them as aspects of the study of the relationship between the individual and the collectivity and of the connection between irrational and unconventional individual behavior and their social roots and foundations. Additionally, from these concrete and circumscribed beginnings we moved out to an analysis of the larger institutional organization and to the interconnections between phenomena at the individual, social situational, and institutional levels. Thus I found that I was moving in seemingly opposite directions at the same time: on the one hand trying to investigate larger and wider social contexts, such as the institution as a whole, and on the other, trying to gather specific intensive descriptions of individuals and small-scale social situations.

It might be useful to describe my role-person orientations during this phase. I now had a fourfold commitment: (1) to the investigation and discovery of new knowledge and the illumination of unnoted relationships in the ward and hospital; (2) to developing the implications of this knowledge in order to facilitate therapeutic effects; (3) to the welfare of patients; (4) to respect and be loyal to the various patients and staff with whom I had developed friendships, mutual affection, trust, and who had confided in me. This meant that knowledge and its implications for patient welfare had to be balanced with a variety of personal considerations so that the maximization of each and all would result. The degree of success of such harmonization is difficult for me to evaluate.

Because of my involvement with these commitments, it seemed that no matter how much time I spent on the ward, no matter how intensively I observed, it was not quite enough. I felt that somehow an additional hour might permit the fragments to fall into a pattern and produce a clear view of the problem I was investigating. I was expecting the profusion of data to produce the answers to my questions. However, I learned to give up the expectation that data alone could provide what I was seeking. The need for inference, interpretation, and conceptualization to order and direct my observations and analysis became clear. In addition, I worked out a way of preventing

[6] Morris S. Schwartz and A. H. Stanton, "A Social Psychological Study of Incontinence," *Psychiatry* XIII (1950), 399–416.

[7] C. C. Schwartz, M. S. Schwartz, and A. H. Stanton, "A Study of Need Fulfillment on a Mental Hospital Ward," *Psychiatry* XIV (1951), 225–242.

my morale from becoming impossibly low. It involved deriving gratification from either progress in the research or from progress in the ward. Thus, when the ward was disturbed and morale low, I could maintain my own interest and enthusiasm by viewing these disturbances as opportunities for study and discovery. The situation then was not a total loss because I could gather data about the disturbance and make it a source of fruitful inquiry. Conversely, when the research was not going so well, I derived emotional sustenance if progress was being made on the ward. The periods when halting progress on the research coincided with ward disorganization represented the most difficult periods of stress and discouragement.

At times I tried to identify the effects of my presence and role on the ward. During the initial stages I was obviously a "foreign body," but after the transition phase my presence and the project I represented seemed to be instrumental in singling out the ward as special and different. The research lent it some prestige in the hospital and eventually outside. The ward participants had acquired a public (outside) but protected recognition, as well as a private (internal) recognition. Although anonymous, the world at large knew of them. I doubt that many patients felt, as I did, that they were making a contribution to the fraternity of patients at large although some ward staff seemed to derive satisfaction from this.

At the end of this phase we had published a few papers and developed the broad outlines of our book.

Ending and Beginning

As the project drew to a close at the end of four years the major task remaining was to complete the publications in process, especially the book that we had started. In addition, we wished to close the project in such a way that it was not disruptive for the institution or patients.

In actuality, my departure from the hospital was only a short vacation, rather than a leave-taking, and, therefore, at this time I did not have to face the problem of disengaging myself from the relationships I had formed with patients and staff. As a consequence of my increased involvement in studying mental hospital social structure and my commitment to carrying on action in conjunction with research, I had applied for another grant. Although Dr. Stanton was leaving the institution, I planned to stay on and work with the administrator who replaced him and the ward staff with whom I had by now established a firm and effective working relationship. My grant was approved and I soon found myself gathering data and focusing data analysis primarily for the purpose of planning interventions. Thus my desire to make the research of use in facilitating patient welfare and my wish to test some of the hypotheses I was formulating took the form of another project on the same site. This time, however, I could indulge my desire to be active, both directly and indirectly, by using knowledge in the service of therapeutic ends.

Our book meanwhile took three additional years to complete. Our papers had stimulated the recognition of the importance of the milieu in the treatment of hospitalized mental patients. The book had a considerable impact on the ways of thinking about mental hospital patient care and stimulated a field of inquiry and practice whose central focus was the relation between social milieu and individual pathological behavior.

Standing back from the experience just described, what general statements might be made about the kinds of influences and processes that are operative in such a research enterprise?

It would be unfortunate if the personal framework in which I set my discussion leads one to believe that the character of the problems and issues I identified stemmed only from my personal preoccupations and difficulties. It is clear to me that these reactions and problems were a mixture of personal processes (uniquely my own), role processes (an integral part of a social structure), and simply human processes (those I share with all other humans). Each fed into the other and crystallized into the unique forms they acquired in the research project. From this point of view the task of the investigator is to identify the ways in which each enters into the social process, to explore the nature of their interrelations, and to evaluate the relative significance of each in organizing a particular complex pattern. Thus, for example, the confusion, shock, and disorientation I experienced initially was a personal reaction that affected and reflected my personality in many ways. It also was an outgrowth of the innovating and unstabilized character of the role I was trying to develop. And, finally, in part it was attributable to the meeting of strangers with incongruent sets of cultural expectations.

Similarly, my anxiety and responsiveness to the emotional currents in the ward can be characterized in personal, role, and simply human terms. The way anxiety and other emotional currents affected me, the nature of my susceptibility, how I handled and finally came to terms with them all were uniquely personal transactions. But the nature and kind of confrontation to which I was exposed (a large number of disturbed persons in the same place) and the generators of anxiety built into my status and role (the lack of clarity of role definition and the necessity for continuing reciprocal relationships with disturbed persons) were consequences of social structural arrangements. Finally, it was inevitable that my sympathetic, empathic responses—reflections of my human nature—would be called forth and involved in a situation suffused with strong affect and participated in by persons whose lives were maintained on an intense emotional plane.

Similarly, the poignancy of the patients' condition: their suffering, wasted potentialities, sensitivity and attractiveness, violations of norms and repulsiveness, intuitive gifts and self-destructive prodigality, and penetrating accusations and silent pleadings elicited personal involvements and identifications on conscious and unconscious levels. But these involvements also were consequences of the nature of my role definition: that is, being an "insider" as well as an "outsider," and submerging myself in the life of the ward in order to understand the subjective life of its participants. Finally, these poignant situations engaged not only my person and role but also touched and shook my inner being; they were occasions for recognizing and implicating my simple humanity; and they were reflections of a common human bond that emerges when persons are in open communication and continuing exchange with each other.

Many sociological investigators are warned against permitting non-role factors to enter their research enterprise. When I first began the project I took this injunction seriously, and when I saw how insistent and inescapable these personal-human factors were, I wondered if I was deficient in some way. I now know that the personal-human equation will enter research despite our wishes to the contrary. I believe it is essential to recognize the potency of these personal-human influences, face them, and try to grapple with them and their relation to our projected roles. We have to be alert to our unresolved inner conflicts that make it difficult for us to conduct an unbiased investigation. We have to be sensitive to the disorganizing influence that may be generated by and in the research project or research site. We have to know the weaknesses and strengths of human capacities. Thus rational attempts to define and carry out a suitable research role may be disrupted by the irrational, undetected, and circumscribed characteristics stemming from the person and his human limitations.

One should not assume that we cannot decrease the distortions, inadequacies, and errors that arise from role-personal-human limitations. Rather this decrease will be accomplished when we develop a framework that takes into account all three factors and when we are willing to confront the difficult task of exposing (and exploring) our personal and simply human attributes as well as our roles to the powerful light of self—other scrutiny.

4

Nigerian Discovery:
The Politics of Field Work

Stanley Diamond

[This essay, describing in subtle detail the initial stages of an anthropologist's encounter with Nigeria, illustrates almost all of the issues and complexities that countless other anthropologists have most surely experienced, but either have not seen or, if seen, have never reported. For present purposes Dr. Diamond carries his report up to his reference to his first visit from the Nigerian police. A later, full-length study, to be called *A Field Trip That Failed*, will complete the discussion begun here.—Eds.]

Introduction

From the beginning it was a star-crossed field trip. In August of 1959, accompanied by my wife and daughters, I had flown down from Rome to Kano, across the Mediterranean and Saharan Seas, from the most permanent and vulgar of European to the most typical and enduring of Hausa cities. For centuries the town had been a customary port of entry for the caravans that converged upon it from the trans-Saharan routes. Kano had been one of the original seven Hausa states, founded, according to the Chronicle that bears its name, in A.D. 999. Today it is the largest and most important city of the western Sudan, the very essence of Moslem Africa. It is the economic hub of northern Nigeria, a rail and road depot, and the center of the export trade in groundnuts, the most important cash crop of the Northern Region (directly supporting at least five million people), and, along with cocoa and palm products, the mainstay of the country's economy. Since I had decided to undertake a field study of a pagan people on the Jos Plateau, it seemed appropriate to enter the country through this ancient gate. We floundered down through the savage squalls that are characteristic during the height of the rainy season in northern Nigeria and landed at the International Airport at five o'clock on a bleak morning. The trouble, which seemed minor at the time, began at customs. The immigration officers wished to know my purpose in entering the country. I produced my credentials, gave them a letter of introduction, and was asked my place of proposed residence and the name of the organization with which I would be associated.

It should be realized at once that Nigeria was not a settler's colony. Unlike Kenya and the Rhodesias, Nigeria, along with the other British-occupied territories in West Africa, had adopted a policy of strictly controlling the number and kinds of Europeans permitted to enter the country. The usual explanation for the origin of this policy had been that climate, disease, and terrain made the place uncongenial for European settlement. These may be factors, but they do not constitute an explanation, for if they were sufficient then no formal policy would have been necessary. A political issue seems more pertinent.[1] Settlers eventually will cause trouble for the mother country, which then has to choose between the interests of the native people, who will look to the Metropole as the Iroquois tribes did to the British, and its own subjects. The latter may antagonize the local people by land grabbing and social prejudice, and the related forms of exploitation; and/or they may develop so vested an interest in the colony that the ties with the Metropole are severed. The history of the New World where England learned this lesson too late is ample evidence. In any case a settler's colony cannot be accommodated to the classic pattern of indirect rule, in the modern British experience, pragmatically initiated in India and pursued by design by Goldie and Lugard in northern Nigeria. Thus the strict control of immigration and the rules of residence and work have the effect of maintaining metropolitan sovereignty (and securing overseas economic opportunities), while apparently reinforcing the well-being of the natives.

The Nigerian officials had become understandably jealous of their prerogatives in this matter, particularly during the period following self-government and preceding independence. When I sought to enter Nigeria, there were no more than sixteen thousand Europeans resident in a country with a population of forty million (now contro-

---

[1] Of course, the nature and extent of economic resources peculiar to a colony, its geopolitical position, the politicomilitary power of its inhabitants are factors determining whether an area developed into a settlers' colony. But other things being equal, a nonsettlers' colony is a happier one for a metropole.

versially counted at fifty-five million). The great majority were clustered in the cities of the south, particularly in Lagos. Controls were stricter in the Northern Region where the political structure was more rigid than in the East or West, since the British had utilized the hierarchical Fulani apparatus, itself superimposed upon the previous Hausa structure, in order to rule the region. Northern Nigeria, constituting three-quarters of the land area of the country and containing more than half the total population, had always been considered a most successful experiment in indirect rule, enabling the British to maintain the colony with a minimum of investment, a maximum of trade, and the least possible political ferment. These efforts had failed in the Eastern Region because of the democratic and decentralized character of Ibo society. Indeed, the women's riots at Aba in 1929 symbolized the inception of the mass movement toward freedom in West Africa: they swept the colonially appointed chiefs out of office and, symbolically enough, in that year of universal economic depression, these women traders, incensed by rumors of taxation, wrecked the trading companies which were buying cheap and selling dear, and doing so under the protection of an alien political apparatus. The riots summed up the colonial business, which the Ibo grasped from the beginning, in a nutshell. In the Western Region, indirect rule had gained leverage with the Yoruba-speaking peoples because of their system of paramount chiefs, but this was complicated by the existence of traditional counselors and other customary checks on the power of the Obas. Moreover, in both the east and west as opposed to the Fulani-Hausa north, a university-trained élite had begun to develop between the world wars. The élite did not fit into the administrative structure; they constituted a force toward new party and parliamentary institutions: the first wave of the colonial revolution, but by no means the last. Of course, it was only in the Fulani-conquered areas of the north, the anchor of British sovereignty in West Africa, that indirect rule worked smoothly. In those sections that had not been penetrated in depth by the Fulani, particularly the pagan areas of the Jos Plateau to which I was headed, indirect rule had foundered because of the difficulty of finding appropriate native authorities. Chiefs, who were often only messengers, were supplied for the uses of the conqueror under the threat of force.

But I was only to understand these political processes later when I became inadvertently involved with them and learned, the way anthropologists are said to learn, by participant observation. At the time that I was asked my address and purpose at the immigration desk at the International Airport in Kano, I did not realize the full background and import of the question. As it happened I did have a prospective address, but it was imprecise. I had arranged to rent a house several miles from the city of Jos from a tin company that had recently been bought out by a large American corporation. Jos had developed into a bustling city of about seventy thousand on the basis of the tin fields which had first attracted the Niger Company, the fine point of British penetration in Nigeria, to the High Plateau. Tin was the leading mineral export of the country, and its high-quality oxide ore was found in an area that was ethnographically hardly explored. The pagans of the High Plateau were among the most primitive peoples still functioning in Africa; and the conjunction of a remote and inaccessible area, a primitive population, a modern industry, and a relatively new urban center made the plateau a particularly inviting place for anthropological inquiry. Moreover, the native peoples of the plateau, indeed of the Province generally, were known for their independence and disinterest in the civilization that was growing in their midst, and I found that prospect attractive, also. As it turned out, there was a further problem of which I was unaware. The fierce desire for independence which had kept the Fulani at bay, and had later frustrated the classic British design for indirect rule, was now finding political expression, feebly at first, and haltingly, as Nigeria approached independence.

The plateau had become the vanguard of a movement challenging the dominant political party of the Northern Region, the Northern Peoples Congress. The Congress was the party of the emirs, dominated by Fulani-Hausa elements, and had been encouraged by most British colonial officials. But dissident groups, connected with the major political parties in the Eastern and Western Regions, had begun to crystallize—notably the United Middle Belt Congress (allied with the Western Region's Action Group) and the Northern Element's Progressive Union (allied with the Eastern Region's National Convention of Nigerian Citizens). Much of the activity of these parties was concentrated on the plateau where, of course, the local cultures had no historical connection of any kind with the archaic Fulani-Hausa political apparatus. Indeed the societies of the plateau pagans had been fundamentally uncivilized, that is, they were not politically structured. The U.M.B.C. and N.E.P.U. had hoped to attract pagan support, not only on the plateau, but throughout the Middle Belt. Indeed, in the new and independent Federation of Nigeria, which was about to be discussed in London, the platform of the U.M.B.C. called for a separate Middle Belt State (N.E.P.U., which drew its strength from dissident Hausa elements, was proportionately less positive on this matter). Obviously, the establishment of regional autonomy for the Middle Belt would have weakened the North critically; the population would have been reduced by one-third, and the land area by one-half. Instead of politically, geographically, and demographically dominating the Nigeria that was approaching independence, the north would have shrunk to more historically justifiable boundaries, thus permitting a more dynamic and progressive national government. The Middle Belt issue was critical, and the Jos Plateau was considered by the Northern Regional Government as one of the most prominent threats to their continued sovereignty.

I was, then, journeying to an area that was ethnographically important, which I knew, and politically explosive, which I did not know. Yet there was no better vantage point from which to view and assess the local roots and national turmoil of Nigerian politics than the Jos Plateau. There, in the cockpits of the Middle Belt, parties and peoples of the three regions [2] of Nigeria met, mingled, and fought. The predominantly pagan population of the province, numbering more than half a million, created an enclave beyond the immediate reach of northern officialdom, in which riotous political discussions and criticisms had to be tolerated. Southerners, notably Ibo and Yoruba, were at home in the city of Jos, and even the colonial officers were less committed to the monolithic north that was emerging out of indirect rule than were their counterparts in other provinces of the region. Moreover, the typical Hausa peasant, habituated to centuries of oppression, and thus, on the surface at least, resigned and fatalistic, was rarely encountered on the plateau or in the province at large. In retrospect, it is clear that by 1959, in the view of the N.P.C., the plateau was a bone in the throat of the north, and all the more so since the indirect income from the tin mines was the biggest single item in the budget of the Northern Region. Yet, in order to understand this, it was not enough merely to visit the plateau; one had to get a taste of its politics. Fortunately, or unfortunately (who can weigh the balance?), that is what in small measure happened to me. I was transformed inadvertently from a sophisticated, if innocent, bystander to a naive, if observant, participant.

Entering the Field

The business began when the customs officer at the International Airport at Kano, after checking my credentials and keeping a copy of my letter of introduction, filled in my entry permit. Since I had made arrangements to rent the house from the tin company, he simply

[2] Since this writing, a fourth region, the Midwest, has been established in southern central Nigeria.

assumed that I was employed by them, although I had explained my mission in detail and indicated this on the back of the permit. It was a logical error on his part. There were no unconnected residents in Nigeria. A man was either a civil servant or a company employee, that is, if he planned to stay in the country for any length of time. There was hardly any category into which an anthropologist unaffiliated with Nigerian institutions could readily be put; moreover, Europeans or Americans, planning to settle in Plateau Province for at least a year, more likely than not would be associated with the mining of tin. But I failed to notice on that weary morning that my purpose in coming to Nigeria had been misinterpreted on my entry permit. Some months later this was to be pointed out to me by an Anglo-Irish assistant superintendent of police, a man with a confidential manner and cold eyes.

We stayed in Kano for a few days—just long enough to get the feel of that bright, harsh city that casts stark, Islamic shadows under a cruel sun. I plowed through the theatrical, filthy markets (Islam has a private, not a civic conscience), appreciated the big clean-lined mosque, and marveled at the cheerful beggars, the happy blind, at the dignity that endures under the surface of self-abasement among the swarming poor in Afro-Asian cultures. But the children with the fly-encircled eyes, that unremarked symbol of social decay throughout the Sudan and the Middle East, repelled me here as it has elsewhere. I wandered, also, through the introverted alleys of the old town, where Islam turns a blind eye to the world yet lives so intensely and indecipherably within, each devout or unspeakable in his measure. But even here, in northern Nigeria, one could sense the body of Africa throbbing under the cloak of Islam, like a great bird under a hood. I was familiar enough with the Middle East; it was Africa I was after, in order to quicken an academic specialty, and we were not sorry to leave Kano. But first I was able to arrange, by lucky circumstance it seemed then, for a Hausa- and English-speaking Ibo cook, steward, interpreter, and general factotum to join us at a later date at Jos.

The trip to the plateau, a distance of perhaps three hundred miles by road, was trivially eventful. We drove southwest of Kano, through the zone of most intensive groundnut cultivation that forms an ellipse around the city, onto the broad empty Sudan savanna, in the direction of Funtua, a small divisional emirate in Southern Katsina Province. We had to abandon the taxi after all four tires had blown out, but finally managed a lift into Funtua in the glossy American car of a prosperous, inquisitive, and unusually talkative Lebanese trader, a groundnut middleman, who was returning to Zaria from a business trip to Kano, and would soon go home to Beirut rich on small steady profits and parsimonious living. The three focal points of activity in Funtua town were the petrol station, the Emir's palace, and the local office of the United Africa Company. The palace was surrounded by retainers of one kind or another, who were curious but not helpful. The Emir was inaccessible, asleep, and no one would dare predict the time of his awakening. From time to time the petrol station sprang to life as a produce truck or Mammy wagon, lopsided with passengers, pulled in for service, rest, or refreshment from the trays of white-robed, itinerant Hausa peddlers. It took courage of a high order along with faith in God (a message inscribed in a variety of metaphors above several windshields) and the capacity to live dangerously in the moment to drive or trust oneself as a passenger in these vintage vehicles. They seemed to have been picked off the junk heaps of Europe; actually most were assembled in Nigeria from imported frames to meet local needs, while maximizing profits. Their wrecked and burnt out carcasses were a familiar sight on the native landscape. But what I remember best about Funtua is the soft-eyed, beautifully maternal African woman, who seemed a single being with the swooning child on her hip as she stood and gazed at us in calm inquiry from the center of the jabbering crowd that surrounded us as we walked.

After a delay of several hours, I was able to find a truck bound for Zaria that was willing to take me and our baggage; my family had driven on with the Lebanese. We turned southeast into Zaria Province, through typical Guinea savanna country, broken by occasional plots of Guinea corn and millet, and empty of human habitation, as all African landscapes appear to the unsubtle, urbanized eye of the stranger. We spent that night in a government rest house on the outskirts of Zaria town (most northern provinces are named after their principal towns); there, while being served a Hausa interpretation of a depressing English meal by a Kanuri waiter with cheeks slashed as if by swords, we had our first contact with British colonial officials on tour. Each seemed an island unto himself, remote, ostentatiously self-engaged in trivial ways to avoid intercourse with another. They were a pale and miserable company. The administrative adventurers of the nineteenth century—Lugard, MacLean, Burton— had dwindled to clerks charged with foreclosing the empire in its last great frontier. Yet, despite the social distance of each from each, they seemed not uncomfortable together.

The following morning we rented a taxi in the old town, less Middle Eastern, more open, frank, and African than Kano, and headed southeast, climbing up through park land and wooded hills to the Jos Plateau. Later this brief trip from Kano through Funtua and Zaria to Jos was to be inflated as a survey of the northern provinces, including Borgu division, a Yoruba center, and that is why I mention it here.

The tin mining company, from whom I had rented the house, was situated about five miles northwest of the city in a village area called Gwong. The main office and staff dwellings were strung out along the road that disappeared into the hills surrounding the city. The land itself was rented by the company from the local pagans—the Anaguta, I was to discover—for a nominal yearly fee, since no expatriate organization was permitted to own land outright in any of the major regions of Nigeria. The company had moved its mining operations off the plateau and out of the province to Tiv country in the Benue area, and columbite had surpassed tin as its major commodity. The tin fields of the plateau were approaching exhaustion, having been worked out by the European companies who displaced vast areas of top soil in the process; and by 1958 the international quota on tin production had driven most prospectors out of the business and drastically cut back the profits of even the largest operators. But the director of the company with whom I had negotiated, a Greek by birth, who had been in the country for thirty-five years, first as a trader, then as a prospector, and finally as an executive, had sensed the trend in the early years of the war. He had been able to switch to columbite, which is found in association with tin ore, and had become an important producer of that strategic heat-resistant mineral. But although three-quarters of the world's columbite supply is in Plateau Province and adjoining provinces, its industrial future is uncertain; present use is quite specialized, extraction is difficult and expensive, and requires a high price per ton in order to keep operations profitable. American stockpiling until 1955 had led to a columbite boom, but the market was now declining rapidly and the director of the company was pleased to sell his majority holdings to a large American corporation. Like many expatriates, he felt the old colonial Nigeria dissolving under his feet; independence was looming, his friends were leaving, his money had been made, and he was looking for a country that would not tax his bank reserves too drastically. But I had come to study, and to associate with, Africans, and had no direct concern with the problems of expatriate businessmen.

The house was well situated. A tiny compound of beehive huts lay nestled about seventy-five yards from the rear entrance in a Guinea corn field that stretched to our back yard. This, as it happened, was one of the compounds of the nominal chief of the Anaguta. There was a constant, casual traffic of women naked to the waist, bearing head loads, to and from the hamlets that lay a short distance on all sides of the company dwellings. By late afternoon we could hear the sound of drums echoing against grim and rocky hills, where the pagans lived in compounds that we knew were there but could not see. Moreover, we were less than a quarter of a mile from the strangers' settlement, the Sabon Gari, or new town, a kind of suburban slum in which Nigerians from other parts of the country clustered on the edge of northern cities. Sounds of joy floated up from the strangers' settlement and, mingled with the pagan drums, lit up the darkest of nights. This was an excellent field headquarters.

None of the tin company personnel knew the names of the pagan villages in the surrounding hills, nor had they ever visited them; they were vague about the tribal name. Without exception they were afraid of Africans like these pagans, whom they could not dominate, and contemptuous of Africans they could dominate. The colonial officers in Jos, who were turning over at an alarming rate as independence approached, were equally uncertain about the Anaguta, and this honed my curiosity further. The Anaguta had never been studied, although there was an occasional reference in the literature; they were, it seemed, a most elusive people, yet they were the aboriginal owners of the territory on which the city of Jos and its environs were located. Here was a sort of suburban primitive culture, buried in its rocky habitat, difficult of access, yet only a few miles as the crow flies from the most Europeanized city in northern Nigeria. I had not decided on a people with which to work before leaving the States—the Jarawa and the Birom were likely prospects, but both were somewhat better known than the Anaguta and, it was said, easier to reach. I decided to take things as they came, and set out in pursuit of the Anaguta.

A few weeks after settling down at Gwong, the Ibo factotum whom I had hired in Kano joined us with his pregnant wife. Pius was an intelligent, adaptable, quick-witted young man, a baker by trade, with a varied and sobering experience of colonial housewives. His native hearth was a hamlet in Owerri Province in eastern Nigeria, the most heavily populated area in West Africa, almost as dense as the Nile delta. Like many of his countrymen, he found it necessary to leave home at an early age because there were too many children, too many legitimate claims, and not enough good land left in his family. Being an Ibo, he was also af a litigious turn of mind; and, of course, he was eager to learn and explore. Pius knew the north, having lived in Kano for many years, and had a mild contempt for the genuflections of the

Hausawa before their social superiors. No Ibo, he would say, ever bows to any other: "we are all equals, we are all brothers." He was even capable of patronizing the political leader Zik. "Zik tries," he would repeat, with sly disapproval, "Zik tries." But of course, as with every other unsophisticated Ibo I have ever met, Zik was the apple of his eye, the symbol of his pride. I had hired Pius, through a hotel steward whom I had met in Kano, for his excellent English and Hausa, and because, being an Ibo, he would serve as a knowledgeable guide on a trip that I planned to the Eastern Region. I had hired him also to avoid any possible complication that might arise from employing a local man in my household.

But Pius created local associations. His full name, Pius Owerri, whether conferred or adopted I did not know, was a conjunction of statuses that placed him at once. He was, first of all, a utilitarian Catholic, and a conventionally religious man. On our trip to south-eastern Nigeria we were to discover a relatively relaxed and apolitical Catholicism that melted self-protectively into the cultural and physical landscape. Framework churches, open to the sky, flourished in Pius's native province, thrusting themselves up through the bush every few miles, looking like so many unfinished Gothic sketches. Owerri, Pius's patronymic, announced his birthplace to any Ibo anywhere in Nigeria, and put him in immediate touch with his countrymen. In no time at all, Pius, a stranger on the plateau, had established contact with an obscure Catholic mission where his wife was to be delivered some months later. And he had joined the Owerri branch of the Ibo Progressive Union in Jos, a combined fraternal, insurance, uplift, recreational, and marching and chowder Society, undeniably but elusively political, that exists wherever Ibos congregate. Other West African peoples may be as itinerant, out of choice or necessity, as the Ibos, but none has developed this remarkable method of maintaining social ties, cultural activities, and an unspoken political solidarity. Ibo particularism is strong, yet it does not contradict their nationalism, for Ibos claim that the creation of a united Nigeria is precisely their *special* mission. This conviction did not endear them to the colonial or Hausa-Fulani authorities, nor did the old colonial residents ever forget that it was the Ibo who first exposed the inadequacy of indirect rule. Moreover, Ibos made stiff-necked servants: their inclination to talk man-to-man was considered presumptuous. And their mutual aid groups, set up in foreign provinces by a people who were notorious for their political irritability, although legitimate and within the law, helped fix the image of the Ibo as a natural subversive.

Pius was politically aware, but he was not, at this time in his life, politically engaged. He had his hands full trying to keep house, placate a homesick, scolding wife, and maintain his intricate finances in order. He had spun out his connections in and around Jos as innocently as a bird builds a nest, and he joined the Union as a matter of course. While Pius went about his business, I began to make preliminary contact with the Anaguta, whom I had first mistaken for Jarawa, climbing through the hills in the company of a Jarawa farmer in Hausa dress who had visited us one day out of curiosity. It was necessary to hike ten to twelve miles daily in order to visit several of the widely dispersed compounds, jot down a few words, and make my presence known to astonished and amused natives. The adults, of course, had seen white men before in the Jos area, but with few exceptions, from a distance. But no white man had ever visited these compounds. Many of the younger children, who had not yet strayed beyond their hamlets, fled, unbelieving, at my approach; and many a babe in arms screamed in outrage. European contacts hardly existed, yet the European presence hung over these hills.

It was easier, perhaps, for me to get used to them. I quickly came to appreciate the mature, deeply experienced, deeply incised faces of the older people. Firm lines of laughter and gravity, of suffering and joy blended with the intricate tribal incisions, so that each face was a tapestry, a work of art, a map to be read. These were the most expressive, most fully human faces I have ever seen; and they made me feel pity and shame for the cosmetic, contrived, acquisitive, vain, uniform, despairing, and empty faces that are familiar even, God help us, among the elderly in the cities of the West. Every conceivable emotion was etched into the faces of the Anaguta as deeply and as harmoniously as the herringbone scarifications that ran symmetrically down each side, from temple to chin. No single emotion or idea dominated; there were no caricatures, no masks.

I had worked briefly among mountain Arabs in Israel, and they had impressed me immensely by their familism, individuality, and dignity. But for centuries they had fluctuated between being peasants and predators; they understood the market, the elementary tricks of statecraft, and had an instinct for the city. Most of my field training had been among Europeans, or European-derived peoples in Israel, and although my theoretical and monographic reading had led me to think otherwise, I had about reached the conclusion shared by most contemporary, academic anthropologists, that primitive peoples are really just like us. Or, if characterological differences can be noted, they are variations on a common human theme, molded within cultural, but not cultural-*historical* dimensions. I no longer believe this.

There are profound qualitative distinctions between primitive and civilized peoples, glossed over by anthropologists anxious to remove the stigma of inferiority from the term "primitive" and still embarrassed by Voltaire's impertinent attack on Rousseau. Whatever their cultural styles, civilized peoples resemble each other much more closely than they do primitives, and of course the converse is true. The human constitution is everywhere the same, and human needs are universal, but they are more completely realized, if in inimitable ways, and perhaps grasped, by primitives than among ourselves. That is, primitive peoples understand the preconditions of a human existence. That is what struck me when I first looked into the faces of the Anaguta, and then looked away (the word embarrasses me) *reverently.*

The only face in that gallery I remember so distinctly, which seemed ordinary, was that of one of my interpreters. He was a young man, the first and only Anaguta to have attended secondary school, the only Anaguta who spoke any English, and one of the dozen or so nominal Christians among them. His features were mobile but blank; nothing was engraved on them. They moved from feigned innocence to a frank, low cunning and back again. He was the only Anaguta I encountered who was capable of social cringing; and he was hell-bent on improving his worldly status, which meant becoming a nominal Nigerian, a consumer of European goods, and an employee of the Zaria Tobacco Company. But he believed in nothing, except appearances, and he was unskilled at them, for he was an absolutely new bourgeoisie. Yet Andu was a sad and poignant figure, groping his way into the outer world, away from a people that scorned it, condemned by their indifference to be a weak, slippery, unhonored, faithless pioneer. He was the only African I have ever met who smiled thinly, and seemed incapable of laughter.

Just as their faces were tempered and refined by a direct and disciplined experience of life, so were their bodies. The women usually went naked on their home grounds, except for a pubic covering of leaves, although they had adopted a kind of sarong for trips to more modest, and licentious, places. The native working garments of the men were breech clouts or loin cloths, although they wore blankets or cotton togas on more formal occasions. But most of the time, most of the Anaguta exposed most of their bodies. Wherever the Christian and Islamic establishments have penetrated, or the body-mind schism has developed, the body has been conceived as an instrument of sin, so Europeans and Hausa alike regarded the Anaguta as *naked* pagans, that is, natural sinners. Their uncovered bodies were not pretty, either cosmetically or in the sense of having achieved the Greco-Roman ideal of physical perfection. But they were tough, graceful, and used. There were no gross, distorted, or repellent bodies among them; each in its style displayed a natural proportion of working parts and no withered functions. After a while I found these active, unself-conscious bodies beautiful, precisely because they were used and, among the old, weathered by use: even the lank, leathery breasts of women, half empty wineskins, worn in the honorable service of suckling children year after year, dropped in a natural contour from straight backs and appropriate shoulders. These features seemed, of course, ugly—hideous is the word I often heard—to fastidiously concupiscent Europeans and Moslems. Living among the Anaguta was a lesson in anatomy. I learned the proper shape of calf and thigh, trunk and buttock, neck and shoulder, even when somewhat diminished by hunger. And I discovered how epicurean and dissociated was our urban image of the body, how *fetishistic,* in the technical psychoanalytic sense, how shamefully aware are we of what we hide, in contrast to the Anaguta, who scarified and circumcised for symbolic reasons, to mark an event, to inscribe identity, to test courage, but neither feared nor worshiped the body in itself. What the Anaguta thought of European faces and figures, to the degree that they can be scrutinized, I do not know. But I do remember the words of a Jarawa prostitute, drunk in a palm-wine market, who confronted a European, "There is *one Baturi* with a good face." *One* white man. It stuck in my mind.

Pius, of course, was no more primitive than I, although we were civilized in different ways. As an Ibo, a Nigerian, a successfully acculturated man, and a blooming citizen of the world, he was puzzled by the Anaguta, and suspicious of them. His people had been exposed for four hundred years and more to the soldier, the trader, the slaver, and the missionary—generally to the underside of civilization—and had developed remarkable means of coping with it and assimilating what they had learned to their own ends. Ibo familism, equalitarianism, their love of the land, and highly developed social reflexes may have had primitive roots, but the transformations in Ibo society had long since shifted their forms and functions. All that these Africans fully had in common was the color of their skins. They still shared rhythm and laughter, and a certain ease of movement, the psychological precondition of which, though not the cultural cause, was, I imagine, a generous and disciplined gratification of the senses in infancy, but the more civilized the person the less pronounced these traits. Pius could be melodramatically superstitious, as he proved to us one night when we were collecting secret society masks in Ibibio country near Calabar just before a mass burning by missionaries, but his random and shallow superstitions were a civilized rather than a primitive phenomenon. He had a few strategic, self-protective beliefs, but no longer any faith. The Anaguta made Pius uneasy. He considered himself their natural superior and could never comprehend why I spent so much time in their company. As for the Anaguta, they were totally indifferent to Pius.

The First Weeks: Setting Up the Household

After the first few weeks at Gwong, our compound took on an even greater assortment of incommunicants, although from the outside it might, or could be made to, seem that a conspiracy was being hatched. First, we had arrived, creating a flurry of interest, which we did not encourage, among the tin company staff occupying the half-dozen houses in the vicinity of the office. I had asked a few tactical questions of the director, the Chief Inspector of mines in Jos, and several assorted colonial officers, who either knew little of the Anaguta and cared less or had confused them with some other people. There was to be one exception to this uniform unconcern, but I did not discover it until much later. I had listened while these officers and company men, to my surprise, bewailed the character of British rule in northern Nigeria. I had even nodded sympathetically when one important administrator remarked, rather too simply: "We have supported the Emirs right down the line, and when the people rise against them, as they certainly shall—if we have not by that day cleared out of the country, they will murder us in our beds." But I had not solicited his remarks and did not improve upon them. Yet the fear of being murdered in bed seemed endemic among the old Jos colonials, whose ranks, I should add, were being armored by colonial dinosaurs from the most remote outposts of a shrinking empire, seeking one last assignment in northern Nigeria before returning home to the new reality.

We made no courtesy calls, failed to sign the Resident's book, invited no Europeans to our house save a Canadian doctor, a domesticated adventurer who became my enduring friend. We neither socialized nor joined any of the several clubs at which the higher-class English residents of Jos tried to amuse themselves. The fact is that I was not concerned with colonial Nigeria, but with what remained of aboriginal Nigeria, and I could not take seriously the claims or pre-rogatives of the White Man's Nigeria, nor the rigamarole of colonial society. Yet I was to understand more fully later that the only real vulnerability of the British colonial aristocracy is in not being taken seriously. They can survive anything but being ignored. Look past them, fail to be impressed, imply even unwittingly that their day is done, and these finely trained, routinely brave men are defeated.

As a leave center for Europeans throughout Nigeria and head-quarters of the tin and columbite business, Jos had a relatively large, "permanent" European population; and it had developed the character of a tiny settler's colony. The Europeans exchanged their imported amenities within the small area of the city and its immediate environs, holding themselves aloof from the pagans who occupied the further suburbs to the edge of the high plateau and beyond. Even when Europeans and pagans inhabited a common physical space, they moved in different dimensions, without seeing each other. This helped fold the European aggregate back on itself, creating a hierarchy of trivial statuses and an electric circuit of tension and rumor. Unlike Lagos, Kano, Onitsha, Ibadan, or Kaduana, Jos had no great chiefs, no high African politicos, no educated African élite with whom the European could communicate without betraying his sensibilities. One must remember also that every colonial is basically a material or spiritual profiteer. He comes to extract, earn, adminis-ter, win to a cause or faith, and he brings his superior manner and technique with him; he could not be a colonial if he came to learn, humbly, or to experience a common humanity. That would make him disloyal to his government, his company, or his church, or, if he is a social scientist of a certain type, to his profession.

It was into this concentrated "settler's" enclave that we, quite un-wittingly, entered and in which we did not participate. Then Pius, Ibo, impudent, and independent, joined us, apparently a servant but behaving like a friend. Indeed, I was humble in his presence because his native background automatically elicited my anthropologist's re-spect, and I was ashamed that he was my servant. After Pius came Taru, Anaguta, a son of the British-recognized secular Chief of the tribe. It had taken me several weeks to arrange an interview with the Chief, who, I finally discovered, lived in the compound just behind our house. And it took several months before I found out that he was not the real authority among the Anaguta, insofar as they could be said to have one. But Abamu was friendly, and after first passing himself off as a Jarawa, he agreed to send me his oldest son as an assistant. Taru turned out to be a cheerful outcast, an authentic deviant. He was in his late thirties, unmarried, with no compound of his own, and it was said that no woman would stay with him, although they found him attractive. The trouble with Taru was that he was an intellectual who had become inordinately curious about Europeans and other non-Anaguta, and had decided to spend his life observing, although he never showed any desire to join them. His mother was a Birom woman, purchased in marriage by his father, and still the old man's chief wife, dominating his second compound up in the hills; and this divided parentage may have stimulated Taru's curiosity, while making him a willing outcast. For Birom women were formally deprecated by Anaguta, who had not traditionally practiced the bride price among themselves, and, rather ethnocentrically, interpreted it as an insult to the woman's family.

Taru was a natural anthropologist; *he learned by osmosis,* and the strength of his mind shone forth through his relaxed and joking manner as he went about his field work among the Europeans. He wore a garment so tattered and nondescript that I cannot recall its color or shape, and he frankly disliked working with his hands, but he spoke the languages of the Birom, the Jarawa, the Nyango-Irigwe, the Jere, the Buji, and the Rukuba. Unlike other Anaguta who spoke a slow pidgin version of Hausa, he was beautifully fluent in that lingua franca of the Northern Region; and he knew Fulfulde, the original language of the Fulani, still spoken by the pastoralists, but largely replaced by Hausa among the Fulani of the town. Taru was an indescribably gentle man, with yellow eyes and a ferociously charming yellow smile that could unsettle Pius and make those who did not know him back away; he looked like a black lion. He was my constant guide and companion, escorting me everywhere through Anaguta territory, everyone's friend without trying, a man of natural and impersonal courtesy, but he was not much use as an informant on the routine customs of his people. He was interested only in the unusual—in leading me to old burial urns, sacrilegious to touch, in exploring caves in which the Anaguta may once have lived, or at least sought shelter, in guiding me through the sacred groves, in pointing out stone axes that his people may have made, and certainly used, for cutting sacred wood. He did all this with the utmost detachment and good humor; there was no delinquency in his makeup, no spite. He knew that his culture and perhaps his people were dying out and, as a fellow anthropologist, he understood my interest, but he did not seem to share my concern. He neither respected, feared, nor hated white men, although he considered them less enduring than Africans. "You are not the first *Baturi* we have seen," he would remind me from time to time (meaning, in other words, "we will outlive you yet"). I noticed that he was always very careful not to be exploited by me, even in the name of friendship, and made a quiet fuss about receiving the modest wage for which he had asked exactly at the appointed time, or else he would not stir from our compound.

Taru was indefatigable. He could sleep under any conditions, anywhere, any time. He bathed like a cat, had a body like a whip, and thought nothing of walking twenty miles to a millet-beer market, or scrambling for hours through rugged country with an awkward and heavy load on his shoulders. Sometimes at night we would sit on the ground while he played plaintively on a small reed harp, singing of some obscure event in his peoples' past, in complicated and beautiful harmonies that exhausted the meaning of intimacy.

This internal exile had no close friends among his own people and seemed merely tolerant of his relatives. But he did argue for my support, rather wistfully it seemed, of a younger half-brother who was trying to enter elementary school against the wishes of his father, the Chief. If Taru had gracefully detached himself from his own people, they reciprocated by not taking him seriously, although they neither humiliated nor rejected him. With great amusement, he used to call me "Pozo," Elder, because I had grown a beard, and therefore presumed above my status, for only elders wore beards among the Anaguta; he did not believe that any white man could really be an elder.

Taru was disinterested in Anaguta women. But he had a quick eye for the erectly tall, beautiful, spectacularly gowned and turbaned Fulani women who walked the trails to Jos with calabashes of sour milk on their heads. He could talk to them in their native tongue, and proud and reserved as they were, they always had time for Taru. After he moved in with us, these birds of paradise made our back yard a regular stop on the way to town. There they sat, applied exotic pigments to their faces, and looked for Taru in his quarters.

Our next permanent guest was Audu, my Anaguta interpreter, who was finishing his penultimate term in a secondary school about thirty miles from Jos. Then came Umaru (Audu's brother) and wife; they, along with a third, older brother, who merely visited, became my chief informants on the day-to-day life of the Anaguta. Audu's family was unusual. They had been recommended to me by Taru's father and the Rukuba teacher at the local native administration elementary school in Gwong. They were the only "upwardly" mobile family among the Anaguta; and Audu had become their trembling vanguard. Both parents were long deceased, and the older, middle-aged brother had assumed the father's place, and was responsible for the family's upward and outward thrust. Atypically Anaguta, from childhood he had been awed by and drawn to the white man's technology. Many years before he had walked thirty miles to a mining station out of curiosity, and there had heard a radio, but he was ridiculed as a liar when he tried to describe it at home. When the Europeans began to come in greater numbers (in the 1930's) and Jos took shape as a city, with roads on which four-wheeled animals appeared, he realized that the Anaguta would have to adapt themselves to the new ways if they were to survive. Despite his dissenting view of their situation, he never lost caste among his own people, probably because they sensed that his interest was not self-serving. He was highly respected, and was said to have the capacity to become invisible in moments of crisis. This blessing was bestowed, it could not be learned, or even summoned up at will by the few who were endowed with it. Sako never boasted of this gift, or even claimed to possess it; he left that to other people. When he was still a young man, they had seen him pull a leopard off a child; as he grabbed its tail, Sako is said to have disappeared, and the animal fled. There were a few false claimants of the gift of invisibility, the most respected of occult powers among the Anaguta; but people paid no attention to them. A man who sat by a trail trying to foster the illusion that he was invisible would be seen and heard, and humored by being ignored. *The power to become invisible*—what greater gift could a people fleeing before civilization desire?

Indeed, it is possible to climb to the peak of a hill in the heart of their territory and look down on the white roofs of Jos, a few miles to the south; if it is late afternoon in the rainy season, and a mist diffuses the air, the city, insubstantial, shimmers in and out of view. Or, even on blazing afternoons, from the sudden perspective of a mountain trail, its bulk contracts, and it appears as just another bright patch on an endless, ancient landscape. The Anaguta play with these perspectives; from the heights they command they know every visage of the city in each season and hour, but the city is not an optical illusion, however illusory may be the purposes that established it or the ends it pursues. As the Anaguta conjure with the invisibility of individuals, so they conjure with the invisibility of Jos. But the city is there.

How ironic it was that Sako, one of the few possessors of the gift of invisibility, should have been aware of the need to come to terms with the superior power that was encircling his people. Yet they had clubbed him severely and left him for dead when he had enrolled

Audu as the first and for years the only Anaguta student at the district elementary school; but he neither struck back nor changed his course. There were other incidents over the years, but Sako survived them with self-respect. After he had become a regular visitor to our house, he had been charged by a younger man of his lineage with betraying tribal secrets and had been publicly slapped. I was being given rituals, part of the living body of the people, it was said, and it was true as everyone knew, for I had explained my mission to all who would listen. Even the subtler aspects of the charge were true, for what sacred thing was I giving the Anaguta in return for what they were giving me? What could I give them? But the man who slapped Sako—and there was no greater insult—was considered a malcontent, jealous of his position, and secretly interested in getting closer to the Europeans. So Sako was praised for ignoring the insult conceived in hypocrisy. On another occasion, Sako had invited me to a most solemn ceremony—the symbolic reenactment of the Anaguta's victory over the Fulani, which helped keep the Islamic horsemen off the plateau. We had both been under attack that afternoon—he, verbally, by members of the family that had accused him of disloyalty, and I by a frantically absorbed warrior who had made several passes at my head with a tomahawk. The majority of people present stood by observing but not looking at us. When we held our ground, the tension broke, and I, at least, was never to be troubled again. Still Sako, the conciliator, continued to be considered the honorable enemy of his peoples' intentions. Unlike Taru, who was a voluntary outcast, regarded a harmless deviant, Sako was quite conservative, even exemplary, as a husband, a father, a worker, and a believer. Thus his unique desire to accommodate the Anaguta to the outer society was conceived as profoundly threatening.

Sako, however, was not successful. His efforts had been narrowed to the scope of his own family. Audu might escape his Anaguta identity, but he was not influencing his tribesmen. And Umaru, the middle brother who came to live with us, was also preparing to abandon his people, as they were bent on abandoning the world. Both Umaru and Audu were in a pitiful, not a tragic situation, because they were unaware of what was happening to them and were incapable of choice. They had learned the need for change, as the only salvation, from a strong brother. But they had no support from their own people, and were faced with indifference on the outside. Inevitably, with little moral or material capital, finding themselves and their people inadequate, ignorant of the society into which they were emerging, lacking modern, specialized skills with little chance of developing any, and pitifully, pitifully ashamed of themselves, they could only hope to survive by bluff, self-deception, and other modes of cheating. Audu had not worked on the land for years; as he had been his brother's pioneer in elementary school, he was the only Anaguta to have attended secondary school. With luck, this deracinated, yet uncultivated man might become a clerk or a minor civil servant in a country full of peasants. The British are ambiguously grateful for the contribution of these West African clerks whom they invented to do the busy work of empire; these underpaid, undereducated, bewildered boys earned the conqueror's contempt as they bent awkwardly to his needs. And those more glorified clerks— the barristers—earnest, literate, precisely educated men, who were scrupulously intentioned yet served as domestic agents of foreign administration and partners in the enterprise, with few exceptions, helped seal the metropolitan intentions. But technical education or the cultivation of knowledge about Africa, its history, geography, cultural variety, and unity were neglected. It did not fit the half-unwitting strategy of colonialism.

What happened to Umaru I, an unwilling agent of change, saw myself. Umaru had learned a distaste for manual labor from Audu, who had in turn absorbed it from the colonial environment in which he existed. By the time he moved into my compound he, a Christian like Audu, had already considered himself superior to his tribe. He was bursting with abstract piety, but he spent all of his money on European clothing, utterly ignoring his wife, who roamed our back yard naked and finally left him to return to her brother's compound with their two small sons, thus, after the custom of marital exchange pursued by the Anaguta, jolting Umaru's sister out of *her* marriage. This disturbed him but not too much, because he was engaged at that time in wooing a young Anaguta woman who had married a Birom, had lived briefly in Kaduna, and was the only Anaguta who had up to that point left the Jos area and had returned home in disillusionment. She had a sophisticated Hausa air, wore pretty robes, and appeared to her former peers as an empty-headed, preoccupied snob. Finally, Umaru's behavior, which had been satisfactory as an informant, became impossible as an Anaguta. His money wages made him feel superior to his wife, who ordinarily would have earned the few shillings a year needed to pay his head tax by selling firewood or a few garden vegetables. Living in my compound reversed this process; now his wife was immobilized and he had the negotiable coin. This also enabled him to neglect his land. He was unable to hire outsiders, and no Anaguta cultivated for wages. Nor, to my surprise, would his relatives or friends maintain his compound in his willful absence. If he had been ill they would have been glad to help, or if he had needed extra hands they would have organized a work group, but this was sheer neglect, and even if he intended to return one day they felt no obligation to encourage what they considered delinquency. The choice had to be Umaru's, not mine or his family's. And one day the breach was made formal when Sako, on a routine visit to our compound, brought Umaru's hoe with him and handed it over wordlessly. Personal relations remained friendly enough between Umaru and his lineage, but he was now on his own.

On the other hand, Umaru never shared a shilling with his friends or relatives. At first this struck me as pure greed. But I came to realize that the logic was as impeccably traditional as that of his kinsmen when they returned the hoe. Only the context was misapprehended. Umaru was now a wage worker; he was earning his keep by his own efforts, he was not living on traditional land. No fellow tribesman was contributing in any way toward Umaru's livelihood, thus none had the right to a share in his wages. The unspoken principle of Anaguta economics—to the laborer shall go the fruit—was now being applied in a quite different milieu. Umaru accepted this but he did so naively. For he was no longer functioning in a cooperative society; he had no guarantee of productive work, and he had no sense of the intricacy of the new economy that would not, in fact, reward him in direct proportion to his efforts. That is, Umaru had no conception of a market economy, certainly not of the capitalist system or of his terribly insignificant bargaining power. The Anaguta had never developed internal markets, had no system of currency, and were subsistence cultivators. Umaru had not even the chance to acquire the elementary shrewdness of the peasant in selling to the city; indeed Anaguta, who habitually counted by the duodecimal system, often paid twelve shillings for the Hausa ten. Umaru was incapable of a depersonalized business exchange; that was not the way goods and services circulated among his people. Even though he gloried in being a paid employee, he regarded himself as did Audu as a protector, a father, a brother, a kinsman. Umaru imagined that he had exchanged a little compound for a big one that required less work, afforded more prestige, and had many more amenities. I tried to play the part of compound head, although I liked Umaru less than the unsentimental Taru, for whom I felt a real collegial bond. But objectively, Umaru had moved from one world to another; my compound was the flimsiest of shelters, and my heart sank for him and the innumerable others like him whose grand and simple expectations had been, and would be, shattered as they climbed out of what was left of aboriginal society into the modern world. I could not explain this to Umaru. He was right in believing that he had no place to which to return, that he could not go backwards, and who was I to tell him that he had little chance of going forward in the way he had anticipated. So I watched him as he luxuriated in his new European vest and trousers, or in his white Hausa cap and gown, jaunty, confident, apparently free as a feather is free but actually at the mercy of every current of air—and rootless—neither Anaguta nor Nigerian, or pagan, or Christian, a man losing his identity in the pursuit of an illusion. Later, when I could no longer stand what I had come to understand, I tried to discuss these matters with his people, but they had already thought beyond me.

Lucas completed our household. He was a debonair young man, a recent secondary school graduate, an acquaintance of Audu's, who spoke superior English and Hausa. Lucas was an Ankwe, from Shendam division, the southernmost sector of Plateau Province. Like many converted plateau pagans, who had an antipathy to Islam because of Fulani attempts at conquest, and who were influenced by the relatively large number of missions in the province, Lucas was a Christian. He was also an eagle scout, and the conventional excellence of his character had won him a guided tour to England some years before. But there was more to Lucas than that. He had a penetrating, detached intelligence, which emancipated him from interpreting human behavior in racial terms. Yet I had seen him shudder with the repressed mortification that a naturally superior man of low social status is likely to experience when ever so subtly slighted by his merely social, merely European superiors. Lucas had shrewdly sized up the structure of the new Nigerian society, at least in the North, and had calculated his chances. But he was torn between his desire to become a doctor, which would have proven a natural outlet for his quick, warm sympathies, and swifter roads to success. Unlike Auda, he came from people who were rapidly responding to European and Hausa stimuli, and from a family that had been acculturated in depth; his father had been an Episcopalian minister. Lucas's aspirations were understood and supported at home; indeed, he seemed the prototype of the young man anywhere who has left home in order to make good in the big city, except that the colonial experience had made him more adaptable and experienced than his Western counterparts. Moreover, he felt that the fate of his kinsmen depended on his success; he was obliged to reciprocate their support, and this made him rather more socially ruthless and fraternally responsible, more nepotic, if you will, than he otherwise might have been. At the time Lucas joined us as my chief interpreter and research assistant, he had not yet decided about continuing his education and was looking for an interim job, other than clerking, which bored him. He was also curious about America, and had toyed with the idea of applying to an American university for a scholarship, so we met each other's needs. I was glad to have him. After we left Nigeria, he wrote me wistfully about the "charming Anaguta" but he turned down the offer of an American scholarship and decided not to become a doctor. He accepted an appointment at an Officers' Training School in England, no work for a young man of his timber, and especially absurd in Nigeria, but a quicker, perhaps explosive route to the top.

This, then, was our more or less permanent African household—Pius, steward and cook, and his wife; Taru, Chinese hobo of a primitive, guide and companion; Umaru, informant, and his wife; Audu, informant and Anaguta interpreter; and Lucas. Two Ibo, four Anaguta, one Ankwe. Five Christians, three of plateau pagan background, and two pagans. Three literates, two semiliterates, two illiterates. No Moslems, no Hausawa, which, it turned out, was contrary to colonial habit.

Getting More Deeply Involved

Strangely enough, this nuclear group never jelled socially. Each went about his business quite independently of the other except, of course, when the necessity of working with me threw them together. Otherwise, they came and went at random, giving the compound the appearance of a place in which something unusual was going on as, indeed, I hoped it was. This atypicality was heightened by the fact that Africans entered through the front door, and I spent a good deal of time in the yard, which, after the custom of the country, separated the main dwelling in which we lived from the quarters of the Africans. The living room was a working office; those African associates with whom I was not engaged drifted in and out as they pleased. When I was not tracking down a compound in the hills, usually accompanied by Taru and often by my wife with her cameras, I could be seen sitting in my front office with Lucas, Sako, Umaru, or Audu, and later there were others, inquiring into Anaguta society along an English-Iguta, English-Hausa, or English-Hausa-Iguta circuit. At the same time I was bending to the task of learning Iguta, a hitherto unwritten language, by writing down texts, collecting vocabularies, and showing off the little I knew on every possible occasion, which was the best way to learn a little more. Since I had come to the plateau to study a pagan people in the vicinity of Jos, I had counted myself lucky in landing in a house on the territory of a practically unknown group, and had gone right to work on the principle that one can do field work anywhere. It did not strike me that expatriates and official Africans alike would be willing to suspect the bearded man who went everywhere with a miniature tape recorder, whose wife was always taking pictures, who was moreover constantly in the company of natives and capable, or so it seemed, of speaking to the pagans in their own language. Yes, I was said to be an anthropologist, they thought, but was I, or, if so, was that all I was. I had not reckoned with the settlers' colony character of the expatriate community, which could amplify a stranger's footfall to the sound of a marching army. Nor had I realized the critical political importance of the pagan areas of the Middle Belt to the dominant parties of the (then) three regions of Nigeria, but especially to the Northern People's Congress, as frustrated in winning the allegiance of the plateau people as the Fulani had been in their efforts to conquer and the British, indirectly, to rule them.

I had considered the possibility of moving into an Anaguta compound and settling my family in Jos; even if the Anaguta had accepted me on such short acquaintance, the idea would have been impractical for a Mary Slessor. The euphorbia-enclosed compound was a maze of tiny interconnected huts through which a family's social and sexual life pulsed. I could not learn to live and work as an Anaguta, and anything short of that would have been a waste of my energy and an outrage on their privacy. I could not have survived on their staples: millet beer or acha gruel, or withstood the cold nights of the long dry season or the violence of the rainy season on that steep ground, without access to civilized shelter. There were, of course, no utilities available; and supplies would have had to be carried in at great inconvenience. Moreover, I would certainly have been an early victim of one or more of the water-borne parasitic diseases for which the region was notorious. I would have had to spend an unreasonable amount of time boiling water, cleaning food, and so on. This was imperative in European quarters; in a native compound it would have been impossible, unless so stocked and transformed by modern equipment that it would have ceased being a native compound, and that would have defeated my purpose. I was fortunate that our house was well within the borders of Anaguta settlement.

At night, if I did not hear the sound of ceremony in the Anaguta hills, I would often drive in to Jos and roam the native streets, listening and observing, usually ignored, occasionally insulted as someone whom I could not see spat "*Baturi* bastard," mistaking me, I told myself, for the other kind of European.   Still I shuddered at being stereotyped and forced to share a guilt that I felt had been personally expunged by training, insight, and sympathy.   My mode of life, my opportunities, the very clothes I wore were an insult to these disinherited.   From a little social distance, anthropologist, colonial administrator, business man seemed alike.   From a greater distance, only the color of the skin was visible, and beyond that any man on the social horizon might be an enemy.   Colonizing civilization had created these distances; good intentions were merely precious and sentiments cheap.   The Africans who called out to me in town were no better men than I.   But once human hatred finds an affective occasion and a plausible excuse in the repressions and inequities of civilization, it is implacable.   What could I reply?   We are all guilty, my friends.   We are all responsible for everything in this modern world.   But could I, a Jew, forgive the Nazis?   It was not so easy to hate the crime but love the criminal.   It was not even simple for most of us to purify ourselves of our small, private enmities.   Certainly, if the church understood anything, it understood that.   Had the missionaries come in fear and trembling before the judgment of their own history, to be forgiven, or had they come, insensibly, merely to forgive?   Sometimes at night I could hear thinned-out African voices rising in the childish, rote refrains of Protestant Sunday School songs, from an enclosure run by a missionary sect, rigid with abstentions.   Once later, in Ekot, in the steaming bush near the Cross River in southeastern Nigeria, we were to be put up for the night at a mission hospital by a young Irish priest with a gleam in his eye.   I had been richly wined and dined in his quarters, he having changed from habit to civvies, and the evening closed with his singing "When Irish Eyes Are Smiling," accompanied by an ancient record, long after I had retired to his absent colleague's bed.   He had become a priest, he said, because it was a good job for a likely Irish lad (like Pius, he has too many brothers and too little land), and he believed in spreading the Gospel.   He kept in touch with the outer world by reading *Life* magazine religiously; the Africans, whom he confessed through a slit in the concrete wall of the rectory, hardly existed for him.   He stated, in so many words, that his mission was to save as many souls as he could by applying the essential formulae.   His senior colleague had been physically close enough to the Africans to have been the father of several children, but I imagine that he felt the same way. When I left he said, with the air of a man conferring a small, impersonal favor, that he would pray for me, and I said, "Thank you, Father," in appreciation of the uproarious evening we had spent trying to communicate from his planet to mine.

But afterwards in Jos I encountered a missionary of another kind, a member of an obscure Irish order, who had been in Nigeria for forty years. He was so keenly indifferent to this world, so experienced in suffering that he was able to identify fully with the Africans who had been hurt by it, as he could, I am sure, with any creature that breathed and had been hurt; and he looked upon the rich and neurotic West with casual contempt. But Africa was leaving itself and him behind, and he was preparing to die without returning home. As I walked the streets of Jos, it seemed to me that the earth was stiffening in abstract, stereotyped hate. How were we to recover our primitive capacity to let hate flow so that we might love. The crucifixion was, for Western man, an indelible symbol of this need, and of the possibility of its transcendence. But that was not exactly a subject for missionary discussion with the natives. How were we to turn hateful energies to creation before we perished through ice in fire; how were we to ride the back of Blake's burning tiger? That was why, I discovered, I had come to study primitives, or what was left of them from a culture strangling in abstractions. And that, I finally realized with relief, was why I had become an anthropologist.

In the towns African humanity is arranged in fluid masses around market stalls, mosques, dance halls, stores; any flickering point of interest attracts a geometric crowd. The world's goods are distributed very thinly through these masses. It is possible to buy things—even parts of things—in microscopic quantities. Once I bought a single match from the head tray of the ultimate retailer. The original shipment, no doubt, had descended in diminishing lots from importer and wholesaler to stores, stalls, and trays, swelling the profits and the number of profiteers while bringing the over-prized ware to the most impoverished consumer. In one sense these new cities of Africa were no more than elaborate depots for the trading companies—everyone buying or selling something in the redolent, swarming markets; under the wings of vultures, a wilderness of petty entrepreneurs. Big traders gave birth to little traders but never cut the cord; and they held the peasants in their credit also by subsidizing the production of peanuts, palm oil, or cocoa. Cultures have been ruined for the sake of modern mercantilism, and societies conquer so as to secure unimpeded trade. Millions of people, stimulated to produce for the Europeans in little lots that converged to enormous shipments, bought back, in towns like Jos, some small expensive thing that seemed cheap because of its size or inferior quality. Tiny individual measures of production and consumption, but they commanded all the surplus sinew and strength of British West Africa. No wonder Europeans were uneasy around Jos. The "white man bastard" was the unseen presence, the invisible master. He rarely materialized; his goods stood up for him. Conquest by trade was indirect conquest; indirect conquest was best served by indirect rule.

The city laughed and chattered at night in a hundred tongues, but it seemed to me to be groaning; was there an African Breughel somewhere who could reveal its burdened and demonic spirit? It was always a relief to leave Jos, and take up my pursuit of the Anaguta, who were matching invisibility against invisibility, indirect response to indirect rule.

As the weeks rolled by, our presence became more conspicuous by our absence from European circles and the flowering of our compound into a web of African activity. Pagan women, wearing head-boards and with babies wrapped on their backs, used our back yard as a short cut home from market. Taru's Fulani friends primped every morning beneath a particular tree. Drummers, flutists, and other musicians were always welcome for a recording session. And there were many occasions when the cement walls reverberated under the powerful, intricate rhythms of the big Anaguta drums. People danced frequently in our back yard, and once several dozen warbling Jarawa women, trailed by a large crowd, suddenly arrived in front of the house, adjoining the tin company office. And then there was the time that we invited the Miango [3] troupe, the most explosive dancers in northern Nigeria, to perform in an open field across from the local court not far from our compound. Armed with a police permit, they moved across the city from their settlement to ours, leaping, their bodies curved like brown fish in the sun, drumming, piping, and singing, followed by most of the Miango community. They put on a show that rocked the countryside for us, themselves, and hundreds of Anaguta who filed down from their compounds, and sobered a passing British doctor who had spent twelve years in Lagos and could not believe what he was seeing. At that time I had no way of knowing that the Miango, the most consciously and intelligently acculturated of plateau pagans, and the Anaguta, the most elusively defiant, were making common cause against Birom control of the Jos Division native authority. That is, the Miango and most of the Jarawa in the neighborhood of Jos were ready to use traditional Anaguta claims to the city and its environs to depose the British-supported, Hausa-oriented

[3] The local name for Jos Nyango-Irigwe.

Birom Chief and to lift the pagan areas around the city out of Birom control. The Miango and Jarawa were already under the Anaguta Chief of Gwong District. Unfortunately, Abamu, the Chief and Taru's father, was, of course, an illiterate, and moreover was of little consequence among his own people. At any rate the Anaguta were unconcerned. But it was now possible for anyone who was compiling a dossier or making mental notes to have me involved not only with national but local politics.

The Authorities Are Threatened and Become Suspicious

My alien presence in Gwong already had given rise to unfriendly speculation by the authorities. I had tried, for example, to interest the Divisional Educational Officer in the case of an Anaguta elementary school student who, oddly enough, wished to continue his education. We had had a quiet, unfruitful conversation. The officer was perhaps a bit too frigidly polite, and I a trifle too enthusiastic. We were also paying the tuition of some twenty Anaguta children at the local elementary school. It was only about twelve shillings per term per child, but their parents could not afford the fee. And we had enrolled a Jarawa waif, who had attached himself to our household with the consent of his sister. The sister, a speechless prostitute in the New Town, had vermilion eyelids and rose cheeks, and a face clenched in the agony of such pleasures. Some years earlier she had left a disintegrating compound in a half-abandoned Jarawa hamlet, taking her brother with her, to take her chances in the city.

In one form or another these modest and unofficial efforts echoed around the colonial circuit, and word came back to me from an acquaintance in the next province that some presumptuous American was raising a hell of a row insisting that hill pagans be sent to school, which was not the case at all. But it took several more concrete events to precipitate the action that was now in suspension.

The first of these occurred a couple of months after our arrival in Gwong. Pius's wife had returned from the hospital, and he, having by that time knit himself snugly into the Ibo community, arranged for the infant to be unveiled at a naming ceremony in our compound. On the appointed day a group of his fellow townsmen from Owerri Province, whom he had met at the Ibo Progressive Union in Jos, arrived bearing gifts and prepared, through their senior member, to bestow a name on their compatriot's daughter. It was an impressive display of Ibo egalitarianism. Pius was a servant, but the dozen men ranged around the table he had set up in the back yard, and drinking the beer he had provided, included professionals and businessmen, merchants and mechanics, and a single policeman. The latter was so obviously Ibo that, even if I had then been aware of the possibility, I would never have taken him for a police spy, although the species, official and otherwise, was common in northern Nigeria. Moreover, the man was in uniform.

The women in their Sunday robes clustered like dark flowers around mother and daughter. The men drank their beer, ribbed Pius on his fatherhood, and spoke of home. The yard hummed with gaiety. Pius had asked me to share a glass with his guests, which I did, responding to a toast to Zik, now President of Nigeria, but then the Premier of the East and head of the N.C.N.C., not then in compromising coalition with the N.P.C. at the Center.

Immediately thereafter, I left to take my family on a drive through Birom country, south of Jos. When we returned, about an hour later, the compound was deserted, and Pius was standing bowed and withdrawn, drying glasses in the kitchen. It seems that the chief assistant to the director of the tin company, who lived in a nearby house, had suddenly appeared, inquired whether I was home, and then suggested that the party be broken up. Although he was not a pious man, he had given Sunday, along with my absence, as the reason. This chief assistant was a hearty, strongly built, busy fellow, with a tea strainer of a moustache and a face like that on the label of Beefeaters' Gin. But he was also a devious bully, haughty before the submissive Hausa clerks who worked in the office, and humble before the boss. It comforted him to think that the boss was just a Greek, some kind of a Wog, despite his carefully trimmed British accent, which almost but never quite betrayed him, and his languorous, pale white, unoccupied, upper-class British wife. Beneath the bluff, Sergeant Major exterior, the chief assistant was a terrified small bourgeois, who had found his way to the colonies, horizontal mobility being a good substitute for the upward mobility that he could not have achieved in England because of his limited chance for education and inconsequential connections. He had lived well in northern Nigeria, playing an upper-class charade, buying service and respect in a passable accent, and he dreaded above all the prospect of returning home to descend to what would be considered his rightful place in society. So he courted the boss like a lover, for his dismissal would have voided his entry permit, and neglected his wife; his marriage was misbegotten anyway, and from time to time he drank himself helpless. His wife, an angular, intelligent English woman, was once a schoolteacher but was now growing incompetent in the colonial atmosphere which rusted her skills while inflating her prestige.

For that reason she feared the return home as deeply as her husband. Later she made an effort to reach us when the going got rough, but fell back exhausted on the other side.

The chief assistant was hardly the man to stand up to assembled Ibos in someone else's back yard. He had to be selective about the Africans he insulted—so as not to endanger his stay in Nigeria—just as he clung to the Levantine boss who enjoyed insulting this Englishman he owned. He had been polite, I am sure, to Pius and his friends out of fear. This was a job for the director, who was less discriminating in his approach to Africans. The director habitually referred to the Africans as bastards and was always trying to make his Hausa employees and servants jump by shouting at them at the top of his voice from the shortest possible distance. The idea seemed to be to catch them unaware, a sport that he felt was appreciated all around.

The Ibo were not impressed by the director's argument—in my back yard and on Anaguta land—that African celebrations were not permitted on *his* property. He was obstructing a naming ceremony, and they argued with him man to man. In a shorter time than it takes to tell it, the director threatened to call the Senior Superintendent of Police, with whom he was on friendly terms, and shouted that Pius and his baby were bastards, and who could properly name a bastard. He went on to charge them with creating a disturbance, which was not true, and at this they reluctantly left. Pius was ready on the instant to take the case to court, but the others would not have it. Southerners were, just then, suspected and disadvantaged in the North. The political battle against southern associated parties was gaining force and "northernization" of business and government was gaining momentum. Charges could easily be trumped up against these southerners, and they were uncertain about the extent of the tin executives' influence.

The next day I went to see the director. Pius had been humiliated in front of his friends; he looked uncertainly to me, "the other kind of European," for moral support, and I would not have people interfered with in my house. At the outset the director and I were patient with each other. I explained to him, as one expatriate to another, that Nigeria was not a settlers' colony, that it was impractical and immoral to push Africans around; and I gave him a short, cordial course on the deficiencies of the colonial mentality. He responded by assuring me of his respect for me and my work, and then read to me from the unwritten manual on old colonial behavior. Africans, he said, were children; it took decades to understand them and no amount of book learning could equal his experience. They had to be treated with a firm hand since they had no direction of their own, and if you gave them an inch they would take a mile. If they were not biologically inferior to whites, they were at least a thousand years behind them. He said he had really been guarding the propriety of my house in my absence, and also the little frontier community in which we all lived. And he told me how Africans were prone to committing atrocities. This, I recalled, was a favorite topic of conversation of his new English secretary, a preternaturally competent, good-natured, earthy woman, neat as a pin, who had spent too many years in the Rhodesias where she had been briefly married and widowed, and who clothed her unusual sexual fantasies in African dress. I informed the director that attitudes such as his were making it difficult for the white race. I told him that he was never to interfere in my affairs again. He said that my affairs were public affairs; he had recognized two prominent members of the Jos branch of the N.C.N.C. among the party in my compound, and if I thought that that was a baby-naming ceremony I was laughably wrong—it had been a political meeting, and he was within his rights in breaking it up because all political meetings in northern Nigeria required a police permit. Moreover, they had been toasting Zik when he interrupted them, and what further proof did I want. Ibos, he said, his eyes turning red, were arrogant and tricky. He was beginning to shake, afraid to insult me directly and afraid not to, so I walked out, telling him to stay away from my legally rented premises, knowing that only a religious conversion could breach that wall of prejudice and frustration.

But I did not know that he had already informed the Senior Superintendent of Police that I had subsidized a large and noisy rally of the N.C.N.C. in my compound. At that time Hausa-Ibo tensions in northern Nigeria were high; the conception of the coalition government composed of the N.P.C. and N.C.N.C. had not yet taken shape. The Ibo were politically active and outspoken, and the memory of bloody riots between Hausa and Ibo in Kano was still strong. This added another complication to the complex and (to the N.P.C.) dangerous balance of forces in the province. In a matter of weeks the colonial circuit of rumor had amplified Pius's private naming ceremony to a lavish reception arranged by me for a hundred prominent members of the N.C.N.C., honoring that southern radical and suspected enemy of the north, Zik,[4] on his birthday. Word even spread to adjoining provinces and frightened a fellow anthropologist

[4] Dr. Azikiwe ("Zik") took office as Governor-General of Nigeria following independence in 1960; after Nigeria became a Republic he was installed as President by the coalition N.P.C.-N.C.N.C. government.

who was professionally addicted to looking at social processes objectively, and had a strategically healthy respect for the status quo.

By that time I had attracted the attention of the British police, who were determined to keep northern Nigeria a model of colonial stability; but I do not think that I was under direct scrutiny. I was known, however, in African and European circles for rather different reasons, so it should not have surprised me, as it did, when a newspaper reporter knocked on the door one day and asked for an interview. He was a representative of the *Daily Times,* the leading national newspaper, published in Lagos in English, as were most Nigerian papers. He told me that he had heard that an anthropologist was studying hill pagans in Gwong, and would be grateful if I explained this newsworthy mission to him. I did not object in principle and, feeling that I could learn as much from him as he from me, I invited him in. I followed the Nigerian press carefully and was well aware of its shrewd, but figurative, interpretation of the news. In the American press proper facts are typically made trivial in shallow and uninformed contexts. The Nigerian press was the converse; it had an instinct for the sense of events, with or against the facts, although it was capable on occasion of reaching heights of fantasy. I was forearmed, but Patrick, the reporter, was a disarming chap. He was of Ibo parentage, born in the north, personable, poised, and eager. I explained at some length my efforts among the Anaguta, the auspices under which the study was being conducted, and he seemed interested but took no notes. He had come with a colleague, who was so quiet and inconspicuous that I was completely unaware of him; indeed, I never saw him again or found out who he was. Presumably, he was a witness to my remarks, but whether innocently, that is, journalistically, or in some other capacity, I did not know. But one way or the other, in what were to be fairly frequent trips to the office of Patrick's newspaper, he was never in evidence.

Patrick finally asked me my opinion and impressions of the current Nigerian scene. I said that I only had some general ideas about the North, not having visited the other regions, and would discuss these with him but strictly off the record, not for publication. He agreed at once and we began a lively discussion.

The gist of it was as follows. The north was a terribly poor and economically underdeveloped area. This was due in part to indirect rule, which had paved the way for, and encouraged, small-holder cash cropping. Indirect rule had been successful where Fulani sovereignty had been strongest, and unsuccessful in the pagan areas where political chiefs had had to be appointed by the British in order to collect taxes where none had been collected before, and to keep the King's peace in the vicinity of trade routes. The N.P.C., the party of the Emirs, grew out of, and merged with, the administrative structure of indirect rule, and therefore could not and would not encourage democratic participation in government at the grass roots. As was well known, Lugard's system was fundamentally undemocratic in application; it rewarded and strengthened those already in power, made them dependent on the Colonial Authority, and disengaged them further from any connections they may have had with the people at large. In theory, I indicated, indirect rule was supposed to use native institutions, not merely established or appointed political chiefs, but it had failed to do so. Had any real effort been made, for example, to transform traditional, cooperative economic systems, or native authorities, into modern agricultural, marketing or labor cooperatives? Actually, the British had done very little *directly* to develop the North; there was hardly any evidence of capital investment beyond the necessary transportation grid in the service of trade. The colonial process had been one of pacification and extraction. Or, rather, the British colonial apparatus had been superimposed upon the cruder, tributary, and slave-ridden Fulani system, itself a type of archaic colonialism. It was also interesting to discover that where the Fulani had not conquered, indirect rule had failed and the N.P.C. had not taken root, as among plateau pagans; and opposition political parties making a direct appeal to an untutored electorate had emerged but these had been stimulated by southern elements. It seemed incongruous, I concluded, that the Colonial Office should consider northern Nigeria the prime example of a successfully managed colony, particularly when so many English officers in the field, in administrative generations gone by, had written so many reports and books criticizing the nature and assumptions of the undertaking.

Patrick, a member of the N.C.N.C., grew very serious, agreed emphatically, and contributed interesting material of his own. When he left, he promised, at my request, that he would submit to me any item intended for publication, and would prepare a brief notice on my study of the Anaguta, but would not, of course, use any remarks that might be interpreted politically. Being a certain type of journalist, this promise he failed to keep. Several weeks later a prominent story appeared in the *Daily Times*, misidentifying me and quoting me selectively and luridly on Lugard and the essential lack of democracy of indirect rule. There was only a single passing reference to my work among the Anaguta, the supposedly original intent of the interview. No mention was made of regional politics, but the north was characterized as the most backward area in Nigeria. Patrick had obviously used me for his own purposes. Breach of confidence aside, the story was inaccurate enough to justify a letter to the editor. But I decided that it would be unwise to attract further attention, and let it go. After all, the Nigerian press was full of statements by natives and visitors evaluating and criticizing every aspect of the local scene. Patrick's story, in contrast, had been relatively modest. But later it was easy enough to visualize official thought processes: an American anthropologist lives in Gwong, apparently studying pagans whose claim to Jos is being used in an effort to shift the balance of power in the area; he considers indirect rule undemocratic, and the north a most impoverished region. Exploiting academic license, he has planted a story in the press which can be used by enemies of the established regime. Obviously, the man is an agent of some kind, probably an agent provocateur. If not, he is having that effect and it is all the same. Perhaps the Americans want a democratic north as soon as possible. After all, Azikiwe and Nkrumah were educated in the United States; both are notorious enemies of political chieftancy, colonialism, and indirect rule. But the man may not be acting in the interest of the American government. Perhaps he takes his orders from the Soviet Union.

Logically enough, anthropologists are frequently taken as spies because of the inquisitive nature of their work; their concern with local affairs in the remote places to which they go, their tendency to fade into the background of local custom in living up to the canons of participant observation. They have, also, a certain limited academic immunity; they travel freely, and what better cover could a secret agent desire. A logical case can be constructed, and often has been, against any anthropologist in the field almost anywhere in this era of active and reactive crises that echo to the uttermost ends of the earth. Of course, in the spiritual sense anthropologists are Kierkegaardian double agents. That is, engaged in a search for the varieties of human experience, they are marginal to the commercial-industrial society that created them; and they are transient, if eager, participants elsewhere. Anthropology is a scholarly discipline, but it is also a kind of secretly structured revolt, a search for human possibilities. Police agents, who are not known for their theological sensitivity, instinctually suspect that sort of thing.

Perhaps a few anthropologists have actually been government agents or, less officially, have reported unpublished findings to appropriate government agencies for aggressive purposes; and they are beneath contempt. But most such suspicions originate in the psychologically totalitarian concept of "objective guilt." That is, the effect of a man's behavior, measured against the intentions of a dominant political power, becomes sufficient cause for him to be identified as a spy, a traitor, and so on. His own intentions, or actual official connections, are irrelevant. Ultimately, on that basis, a case could be constructed against any citizen, anywhere; it would be unnecessary for him to be an anthropologist. But the theory of objective guilt has the curious effect of creating opposition to any system or agency that makes use of it. To fear being mistaken for an enemy of a regime is the beginning of political wisdom, that is, it is the first step for men of conscience toward becoming an opponent of any regime that will not tolerate dissent. This then is not merely an anthropological matter, although anthropologists are perhaps in a good position to make inquiry. Nor is it even a national or colonial affair, but it is a familiar and universal threat in an age of ecumenical terror to citizens of the world, whose first loyalty must now be to mankind, that is, to the human possibilities of men everywhere, and not to nation states as such and not to systems. Still, I had no intention of becoming involved "objectively" or otherwise in Nigerian politics, and I realized that my private talk with Patrick had been an error in judgment.

By December I felt that the initial phase of my work in Gwong had been completed. After involved negotiations I had finally met the real, traditional authority among the Anaguta, a Priest Chief, a holy *primus inter pares,* whom I was permitted to provide with millet beer at forty paces (to approach him more closely would have contaminated him). Three months later I was permitted the right to talk to him, providing I did not look at him. Thus we decided to undertake our planned tour of southeastern Nigeria, including a visit to Pius's home town, and the southern Cameroons. The purpose of the trip was to see Iboland, to visit a few plantations north and east of Calabar, which are rare in British West Africa, and to collect, if possible, artifacts for a university museum. The southern Cameroons was then a separate region within the Federation of Nigeria. The beginnings of a plantation economy had been developed there under German administration prior to the First World War; and the highlands were also celebrated for wood carving and bead work. There had been some agitation for an independent Cameroons, reported in the Nigerian press, and a plebescite was to be held in 1959. But it was generally felt that the electorate would choose to remain connected with Nigeria. At any rate that was not then a problem of concern to me.

Our trip lasted about a month, including a strange tropical Christmas Day in the Oban Hills, where native ceremony was expressed in bizarre versions of Christian mortification of the flesh.

We toured the bush trails and brisk towns of Iboland, crossed rivers in every conceivable way, including a poled raft, and climbed the new trails north of Calabar to the one-way road up to Bamenda, the highland center of the southern Cameroons. The plantations were open-air factories that had stilled and routinized the bustle of African life, and created a restless labor force. Featureless rows of concrete dwellings had replaced the lovely, lofty, thatched, triangular huts of the region. I was content that these plantations had no real future in southern Nigeria. But the arts of the carver and potter were still alive in the villages.

In Bamenda I was directed to speak to a Mr. Foncha, who was connected with the Antiquities Commission, to determine whether certain objects for which I was negotiating could be taken out of the country. It turned out that I had a good, long, hair-raising talk with him about many things while he was immobilized in his compound with a fractured collarbone, and a rainstorm of unimaginable violence kept me at his bedside for several hours. Foncha, it developed, was the head of the Opposition Party, which was working toward Cameroonian independence and which to everyone's surprise won the election some months later, catapulting him into the Premiership. This was taken as a blow to Nigerian prestige in general and a threat to northern territorial integrity in particular, since the precedent set by the southern area could have been followed by the northern Cameroons. I had traveled, in short, from one sensitive Nigerian area through Iboland, itself a region suspect in the North, to another politically uncertain place. From Plateau Province through southeastern Nigeria, the southern Cameroons, and the return. I could not have followed a more sensitive itinerary if I had planned it that way. Shortly after returning to Gwong, I had good reason to recall my first visit from the Nigerian police.

Part Two

Community Sociology
as Self-discovery

5

Crestwood Heights: Intellectual and Libidinal Dimensions of Research

John R. Seeley

[The three essays that follow are published together because, quite apart from what they deal with intrinsically, they demonstrate one more aspect of sociological action: differential reporting for different "audiences." The first essay was ostensibly addressed by a professional to his own senior colleagues; the second and third were addressed to graduate students in a seminar concentrating on "Applied Sociology" at Brandeis University.

The differences among the essays reinforce one major point: that above all in "reporting"—though not only there—the sociologist is functioning supremely socially. What he tells—how, with what emphases and shadings intuitively calculated toward achieving what effects—is a function of nothing so thin as "role" and "social structure," but rather a function of his *inclusion* as an actor in a full-scale social drama. What passes as "pedagogy" depends so little on instrumental and "rational" considerations and so much on an intuitively apprehended *Sittlichkeit*, a sense of and for form that is the opposite of formality and the analogue of artistry. The epitome of bad teaching would be precisely that "same for all" at which mass education aims.

One major problem of sociology—as of life—is what to tell whom about what from among the things we "know." What *should* happen is a difficult question. But a study of what *does* happen could begin with a careful examination of the different messages of a sociologist to different co-actors with regard to the "same" matter. For such a study, essays such as these might be data.—J.R.S.]

PERSONAL DIMENSIONS AND SOCIOLOGICAL ISSUES

It is the commonest of commonplaces in our professions to say that the meaning of an act observed is not immediately evident, that before we can begin to understand its significance we must have access to a great deal of the lifeway of the actor or actors concerned. That is one reason why we do community studies, or, if not a reason, a justification.

Subjective and Social Dimensions of Research

On a second view, the making of a community study, or, indeed, the performance of almost any sociological act viewed as a social act, is unintelligible without access to the lifeways of the participants: those "studying" and those "studied." The original sociological product, the study itself, is an "artifact"—to use the jargon—and should be no more immune to examination than the activities it examined. Indeed, an understanding of the study, in addition to what is studied, is a matter of paramount interest socially and sociologically.

The social interest in just what it is that the sociologist is doing surely should require no extensive elaboration. From the viewpoint of the society, an active sociology has emerged as a new force, allied with God knows what among preexisting interests. American sociology is no longer represented by some dear old men sitting in their offices classifying the "forms of association," or trying to illuminate themselves and confound each other by etymological or semantic analyses. (Not that even these enterprises were free of consequence.) On the contrary, American sociology is represented by a multitude of not-so-old, not-so-dear men actively poking about, and (by a bias of the profession) poking about as far as they can in many places where they are least wanted.

I know it is fashionable among sociologists to pretend—even though to do so has a spurious air of humility—that sociological inquiry is no great force, while at the same time knowing that motive and morale among sociologists are sustained by the belief that their work is a very great force indeed. It is no professional secret since W. I. Thomas (if not before) that social facts are what they are defined to be. And what is the content of sociology except the redefinition, and hence the reconstitution, of social facts? Social facts for whom? Not social facts for the sociologists, but social facts for the society. The sociologist substantially makes over the culture—

not merely the professional subculture which has to be sought and broken into, but the culture proper which one is drawn into in one's formative stages and from which it is hardly possible later to become disenmeshed.

It is difficult in the new, postsociological society for a person even of the most modest literacy to avoid thinking in Weberian terms—not necessarily in Weber's words, but with his set toward the Puritan ethos and his notions (roughly) as to the roots of work attitudes in a religious faith now largely inoperative in practice. It is not possible to be a youth in even middle-brow surroundings without struggling, almost in so many words, with the problem of "other direction," named by Riesman, and, therefore, in its current form, *constituted* for others as the experience of others by him. Warner's analysis is in the culture via *Life* magazine and Vance Packard. The Bethel Laboratory is in the school and is absorbed there directly and indirectly from Madison Avenue. We are not far from the point where what the social scientist said yesterday is part of today's mores (in Sumner's strict sense of unquestioned and unquestionable thoughtways). Who *can* think, talk, or write today without explicit or implicit use of terms such as mores, folkways, social structure, culture, role, self-conception, and social status? (Some weeks ago I saw two little boys, one nine, one ten, banging the front wheels of their bikes, one old, one new, together in a primitive attempt to settle the right of way. Said the owner of the older bicycle to the other boy, "Whatcha tryin' to do? Pull yer social status on me?") How many college students have used Kinsey to justify what they otherwise might not have done? The transforming of the otherwise private to the public sphere by the public presentation of the sociological report may constitute a form of legitimation for the actions described: "If they can do it, why not I?" The effect may also be to illegitimize by rendering open what was previously legitimate only because it was a secret of common knowledge.

I do not think we can deny our defining role and sometimes our definitive ability to specify reality by the terms we introduce. That the wish among us to deny that intent and effect should be so widespread itself invites sociological speculation and investigation. Detached sociological innocence is no longer possible as a defense for the practicing sociologist.

With the emergence of a new social force arises a legitimate social interest in the understanding of it, and, unless we are to have a new profession of metasociologists, the social understanding of sociology must come to society through further sociological thinking.

But independently of the social claim (which we may have to be the ones to press, *faute de mieux*, against ourselves) there is a vital sociological interest at stake. The metasociology is not some footnote or addendum to the sociology of anything: once recognized and treated it alters and makes over the sociology itself, just as the sociology makes over and alters the society. Each next stage thus creates its own new reality.

Let me try to make what I am maintaining crystal clear. The analogy with the psychoanalytic process will serve us rather well. The psychoanalytic profession maintains, and, I think, obviously rightly, that it is not possible to practice psychoanalysis without both having been psychoanalyzed and virtually reanalyzing oneself in every analysis of another. Note both points. It is not possible, on this view, to perform an analysis in virtue of any amount of knowledge about analysis; the learning about analysis in its major aspect is a consequence of the undergoing of it. And the virtual reanalysis with every fresh analysis is a tribute to and recognition of the fact that neither patient nor practitioner, analyst nor analyzed, is left the same after as before the analysis. A set of "bad" practitioners can be imagined in an ordered series (a real Guttman scale?): those who thought they could practice by mother wit [1] and in the light of nature; those who thought they could practice by merely adding knowledge about psychodynamic theory and consulting-room practice; and those who thought that all that had to be considered was their own once-and-for-all analysis.

We have a corresponding series in sociology. Very few, I suppose, hold that they can adequately analyze or describe society by mother wit and in the light of nature; nevertheless, even this is evidently a non-null class. The vast bulk of our fraternity not only has been indoctrinated into the second position, but stands there, and indoctrinates its students therein: the position that it is possible, meaningful, and satisfactory to do sociology, to pursue social analysis in virtue of knowledge *about* social theory, sociological method, and social status and dynamics. The very sophisticated save themselves from the most obviously self-damnatory implications of this position by some slight and informal apprenticeship procedures plus some formal exposure to the sociology of knowledge. The first of these "safeguards" is too trivial to speak about. The second is analogous to telling the would-be analyst, the psychoanalytic candidate, *about* what happens

---

[1] By mother wit I mean what others mean by God-given wit, the natural wit with which we came into the world. The transposition is interesting!

in analysis, about the epistemological status or psychological roots and implications of the communication events in the consulting room. It is surely strange that we should say insistently that the meaning of what is learned depends substantially on the social context in which it is learned—and then turn away our analytic eye and hush our didactic voice both in reference to what our students are learning and what we ourselves have learned and reported upon. I do not believe that sociology can be so taught any more, or any less, than psychoanalysis can be so taught. Becoming a sociologist must be a matter of self-consciously entering a special society (in one sense a subsociety, in another a super- or extrasociety). At the beginnings self-consciousness must be at a minimum, but at every point in the subsequent social relation, the normal, uncritical, or unsociological perspective is increasingly made over.

It is true that a little of the latter goes on without anyone taking direct thought of it. When a Warner or a Hughes lectures to a class or has lunch with a student, a little of the significant matter is allowed to show forth. One knows when the matter *is* significant by seeing how the students come alive. It is not only that the instructor's heightened color and brightened eye communicate some mere undifferentiated excitement that the students cannot find in the text. It is much more. What the text and the formalities *conceal,* he reveals by his emotional involvement and commitment—his involvement as a whole human being, not merely setting out to solve some intellectual problem or to see something interesting, but as a man with a personal and social agenda, manifest and latent, overt and covert, praiseworthy and reprehensible, kind and malicious, in recognizable mix—an intelligible human object. Without too much effort, we can see the meaning for the sometime minister's son in treating dead-pan, in acadamese sociologese, the time-honored sacred objects: "religious affiliation," "cult," "hierarchy," "table showing relation of religious denomination to class level," "The Church in the Power Structure of the Community," "The Parish as Social Unit," "sect," "church," and so on. What appears in these momentary flashes is that the speaker is not "objective" (whatever that could mean in reference to human affairs), not neutral, not detached, not unbiased, not "scientific," not nonpolitical, not noninterventory, not disengaged from or "above" the battle he purports to describe. Even in the most rigid "scientists" total repression happily is never achieved.

But note that I say these leakages of involvement are momentary flashes; and the didactic status they have is not only unsystematic but largely that of the smoking-car story. They are, in the first instance, breaches of a conventional order of silence. Second, they meet in most places explicit denial or, more generally, explicit assertion of their contraries. Third, if the silence is broken and the facts given partial acknowledgment, they are rendered *déclassés*, by being confessed as lamentable weaknesses attributable to personality quirks which it is the business of more or better training to counteract. The subjective basis of all sociology is thus distorted out of all recognition to the point where objectivity has become a cardinal canon, a dogma not to be questioned by the pious.

The Shared Illusions of Sociologists

At least so my experience ran. And not for want of exposure to the best minds at Chicago, in the Sociology Department, in the College, and elsewhere. It was more than a formal exposure; indeed, it was unusually sociable, protracted, and profound. And there was no want either for discussion with peers. True, in class and out we kicked around the classic chestnuts: "Is sociology a generalizing or nomothetic science?" But despite the maturity of that postwar year's students, we might as well have been prepubescents discussing the joys or fatigues of defloration. We might know in a lexicographical sense what the terms meant, but that is about all. What was communicated to all was the sense of an ongoing intellective process, in reference to society, of essentially the same kind as the process of the sociologist's natural science counterpart in reference to pendulums or amoebae. When the metatheory that ought to have raised disturbing questions about this stance *was* discussed, this discussion too had an aseptic tone, as of gods discussing their godhead—to be reviewed but never to be altered or hurt, much less made or unmade by their discussion. No one to my memory asked or faced the question, "How does my role differ, if at all, from that of minister, social worker, or politician?" In fact, in headlong flight from just such possible dangerous identifications, those who spoke at all showed directly and by a stylized, ritualized expression of contempt that they regarded as total antitheses what now appear to me to be minor distinctions. There were sects and heresies *inside* the established sociological church, but no act comparable to the heinous one of an apostasy in which the apostate once asserted that what divided the faithful from the pagan was less and other than the faithful thought.

I have so far accounted for the blindness in myself toward the logical and operational status of my discipline in terms of a social system, composed of my peers, my teachers, and myself. Surely, this is legitimate enough and, on a superficial view, sufficient. But a minimum degree of honesty should drive me to ask myself how it was, when I had so easily so often in the past seen through so much, that I was not able to penetrate this most penetrable of pretenses. I had but to look inward to see what I was doing and experiencing. I had but to look around to see or sense what my professors were actually dealing in and concealingly revealing in their flashes.[2] I had but to use on "us" the analytic methods we learned to use on "them," analytic methods I had found easy to use in a two-year participant-observership in the slum which I was taking part in concurrently with University study. Such methods here had stripped away easily the conventional nonsense about crime, delinquency, and such. Why did I look there and see, and look here and *not* see?

Contributing to that inability to see the obvious (if not sufficient by itself to account for it) was the existence of a known but not at all adequately appreciated massive investment in the illusion. The investment was personal and social. On the social side was the same set of weights that bore so heavily on my professors: the need to distinguish a distinct profession, with all the returns in income, deference, and safety that it entails; the need to leave, therefore, the core of the professional creed unquestioned; the need to separate oneself from previously discredited professional intervenors by further discrediting them (by homily and by "studying" them, if need be); the need to retain academic and intellectual respectability by claiming the posture of the disinterested scholar; the need to invoke the sacred name of science to cover the new magic, sanctify the new juju; the need to define a social role not dirtied by direct or close involvement

---

[2] I should not overexaggerate the ease of unmasking. One professor with whom I was intimate and to whom I was deeply attached was himself a supremely skilled participant-observer in the higher echelons of Chicago's underworld. He was moreover a man who let passion show. We even did field research together. But he left me with the impression—designedly, I think—that his passionate espousal of the criminal was for the sake of *intellectual* honesty, i.e., for the sake of scientific exactitude, for the sake of sociology. All his subsequent career— at this distance—denies that view. The sociology is (was) an intermediate term, not an ultimate one. He was and is essentially a reformer, not of the type of the "Christers" and "do-gooders" for whom he had so much contempt (because they were incompetent), but a reformer of a much more revolutionary type. His sociology functioned as an attack on conventional justice for the sake of a higher justice. And the function was the same as the motive. He had been like that even as a boy. I do not think he knew it then; he may not know it now. At bottom, he was an intellectual (and more effective) Robin Hood.

in a too obviously dirty world of action. The tremendous force of an enlightened outlook with regard to the value and consequences of the pursuit of "truth," as necessary or sufficient to other goods, made permissible intellectually what was profitable socially: the stance of "science" in reference to the social. The "great day coming," if one allowed onself even that much involvement, would occur when man understood himself sufficiently to enter (largely) into the control of himself and his destiny. Even bare *logical* analysis should have raised doubts as to what intelligible meaning could be given to *that* slogan. The capacity for professional self-deception is proportioned precisely to professional necessity.

Even given these odds on an initial entertainment of the conventional view of social science, it takes, I think, a further line of explanation to make intelligible why it was penetrated (in my own case) so little and so late.[3] The supplementary line of explanation must be personal.

This is not the place for some sort of psychodynamic self-exposure. Not that it would not be scientifically apt, but that it would be socially inept. It would be seen as in bad taste. It might create pressures on my friends and colleagues to do the like. It might embarrass me later or put me at a "competitive disadvantage." (In any case, self-disclosures at any depth have to proceed like disarmament negotiations, each step on each side making possible the next step on the

---

[3] Throughout the period of intense participant-observation in the delinquent and other youth groups "Back of the Yards," I was able to preserve somehow some strange duality of perspective: when I was with them, I knew that what I knew was in their service; when away, I was able to believe that these friendships were primarily instrumental, prices paid (albeit pleasant paying) for enlarged sociological mastery. How passionately I was on their side, or the side of what they stood for, so that the carefully "scientific" sociology was partly preparation for advocacy and partly an advocacy in itself! Not only the direction of my interest, not only the sharpness of my probes, but also the selectivity of my (in themselves perhaps accurate) observations was governed by my growing perception that the social workers functioned by and large as confusers of issues and blunters of the edge of social discontent, Meddlesome Mary's who in the act "done no one no good." I did not, therefore, turn an uncritical eye on labor union or church leadership which had much the same effect but much less; but I had my hidden hierarchy of villains, and the social workers headed it because (a) they were so much more pious, and (b) they were women. What, might one infer, would pious, meddlesome women, who prevented justified rebellion from becoming self-conscious and open, be likely to represent to a male "lover of truth and justice," himself not a decade away, even chronologically, from adolescent rebellion? The conscientious sociologist I aimed to be would not on this ground admit any untrue facts to his reports; but who can control selective vision of what is clearly there to see?

other. What could be done by social agreement and in mutuality, therefore, is not even instrumentally effective as a lone, quixotic, rather than heroic, act.) In any case, detailed psychodynamic stories may involve and damage living persons, a consideration that raises social, emotional, and ethical problems, which go beyond the purview not just of sociology but also of available codes of personal conduct.

Suffice it to say that I had quite special (personal, idiosyncratic) reasons to believe in the value of thought, in the efficacy of knowledge, more particularly "scientific knowledge." I had had the catastrophic childhood that seems to be the fairly common lot, so no special tears are called for there. What is germane is that my childhood was, for the greater part, so Kafkaesquely absurd as to defy comprehension without one of two lines of "explanation": that the principal significant figures therein were monsters of malice of an unconfrontable order; or that they "didn't understand," that is, they lacked knowledge and skill which were or would be somewhere available. (The middle position, that they might have been slightly or severely mad, did not occur to me as a real possibility till much later, and when it did it seemed like a certainty.) The "malice" theory yielded to the "misinformation" theory, if only because what would have required an accounting under the former taxed even a child's lively capacity to imagine human evil. The belief in the susceptibility of atrocious behavior to education thus received a heavy charge of plausibility from wish and need. And the prototype of what my quasiparents had seemed not to know was precisely the kind of view that the social sciences were delivering as their product. Hence there existed in me a *need*, whose presence I recognized but whose distorting force I failed to adequately assess, to see in the beloved, the Social Sciences, those matchless virtues that her professional protagonists said she possessed, but which a second glance should have told me she did not, and a moment's free thought that she *could not*. For me, social science was not just cathected, it was libidinized.

Even so, with this much more than the usual told, what was going on is not really intelligible. The same "weapon," social science, that was in one sense supposed to "legitimate" the quasiparents (and thereby me) by demonstrating that they were *merely* "ignorant," was also supposed to serve to discredit them by demonstrating (compatibly but quite inconsistently) that they *were* ignorant, and moreover ignorant of easily-come-by knowledge, that is, that they were negligent and wicked.

To this barest sketch I must add what almost goes without saying: that in a trivial sense I knew these things, but in any meaningful sense I did not. The sense in which I knew them was that, had I asked myself or been asked the right questions, I should undoubtedly have given the right abstract answers. But, necessarily this meant I knew nothing of detailed interconnections (which are of the essence) or the force of the forces that animated me and, as far as I know, animate us all.

The point of all this is not meant to be idiosyncratic or autobiographic, except incidentally. It is rather to make forcibly another point: that every sociologist I have met before or since is recognizably playing out in his science a very complex play, intimately related to, if not ultimately governed by, the original drama experienced and played out by him in his "family of orientation." I should add that, surely, on the showing of our sciences themselves, it cannot be otherwise; and as a footnote, it is strange, passing wondrous, that we should ever seriously have "thought" otherwise.

A third play in which the social scientist is clearly enmeshed, but which has received too little attention, is the play that he shares with his colleagues in his own discipline—surely, for him, a major "reference group." The nature of that play also will not be unaffected by the primitive drama just referred to, but it will have in addition a very important determinative effect of its own on what he does. We point with pride very often, in public, to the disciplinary effect of the scientific group, and we are inclined, perhaps justly, to see this social bond as constituting or underlying the very discipline of science itself. But so powerful and significant a society can no more be productive of purely beneficent results, for science or the scientist, than the similarly powerful family group can be productive of discipline without damage. Here again there is a scuttlebutt of such things, but no well-articulated, intrafraternity knowledge or culture, let alone an open, public understanding. The high premium set upon distinction, for instance—not meaning here distinguished work, but only *distinct*— in a field where almost anything may be said with credibility, clearly puts a premium on what is actually observed: the constant shifting of attention from one field, topic, or aspect to another, if only to find a relatively noncompetitive niche. (This centripetal force, rather than alleged theoretic difficulties, may well account for the fragmentary, noncumulative nature of sociological knowledge.) A perhaps easier way to preferment is to become distinguished (distinct) by achieving the dramatic, which, given the earlier alluded-to bias of the profession, invariably means the scandalous. Two such avenues to notoriety through scandal offer themselves: social scandal (and sociological social scandal) is typically achieved by demonstrating, for instance, that incest is for some enduring group a stable way of life; sociological scandal is achieved by upending a cherished sociological theory or oversetting a widely accepted fact.

I am not saying that these things are good or bad in and of themselves. I suppose I am saying that I find it odd that we refuse the social medicine we prescribe: a sociology of the profession finally integrated with and incorporated in the professional training.

We (not only I but, I believe, my colleagues also) were innocent of all this when we came to Crestwood Heights.

The Crestwood Heights Research

The enterprise in Crestwood Heights was not, of course, any simple community study to begin with, even at the ostensible level. I cannot find any simple term, not even "operations research," to describe it. There are many reports on what we intended to do, and on what we did and did not do, so there is no point in repeating these, except summarily, here.[4] In retrospect I am still not a little frightened at our temerity, though I was not so at the time.

Briefly, as part of the Crestwood Heights enterprise we had:

(a) A set of "clinical services" for "disturbed" children and their parents. This was intended partly as direct service to the community, partly as a demonstration and education source to Crestwood teachers and educational administrators, partly as a "research tool" (a source of information) for the community study, partly as a demonstration for other educational systems, and partly as a testing and training ground for psychiatry.

(b) Also for the children we had an extended series of free discussions ("human relations classes") that were intended primarily to be a directly beneficial mental-health intervention (my "venture in eupaedics"), but also were designed to provide a rigorous test of the efficacies, emotional and educational, of the intervention; to demonstrate to teachers and educators inside and outside The Heights system what children could do and would say; to train an intended

---

[4] See, for example, John R. Seeley, R. Alexander Sim, and Elizabeth Loosley, *Crestwood Heights*, New York: Basic Books, 1956; J. D. Griffin, M.D., and John R. Seeley, "Education for Mental Health: An Experiment," *Canadian Education*, 7, No. 3 (1952); John R. Seeley, "The Forest Hill Village Project," *Understanding the Child*, 23, No. 4 (October 1954); *ibid.*, "Basic Approaches to Mental Health: The Forest Hill Village Human Relations Classes," *Personnel and Guidance Journal* (February 1959).

new profession of "liaison officers" (personnel "between" psychiatry and education); and, perhaps as important as anything, to provide massive inside data on the children's lives as perceived by them, in considerable content and great depth.

(c) For the parents of school children, we had or participated in a program of parent education, sometimes extensive, sometimes intensive, partly functioning as an explanation system of what we were doing otherwise, partly Socratic, partly indoctrinatory, above all functioning, like the special classes for the children, as a massive source of material as to how the parents saw life, school, children, the entire range of matters discussed. Incidentally, without original intent on our part, this "parent education effort" yielded a corps of researchers ("participant-observers") about as good as one could hope to train in a graduate program.

(d) For the Crestwood Heights teachers, we had a formal program lasting several years. We took part at policy and operation levels in the schools' inservice training program; we counseled counselors; we collaborated with the guidance system and drew the teachers deeply in, and again, of course, we listened, recorded, and made use of the material for the community study.

(e) For the teachers from all over Canada whom we brought into our university for the equivalent of a full year's full-time retraining, we provided an intellectually stimulating exposure to the social sciences as they bear on education, an apprenticeship in the psychological and "human relations" services, a group experience, and "therapy," formal and informal, group and individual, as necessitated or recommended by the impact of our operations on their lives.

(f) We participated in the semiformal community life in matters from "interfaith relations" to "teenage dances" as opportunity offered or diplomacy required.

(g) We provided incidental services ranging from short researches into some correlates of success in learning Latin to running a rather unexpectedly extensive psychiatric referral agency for all kinds of people who somehow just thought we would know who was who and what was what in this connection.

(h) For students in many departments of our university, we provided a research field, research opportunity, supervision, training, and the usual aids to academic progress.

I could go on describing functions. Suffice it to say we were busy, our lives were complex, and our lines of communication were highly intertwined, if not tangled. But it is important to distinguish between mere tangling and conceptual confusion. At the time the various supposed roles were held clear enough in administration, in everyone's mind, in practical arrangements. Whatever my subsequent views developed from, it was not an antecedent confounding of the therapeutic, teaching, scientific research, administrative and political subenterprises of which the whole project was composed. It may have been helpful to participate in all these enterprises personally so that the distinctions between them, if invalid, would be continuously hammered at by experience; but even that is uncertain, since in the different roles, supported by different associates, I was also supported by the normal conventions that we were doing very distinct things in each, and that these distinct things were governed by distinct and stable professional canons of performance.

Against all self-interest,[5] a new definition of what we were doing forced itself into recognition, largely by the logic of the process, the nature of the data, and the presenting situation.[6] Let me deal with the last first.

Crestwood Heights, it will be recalled, had, among its extraordinary characteristics, its self-conscious "ethnic composition" (roughly, half Jewish, half non-Jewish), its dedication (or the dedication of some large part of it) to values similar to those of the researchers, its high degree of literacy, its degree of participation in "the high culture" and its long historic exposure to "experts" not very different from ourselves. The bearing of the first of these facts may be least and the bearing of the last of them most obvious

The polarities thus present in the situation were for both sides unusually heightened, unusually conscious, and unusually ambivalent. Our "subjects" wanted, sometimes passionately, to be regarded as virtually part of the research team itself, as also highly "educated" professionals in human affairs, at least as semi-experts. They also wanted to retain a sharp distinction in the same realm, a distinction so sharp and so "morally" loaded that it almost amounted to an antithesis between secular-sacred, lay-religious, disciple-leader, acolyte-priest. And the ambivalences of at least some of us were equal and complementary. We too wished to be of them and not of them, to

[5] At least against self-interest in any obvious sense. The pretenses of the podium, the consulting room, the "social science laboratory" are *protections*, internal and external, primarily for the teacher, therapist, researcher. To abandon them is to expose oneself to dangers: from within, in terms of stability of image and level of self-esteem; from without, with reference alike to client and colleague.

[6] I say "largely" because it is not possible abstractly, or in the given case, to exclude mere masochism as an explanation. But I suppose it is a necessary rather than a sufficient one. And it permeates much if not most social science.

redefine ourselves now as in, now as out, to accept and to reject the counterposed definitions offered. We oscillated, as they did, between the detachment or pseudo-detachment in which we had been trained, the stance or sub-stance of lofty leadership, and the kind of encounter that, shattering in its intimacy, sweeps away conventional pretense in its preconditions and its consequences.

We walked the brink of a crisis or a succession of crises of identity, individually and collectively, and we led and were led in so doing. The crisis focused on the operation and its aims, the nature of the "team" (or whether indeed it was a team), the division of labor, the intended product, the nature of our sciences "pure" and "applied," and actually, for some, who we were and what we were doing here. Interpersonal conflict, overt and covert, increased, and so did intrapersonal stress, for some of us, to the point of threatening or breaching habitual defenses. Hardly one of the senior personnel involved failed to show a sharp career break, objectively visible as well as subjectively palpable. Two of the senior authors ceased to be practicing social scientists, and one retained the definition but played a then largely anomalous or unconventional role.

Indeed, for at least one of us, all the conventional poses and postures—"teacher," "detached observer," "lecturer," "reformer," "community organizer"—became untenable, and ethically intolerable. Precisely what had been most well defined became most problematic. Problems of possibility as well as problems of legitimacy presented themselves in a new light and had to be faced at precisely the moment when all the normal supports for facing such shattering questions were wanting. The shaken psyche could be repaired, but the world in which it had lived could not be reentered. The man who coined the term *Entzauberung der Welt* retained nevertheless the aura of the wizard and created a wonderland of his own; but *we* had deglamorized the glamorous-deglamorized, and could not reinvest our world with any available magic.

Personal Consequences

One upshot for this author was a necessary formal turning to the exploration of his own inner world. What might have been desirable in any event became mandatory, psychologically, socially, and intellectually. This is not the place for a "story of my analysis" except as it bears on the present topic. What emerged, as far as that is concerned, was a recasting of point of view with reference to the whole drama in which we were acting, *including* the supposed formal observation of the drama that we call social science.

This "professional activity," as much as or more than recognized "projective" material, such as dreams or TAT responses, became visible with increasing clarity as the playing out of a drama of the same sort, complete with replicates of or surrogates for the earliest infantile dramatic figures. First for myself, and then for others, "social science" appeared as a palimpsest, with interesting enough depiction of a sort on the topmost layer, but a much more interesting, highly colored, and significant message underneath. Indeed, the figure of the palimpsest breaks down, for in the case before us, unlike the analogy, the surface script can be only superficially understood without access to the layer or layers underneath.

By a perhaps necessary but certainly destructive courtesy, such recognition is commonly barred. It is permissible for a Freud to explain the life of a Leonardo da Vinci in terms that render his acts clear as functions of his unconscious needs or drives; but it is usually regarded as unnecessary or immodest in a Freud (or impertinent in a colleague) for a similar explanation to be supplied of the analyst's analysis as itself an expressive, projective, and symbolic gesture. The "rational" or polite reasons why a Freud might turn to a da Vinci and place him in just that light are acknowledged; but that he may, indeed must, be playing out for himself a much more complicated and covert play in so doing, is either unacknowledged or passed over (suppressed) with a mere "Why, of course . . . ," followed by rejection of the obviously necessary implication.

We have good reason as well as bad for refusing to follow this lead. For one thing, it poses serious problems for self-relation and social relation (but then so did psychoanalysis in the first instance). More seriously, perhaps, it takes us into an infinite regression (but then we have never let that stop us, in any practical matter, from going as far and stopping as soon as we wished).

We also have good reason as well as bad for following more deeply that earlier lead. Social science so seen is not impoverished but enriched. We continue to ask questions about adequacy of description, accuracy of observation, validity, reliability, the usual "reality checks." But we may also hear if we choose, in any serious piece of social science writing as in any poem, the cry of a soul calling attention, obliquely but obstinately, to who he is, what he wants, what he suffers, where he is, who is with him and against, what is struggling and reaching for dramatic recognition, in the existential flux which neither he nor the poet can overfly or escape. It is not enough to say that, even though social scientists, we are still people talking to each other, even if we were to recognize the ambiguities of every word in the sentence. The contention is rather that the formalization of social science misleadingly inclines us to believe we are doing something much other than singing love songs to each other. A fine distinction (not to be denied, but not to be overstated) is thus exaggerated into a false antithesis, and under its cover a drama that need not be covert, and should not be if social science is to be useful, is smuggled in and played out. It would be better to overrate the identity. If we could see ourselves as fighting similarly in our lectures, on grounds equally obscure, for the things we fight for in our families or our politics, we should be closer to the truth. We could then afford to *inquire* as to how the scientific element in social science affords a marginal safeguard for "substantive rationality," rather than to take for granted what we ought most to question. We might still see in every topic chosen, in every word used in its treatment, in every turning of differential interest on this rather than that aspect, a re-tracing of paths early laid down for us (or an attempt to run counter to those groovings), but we should be less certain, less simplistic, less likely to "take in" ourselves or each other or our publics. The cost would be, is, great; but the gains would be, are, incalculable. We might find ourselves without firm foundations if we renounced false firmities. But that is, I think, worth daring.

And even as such complexities drove me into Crestwood Heights as a community and an enterprise, so that community and that enterprise drove me into these complexities. With an eager reluctance I rejectingly embraced what I had unwillingly sought: a clarification, even if clouded, of the I-we that is presumably the basis of sociology.

APPLIED SOCIOLOGY AS A VOCATION

The Meaning of Vocation

We generally reserve the term "vocation," I think, for a "high call-ing." A calling is deemed high when, by the judgment of ordinary men, the worldly standards, demands, or tasks to be performed are very painful or exacting and the returns, by the same standards of judgment, are correspondingly low. A priest or monk who lays his sexuality (and perhaps also his aggression) on the altar of service to God and man, and who receives in return little, materially, but his sustenance has, by common consent, such a high calling. If in the course of his career he either diminishes the element of sacrifice or increases the return upon it (in other than a "spiritual" sense), he is said to be making a business out of his career, to have lost his vocation, to have betrayed his call. Similarly with the prophet in the wilderness, subsisting on locusts and wild honey while performing that most thankless of tasks, recalling a people to its destiny, or people severally to their own "higher" possibilities. The statement that something is a vocation or a calling is equivalent to saying that it makes no economic or common sense; indeed, that it is the inversion of these, the uncoerced furnishing by the supplier of more for less.

It is this contrariety to common sense that makes the term "vocation" appropriate: for such behavior would have to be explained away as madness (as it sometimes is explained) or accepted as a reproach (which cannot be long allowed) unless a quasi-coercive explanatory element is introduced. The explanation cannot be in terms of raw coercion because that would obviously rob the behavior of its social significance and utility; but it must have a quasi-coercive character lest the appearance of pure voluntary choice indicate too uncomfortably forcefully for everyone: "Go thou and do likewise."

The precisely right term is then the "call." The call is not a command backed by this-worldly sanctions. But neither is it a casual invitation to be accepted or declined at whim or will. It is a call from something or someone whose authority is moral—preferably, *purely* so. In the mixed case where purely moral sanctions are joined to those of other kinds we evoke, no doubt, the contempt expressed by Swinburne: ". . . as for the Gods of your fashion, that take and that give, In their pity and passion, that scourge and forgive, They are worms that are bred in the bark that falls off, They shall die and not live."

The possible sources for such a "call" are: in the sacred realm, God or the highest of ideals (acting as "forces," but almost personalized); and in the secular realm, the inmost self, or some sufficiently great "cause." Note that where the inmost self is allowed as a legitimate source of "call," it has already been assimilated to the highest good (or to God: cf. the Quakers' "light that lighteth every man that cometh into the world"); and where a great cause is allowed, its imputed greatness is held to be in its relation to the same.

The difference between "following a vocation" and "being under a spell" does not lie then in either the externality of the commanding agency, its semicoercive force, or its lying in the realm of morality. The difference lies in the polarity of that commanding or responded to in the dimension of good and evil.

The notion of a call is commonly associated not only with an external source of call but also with the notion of selective calling by the caller and selective capacity to hear (as well as follow) the call in the called. Many may be chosen, by one means or another, but only a few are called. Only in relation to the number who both hear and follow are the called a considerable quantity. For the aspirant to priesthood (or the vocation of nun or monk) the quite agonizing, protracted first step is the assuring of oneself (and sometimes others) that the call was genuine and not something imagined on the basis of inner needs or low motives (or, indeed, high ones!).

Even when we quite secularize these explanatory principles we are left with a high something that is held somehow to have a differential claim on us (severally), a selective sensitivity to that claim, and a selective "willingness" to attend to what is intimated by the interaction of both. Thus a nurse, if held to have a vocation for nursing, will be presumed to have a differential attraction to the high aim of relieving certain kinds of human suffering (a high value) by nursing, and a differential willingness to respond to that attraction at the cost of other possibilities in herself and for herself. If, *per contra*, she "uses" nursing as a stepping-stone to marriage to a doctor for reasons of economic and social race winning, we might say she had a talent, but hardly a calling.

Vocational Defenses of Sociologists

For a generation that has grown up since my own, it may be necessary to make the point that sociology in my day was a calling in these terms. (It may not be all that clear nowadays, because sociology has since gained some modicum of deserved or undeserved respectability *and* reward.)

When I entered the profession, a sociologist was a poor man, concerned with what were widely thought to be poor problems: problems either that few understood or that everyone understood as well as he. They were men talking in a strange language about familiar objects, challenging comfortable views and preconceptions (when intelligible), and in general living a very laborious life with little income, deference, or safety—even when, as sometimes happened, they were not mixed up in the popular mind with socialists. The lack of safety, of "security," was of two quite different kinds, only one of them of the sort intended in Mr. Lasswell's triad. Of course, there was uncertainty or insecurity or lack of safety in terms of employment at all or employment that would at all substantially use one's talents, but this was true also in those days for other academic men of many different kinds. What was most insecure about sociology was its *inner* safety (and therewith its safety in relation to the other "disciplines" or vocations themselves). For, whatever brave show sociologists might put on for others, and particularly for one another, doubts would not die down (and have not yet) as to what sociology "is"; and, given some definition of what it is, as to whether such an enterprise is possible; and, given its possibility, of positive, zero, or negative utility. The endless discussions of "methodology" were greatly similar in many ways to the Puritan's agonized self-examination on the question of his salvation, and the sorting and resorting of evidence bearing upon his "election."

The less modest probably talked in terms of a "science of man," and the very stridency of its arch-proponents (a Lundberg, for instance) served only to heighten the doubt as to how such a thing could be possible. No one doubted that sociologists could pie up formal glossaries of terms (von Wiese comes to mind), and make formidably fine distinctions where none had been seen to exist before. But that they could thus—or otherwise—talk fruitfully or illuminatingly about the life of mankind, or the problems that beset us, remained yet to be determined and was not encouraged of a positive answer by the performance of ourselves or our predecessors.

I must not exaggerate or make myself seem older than I am. I do not antedate Durkheim or, for that matter, Park and Burgess, or the Lynds, or Reckless, or Zorbaugh, or Parsons.

These people were or had been; their products were there for perusal and their example was before us. But, with all due respect, for me as for many others, inside and out, the most fundamental questions had not been settled or even perhaps well posed. We passed with terrifying casualness over the profoundest philosophical and intellectual precipices, glancing down perennially but with a sort of blurred focus lest we lose such seeming balance as we had and plunge into a pit from which we might rescue neither ourselves nor our "discipline." We strung words together with all the satisfying complexities of the Athanasian Creed, but with all the dubieties as to what it all really meant or whether indeed it had any ultimate referent in "reality."

We talked of "social forces," and the people who used such terms could name examples of what they meant, but in what sense they were "forces," in what medium, deriving from what and impinging on what or whom, and whether "social" because of source, medium, or "sink" never became clear. The words gave an air of analogy with physical science (which was rapidly abandoning such anthropomorphisms). But *was* there an analogy, and if so, in reference to what elements, and with what utility and effect? We talked of "society" and "the person," and how the two were or could be related; we even came out with such comforting formulations as that the two were the "collective and distributive aspects of the same thing," but I do not believe any critical mind believed we had really formulated something that retained the most important aspects of the experience that makes us speak of "I," "we," "they." We spoke of "social structure," and that tended to resolve into "social class," and that turned out to be susceptible of anthropological analysis in Newburyport, where patently people had a rating scheme of some sort that corresponded with life patterns, life chances, and so on. (Finally, we concluded that we could class-type a man by his housing, education, area of residence, and the like.) But what a class *is* was never settled (on the assumption, I assume, that we may define terms in any useful way), although almost everyone in a class society knows what class means, and that to be a member of a class is to take on a class-defined, class-approved, class-demanded set of behaviors, attitudes, loyalties, enmities, and value and idea standpoints.

I do not want to go on indefinitely like this, particularly since, as I make the contentions more detailed, I risk debating the details and overlooking the force of the whole. My point is that, from within and without, sociology appeared in a gel state rather than a sol state, if I may use such an analogy. Unlike a liquid which invites very few to walk its surface, or a solid which normally sustains all who do, a gel looks inviting but is incapable of furnishing firm footage. (I do not know how far the present state of our discipline departs from this image; I think, despite the multiplication of "middle-range" studies, or because of them, very little.)

The general way in which sociologists I knew coped with this situation was not too dissimilar from parallel behavior in other pariah groups. There was an air of great urgency to find true dogma, to show oneself scholarly (almost Talmudically scholarly) in linking current argument to prior high authority. There was disputatiousness and, growing in part out of it, the formation of "schools" and sects that recruited, rewarded, and penalized, scanned for evidence of the true faith and demanded loyalty and forensic fire. Revealing of the true meaning of the rather fierce rivalries within the group was the fact that differences of opinion were rather readily extended into differences in the imputation of intelligence (a not unnatural conclu-

sion, perhaps) and hence into differences in imputed worth or, ultimately, goodness. This is just about the normal way of defining the
heretic; a person worthless or worse because of unwilled or willful
blindness, but, in any case, "invincible ignorance."

Again, not atypically, despite these desperate dissensions within, all
were expected to share, and largely did, in a common set of attitudes
toward the outgroup: the barbarians without the gates, the gentiles
upon whom no light shone. And again characteristically, the more
nearly the outsider resembled in some vital way the insider, the
stronger became the invective, the more developed the structure of
reasoned contempt. The deviant is more dangerous than the enemy,
just as the apostate is worse than the pagan.

The humanists, like the Negroes, were all right, I believe, as long
as they knew and stayed in their place. That place was to embroider
and enliven life, not to explain it. Explaining human life was a task
for the social scientists, but among them some were far and away
more equal than others. The sociologists were clearly the most
equal of all. Cultural anthropologists were tolerable, at least in the
abstract; economists and political scientists were tolerable as long as
they did not overassert their claims or overextend their dominions.
The greatest unease was felt (within the "formal" disciplines) about
psychologists, who seemed so wrong-headed as to attempt the explanation of virtually the same realm of phenomena by other means.
Indeed, worse, they seemed to make sociology derivative from or
conditional upon psychology, whereas it was plain to the faithful that
the opposite was true. But even so, all abstract disciplines were
somehow within the pale: a church in heresy or schism is still a
church, not an antichurch.

So low on the ladder of contempt as barely to deserve mention
were the two groups to whom I later, much later, came to believe
we were most nearly related: the social workers and the applied
sociologists. (I preserve the distinction between the two, partly because the social workers were "applying" much else besides some
sociology, and partly because most such applied sociologists as there
were had at one time been "respectable," which social workers had
not.) These two groups threatened the purity, and hence the existence, of the pariah people proper in two quite different ways.

The social workers, also largely pariahs then, functioned like a
"related people," whose whole way of life both competitively threatened ours and was likely to bring all of us into disrepute. The
feeling was perhaps not unlike that between Bedouin and pastoral
people popularly identified as belonging to the same stock as, for

example, in Biblical Palestine. Indeed the "relationship" was held to exist only in the popular mind, whereas in our minds differences exaggerated into antitheses were held clear to override mere superficial resemblances popularly exaggerated into significant similarities.

It was not merely that the social workers were less intelligent, which, given the recruitment problems of those times, may well have been true. It was that they were less intellectual, patently putting a lower value on thought itself, indeed rather regarding it as a means than an end of action. They also used a rival, partly overlapping jargon —like two varieties of Yiddish—hence threatening all jargon. They were activists, interventionists, meliorists and, perhaps worst of all, unwarranted optimists. There was a strong feeling that, by a sort of Gresham's law, their bad currency of discourse and *Weltanschauung* was driving out our good currency of talk and frame of reference. There was a worse feeling that while we patently waited to be called in as the only appropriate Grand Viziers to such Sultans as Hoover and F.D.R., the social workers, not content to be powers behind thrones, were insidiously filtering in to the palace and its surroundings and beginning to occupy seats of power. It was not even clear that once they had power *de facto* they would have the good sense to seek power *de jure*, to legitimize themselves belatedly, by calling in their self-evidently appropriate mentors, ourselves, who, equally patently, had what they lacked.

An additional, seemingly peripheral but quite unforgivable, crime was that they used the word "social" in their style and title as social workers, and invited confusion with social scientists, which was nearly as bad as the usage of Christian in "Christian Front" to cover a counter-Christian (as well as anti-Semitic) movement.

Given this major battle order, the major charge against the applied social scientist (besides the instrumental imputation of lower intelligence, lower intellectuality, and lower motives) was that he tended still further to confuse vital distinctions by his willingness to engage in or to influence action (openly), and by what was properly presumed to be his melioristic stance. It was not merely that he was led away into action (from theory) like going a-whoring after strange gods; it was not just that by permitting himself to be so led he acted as a potential decoy for others; it was also that he threatened thus further to confuse the already excessively confused popular mind as to what it was all about. Like a "working priest" he confused equally what it was to be a priest and what it was to be a worker. To engender and promote such confusion, when a beleaguered minority is striving to protect itself or establish a position of minimum safety at least, is to commit high treason at a very deep level.

I am sure not everybody's experiences were the same as mine; nor that, even when they were, identical conclusions, logical, social, and emotional, were drawn. But I think I have made a fair sketch rather than a caricature.

What we now need to ask is who was called (and why and with what consequences) into such a calling. My answer must be partly general and speculative and partly personal, autobiographical, and still speculative. (About ourselves each of us has only an opinion!)

Tensions Between Pure and Applied Sociology

If I am going to generalize without fourfold tables and "hard" evidence, I had better allow myself the usual exit by saying now that I do not suppose that what I consider "typical" excludes the possibility of a small (or even a substantial) number of atypicals. It may be, for all I know, that some small number just "happened" into sociology and stayed there by accident, just as some people happen into pregnancy and stay on for motherhood. It may also be that for some, though I have never encountered any, their being and staying was a result of intellectual curiosity, pure and simple, and its being sociology they stayed in, because they found society just another fascinating object of attention. I doubt that the numbers of such were (or are) large.

For the greater part, I think we require a great deal of explanation as to how and why they heard the sociological call, heeded it, and then went on deeper into the wilderness by recognizing and proclaiming themselves "applied sociologists." Let me deal separately with the two steps.

Although sociology was perhaps the latest of the social sciences to arrive, I never met anyone "in" it who was there because it was *dernier cri*, like folk music at present. We did not think we were "fashionable," or shortly about to become so, any more than the Christians in the catacombs had the feeling that they were fashionable or were there because of that. Indeed, the image may be extended: there was an earnestness, an air of having the true gospel not likely soon to be accepted, that makes the association something more than accidental.

For only a very few, I think, was the major attraction the sort of interesting, not to say fascinating, facets of social life thrown up by the enterprises of Professor Park and his school: the intimate looks at gangs, taxi dance halls, lives of waitresses, juxtapositions of gold coasts with slums, stories of delinquent careers, distributions of mental conditions, glimpses into the lives of the hobo and the homeless, the Negro family or the family wrung in the wringer of depression. As material of interest in itself—apart from its bearing on a theory of society—I believe it held no primary place of interest: largely gone already was the evident delight and excitement in the variety of The City and the variety of human behavior that clearly animates Park's writings and those of his nearest followers. Not that they were uninterested in scientific sociology, but they, much more than we, were evidently entranced at the sheer wonders that the travelling telescope of field work revealed readily to the even moderately steady eye.

We were, I believe, a different breed. Something of the assurance, the urbanity, the gaiety almost, the detachment, the optimism, and the spaciousness of a Park and his time were wanting. For one thing, I do not think that we had the feeling, which he or Giddings or Small seemed to convey, that there was lots of time. The older of us had lived through the Great War (the "First World War" now), the collapse of societies with which we were identified, and the sweeping away of ways of life for which we had been made ready, the wracking revolutionary and counterrevolutionary years that followed the "Armistice," the disappearance of even such working certainties as the value of the currency in one or other of the great inflations, the general economic collapse of 1929 and the depression that followed. We were the children of catastrophe in a quite different way, I think, than were our immediate predecessors, or even those earlier notables like Durkheim, whose work was in its way their response to the French Revolution.

I think many of us were unrevolutionary or anti-revolutionary revolutionaries, and for us sociology held the promise of being the continuation of revolution by other means (just as trade and diplomacy are the conduct of war by other means). When I say that we were nonrevolutionary or antirevolutionary I mean that we held the strongest preferences, conscious and unconscious, against disorder and violence. (Indeed, a utopian, latent hope was that man's self-understanding out of sociology would make disorder and violence diminished or nonexistent.) When I say that we were revolutionaries, I mean that we looked to an altogether other society that might be brought into being, or at least assisted at birth, by our efforts. We were nonspecific revolutionaries, as we had to be, since we represented, so it seemed, *werthfrei*, value-free, social science, a social science above and outside and beyond politics. We had, I believe, a revolutionary sense, but without a revolutionary aim. (When I say "we," I must concede there was still a substantial number of "reformers," or middle-range utopians.) We were then, I suppose, revolutionaries of process rather than product, men who might teach man to think about himself in ways so different as really to change the conditions of human action.

But even this could not be openly discussed, so that insofar as the ascription is at all true, we were covert revolutionaries. The high hopes we held of our discipline, which appeared to connect our professional performance with the concerns from which it sprang, bade us in effect to be wise as serpents and gentle as doves: wise in maintaining the even tone of detachment, and gentle even in presenting our findings dead-pan in analogy with a good biologist's professional description of the flora and fauna. We spoke blandly *because* cumulatively we expected to have all the more radical ultimate effect.

We were able to do all this in good conscience, I believe, because momentarily the social scientific claim seemed credible, just as the Marxian claims once had seemed credible to others with other canons or other creeds. It did *seem*—I cannot quite tell how, even today— that one could write from a position as if outside of society, representing a more general or higher interest not specifically declared. Perhaps the sociology of knowledge was too new and recent for us to sense its full impact in its application to ourselves. Mannheim, in *Ideology and Utopia*, while generalizing the term ideology to permit the unmasking of the partiality of perspective and speciality of position and interest in all social argument, seemed to have saved a special position, not open to the dissolving acids of his own attack, for the arguments of the sociologist. The position is not logically impossible: even the statement "all propositions are lies," if clearly seen to lie in the metalanguage about propositions, is not self-contradictory. Whether indeed the sociologist had a position so special should have been less a matter for logical argument and more a matter for honest and open-eyed inquiry.

Those who were drawn into sociology at that time were, in my memory and opinion, utopian, revolutionary in intent, and, of course, concentrated on the diseases of society, their social etiology and social remedy. Despite—or because of—what they had seen in Europe and indeed all over the world in the unchaining of the tremendous forces of the irrational, they retained a faith in the power of thought to affect or control events that was, to say the least, magnificent. Even as Freud was able to say and believe (in his optimistic moments)

that "Where id was, ego shall be," so were we able to believe that
rational study of the irrational would be the taming force upon it—
or, if we did not believe, we acted as though we assumed such to be
true. By another irony, although we believed with Max Lerner that
"ideas are weapons," we thought of ourselves simultaneously as idea
bearers (and idea makers) and men of peace. We were certainly not,
as sociologists, *in* the battle in which ideas were weapons, perhaps
ultimate weapons. Implicitly, I should think, we must have believed
that our ideas were of a different order of weaponry, or that we could,
like classic arms manufacturers, be indifferent as to which of the
contending parties used our weapons for what purposes and how.
I think the "approved line" was closest to this last position: we could
not be partisan politically; we could not prevent men in their wanton
folly from misinterpreting and misusing ideas, including ours; our
task was to furnish good ideas (valid, relevant, encompassing) and,
I suppose, send them forth to take their chances in the idea market.
There was on the other hand, as I have indicated, an anything-but-
laissez-faire attitude, an attitude of hope and desire for a better world
in which our effort had meaning, a setting toward what I have called
elsewhere the support of the generalized underdog (after George
Herbert Mead), the utopian, revolutionary spirit of which I spoke.

Similarly unreconciled in our minds were two strains of passionate
belief, one in wholism (the other in piece-mealism) with reference to
etiology, definition of the problem, and remedy. There was a strain
toward isolating "social problems"—broken families, delinquency,
mental disorder, poverty (barely mentioned), and so on—from each
other, and to encourage the separate study of them even if with
similar concepts, on the obvious implicit assumption that the condition of society might be ameliorated by the mitigation, reduction, or
cure of these problems, as though, to say the least, the state of society
might be improved by improving the state of social subsystems. On
the other hand, we were equally insistent on a view, caught up by
Lawrence Frank in a different context, that society was the patient,
and that these various manifestations of symptoms in subsystems were
of interest only as indicative of deep-seated disease in the whole,
which had to be addressed directly before any benefit could accrue
to the subsystems (which might then also take care of themselves).
We were thus radical reconstructionists oriented in a whole-to-part
direction, and moderate meliorists set in a part-to-whole posture.
I must admit that this particular conflict lay not always unresolved
within persons, but sometimes as a matter of dispute between them,
so that there was a recognizable party that opposed and looked down

on the social problems-social pathology boys as both in intellectual error and, to some degree, in social sin. But many or most of us carried around a both-and rather than an either-or model. An observer might have said, kindly or unkindly, that we were latent opportunists, intending to base action or argument on either set of beliefs as need or opportunity might dictate. (This is, I believe, roughly what the British mean by "muddling through," and it seems to have served them well practically, although leaving them with less apparent intellectual respectability than Continentals. I think we each wanted both practical successes and intellectual respectability, on American and German models respectively).

Besides this *implicit* left-of-middle-left (the radical reconstructionist theorists) and right-of-middle-left (mild and moderate meliorists) dichotomy, I think there was another unacknowledged (and perhaps, unconscious) split, to which Bramson has drawn attention in *The Political Context of Sociology*. This amounted more nearly to a slightly-left-of-middle sympathetic inclination with a considerably-right-of-middle effect. The first represented our heritage from our essentially "liberal," intellectual ancestors in America; which, for example, led Burgess and his school into many productive small-scale-reform-potential studies (e.g., marriage and "probation"). The other represented the unforeseen effects of intellectual tools more commonly derived from European preoccupations or from other sciences, such as led to a focus on system, equilibrium, social order, mores, social structure, social control, system stability—even, or particularly, our preoccupation with and preference for *Gemeinschaft* over *Gesellschaft* —which had patently supporting and comforting effects for a moderate or radical conservative ideology.

I am not saying, not even faintly suggesting, that we were stupid, unsubtle, or unperceptive. On the contrary, I am saying that we came to sociology, itself a social product in a *given* state of social development, with social problems of one kind and not another, stemming both from the given state of society at the moment and our own personal social development. I am also implying, I suppose, that in addition to all the other qualities involved in the answering of the sociological call must have been a high capacity to welcome or sustain the strains implicit in holding, or attempting to hold, these difficult intellectual and social positions. In their nonresolution lay a role crisis for sociology, I believe, which it still has not worked out; and, for many sociologists, an identity crisis, which, for many sociologists, also is still unresolved.

I think that, by now, many analogies between the vocation of the religious religious and the secular religious of sociology must have become clear—as well as some disanalogies, since few of us took vows of obedience; and still fewer, of chastity. The ascetic elements of great labor for little material return, of a special relation to the world such as to separate the sociologist in a sense from it (noninvolvement in one of its senses), the commitment to high ends and a hard discipline, the strain growing out of the complexity of explanation and the uncertainty of perception, the difficulty in catching *clearly* the object of attention, all gave us as students more analogies with seminarians than I would at the time have cared to admit. Disanalogically, we were not assisted either by church (or an admitted one, at least), ritual, singleness of dogma, common discipline, long tradition, or explicit agreement on a creed that would give at worst the semblance, and at best the substance, of unity. Analogically again, we had focused our attention and our causal-ascriptive activities on (next to God or the universe) the largest possible unit of explanation—society—from which all originated and to which all returned. Involved, I believe, was a parallel modesty about individual man (even, perhaps, sometimes ourselves) since ultimately he was whole and entire a social creation, and his effect was, must be, upon and through society. (Quite inconsistently, we appeared to think we, or men with our aid, could make over or reconstruct society, so perhaps we were inconsistent or held some covert reservations with reference at least to our professional selves and their merely social causation.) In any case, I mean to contend no more than that we were called out by and called into a rough analogue of a not very well-established, not likely soon to be established, somewhat covert or curiously non-explicit, secular, utopian-revolutionary, sect-like movement that must have appealed to profound inner needs to keep its votaries in the face of very high demands in relation to any this-worldly, common-sense returns.

Who in the society would be differentially likely to hear, attend to, and remain attentive to such a call, invites lines of social and psycho-dynamic explanation to which I invite speculation, each for himself, but to which I do not propose to, cannot, give adequate attention here. Certainly there should be food for reflection in such matters as: (*a*) the compresent beliefs in the power and ultimacy of the irrational and the belief in the power of thought, particularly scientific thought; (*b*) the selection for causal ascription (and, occasionally, "praise" but mostly "blame") of the largest possible human system; (*c*) the indirection involved in the reformatory or revolutionary intent so that we counted on changing radically the going order without direct clash with it or without a clash in which we could be hurt (in contrast with the everyday revolutionary's or political reformer's commitment and risk); (*d*) the selection (or arrogation) to ourselves of a most peculiar role in the society, at most modest, like Simmel's stranger, simultaneously near and far, within and without, and at much less modest somehow outside and "above" or "in advance of" the society that gave us birth (a parent analogue) and the society that surrounded us (an analogue for the sibship); (*e*) and a moderately or sizably high preoccupation with or practice of "unmasking" or tracing unanticipated consequences with reference respectively to the ideology and acts of others, while carefully preserving our own professional preserves from such probing.

Out of many persons so selected had yet to come a further selection for applied sociology. And, as I have indicated, that selection was rather against than with the professional grain, so that having once faced all the risks attendant on being called out of this world into "the profession," they had to face the new set of risks involved in being called out of the core of the profession into a not highly esteemed variant.

There is great difficulty here in distinguishing what was meant by "an interest in applied sociology." (Note parenthetically that at this career stage the problem was the problem of electing an interest and a definition, not of *becoming* an applied sociologist which would have to happen, if it happened, largely following the apprenticeship and largely out "in the world.") It certainly did not mean more closeness to living data; or starting from, or descriptively with, the problems some people claimed they had. Nearly all American sociologists "believed in" closeness to data, and, for many, the problems of others, as stated by them or others still, were at least data of high interest and perhaps beginning points for reflection.

It would be too easy to say that the crucial difference between the applied and nonapplied (pure?) sociologist was a difference in belief as to which existed for the sake of which: theory to illuminate or alter social practices, or practices merely as matter for theory. Both sides might even then have conceded that something of a conversation takes place in history between theory of society and social practice. And yet something of a difference, driven further into a distinction, did appear to animate the definition—as though the question were "Which is the *ultimately* more important term in this conversation?" Something attended and imbued the discussion that was closely analogical to one view, derived from much of ancient Greek high culture, that thought and thinking (and the thinker) are "high" (and perhaps eternal) in relation to all other aspects of life. The opposing view, derived from much British empiricism culminating in American pragmatism, was that act, action, and actor (and "life") are high, and that thought derives its value from its capacity to illuminate situations and alternatives, and its capacity to direct an active process in which it is only a phase toward its own up-building or enrichment in many dimensions other than or additional to thought itself. Substitute "theory" for thought and "application" for action, and you have a more or less close analogy with one of the arguments that was thought to point toward one of the distinctions.

But more than this was involved. Anyone interested in applied sociology had to be interested in application *now*. The antagonist or counterproponent merely had not to be interested in applied sociology *yet*, either for general reasons or for the very practical one that sociology was insufficiently developed theoretically to be of valid or practical use as a source of guidance in action at any important level. Those who differed on this point, that is, believed in action now, had to believe that sociology was ready, or that necessity dictated, or that sociology never would be ready unless the effort were made. I think for most a combination of all three arguments was allowed to overbear doubt. ("Necessity," be it noted, could be external or internal to the sociologist.)

There was at least one other dimension in which a difference had to lie. In the stage of social development of that day, the intending applied sociologist would expect to work on, to test application in reference to, something below the level of ultimate or largest-scale social problems. He would not expect to be called in or admitted to the planning of a world society or the replanning of a national one. He might be given an arena for action with reference to standard textbook "social problems"—like delinquency, neighborhood renewal, housing, "race relations" (meaning, I presume, diminution of violence and discrimination between whites and Negroes and between Jews or non-Jews *without* radical reconstruction of anything), mental health, alcoholism, or what-not. Application, even as an interest, did thus imply a shift from global to partial problems, from revolutionary beginning to reform beginning, in part from self-set problems to other-set problems (other than self and other than other sociologists), and perhaps to the "worthy poor" as the probable ultimate beneficiaries of success: those "underprivileged," but by no means the unworthy underprivileged. The worthy poor are, of course, the clientele at any time of the most liberal of social agencies, who in turn largely determine (or did) what are (textbook) "social problems," which in turn define the applied sociologist's most likely field of operation. (The unworthy poor must, I presume, be the interest and concern only of others, like themselves, who are in some sense outlaws.)

Those who could and would accept such sizable constraints, particularly drawn from a fraternity that would view each constraint with alarm or disdain—and the yielding to it perhaps with contempt— had to be drawn or driven by strong attractions or forces. One of the strongest such drives was to secure reassurance, social and psychological, that one's discipline (and therefore, perhaps, oneself) had a bearing on practical affairs, could be of use in the practical activities of (ambivalently viewed) practical men. One of the strongest such drawings, analogical perhaps to what might draw a man out of biological theory into medical practice, was the appeal of common humanity from which withdrawal—even "in the short run for the sake of the long"—had been achieved with something short of enduring completeness, at least for some. This lack of an enduring and severe self-severance is not self-evidently to be praised or blamed. How it is to be evaluated is not *in abstracto*, but in reference to some judgment about actually available goods or avoidable evils in a concrete historical context. For those of us not driven by necessity, who made what is called a free choice, it must have appeared that, on balance, more was to be gained than lost (for society, for sociology, for us?) by an attempt to apply, with all its attendant risks and costs, than by refusal to engage on the actual terms available.

As I recall it, those who were willing to go on to application were not differentially distinguished by their sentimentality, though there may have been an element of that. I think they may have been distinguished by what would seem to some to be impatience, but to others was sensitivity to the pressing claims of those seriously interested in testing collaboratively what sociology could do for them on their small, particular, but no less excruciatingly urgent segment of the social front: the family, the school, the mental hospital, the probation service. The appliers also had a different estimate of the pedagogical risks involved: against the no doubt valid warnings of the nonappliers as to the risks of contamination, loss of perspective, desertion of grand theory, segmentalization, becoming labeled (with the name of the field of application, as for example, educator or mental health specialist), the appliers set the possibility or likelihood that precisely in attempted application would new problems, new insights of the highest theoretic importance, come into view and thus their education, even as high-level theoreticians, be quite probably differentially furthered. We also saw the possibility either within large segments of our career, or even within the day-to-day activity itself, of shifting gaze rapidly from primary preoccupation with theory to primary preoccupation with practice, with probable, otherwise unattainable, net gains to each.

Again I invite speculation, but do not propose to treat either the social or psychological characteristics that would make for this second selection from among the previous select. Social origins, retained or looked-forward-to social connections, estimates of social possibilities, previous preoccupations with problems functioning in their own right or as symbols of other things (cf. Lasswell's *Psychopathology and Politics*), security needs of various kinds (and evaluation as to what was more or less secure), different attributions of importance (on rational and nonrational grounds) to "action" or "completion," different access to different opportunity systems, different life-chances estimates, different tolerances of different risks or certainties of alienation (from one's colleagues, from one's noncolleague contemporaries), different attractions from community as over society—all these and many more must have entered in various weightings into most such decisions.

Once the fundamental decision to risk application was made, a quite different process took over in which the sociologist became what he did become out of an interplay between theoretic considerations of the kind he had had in lively consideration in college and graduate school and a practical *entrainement* in which career choices flowed more evidently and intimately out of previous career choices and decisions. But this description is the matter of another paper, so that I leave the matter here with the applied sociologist set upon the verge of his career rather than launched into it.

CRESTWOOD HEIGHTS AS A PERSONAL EXPERIENCE

Personal Background to Crestwood Heights

On looking back over my professional career, I see that a sociologist may, by intent or inadvertence, be doing so many things at any one time that it is only by "forcing the data" that he can classify his activities, and perhaps by a further forcing have them make sense (or at least yield pattern) to himself or others. For your sakes, mine, and sociology's, I do not wish to do that much violence to the data.

Even those who may feel that in this career they have always and only been doing "one thing" would probably find on inspection and reflection that, in the complex play of motive, intention, effect, and the interplay between these, they were almost sure at any given moment to be really doing something different from what they had been doing the previous instant. And yet that is not right or not quite right: for example, we may, in considering motive alone for a moment, be struck with its immense and rapidly changing variation, and then in another light be struck with its almost unvarying fixity. We may, for instance, believe that we see in a given career a serving both of affiliative, tender, or affectional needs and of needs for power accumulation, dominance, and so on. And we may be right. We may, taking a closer or different look, see rightly that one motive was always, altogether, or largely in the service of the other—and thus conclude to inexorable fixity of motive and virtual unalterability of purpose. Analysis may also run the other way and reveal in what looked like monolithic motivational unity a vast flux of "real," deeper, or more ultimate motives masquerading under a single cloak. Tenderness, for instance, in our society, in our day, in certain social strata, is often thus concealed.

I am only saying so far that, even limiting ourselves to one category, such as motive, it is very difficult to tell in retrospect what others were doing, let alone what we ourselves were doing, without introducing fictitious unities and simplicities. There is also the opposite, and perhaps equal, risk of failing to discover and report a real unity concealed under a factitious diversity. And what is true for motives is, I think, equally true for intentions, both those in the forefront and those on the margin of consciousness. As for effect, we know in any case very little, but we do not have to talk frankly to many in our ambit of acquaintance, or one-way or reciprocal influence, to discover that we have been many things to many people, useful and useless in countless and often unforeseen and unforeseeable ways. Perhaps the elaboration and illustration by example of these complexities would be more instructive than an attempt to describe a pattern at a simpler level, but it is the latter that I shall have to do, if only because the time I had for self-searching and the time I have for presentation will not allow me to do more. I shall simplify, chiefly by saying little about motive, dealing with intentions in terms of dominant, conscious ones at a given time, and restricting effects to most obvious ones. I shall deal with the interplay of the three as best I can.

I have equal but different difficulty in drawing, except at the outset, even reasonably neat boundary lines around sociology-connected enterprises that might be thought to be at least conceptually distinguishable.

I should have been inclined near the end of my student days, I believe, to recognize, legitimize, and sharply distinguish between three such major enterprises: sociography, sociology, and applied sociology.

I would have thought that there was a recognizable activity of sociologists that consisted essentially in the description of social situations in acceptable and (for the moment) established sociological terminology. The formal purpose here is not to test hypotheses, to make generalizations, to seek new laws, or indeed anything else except to bring a social object (e.g., this gang, these gangs) rather fully into view, in terms then thought useful to or usable by sociologists. Such description, analogical to historical description, may have richness and interest of its own, and thus be justified if justification is needed; or it may be "raw material" for sociologists sociologizing, but some perhaps using it as an illustration of one thing and some of another (in the gang illustration, "subculture," "small group behavior," or "deviation" or "counterlegal organization," for instance). It is evident that a man trained in biology, without any eye toward the further development or the confirmation of biological theory, can send in valuable accounts of the flora and fauna, and perhaps the particular ecology, of his *nova terra,* his new-found land. And since society is ever changing through time, and inexhaustible in objects of interest at any one time, sociography is an endless enterprise of never-diminishing justification. This sociology-connected enterprise is most clearly idiographic, though I should hasten to add it must assume universal terms to render particulars intelligible.

I should also have assumed at the same time that there was a distinct enterprise called "sociology" whose intent and achievement it was, in a phrase of Louis Wirth's, "To discover and describe the laws of human behavior insofar as it is affected by membership in groups." Since so little is not so affected, and particularly so little that is of interest, the mandate seemed virtually equivalent to a demand to develop the laws of human behavior, period. I not only assumed that this was not self-evidently (logically) impossible, but also that there was no practical bar to possibility and, further, that our predecessors had already gone some considerable way toward such statements of significant invariances under the sign of eternity (which is the hallmark of the idea of science and the guide to its daily practice). I should have regarded this activity not only as possible, distinct, and justified, but as vested with the highest eschatological hope: the vehicle, if there were any, of man's secular salvation via self-comprehension to such self-control as is possible and serenity where it is not. The vision evidently makes full use of man's capacity and desires for activity and passivity, but distributes them rationally respectively over the possible and the impossible, chiefly by the continuing clarification of the difference.

Third, I should have assumed as possible, distinct, desirable, and open to immediate exploration, if not conquest, a realm of "applied sociology," in which known general principles, applied to known particular cases, permitted (and humanely enjoined) partial remedies for part ills, the sum of which might not be social perfection but would at least not be inimical to more general improvement.

I was shortly to learn, as the issue will show, not only that in practice these things were not all that distinct, but—much later, and gradually—that even conceptually the distinctions could not be drawn without violence to the nature of society, the sociologist, and sociology. Beyond this I certainly had not distinguished as a part of or apart from "applied sociology" the mere diffusion of the sociological attitude or set, sociological methods and sociological knowledge, which is something we all do a great deal of without much reflection on just what it is that we are doing or intending. And also I had not clearly set apart mere action on the basis of sociological knowledge, which is an inevitable aspect of the action of any sociologist, but quite different generally in intent and always in effect from what I had separated as "applied sociology" initially. I was finally to be brought to a quite different standpoint, hardly connected in any way with my point of beginning except for the thread of a single experiencing self on which the beads of revision and re-revision were bindingly, if not brightly, strung. My personal *pons asinorum* was Crestwood Heights.

I should probably preface my statement about Crestwood Heights by saying, in case it should prove to have a significance that I do not attribute to it, that I had had about five formal encounters as a sociologist with "the world" before I came to "my community" (of study, not of membership). I had had a three-year experience in the Canadian Army at Army Headquarters in Ottawa and London and in U. S. and Canadian training centers, in personnel sorting and officer selection, but primarily at highest level acting as a kind of intellectual broker (and community organizer in a sense) between psychologists, psychiatrists, social workers, and so on—largely the advocates and protectors of the soldier as a human being rather than a mere body in the Services. I do not know where this fits into my fivefold scheme, except that it clearly was neither sociology (I was building no theories, formally testing no hypotheses) nor sociography (I was acting upon, not reporting on, the Canadian Army, where I touched it). I was not primarily oriented to the diffusion of sociological knowledge or the sociological *habitus*. Nor was I merely quite "acting in the light of sociological knowledge," since it was quite clear that I looked on things, spoke about things, and raised questions about things that cast them in a different light from that habitually shed upon them by common sense, any of the represented disciplines, or army habits of thought. I was a puzzle, an annoyance—what people mean by "a stimulus"—an indigestible foreign body, but also somehow a bridge maker (if I may so mix my metaphors) to top brass, to those to whom I was "scientific advisor," and even upon occasion to the presidents of courts-martial (of other soldiers, not me) or directors of penal camps, "neurosis centers," and camp commandants. I still do not know quite how to define that role, but it was a sort of combination of a generalized Socratic probative questioning and a role not unlike that of Simmel's stranger.

I had also had three briefer experiences, to none of which I should be inclined to attribute much significance: the gathering of some ecological-psychological data in Chicago for a doctoral dissertation (never written), a "mental health survey" of an Ohio county, and a study of the structure of neighborhood disorganization around the University of Chicago for the University of Chicago.

The fifth experience undoubtedly had significance. It began with mere friendliness and curiosity, went on to a sociographic study (with intent to report, but not to write), had strange aspects again of the sociologist as the stranger, and wound up with friendships and, for me, a rather profound initiation into the delinquent (and, to a lesser degree, the criminal) culture and society of a part of Chicago nearly twenty-five years ago. Somewhat like William Foote Whyte—but more immersed, I believe, because I had no formal reporting responsibility—I was for two years a virtual member of street-corner society, a jacket- (or sweater, in those days) wearing member of several gangs, their protégé and pupil, their highly participating questioner, only in small degree a representative of and certainly not an ambassador from the overworld or the incredible middle-class and University society with which, they knew, I was somehow involved—like a potentially good boy who has got into bad company. I became a true and somewhat more than honorary member when someone of loose tongue, influence, and fertile imagination spread a rumor that I had a racket (blackmailing middle-class ladies, I believe) which made me at heart one with them and explained my need to be circumspect with regard to V.D., robbery, and a few other matters. I did not disillusion them, since they needed to believe it and I needed them to define me as they wished. They spoke of it in my presence, but never questioned me. Thus—to each other—"Don't ask him to do nuttin' like dat; 'e can't take no chances on dose mudderjumpers findin' out an' holdin' it over *him*."

Whatever else I was doing here, it was not applied sociology. If anything was being made over it was the sociologist and not his new society. If I had any reform impact, it was not upon my slum world, but on the third world in which I lived, the company of the good social workers of the University of Chicago Settlement, who thought of themselves as subsociety rebuilders, and hence, perhaps applied sociologists of a sort. Though I could tell these good people very little in particular—the first law of the street was "Dem's social workers, see! Don't tell dem nuttin', you"—what I could tell them in general would tend to call into question and move toward reconstitution of the Settlement rather than the slum. But that was a side issue. The main issue was understanding so interfused with affection that to split them apart in retrospect into participant and observer elements is to make the experience false. Within my limitations, and conscious that at best I could have only an extended visit, I belonged as far as I could, I made the initiation as genuine as possible, not on an "as if" basis but because I wanted to belong, for its own sake, to so fine a company, beside which much company I had known and was yet to know would seem pallid or corrupt. So, anyway, the prelude to Crestwood.

Objectives of the Research

I had better abandon for a moment any attempt to be orderly in classifying activities and, speaking in terms of conscious intents, set forth first the vast variety of activities that composed the Crestwood Heights Project.

The following enterprises were operating simultaneously.

1. A community study. An attempt to describe the life and hard times of the relatively rich: the upper-middle class in a suburb, self-consciously dedicated to "liberal" values and, self-consciously again, about half Jewish and half non-Jewish.

2. An experimental study. An attempt to determine (and demonstrate) the effect of free discussion—in a sense to be defined later—on the feelings and behavior, the "mental health," of children aged six to eighteen.

3. An operation in and on the community's schools, by a variety of methods, to secure a new vision, a revision, literally, of the whole educational enterprise, of the meaning of "the child," "teaching," "the teacher," "the community"—as seen in heightened consciousness and depth, in general, and in the perspectives of psychoanalysis, sociology, and social psychology in particular.

4. An operation not in but on the school systems of the remaining provinces of Canada, by organizing a new subprofession within the teaching profession, recruiting carefully for this profession, negotiating agreements for the teachers' proper employment, and then training them (a year each, a dozen at a time) for their new role.

5. An operation in and on, finally, the community itself—or, more precisely, key officials, functionaries, and parents within it—in which some of us were counselors, educators, questioners, psychologists (individual and social) acting "therapeutically," discussion leaders, redefiners of situations or issues, sometimes participant-*observers* but also frequently *participant*-observers.

6. An operation in and on the psychiatric community (after all, I was a member of the University of Toronto's Department of Psychiatry, related primarily to psychiatric colleagues and partly responsible for teaching psychiatrists) in which it was my minimum aim to provide a better picture of the (statistically) normal lives their patients live, to set against the standard psychiatric fantasies and projections. (I had so often, in the Army and in clinical case conferences at the hospital, heard behavior, which was culturally normative in the patient's culture of orientation, explained in terms of idiosyncratic psychopathology largely because no one at the conference knew the cultural or social circumstances, or sometimes because no one knew that not all North American subcultures are standard, lower-middle class, modern, urban, Western.)

These at least were the principal overt intentions. What some of the covert intentions variously were, I only gradually realized. How serious a part the overt and covert intentions of the subjects of study would play both in illuminating and reshaping our intentions, and certainly in affecting our effects, was yet to be discovered in the particular situation and yet to be reflected on for its general implications for sociology or for sociology-connected activity.

If I may return now to my original scheme, we had one socio-graphic aim: the description of the community, which was to eventu-ate in the book, *Crestwood Heights*. We had one sociological or social-psychological aim in our "human-relations classes" or "free-discussion groups": to make a contribution to mental health or social-ization theory by testing for the predicted effects of a far-reaching intervention. The remaining operations may be called applied soci-ology, or the application of sociology, though I would now reclassify a great deal of it as sociological diffusion (whether for its own sake or as designed, active, meliorative intervention), and mere action on the basis of sociological knowledge. We came to have one other aim in substantial conflict with all the other intentions taken severally or together. Despite anything we were able to do to maintain dis-tance and due detachment (or just because of these acts), we were drawn into genuine, profound, human, and affectional relations that gave, as a minimum additional aim, the preservation so far as possible of these priceless bonds and the protection and preservation of those with whom we were thus socially (morally and affectionately) bound.

What came out of Crestwood Heights for me was not primarily a book, or a series of papers, or new sociological knowledge (though these did issue). What came out of it was a shattering encounter, whose consequences I have not yet by any means fully worked out. What was shattered beyond redemption, and is still in process of slow and laborious reassembly, was the connected series of "views" I held regarding myself, other sociologists, the nature of sociology, and its connected operations. Simplistic, false, and illusory views that may have had peculiar personal force, but that were the common heritage, reinforced by education and professional training, fell victim to the realities of the experience, which by a self-chosen fate we had made ourselves morally bound to look at.

I would like to forestall a line of thought that no doubt will arise in your mind: that whatever eventuated may have been largely due to our having cast ourselves in a number of different, perhaps incom-patible, and not sufficiently distinguished roles. We might reason-ably be expected to have reaped confusion at the end if we had sown it at the beginning. I want to forestall this line—not to declare it out of bounds, of course, but to warn against letting it blind you to other possibilities—because, naturally, it was the first line of explanation to occur to all of us; it was the most personally, professionally, and socially acceptable, the most obvious, and, as I finally concluded, the most misleading explanation. The premises, for one thing, cannot be supported by the facts: we *did* sharply distinguish roles and, so far as such things are ever possible, we got others to distinguish them progressively more sharply the same way. If I finally concluded that the distinctions were false, and like all major falsehoods due to obscure purposes and all the more endowed of strongest affect, it was not because they were not made to begin with, and sustained with skill, by common desire and consent. If I may anticipate the end of the argument, I should say that I did not revise my opinion of sociology (as well as sociologists and myself) because I was doing so many things in its name, but rather the reverse, that I was doing so many things because all of them are and must be implicit in the very idea of sociology. (Surely I should have known, even as a student, that the very strength of certain professional denials was a probable pointer not only to a hidden truth—hence an assertion by negation—but to a truth of consequence and painfulness. That I did not note what I should have known—did "know"—points merely to the serviceability also in my personal economy, as of that time, of the shared madness, the common myth.) I do not know how much of this I can make clear, since much of it is not clear to me yet.

The Education of a Researcher

The views to which I was led, by seeming inevitability, confounded the distinctions between kinds of enterprises that others had drawn for me, and that I had accepted. I was led to the view that all sociology is applied sociology, if we mean by that an activity that alters the society by the activity of the sociologist acting as such; and, more particularly, that the activity is most applied that is most "theoretical." (A new theory of society *is* a social revolution; all that follows is mere acting out.) Inevitably, I came to see the sociologist largely as an actor; more actor in the society than the "actors" whom he observes and upon whom he reports. Value neutrality, insofar as it was not nonsense or fraud, was a value position with extraordinary practical effects as operating in society by the force of the sociologist's example; partly, in reality, impossible, but, insofar as actualized, bathing all things in a new light, like the counterpart of a mystical experience, and, like that experience, making all things new. I came to see judicial, legislative, and executive functions as central to the sociologist's acts *qua* sociologist, whether in research, theorizing, or educating (diffusing). I came to see elements of priestly and political roles, only best concealed and hence most potent, in the classic sociological role definitions. Needless to say, I came to question the pose of the social scientist as somehow to a significant degree outside history, outside society, outside culture, and to ask sociologically how that could be and *where* then he could be. I began to observe effects, and gradually became convinced that they corresponded to intents, whether unconscious, merely undisclosed, or just hidden. I came to a focal interest in the psychology, sociology, and "philosophy" of sociology (the metasociology) which seemed at least as integral to sociology as the history of philosophy is said to be to philosophy (that is, philosophy, on this view, *is* its own unfolding; they can be distinguished only illusorily). I came to see the student of culture, particularly his own culture, in many lights, both with reference to his effect and intent. (If the culture is the womb, the common matrix with the siblings, what? If the mother's breast, the source of our common nourishment, the very substance of our substance, what? If the culture is a set of constraints, even if also "liberating" directives, the echo and enlargement of the father's heavy constraining hand, what? If an edifice, a structure, an elaboration of towering levels, a super-phallus over against nature, our mother, what? If the "culture bearers," our erstwhile sibs from whose company and culture we must go out if we are to attain "perspective," are our subjects or objects of study and contemplation as if from afar, what Joseph-in-Egypt-and-brethren-in-Israel relations have we not instituted between us, with what causes and consequences for us and for them?) In another view, the sociologist, particularly the cultural anthropologist of his own culture, appears to have inherited the role of the singer, the minstrel, as Uhland sketches for Bertram de Born:

> Du der kamst mit Schwert und Liedern,
>   Aufruhr trug von Ort zu Ort,
> Der die Kinder aufgewiegelt,
>   Gegen ihres Vaters Wort . . .

or, in *very* free translation:

> You who came with sword and singing,
>   Uproar bore from place to place,
> 'Gainst their father's word upbringing
>   E'en his children, out of grace . . .

The "uproar" is the ferment of ideas and attitudes in the world, which flows from the operations of such persons as social and personality theorists, chiefly, in practice, sociological and psychoanalytical theorists, who pose in their products (and even more forcefully by their "sacrilegious" behavior, as examples) ever-new impossibilities of rest, ever-new demands for change, not at the trivial external level where we often think such problems lie, but at the inmost level of individual and collective self-image, and hence of proximate attitude and ultimate set. The carrying of the unrest from place to place is the essence of and reason for publication, ultimately popular publication (whether by self or others makes little difference; it is one integral act, invariably with that effect and commonly with that purpose). The sword is the body of sociological knowledge; and the song, the public lecture. The "father's word" against which the children are stirred up is of course the received culture, the conventional wisdom, which must be the object of reexamination (read "reevaluation"). Even when the intent is conservative (at least the conscious intent), as, for example, in Durkheim in reference to religion, the support that is given is the kiss of death, for a religion that is justified by social utility in terms of its power to create social solidarity is no longer a religion as such, but a social gimmick or instrument of social control. If religion as religion is necessary to society then surely the society that knows this (by the working of the sociologist) can no longer have religion, or at least not in the same sense. (If God is loved because it is good for one's health, mental or physical, the love of God dubiously has any of its alleged curative or preventive properties.)

Nor, as I finally came to see and feel it, was it sufficient for a responsible sociologist to have such insight as he could into what sociology "is" in general or how "sociologists" operate in general. Of overwhelming importance, for him as for the psychoanalyst, is an understanding not alone of the play and the parts, but of his own particular, private, and personal version and variety of the play and style of playing out the social part. For, as with the prototype of all symbol systems—as Norman Brown out of Sigmund Freud reminds us—the primitive first symbol and its successors function as play material, weapon, property, and gift. But which of these in what proportions, combined how, why, and with what effects is what the practicing sociologist most needs to know and is, in the nature of things, both least likely to know and least desirous of knowing. The styles in sociology—shocking, mischievous, superior, snide, indulgent, falsely detached asserting by negating, falsely committed negating by affirming, remote, simplistic, overcomplex, turgid, spuriously transparent— all cry for understanding, because they are of the essence, not the accidents, of what it is, and therefore of what the relation of society to sociology and sociologist can and should be. The anecdotist is asserting to and pretending one thing, the systematizer another, the middle-range theorist a third. Even preferences among Stein's Trinity (history, system, drama) have more than their ostensible utilities to recommend them; they involve, at the least as conditions of tenability, sizable shifts in the self-image (and the held-out other-image) of the sociologist who holds them, for somewhere within his preferred scheme or metaphor he must find a place for himself both as a sociologist and a self among selves.

Still later I came to see, in generalization from W. I. Thomas' "definition of the situation," that the greater part of social facts, and those the most important, are and forever will be constituted by their definition (brought into being, and so sustained, by faith); that a redefinition is no less, rather more, a definition; that the sociologist's profession is to initiate redefinitions of society or subsociety; and that hence he is in the business, necessarily, of the continuous re-constitution of society, whether he does it ill or well, effectively or ineffectively.

Thus this innocent abroad, this *rapporteur* merely or *raconteur*, this urbane student of the social scene, is a crucial actor within the play he appears and purports merely to watch, only to record or enjoy. Even by his refusal so to see himself he decisively affects the drama, holds himself only from the consciousness of his history making, and deceives himself as to his place in the system.

The questioning of the actual set, posture, and effect of the sociologist in society not only led me to revise and reexamine what was involved in selecting particular objects (say gangs, communities, or suburbs) for attention, but what was or could be meant by imputation of social causation where the canons that guide the nonhuman sciences —convenience for intervention—have no clear meaning, or a radically different (political) one. I became interested in or curious about the actual social uses of sociology: a Vance Packard, seeking status and clad in the symbols of successful seeking, lecturing an audience on "the status-seekers" as though the term referred to them, or to others, but not him; or grade-school kids recasting ancient child disputes in our terminology. At a more vital level, I watched more intimately young college and old high-school boys and girls explaining their acts in terms which we had given them to attribute for causation to history, the social structure, the culture or what-not.

The whole matter comes to one beautiful, practical—but only illus-trative—sort of crux in the decisions over the last few years from the bench of the Superior Court of the District of Columbia, particularly the decisions of Judge David Bazelon. The record is there to read, and should be read. Suffice it to say that, taking psychic determinism seriously, he has sought to extend and has extended, not into the mitigation of punishment or the assessment of extenuating circumstances, but into the determination of criminal responsibility and guilt (the central doctrine of *mens rea*), a set of notions of how human acts come about without the intention (or negligence) of the principal actor. And similarly he has sought and is seeking the admission of what might be called sociological evidence to adult trials, so that, in principle, if a competent sociologist could convince a jury of the "social causation" of a given act, then clearly it would fall as far outside the realm of culpability and criminal responsibility as if it had been committed as a consequence of mental illness, or, in the older terminology, "while of unsound mind." Clearly, we are not much longer going to be able to have our causal arguments both ways, and we may well be required to come to some crucial decisions (or have others do so for us) in connection with the criminal law. The direction I see events taking is a much diminished notion of individual responsibility for personal acts—the notion in turn then altering the facts—with a much increased individual responsibility for the collective acts (e.g., segregation) which furnish the conditions and limits (or causes) for personal acts. If, as seems entirely possible, such individual responsibility for collective acts cannot be borne or adequately responded to by individuals, the likeliest outcome seems highly increased centralization, benign no doubt in intent, going toward an iatrocratic sort of society, with still further consequences for the idea and possibility of personal potency and responsibility.

Unanticipated Consequences

Some of these ideas may be assessed or debated on their merits, no doubt, in due season, but how did they come out of the experience in Crestwood Heights? They came out of Crestwood Heights because the circumstances, the nature of the enterprise, and my own and my colleagues' "readiness" (if you want to call it that) forced a collision between theory (or professional ideology) and the facts that we were ostensibly there to look at. I can touch only lightly and illustratively on what I mean.

First, it became evident that what we were actually "doing" at any moment in any part of the enterprise was a function not so much of our intentions and techniques, nor our definitions of what we were about, but of what others, individually or collectively, imputed to us as the motives and nature of the operation. Thus, to take a crude example, some people thought that the psychiatric clinic we installed was, despite our claims and disclaimers, altogether or primarily a research station, and they responded to it as such. Depending then on what they "thought" of research and therapy respectively, and, more covertly, on dispositions to help, be helped, or enter into specific help-exchange bargains ("I'll tell you this, if you tell me that"), the consequences might be therapeutic, countertherapeutic or therapeutically neutral not only for the client but for the aid-tendering professional. What people "thought" the clinic was, and hence what it practically came to be, was, of course, not just a datum. Nor was it a result of our conscious defining of activities. Any definition at any time—and, with the definition, the temporary, tentative operating reality—came out of an obscure conversation or transaction in which the overt and covert interests and needs of both parties to the transaction —the professionals no less than the clients—were of the essence of the outcome. And as to what either of these terms, "research" or "therapy," meant to the participants at deepest levels, initially or sequentially, it also turned out to be ultrasignificantly affected by the initially unknown life experience which on the one view would be the subject of study, on the other of "helpful" intervention. Thus "research" might really mean something like early-experienced (in reality or fantasy) parental investigation leading to guilt or punishment; or it might fall into a matrix of "ego-syntonic" experience of self or others, where investigation had been the prelude to reward, satisfaction, or coming to terms with reality. So not only the defining terms and what the definitions "really" meant, but further depths were involved: that is, "help" as something to be welcomed or feared, what the clinic was, and thus what we were doing from their viewpoint, and thus, in consequence and by reaction, what we were "really" doing in the clinic. All this was a shifting consequence of a social action initiated by both sides and controlled in any vital sense by neither, and only detectable in sketch or impression by listening with a most attentive "third ear" to our own nonexplicit expressions and theirs. And note the circularity: the desire to know what is actually going on is primarily, formally, a "research" interest; but the discovery of such subtleties rests primarily on a "therapeutic"—or, at least, benevolent and mutual-aid—relationship and definition of the situation. No set of assertions, no education campaign or public-relations program can more than touch these fundamental facts; for each of these facts in turn depends on the same set of complexities.·

I chose the clinic for an example because it was separately staffed and located, most easily recognized in conventional terms (in a psychiatrist-using and child-education and child-raising-centered community), most protected by established professional practices designed to safeguard professional definitions, and doing mostly one thing. For children, teachers, principals, school officials, parents, outside observers, professionals involved, as groups or severally, it was far from one and the same thing; and patently what it was operationally had small relation to what it was initially and officially defined to be.

And, if so for the clinic, *a fortiori* so for all the other less conventional enterprises.

Again, and more generally, it turned out that the principal—most common and most significant—effect of what we were doing bore very little relation to what we were actually doing. For the project as a whole, for instance, one principal effect was the raising of community morale and pride because this community was selected as a place for operation and a subject for research: its inhabitants were evidently, by implication, even more interesting to people of a type they admired ("experts") than they had ever thought.

In a "concession," whose politics I leave you to guess, we conducted for several years a graduate seminar for women, not on Crestwood Heights or anything we were doing, but essentially on culture and personality, just as we would have done in our universities. The effect of this peripheral activity went further, perhaps, than any one thing we officially did, in the direction of applied sociology. Our observers at P.T.A. meetings, or still more informal but vital meetings, could roughly trace the spread in this sophisticated, literate community, not only of a body of knowledge, but a way of looking at problems, that was seriously to question previous received doctrine on which institutions (school, church, temple) were operating, as well as to cause practices previously accepted there (and in homes and families) to be seen in a different, unfamiliar, and action- or adjustment-requiring light. So here, where we were most abstract, theoretical, academic, we had the greatest practical impact.

Similarly, "clinical conferences" with teachers and "guidance personnel," designed to secure consensus on the handling of a given child, turned out to have their principal effects not there, but on the social organization, status system, and system of alliances within the school, in precipitating new individual and collective self-images, and, in many cases, in affording a therapeutic or cathartic outlet for the teachers who were ostensibly involved, not thus, but in their role as caretaker-educators.

The one most clearly labeled "scientific experiment"—the attempt to measure the effect psychologically and sociometrically of "free discussion"—turned out to furnish one of the most vital and detailed sources of information for the sociography, information we could have got in no other way short of mass psychoanalysis. For before our very eyes and around our very ears unfolded in dynamic fashion—a social analogue of personal free association—the concerns, worries, coping ways of these children as embedded in their personality and social structure, inside and outside the school. We got living pictures, not undistorted, of course, first of the idiosyncratic and then, under discussion, the communal experience of being a child in Crestwood Heights, as seen by children of the several sampled ages.

We not only got something other than we aimed at, in this fashion, but something additional in the experiment itself: mere serendipity, to use the current jargon. Our "experimental subjects" not only made notable, "significant," and substantial gains in the mental-health (or psychological) directions predicted but, quite unexpectedly, dramatic academic-grade gains even in subjects they had to "sacrifice" in order to permit time for the discussions. Also, unanticipatedly, not only the method but the underlying attitudes were "brought home" by children and adopted or imitated by some parents, quite a few teachers, and even some temple personnel with extraordinary results. Indeed, the method and more carried over into school staff meetings (nearly oversetting the structure of the one authoritarian school) and, believe it or not, into the youngsters' own, "extralegal" fraternity and sorority lives.

Again some odd results. By coincidence or otherwise about three years later, when everyone had forgotten who had and had not been in any experimental group, of five students winning major outside-awarded scholarships, four were experimental children (and one a newcomer) and none were "controls," though there were four times as many controls as experimentals. Again, about the same time, one perceptive teacher said he could (and proved he could) pick out the "experimentals" in the entire three-times-reshuffled grade, by the way they "went at" a problem (in history, his subject) and by the feeling they communicated as to how they saw him and his role as a teacher. Again, at about the same time, an outside and independent team of investigators interviewing the experimentals found (a) each believed he had not changed much as a result of the discussions, but that all others had changed a great deal; (b) most felt it had been a vital experience, but could hardly remember anything discussed; (c) a strange majority thought the object had been to "teach them how to *think*," though most referred to changes in feeling or sensitivity or perception of their social and especially peer world as illustrative. (The double distortion, that we aimed at thought and that we were *teaching* them, gives food for thought about teaching!) Also, and coincidentally, we set off within the teaching staff inside the school passionate discussion and debate on the relation of the school to the pupil, the adult to youth, the place of ethical or other indoctrination in education, the teacher's private conscience vis-à-vis his public responsibility, and so on. Not only that, but among educators and others in the metropolitan area of Toronto and outside, a parallel agitation was set off as rumor or report (or observation) of what we were doing circulated and variously reached various targets. Observers spoke essentially of three things: a tremendous positively toned emotional experience for them; a shaking blow to their beliefs about what children could and would do with such a freedom, how much they unsuspectedly knew, and how wise and responsible they seemed; and a need to go away and carefully consider implications for educational theory and practice (or, sometimes, family theory and practice).

Again, I would be inclined to say either that the principal product lay outside our conscious intentions and designs, or that the byproducts were so numerous, important, and various that they altered substantially what is meant by "the product." Certainly, we had not aimed to illustrate for Crestwood Heights itself what "acceptance," "respect for others" (chiefly children), attention to covert as well as overt message, especially self-direction, and, in essence, free association as against structured attack, could do for participants and, evidently, observers. (If we had been able to have our way, I am sure we would have insulated or isolated our precious experiment for the sake of scientific purity.) Certainly, we did not aim at altering the intellectual-emotional climate of the educational enterprise (parents, children, and teachers). But, more visibly nearly than anything else, this, I believe, is what we unwittingly did.

Similar results were obtained with other aspects of our operation, but I will not burden you with further detail. Even a public lecture in or near the community on some quite unconnected topic might turn out to be more a rite of solidarity, an exercise in sociability, or a genuinely transference-attended situation than any of us, in our then naïveté, would have been inclined to believe.

The Subjective Ambiquity of Reseach

You may have noticed that hitherto I have spoken with almost pedantic insistence on "conscious motives" and witting intents. I did so by design, because I was not aware till much later how much the actual upshots, when they were not wedded to conscious designs, were indeed the offspring of unconscious intents. Not inadvertence but indirection marked the route from motive to effect.

I must compress a great deal into a little space and, although I am sure the generalizations would be true for all members of the project and for all social scientists I have known, I must speak from here on only for myself.

If I had to condense all I propose to say into a single generalization, it would be that a scientific career, like a dream, is a message, telling in detail, for those who can interpret it, of a rich and quite different inner life, a "compromise" solution of an affect-laden conflict, an indication of some unfinished business in the social drama of infancy, a symbolic representation attended by condensation, displacement, reversal, and so on. Of course, just as in a dream, there are accidental factors and elements and traces of daylight purposes, but the significant, dramatic, and illuminating connections are not there, but in the largely unconscious life which necessitates the second displacement. Sociological and psychological studies and careers are, I suggest (beyond this public and ostensible character) partially but significantly, returns of and fresh attempts at coping with the repressed. I say "partially" because like other art—to which they should be assimilated—there is a controlled and socialized element that makes for intelligibility on two planes, rather than one, as in the dream or somatic symptom.

It would not be proper for me and I should be reluctant to burden you here with intimate detail. I should only say that there gradually emerged so fine-grained an appreciation of the connections between my childhood experiences, my present personality, and my scientific operations that I could see and become convinced of even very fine connections between particulars. Thus, in retrospect, and comprehensible only at depth level (though I *can* give also surface-plausible explanations), virtually nothing seems accidental—beginning with the basic turning away from any community of any kind I had ever known and toward delinquency (in Chicago), and the subsequent turning toward a community of about the socioeconomic level of that of my origin, with a special eye to the ideology and behavior of authority figures vis-à-vis the child, a very special eye to the unanticipated consequences (and hence the basic folly) of their acts, even when well motivated, and a particular sensitivity for and interest in emotional consequences. This is perhaps too general. It would be more convincingly particular perhaps to say that the free-discussion groups (or human-relations classes) represented an "experimental" point-for-point upending of my own most important experiences in a very Victorian (and otherwise very stormy, stressful) home. The scientific character of the experiment, I think, is unassailable or as nearly so as these things can be. But, at another level of language, what can be heard but: "Look, if authority figures treat a child as I wished to be treated and was not, may not some good come of it for them (and could have come for us)." Even the serendipitous discovery of the tremendous academic gains made after "wasting" time on discussion only adds with psychodynamic cogency: "And, look, at no cost!" The whole also demonstrated another buried conviction of childhood: "Effective knowledge is assimilated only in affection."

I could go on thus piling up detail after detail from *Crestwood Heights,* or, with reference to friends, from other studies. But by now conviction will likely have set in—or it will not set in at all.

You will have several legitimate questions. Have my primary observations on myself been correct? I believe so. Am I correct in generalizing to others? I suggest you check in yourself and those to whom you have access *if* they have access to themselves. So what? This is more difficult.

So, I think, we certainly can and probably should and perhaps must view our own "scientific" conduct, personal and collective, under the same microscope as that under which we view our subjects of study. I think that this microscope not only enlarges, but—forgive the mixed image—transforms: so that on this second view neither are they so simply doing what we thought they were doing nor are we doing largely or at all what on the first view we so simply thought. Indeed in this transforming vision we may see ourselves engaged with them in a common social life and struggle, much as the other poets, artists, and seers, speaking perhaps in a different idiom, moved perhaps by a different vision, but purveyors nevertheless of a gospel we should be at greater pains to make clear.

6

The Eclipse of Community:

Some Glances at the Education

of a Sociologist

Maurice R. Stein

My contribution to this collection differs from the others because I never actually carried out a community study though I did spend a long time reflecting upon other people's studies while writing *The Eclipse of Community*.[1] In this postscript I will describe some of the personal and intellectual circumstances surrounding my own extended meditation upon community studies.

I

I first became aware of the enormous role played by personal responses in social inquiry when I worked for Alvin W. Gouldner in his study of a gypsum plant and mine during 1947, 1948, and 1949. I had completed two years of military service a short time earlier and found myself in the process of shifting from physical science to social science because the former seemed unable to help me with those questions about my life and about the world that worried me most. I wanted a profession that would permit me to explore a series of personal experiences. While in the army I had found myself eager to enter combat despite personal fears and serious moral doubts. During my period of military service I encountered two caste systems, the standard distinctions between officers and enlisted men and the distinction between whites and Negroes in the southern communities where I was stationed. A third form of caste appeared when I served with

[1] Princeton University Press, 1960; Harper Torchbook, 1964.

the occupation in Korea where I found American soldiers treating Orientals as subhuman, a point that had been reinforced earlier by the bombs dropped on Hiroshima and on Nagasaki. Underlying my reactions to all three forms of caste was my own experience as a Jew which led me to identify with the lower castes in each situation. And, of course, this identification alerted me to the seeds of totalitarianism which caste attitudes manifested.

Prior to becoming a sociology major, I had discovered a comprehensive interpretation of caste and much else in modern life in Marxism. However, I quickly became disgusted with the platitudes of organizational Marxism which seemed to bear little relationship to the realities it purported to explain. At this juncture sociology entered the picture as an intellectual discipline that promised to permit sustained exposure to theories about society which would allow me to understand the world and my place in it.

The choice between sociology and psychology was made largely because the Sociology Department at the University of Buffalo offered a broader spectrum of courses that seemed to include self-study and objective research about social processes. I was attracted to such courses as Alvin Gouldner's Sociology of Fascism, Nathaniel Cantor's course on Personality and Culture where we all expressed ourselves or else, Milton Albrecht's Sociology of Art and Literature, and Jerry Wolpert's full year textual exegesis of Max Weber. Unusual and important as the formal course work may have been, the opportunity to get into the field that becoming Gouldner's research assistant offered was still more crucial. My last two undergraduate years and my semester as a teaching fellow were spent hanging around a gypsum mine and plant which Gouldner describe and analyzed in his *Patterns of Industrial Bureaucracy* and *Wildcat Strike*.

II

In 1952 I wrote with Gouldner the appendix to *Patterns of Industrial Bureaucracy* called "Field Work Procedures—The Social Organization of a Student Research Team." Just as Gouldner's books contain the fullest description of the happenings in the factory we were studying, this essay contains the fullest description of what happened to me during the study.

My main point of attachment to the study was my identification with the gypsum miners. I was proud that I could make the arduous three-quarter mile walk from the foot of the mine to the face where the gypsum was collected and where there was danger of the loose slate roofs falling in. I was pleased when I began to have the recurrent dream that all real miners have and talk about of wandering in dark corridors and being hit by a falling roof. When asked why I liked doing research in such a superficially uncomfortable environment, I gave the classic miner's answer, "It was wonderful to work in a place where the temperature stayed the same the whole year around." I found myself talking like a miner and even taking over their contempt for workers (and for members of the research team) who confined their activities to the gypsum processing plant on the surface. Some of the other satisfactions are shown in the following passage from the 1952 essay:

The team members enjoyed the freedom of movement in the mine. It was pleasant to get into sloppy clothes and throw oneself around the mine without worrying about getting dirty or looking well. Again, most team members liked the language patterns of the miners. Conversations were relaxed and profane. Miners shouted and yelled at each other in a way not permissible in polite circles. There was a spontaneous expression of feelings too often inhibited in academic groups. (*Patterns of Industrial Bureaucracy*, p. 263)

Obvious psychoanalytic interpretations aside, this was a wonderful place to spend my kind of protracted adolescence. I was dealing with the working class and had finally found a section of it which, though generally without political consciousness, still had personal qualities of magnetism, spontaneity, honesty, and physical vigor. In addition, they had the dignity that comes from doing hard, dangerous work, and the ironic humor, as well as the affection for each other, that this kind of work sometimes generates. And I could easily compare favorably the miners with the surface men who had accepted routinization along with the loss of spontaneous language as their lot in life.

Working from notes written in 1948, I find that I was continually comparing mine jobs with surface jobs in terms of the special, preferable qualities of the former. The miners set their own work pace according to the rhythms of their collective work activities. Since they were paid by the quantity of gypsum they hauled out, this raw gypsum became the only "product" that concerned them. They were cooperative because they needed each other to do this work properly and, in fact, their lives depended upon one another's effectiveness. They were doing "men's" work and it was so regarded (though ambivalently) by the surface men and by the people in their towns. There was a minimum division of labor and a maximum rotation of jobs at the face, with everybody, especially the foremen, chipping in and filling in at will. Each day the miners had to make significant decisions such as deciding whether an area in the mine (called a room) that had been blasted out the night before was safe to enter, and, if it was, they had to help the prop man, their institutionalized shaman, to decide where to put his props. These props would really not hold up a roof that was going to fall in, but everybody felt better if their particular prop man was a person who appeared to have great strength.

On a more fundamental level, all of the men working in this mine knew really that they were indispensable. They knew it so well that most of them chose to work a three-day week only, on the ground that mining created such an enormous thirst that they had to spend at least four days tanking up at local bars to get into condition. Though not easily seen by an outsider, mine work had considerable internal variety. The blasts that created the "rooms" left differently shaped walls and ceilings so that each day the mining team had to determine how to get their loaders into the room most effectively and most safely. In the mine one had to be alert, because even an ordinary activity such as walking involved complex sensory and motoric adaptation to irregular, jagged roofs and jutting floors. The miners also felt a peculiar kind of self-sufficiency in carrying the light they needed on their helmets. Miners always wore their helmets when running errands on the surface, though they did leave the batteries behind. In the mine the machines employed to see and to work with were very much under the control of the men operating them. They were much more like body extensions of the men than was the moving assembly line on the surface, which tended to transform its attendants into a mechanical extension of an apparatus.

Detailed descriptions of the work process both in the mine and on the surface can be found in Gouldner's book, but since I am here speaking of its meaning to one member of the research team, let me repeat some of the reflections written into the appendix:

Getting interviews in the mine was quite different from getting them on the surface. In the first place, the miners' feelings about their foremen were different from those displayed by surfacemen. The miners' solidarity was sufficiently strong that being brought into their group by a foreman did not threaten them. Occasionally, it was actually helpful, because the foreman might be a respected member of the group. On the other hand, if miners disliked a foreman, they would tell you so right to his face. If miners saw a team member with a disliked foreman, they would not reject him but would, instead, try to convince the researcher that the foreman was a "s.o.b."

On the surface, however, though workers treated their foremen in a more "respectful" way, they did not *feel* quite so much respect for them. Being introduced by a surface foreman never helped us, and we prevented this in the way described above. Another contrast: Surface foremen were hard to interview, but mine foremen often sought us out, if there were no one else around at the moment with whom to pass the time. In the mine, we could be very friendly with mine foremen and no damage would result; but similar cordiality with surface foremen could have been disastrous.

The team members were always struck by the difference between our rapport with the miners and the surfacemen. We had good rapport with surface workers, but it was qualitatively different from that prevailing in the mine. Our relations with the miners approximated informal solidarity. While we seemed able to get all the information we sought from surface workers, we never got to know them too well as "persons."

The differences between mine and surface interviews should not be unduly exaggerated but there were variations of feeling-tone in interviewing typical persons in the two groups. The miners insisted that we be friendly before they would allow themselves to be interviewed. Surfacemen, for example, rarely tried to draw us out and elicit our opinions, but the miners often did. Again, the miners were far more likely to talk about personal affairs than were the surface workers.

The miners regarded us as people who were "also" interviewers; while surfacemen thought of us as interviewers and established "segmentalized" relations with us. Before a miner was going to tell us anything about *his* feelings, he wanted to know about *ours*. This was not because they were suspicious of us, but largely because they were unwilling to accept the dependent and passive role involved in a one-way exchange. And we not only had to express our ideas to the miners, but our *feelings* as well.

Despite the fact that this seemingly violates the canons of good interviewing, we were all convinced that our best data was obtained during such moments of real interaction. Our experience suggests, therefore, that there are some persons who *cannot* be well interviewed unless the interviewer abandons the appearance of lofty detachment and impersonal interest, and unless he behaves with friendly respect. The ideal role of the impersonal interviewer could be approximated on the surface, but it fell flat in the mine. We tentatively concluded from this experience that the dangers of the interviewer's "over-identification" or "over-rapport" can be much exaggerated, and that it is sometimes indispensable to develop friendly ties with certain kinds of respondents in order to obtain their cooperation.

Certainly, we are not advocating that scientific objectivity be abandoned and, of course, one should avoid expressing opinions on matters of concern to the study which would bias the informant's comments. But deep rapport can be based on mutual identification on broader issues. Furthermore, it is necessary that such identifications be recognized—as we think they have been here—so that they will not interfere with analysis of the data. One of the mechanisms which prevented the interference of such identifications was our use of *collective* analysis of the data, which will be elaborated on later, so that distinctive individual prejudices which arose were canceled out by the group process. Deep rapport has its perils, but to treat the norm of impersonality as sacred, even if it impairs the informants' cooperation, would seem to be an inexcusable form of scientific ritualism. (*Patterns of Industrial Bureaucracy*, pp. 258–260)

These passages point to the heart of the research dilemma which this involvement with the miners posed for me, and to a lesser degree for the study as a whole. Looking back now I can see all kinds of influences that must have been involved. I was working out authority issues, and clearly I chose the open expression of hostile feelings that was characteristic in the mine rather than the repression that was characteristic on the surface. I came from a muddled class background which involved a mixture of lower-, upper-, and middle-class elements that I have not yet been able to disentangle fully. The main point is that I associate working-class settings with emotional spontaneity and middle-class settings with emotional restraint. I never quite confronted the fact that the surface men were as much members of the working class as were the miners.

From a more intellectual standpoint, I discovered that doing research and thinking about research demanded that one be capable of both involvement and detachment, each to be deployed when required. I learned that intensive identification with the miners allowed me to be with them when they were behaving naturally; it allowed me to talk man to man with them and even to go drinking with them and meet their families. No amount of research training could have substituted for the real effect on these men, who valued spontaneity so highly, of my spontaneous feelings about them. The simulation of such feelings would hardly have led me to choose to stay in a place as dangerous and uncomfortable as the mine. I suppose I had to be there for reasons somewhat similar to theirs before they would accept my presence as legitimate.

On the other hand, I was also there for reasons different from theirs. Every evening after a day of participant observation, I spent long hours at the typewriter recounting the events and encounters of the day. In addition, I participated in endless planned and informal discussions about what was happening in the plant and what these happenings might mean from the standpoint of social theory. The descriptive writing became an act of fealty since I felt that writing about life in this setting was my way of being loyal to the people living in it. This writing came more easily than most of my other writing. But the efforts at interpreting the miners' behavior as a product of social forces, and especially seeing it as being in any way strategic rather than spontaneous, left me with profound misgivings.

This study finally left me with an incomplete field experience, in the sense that in the role of research assistant I was never forced to organize, systematize, and interpret the sequences of events that unfolded before my eyes. The writing that I did consisted almost entirely of specific dramatic representations of events and encounters. This was relatively easy because much that happened in the mine lent itself to such representation. I was always aware of how much harder it was to dramatize events on the surface, at least in day-to-day terms. Gouldner finally organized his narrative presentation around the dramas generated by managerial succession and ultimately by the strike. He then interpreted these dramas within a theory of bureaucratic rules. This theory focused on technological and bureaucratic rationalization as it occurred in this plant and on a theory of social systemic tensions which moved to an even higher level of generality. I was more concerned with the former than with the latter and remain most impressed by Gouldner's distinction between responsibility-centered and punishment-centered bureaucracy, a distinction that makes intelligible the human grounds on which the miners and some of the surface men resisted certain kinds of rationalization. In any event my responsibility for writing ended with description, though the research team continually talked over the emerging interpretive themes. Since the daily routine of the mine was peculiarly dramatic, including tragedies such as a cave-in that crippled a foreman with whom I was especially friendly, the main issues that I had to face were the struggles to be objective despite my identifications and to write dramatically within the limits of my literary style. The problems of committing myself to an historical interpretation of the dramatic sequence or to a systematic interpretation of the social structure and processes did not arise, and in these important respects the field experience was incomplete.

III

A summary of my intellectual position in 1949, when I entered Columbia as a graduate student in sociology, might be helpful. As a result of the broad cultural approach to sociology that I had learned from the Buffalo department, I was persuaded that all aspects of the development of society in general, Western society in particular and especially the American version of it, were susceptible to interpretation within the categories of classical and modern social theory. I was well aware of my ignorance about most historical periods and of the difficulties this created in understanding social theory, especially the theorizing of Marx and Weber, but I was confident that such detailed knowledge could be acquired in time. Second, however, I was convinced that detailed knowledge of history by itself could never allow us to understand our own period, nor could simple reapplication of the classical theories serve this purpose. The gypsum study had shown me the centrality of detailed inquiry in empirical settings and had persuaded me that such inquiry was both emotionally rewarding and intellectually justified insofar as it promised to permit the cumulative extension of the ideas and the insights of the classical tradition. Without this open-ended exposure to modern realities, it was all too clear that these ideas and insights became sterile ideologies. Finally, I was certain that sociology would allow me to explore the major issues that I confronted as a member of society, as a member of a particular class and ethnic group, and as a person.

This is not the place to try to do a sociological interpretation of the graduate Sociology Department at Columbia, and I am certain that my limited experience as a student in this department from 1949 to 1952 would hardly equip me to do such a study. We all reflect on our lives, however, and just as the mine remains a setting with which I was deeply involved and which deeply influenced me, so was I involved and influenced by Columbia. In the discussion that follows, let it be absolutely clear that the influence described is written from the standpoint of the involvement of the person with the intellectual concerns just described. Graduate students with other concerns undoubtedly had quite different experiences, and I am certain that a description of the university written from the standpoint of the faculty would reflect almost as much inner diversity.

My impressions while at Columbia were dominated by my strong negative reaction to the prevailing ethos which proclaimed survey research and survey logic as the major ways of developing significant sociological generalizations. This reaction was compounded by the corollary assumption that these methods were devoid of value biases and therefore could be used and expanded for any sort of inquiry. This assumption of methodological neutrality was bolstered by the kind of structural-functional theorizing which worked systematically with abstract, value-neutral categories that could as easily be applied to analyzing coffee preferences as to interpreting reactions in a revolutionary situation. The dominant figures of course were Professors Lazarsfeld and Merton, working, as the latter phrased it, in "double harness." Many of us spent a great deal of time and energy trying to discover what held these two horses together as well as trying to learn what made each of them run.

Looking back on the situation and my responses to it, I can see that the starting point of my negative reaction lay in my conviction from the gypsum study that empirical sociology could never be value neutral, as the survey methodologists assumed their work to be, without excluding vast realms of human experience. Throughout all of my course work in methodology, I was always perplexed by such naive questions as "How could survey analysts working from coded responses to questionnaire items administered to people they had never seen by people whom they barely knew ever achieve genuine insight?" During the gypsum study we had used questionnaires to check out our impressions about the distribution of attitudes, but only after we knew what the historically and sociologically significant processes were through long immersion in the life of the factory. Nothing very much emerged from this questionnaire study, though a disproportionate amount of time was devoted to it. And this remains my impression about most surveys: they yield a very small intellectual gain for the time and the energy they consume.

The issue, however, is not evaluating the survey method because that is impossible. For certain purposes, obviously, the survey method is the only way to obtain data, but it should never become the only kind of data that sociologists gather, for if it does, thought is stopped before it starts. In fact, however, survey logic lends itself to such a thought-stopping role, as indeed does the logic of any method if it is consciously or unconsciously presumed to be the necessary or exclusive method. One of my favorite fantasies is a dialogue between Mills and Lazarsfeld in which the former reads to the latter the first sentence of *The Sociological Imagination:* "Nowadays men often feel that their private lives are a series of traps." Lazarsfeld immediately replies: "How many men, which men, how long have they felt this way, which aspects of their private lives bother them, do their public lives bother them, when do they feel free rather than trapped, what kinds of traps do they experience, etc., etc., etc." If Mills succumbed, the two of them would have to apply to the National Institute of Mental Health for a million-dollar grant to check out and elaborate that first sentence. They would need a staff of hundreds, and when finished they would have written *Americans View Their Mental Health* rather than *The*

Sociological Imagination, provided that they finished at all, and provided that either of them cared enough at the end to bother writing anything.

This imaginary encounter points up the obsessive power of survey logic, which is far more compelling than anyone, Mills included, ever realized. Almost no professional sociologist can write a sentence, not to mention a paragraph, without going through some condensed version of the foregoing dialogue. Luckily, talk is cheap, which is why so many of us are more interesting in the classroom or the cocktail lounge than we are in print.

Several other aspects of survey logic disturbed me as a graduate student. However, they are all matters which at least in principle can be dealt with through modification and supplementation. For instance, the panel study attempts to take care of objections that surveys report only attitudes at a single point in time. But no feasible panel arrangement, and no feasible manipulation of samples, can ever deal with the inherent limits even of such an elaborate study as *The American Soldier* if one wants to address problems of comparative military organization. Knowing how a sample of soldiers felt about combat or anything else at a certain point in the war and in a particular army could not tell us how soldiers felt in other armies in other wars, but it was sometimes assumed through the magic of statistical generalization to have done so. And reanalyzing such time- and space-bound generalizations using a social-psychological theory of reference groups cannot render them specifically useful for studying other military contexts, though it can increase apparent generality of the ideas.

I mention *The American Soldier* here because its publication in 1949 was seized upon by both the survey methodologists and the middle-range theorists as demonstrating the virtues of their kind of sociology. Personally, I could absorb it only as a useful but limited kind of information to be added to ongoing meditations about my own military experience and to other sources of information ranging from Bill Mauldin's powerful Willie and Joe cartoons to the neglected psychoanalytic book by Therese Benedek misleadingly entitled *Insight and Personality Adjustment,* which dealt with soldiers and veterans. The point is that it seemed sensible to welcome statistical information but obsessional to allow it either to become an exemplar of what sociological data about military life ought to include or to allow it to crowd out alternative sources of data.

Whether we graduate students were right or not, more than a few of us at Columbia felt that survey methodology institutionalized in the Bureau of Social Research and in the graduate department was actually restricting the range of possible information that we drew upon and, even more importantly, was restricting the kinds of problems that we could study. This conviction was reinforced by the structure of our situation, possessing as it did certain elements not necessarily present in all other graduate departments. A major factor was the large number of students enrolled compared with the small senior faculty. Since an academic depression, due to the contraction of colleges after the postwar enrollment upsurge of veteran-students, was in progress, the extreme unsteadiness of the job market linked to the difficulties involved in getting the kind of attention that yields good references when so many people were competing for so few places in the sun, combined to create a special incentive for graduate students to want to believe and to study what they assumed their professors would appreciate.

But these special circumstances were compounded by the sense of intellectual mission disguised as objective science which the team of Merton and Lazarsfeld had developed. For someone with the commitments I indicated earlier, this intellectual program was a source of constant concern. If large-scale surveys were the model method, then my field experience with the miners was trivial. If middle-range theories were sufficient, then my concern with large social problems was misplaced. If sociology was to use only value-neutral structural-functional categories, then my commitment to social criticism and social transformation had to be abandoned or carefully segregated within my private life. If classical social theory was simply a repository of bright ideas or general orientations rather than a critical interpretation of Western history, then my effort at understanding historical development in substantive terms was wasted time. If the condensations of classical social theory by Parsons and Merton really captured most of the significant analytic elements in classical theory, then these theories did not have to be studied except for historical purposes, if at all. If scientific sociology was really accumulating, then present-day sociology must contain all that was valuable in the past, leaving us with the sole task of using the new concepts and the new methods to advance bravely into the future. My old dream that sociology could be a source of double insight into my own circumstances and the circumstances of the larger society had to go the way of all prescientific fantasies into oblivion.

It is impossible for anyone who was not present and under the pressures that my generation of graduate students was under to fully grasp why we accepted this perfectly legitimate but hardly inclusive orientation to sociological inquiry as wholeheartedly as so many did. In the first place, its proponents presented their orientation as true science, ignoring what should have been visible to all that it was built upon the special gifts of both members of the team. Lazarsfeld's fertile logical mind equipped him to take any survey results and perceive relationships, whereas Merton's systematic bent equipped him to bring a kind of order out of the apparent chaos of propositions about the sociology of knowledge, about applied sociology, about soldiers, or even out of the entire corpus of classical theory. By appearing ascetically to renounce value judgments and the rich interpretive powers of classical sociology in the name of scientific sociology, they generated a mid-twentieth century version of the positivist strategy which was more subtle and more effective than several earlier versions.

IV

On leaving graduate school and beginning to teach as well as to work on a project of my own, I found myself becoming increasingly conscious of the price that Merton and Lazarsfeld had paid for whatever intellectual gains they garnered by their commitment to middle-range studies, to survey data, and to a narrow conception of value neutrality. I was by no means ready to abandon these commitments, since I thought at the time that doing so would mean abandoning professional sociology and, even worse, abandoning objective science. However, the old undergraduate attachments remained near the surface and were reactivated whenever I read any of the classical theorists or a good ethnographic study. I had come across a statement about the effects of professionalization in psychoanalysis that seemed peculiarly appropriate.

Having made the decision (primarily an unconscious one) to become a professional psychotherapist, the individual enters a new phase of development. In the ordinary course of events, and on the basis of his previous experience in medicine, he decides to implement his decision by appropriate didactic training. This implementation may in some ways be unfortunate. The needs to become a psychotherapist stem from deeply personal and emotional drives within the person of the applicant. The contrast between the academic, didactic atmosphere and the highly subjective motivations which send him into training frequently lead to disillusionment. This results from his failure to obtain at the critical time full satisfaction of the needs which originated his decision. It may be that the objectivity of the training causes him to utilize objectivity as a method of isolating and holding in suppression his personal therapeutic impulses. He develops a series of reaction-formations as a means for tolerating the discrepancy between his patient-need and the necessarily impersonal quality of professional training. He takes on, in the course of his training, a basic conceptual framework about personality which may extend into his concept of himself, and become a limiting factor in growth, both as a person and as a therapist. His intellectual comprehension of the dynamics of behavior and of pathology then become pegs on which he hangs, or categorizes, his deeply personal needs. (*The Roots of Psychotherapy*, by Carl Whitaker and Thomas Malone, p. 145)

The full implications of this argument by Whitaker and Malone took several years to unfold. It did serve at the time, however, to sensitize me to certain processes in my own development, especially the dysfunctions of professionalization, which I might otherwise have been unable to acknowledge. In addition, it allowed me to see the same process at work in my colleagues and students. In miniscule, this process reappears in every sociology department. The introductory course, which draws students into the department as majors, depends heavily on the work of such "popular" sociologists as C. Wright Mills, David Riesman, William H. Whyte, Jr., and others. In doing so it projects an image of sociology that stresses its capacity to provide real insight into the larger sociopolitical work and also into the smaller social worlds in which we all exist. The response of students to this image of sociology would correspond, I suppose, to the therapeutic impulses and the search for self-insight that mark the neophyte psychotherapist. But the budding sociologist, in most departments, finds this syndrome under attack even as an undergraduate. Immediately after the introductory course, with its broadly "generalist" attitudes, he is plunged into rather "rigorous" courses in theory and method which aim at eliminating any infections that the introductory course may have left with him. Classical and social theory, rather than being presented as a living part of the same search for truth about self and society, is usually wedged into courses in the history of sociology, or even worse is presented in a way that shows how modern systematic theorists have subsumed all that is valuable in the work of Marx, Weber, Durkheim, and Simmel among others within currently fashionable structural-functional categories.

My own line of development, as indicated earlier, had been one in which my undergraduate training had encouraged the search for real insight into society and into my own situation. This made the reality shock of graduate school particularly sharp, but it also left me with a far broader sense of the possible varieties of sociological styles to juxtapose to the particular styles being advanced at Columbia. Whitaker and Malone alerted me to the bare possibility that the suppression of sociological impulses in the name of scientific objectivity could serve personal purposes for my teachers and could serve to limit my own growth. It took a much longer time for me to accept the full implications of this position.

V

I shall condense the reflective processes involved in producing *The Eclipse of Community* within a set of categories suggested by the foregoing personal history. I shall try to avoid reproducing the solutions adopted in my book and therefore hope that the interested reader will turn to it for my primary "reflections on community studies." In fact, it contains some secondary reflections, since the epilogue was written two years after the original manuscript. The discussion that follows will fill in some personal contexts and meanings and explore several intellectual issues surrounding the writing of the book.

My interest in community studies began while I was still an undergraduate. Having always lived in a city but having moved within various ethnic and class atmospheres, including second-hand experience with small-town European ghetto life mediated through a transplanted Jewish community, I was afflicted with puzzlement over the ways in which different groups lived. This puzzlement was reinforced by my army experience, which not only exposed me to military life and to Korea but also forced me to spend an uncomfortable six months in the South. The contrast between miners and surface men in the gypsum plant as well as between the plant and the university community, both of which were on my mind in the active sense that I was trying to construct detailed representations of the contrasts, led me to appreciate the achievements of such community ethnographers as Lloyd Warner, the Lynds, and William F. Whyte, whose *Street Corner Society* remained a particular favorite.

At Columbia these "literary" studies were paid little attention as compared with the concern and esteem accorded survey research. My own interest in such studies, however, was bolstered by a seminar taught by Seymour Fiddle which dealt with the methodological complexities of community research. This seminar taught me to appreciate the scientific qualities displayed by good ethnographic field work and reporting. It reinforced my impression, persisting from the gypsum study, that such reporting represented at least as profound a form of objective data as the most ingenious survey. Fiddle's brilliant demonstration of the complexities of community research and his enormous enthusiasm about such studies provided essential inspiration and support for my own evolving attitudes.

Prior to setting to work on codifying community studies, I began a series of studies on problems of work motivation and alienation. These studies included an effort at extracting theories of work motivation and alienation from the classical tradition and linking them together in terms of "propositions about determinate relationships between determinate variables" in the manner adopted by Merton in his essay on the sociology of knowledge. There was also to be a sociophilosophic study of the human meaning of work starting from Marx's conception of alienated labor and class domination in capitalist society. In this framework I continued to work out the problems of combat motivation, and initiated an empirical study of journalism, a profession which was clearly engaged in a direct fashion with problems of objectivity. This project obviously was quite ambitious and each phase of it ran into serious difficulty, but none of the difficulties with the parts ever quite matched the difficulties that arose when I tried to bring the theoretical formulations into line with the empirical studies.

In the first place, my systematic summaries of the classical theories of work motivation and alienation, which placed the complex thinking of such diverse figures as Marx, Weber, Veblen, Durkheim, and many others within a structural-functional context, was so abstract that it sacrificed the distinctive intellectual themes which made each individual theorist powerful and valuable. This experience left me with a permanent distrust of all "translations" of classical sociology into structural-functionalese, whether this be Parsons' collapsing of Weber, Durkheim, and Freud, along with so much else, into a theory of social systems, or the effort at developing a less ideologically slanted "left-revisionist" version of this theory by Merton. Veblen might have been amused to learn that he was really talking about the latent functions of conspicuous consumption but I doubt that Marx would have appreciated Merton's translation of key passages from *Capital* into structural-functionalese. At the time I tended to blame the failure of this systematization on my own lack of systematizing power, but I now doubt that classical social theory can fruitfully be collapsed in this fashion without sacrificing its scope and its power.

The difficulty at the other end with empirical studies of work motivation had similar features. Since many of the empirical studies had focused on manipulating the motives of workers in the interests of management, their integration within a theory that started with Marx's conception of alienated labor was precluded from the outset. And my own study of journalists quickly ran up against all of the difficulties that a study from the outside of a highly literate professional group encounters. In addition, the omnipresent atmosphere generated by survey logic made it almost impossible to acknowledge, no less to generalize, about journalistic patterns from the limited amount of data that could be gathered.

As luck would have it, my first teaching job forced me to undertake a heavy commitment to courses in urban sociology and in sociology of American communities. This redirection of attention forced me back to the community-study literature where I quickly realized my spontaneous interest lay. It allowed me to stop studying work motivation and to start working. The work started with an effort to show how the various community studies could be fitted together both as a mosaic picture of American life and as exemplifications of systematic theory. The initial impetus came from my newly discovered capacity to talk about these studies vividly in the classroom as well as to read them repeatedly with growing excitement. They were teaching me about places where I had been and where I might eventually go. This excitement had the quality of connection to open-ended experience which made extended meditation possible.

The first few years of work were devoted to an exploration of alternatives suggested by my previous training and experience. I started working from the top by trying to extract general propositions about communities from the classical sociologists and then organizing these propositions into a structural-functional theory. Luckily, this process was greatly shortened when I realized that the writings of Robert Park—writings, incidentally, hardly noticed at Columbia when I was a graduate student—seemed to draw together several threads of classical sociology, especially the threads offered by Durkheim and Simmel, within a working theory of urbanization peculiarly suited to the American scene. I almost avoided this recognition because Park's theorizing was profoundly meditative rather than systematic, and his students tended to systematize a fragment of the master's meditations, all too often mistaking their parts, whether it was ecology, demography, the study of disorganization, or the study of urban subcultures, for Park's whole.

Apart from its relatively unsystematic character—and I think multisystematic would be a more appropriate designation—Park's interpretive framework was confusing to me because so much of it seemed based on and peculiarly applicable to the city of Chicago during the period from around 1900 to 1930 when most of the substantive studies were completed. Here, my training in survey method led me to notice that Park's general theorizing was primarily anchored in detailed inquiries into a single city, Chicago. However, my resistance to survey logic led me to wonder if this fact made it necessary to abandon the detailed insights into urban mechanisms and processes which Park and his students provided just because we could not be absolutely certain how representative of American urban processes they might actually be. Having by this time gained a sense of Park's broad range of experience within cities all over the world, and of his capacity to re-present this experience in acute observations and concepts, I felt that some way must be found of incorporating the historical content of Park's observations without sacrificing his important generalizations. In addition, I felt that Park's way of theorizing, despite its lack of structural-functional propositions, had close intellectual affinities with classical sociology since Park, like his teachers, Simmel and James, focused on the perpetual dialectic between individual and community with its human penalties and its human possibilities.

Next came *Middletown,* a study which, like the work of Park, seemed to show deep grasp of the transformations experienced by a single community, but which differed from Park in offering no general interpretive framework. The Lynds had somehow managed to create an intellectual structure which could mediate between the set of experiences with industrialization that any given reader might have had and the set of experiences that they reported as having taken place in Middletown. This communicative structure was effective as shown by the enormous popularity of the book; however, it clearly did not work through abstract theoretical formulations. Actually, it was my reading of *Middletown* that persuaded me to give up the search for a structural-functional theory of community. The Lynds, using a very elementary version of Wissler's distinctions between cultural areas, had succeeded in doing brilliant ethnography and I am not convinced that more recent systematic theories of community emphasizing elaborate functional classifications of institutional structures have gotten significantly further.

Following the lead suggested by my approach to Park's work, but reversing the emphasis, I constructed a set of low-level historical generalizations about the impact of industrialization on institutions and used this to argue that Middletown could profitably be viewed as a case study. By this time I felt far more secure in abandoning the survey-bound requirement of representativeness, because I had begun to understand how case studies could be coordinated to cover a range of situations. I also began to appreciate how much was lost when historical contexts were abandoned in favor of ahistorical generalizations whether these took the form of structural-functional propositions or of survey reports.

My final discovery was that Lloyd Warner's work, properly weighted, could be used to trace the workings of bureaucratization within the same time span covered by the work of Park and the Lynds. With this then, I had an interpretation of the ways in which the processes studied by classical sociology worked themselves out during the early part of the century in American community life. This was quite different from the summaries of contributions to a structural-functional theory of community which my earlier approach had led me to expect, but it seemed in far greater harmony with the style and the substance of classical sociology than a more systematically adequate statement was likely to be. Equally important, such a theory allowed me to codify the substance of the great community studies without losing their human meanings. I was able to place these studies within a larger sociohistorical context.

But this was hardly sufficient to explain modern community life. I wanted a theory that would interpret the evolution of American communities within the context of basic social processes, but the later phases of this evolution concerned me at least as much as the relatively early phases covered by the classic community studies. After all, I was still committed to trying to make sense out of my own experience. Part I of *The Eclipse of Community* involved departures from graduate school expectations about survey logic and systematic theory. It also involved departing from my commitment to joining the great dialogue about Western history, since I was dealing with such a narrow time span and with such a small group of people. In addition, even though I discussed basic social processes, I dealt only with peripheral rather than with central embodiments of these processes. In other words, I was noticeably not writing about either the power élite or the city in history, and these two unwritten books bothered me at least as much as the unwritten systematic and survey books on American communities. One could learn a great deal about what an author does from the books he is consciously, if guiltily, not writing. Chapter 4 contains a great deal of inner dialogue on this matter and can be read as my effort at explaining how I was coming to terms with the demands of history, system, and drama. This coming to terms was always anchored in my respect for the studies themselves, and my growing ability to present their contributions without denying their limits.

The step into Part II is the demand for some kind of total picture of American community types, both as they evolved from the 1920's to the 1960's and as they exist currently. If the theory was to deal with modern communities, then this later evolution had to be charted and the distinguishing human problems of modern communities had to be identified.

The set of fundamental processes taken up in Part I remained somewhat distant from my own personal experience. Chicago of the 1920's, Muncie of the 1920's and 1930's, and Newburyport of the 1930's constituted forms of communal life that antedated my conscious communal participation. I had lived, however, through the last years of the depression, having turned thirteen in 1939, and had spent my childhood in an urban Jewish ghetto of the kind described by Wirth. This last circumstance left me extremely sensitive to both the beauties and the terrors of close-knit traditional communities, and it also left me with both an intense desire for such communal forms and an equally intense dread of them. One could not easily conceive a better formula to nourish a prospective community sociologist.

Part II of *Eclipse* gets much closer to the forms of community with which I did have first-hand contact than does Part I. Each of the five chapters deals with a subcommunity in which I had lived. It was far easier for me to remain detached from the human consequences of industrialization, urbanization, and bureaucratization in Muncie, Chicago, and Newburyport than it was for me to detach myself from the symbolic meanings of the slum, bohemia, the southern community, military communities, and suburbia, simply because each of the latter poses vital personal choices. I did not concentrate on the special personal meanings of each subcommunity taken up in Part II when I began to plan the section and I permitted myself the luxury of assuming that I was dealing almost exclusively with a set of objective problems.

On reflection I feel that I chose the better studies and the more important types of communities. I also find, however, that I was strongly influenced by my own feelings about and experiences with each community in question. This did not necessarily make it impossible for me to present relatively detached case studies of the communities in question, since each analysis was governed largely by the contours of the community which the monograph in question disclosed and by the requirement that the analysis reveal the later workings of urbanization, industrialization, and bureaucratization. In addition, the attitudes of the authors of the studies toward their community sometimes diverged considerably from my own attitudes and provided a major external check.

Let me simply sketch the main issues that underlay my attitudes toward the slum, bohemia, southern castes, military communities, and suburbia. At several points in this essay, I alluded to my early involvement with Orthodox Jewish life. This assumed class overtones since orthodox synagogues in Buffalo were more often lower class, whereas conservative and reformed synagogues served middle-class clients. The neighborhood in which I lived as a child was mixed working and middle class. For complex personal reasons, I symbolically divided the neighborhood into a lower-class segment, which I experienced as being spontaneous and emotionally honest and virile, and a middle-class segment, which I felt to be repressed, dishonest, and effete. This symbolic split manifested itself within my neighborhood, my family, and myself. When I was about ten, my family moved to a dominantly middle-class neighborhood, thus forcing me out of my previous gang associations but still allowing me to associate with the lower-class remnants in the new neighborhood by choosing more delinquent peers as friends, by affiliating with the one orthodox synagogue in the neighborhod, and eventually by electing to attend a distant vocational high school rather than the dominantly middle-class neighborhood high school which stressed college preparation.

Cross-cutting this class symbolism and greatly complicating it was the fact that I reacted against Jewish orthodoxy very early and began to fight my way out of ghetto culture into Western culture. Since I was simultaneously rejecting the middle-class forms in which Western culture tended to present itself, I entered into a series of experimental compromises like vocational schooling, total immersion in literature and music, and finally various kinds and degrees of political radicalism. Even now, despite the abandonment of commitment to orthodox Judaism, or any form of organized religion, when I have occasion to attend conservative or reformed services, the buried orthodox prejudices reappear. I cannot help comparing the devout, embittered, dignified, ironic ghetto Jews whom I knew as a child with their assimilated modern counterparts. The former, bigoted though they may have been in their own way, still knew how to pray, how to handle sacred objects, how to wear prayer shawls, and how to sing, dance, and wail with style. The old men managed somehow to look like old men and not like aging boys.

This is hardly the place to sort out these class and ethnic experiences any further. Their bearing on the themes of Part II should be fairly obvious but let me underscore a few points. In reporting on Whyte's description of Cornerville, I was captured by the central contrast between Doc and Chick, which accurately reflected my own ambivalent relation to lower-class and middle-class culture. In interpreting Greenwich Village, my ambivalent response to avant-garde protest against the middle class was dramatized in terms of Ware's distinction between the authentic Old and the pretentious New Bohemians. There was far less ambivalence in the studies of southern communities, either on my part or on the part of the authors themselves, since the terrible effects of the caste system were visible to all. The discussion of military communities grew out of my surprise at my own eagerness to fight despite real fears and despite profound moral-political doubts about the conduct of World War II. This was my first conscious experience as the object of bureaucratic manipulation and its effects have not yet worn off. Finally, the discussion of suburbia was an outgrowth of my critical response, even to the highest forms of middle-class culture. A search for internal contradictions was all too easily rewarded in the studies by Whyte, by Spectorsky, and especially by Seeley, Sim, and Loosley.

I could easily go on, perhaps endlessly, recounting the personal and symbolic meanings of these communities. The point is simply to suggest the sources of concern and energy that motivated the intellectual operations. Such concern and energy is an essential prerequisite for serious work; the work, however, does not become really serious until the concern is externalized, sources of new information are identified, and a way of finding larger coherent patterns is developed.

A persisting concern in the entire book is the impulse to develop critical concepts of a sort that penetrate beneath commonplace communal self-interpretations to show divergent realities. The point of such unmasking is always expansion of consciousness and communal reorganization on a higher plane, but it can appear to be a kind of compulsive criticism of things as they are. In Part I it was easy to adopt a genuinely dialectical attitude toward the human meanings and human consequences of the fundamental processes. Park was especially helpful in setting this tone since he was so keenly aware of the manifold desirable and undesirable human consequences of urbanization. In Part II, where my own emotional investment was greater, there was more pressure toward unmasking pretenses, especially those of suburbia. It was necessary to develop the argument that, despite the obvious material gains, profound human losses were involved, even in suburbia. In Part III anthropological and psycho-

analytic perspectives are invoked to deepen the total image of communal experience and of communal possibilities in such a way as to
justify my critique of suburbia.

Chapters 10 and 11 of Part III, which present these anthropological
and psychoanalytic perspectives, show my conviction that long-range
interpretations of the forms of human destitution and reconstruction
in modern society depend on humanistic depth of a sort that could
only be obtained from students of man who possessed the broadest
possible perspective. The malaise of the affluent suburb was hardly
obvious, especially since suburbia appeared to offer so many of the
material fulfillments that make up the American dream. I did not
want to render a simple-minded judgment about the diluting of traditional communal patterns because Park had taught me, as had my
experience, that this dilution had desirable as well as undesirable
consequences.

While those chapters were being written, I encountered two anthropologists with a new perspective—Paul Radin and Stanley Diamond—
and indeed Chapter 10 was written for Radin's festschrift, which was
edited by Diamond. The main emphasis of these anthropologists, as
distinct from the structural-functional anthropology which I had
learned earlier, involved viewing primitive existence as a valid form
of existence equal to and in certain ways superior, as in others inferior, to the several forms of civilization in the East and in the West.
Radin showed me how the study of primitive cultures could provide
central clues to the evolution of Greek society and indeed to the evolution of modern Western society. He introduced me to the broadly
historical vision possessed in various versions by several students of
Boaz, especially by Sapir, Lowie, Kroeber, Benedict, and Radin himself. This in turn inclined me toward the kind of philosophical anthropology involving continual meditation upon primitive society,
classical civilization, and modern society practiced by Robert Redfield, Stanley Diamond, and on occasion every anthropologist who
penetrates to the deeper human meanings of the tribe that he studies
and of the world from which he comes. This conception of anthropology led in many directions ranging from the Greek drama and its
interpretation as ritual by Jane Harrison to an intensive study of
Elizabethan society and drama drawing heavily on Francis Fergusson
and others. Some of these seeds are strewn in the chapter but the
fruits are still to be gathered.

The large specific insight that Radin and Diamond supplied was
one that resounded with my own previous experience. No matter
how one might feel about the orthodox Jewish subculture, which I

had caught the tail-end of in my childhood, anyone raised within its purview had some feeling for the ways in which folk or primitive cultures protected and celebrated the phases and transitions marking the life cycle. I was particularly struck by the centrality of the bar mitzvah (confirmation) and the dominance of the old men in the synagogue as analogs to primitive culture, though undeniably of a distant sort. In any event, and perhaps on a still deeper level, the curious mixture of passion and restraint, of bitterness and joy, of irony and innocence, which were given shape in the orthodox community, struck me as strongly resembling the acceptance and integration of ambivalent feelings noted by Meyer Fortes in the long quotation in Chapter 10. Fortes' observation that behavior which would otherwise be the maddest of fantasies or the worst of vices can be transformed into custom and woven into the visible fabric of community's social life points toward the central role of ritual as an individuating force. My association was to the several terms for someone who departs from ordinariness in Yiddish, all of which connote oddness or madness without quite excluding the person so designated, and indeed often including him, in an ironically loving fashion.

We stumble here into questions of great magnitude. I had hoped that I had made it absolutely clear that this search for the emotional virtues of primitive culture did not preclude awareness of its concomitant limitations and that the recognition of such virtues did not constitute advocating a return to the primitive condition, as if any such return were possible. However, this anthropological framework helped me to accommodate another event about which I intend to say little, except to indicate that it has been both profound and protracted. Chapter 11 on psychoanalytic perspectives grew partly out of my own experience with psychotherapy. It stressed the ways in which this relatively recent phenomena in Western society seemed to be an adaptive mechanism for bringing discontinuities in the life cycle that had been ignored or suppressed by the larger society. This lead me to an interpretation of Freud which stressed those aspects of his theorizing about man and society that were compatible with the special attention to security operations and the development of a repertory of communicative styles stressed by Sullivan and with the analysis of identity developed by Erikson.

Chapters 10 and 11 together trace threads through anthropology and psychoanalysis which constitute grounds for the charge most fully developed in Chapter 12 that the dominant forms of community in modern America fail to provide crucial resources for individuation and full human development. Chapter 12 pulls together the several strands of the book in the form of an interpretation of the history of American community development as this was constructed from the community studies and from an interpretation of the crucial problems of suburbia. An effort was made to present the total configuration of American urban subcommunities and to focus on the one, suburbia, that seemed a promising social laboratory. Obviously, other subcommunities could have been selected as crucial and indeed my own research interests have swung back to studying slums, a fact related to recent changes in the total economic picture and their impact on American life. The point of Chapter 12 is that this kind of theorizing very much depends on assessments of the total picture so that events within any particular community or subcommunity are always seen in relation to larger social trends and major events of the decade. It tries to project an image of community sociology that can respond to major trends and changes in community as well as national and international affairs. I tried to suggest the centrality of suburbia during the 1960's as a social laboratory and remain persuaded that it continues to be such. Recent events and studies, however, suggest the urgent need for new research on the culture of poverty. This research should not be segregated from the suburban studies because these latter tell us about the highly precarious nature of the middle-class role playing and help us to understand the serious problems arising when persons reared in the new slum come into contact with the new middle-class world. The point is that both the student of the slum and of the suburb require some sort of *total picture* of the evolution of the American communities and of emerging constellations and converging problems.

The epilogue, written almost two years after the manuscript was completed, continues my meditation on the history, nature, and methodology of community studies. It reflects the sharpening of my awareness that each study discussed necessarily involves the personal qualities and concerns of the investigator at several points. I had developed a way of taking this into account by always commenting on the angle of vision and the social situation of the investigator when discussing the studies themselves. But no amount of account taking could remove personal synthetic elements in research or in reporting, and the presence of these elements rendered the studies themselves as much meditative records as the second-order record of my meditations on them. It now appeared to me that no historical interpretation of the evolution of American communities could be offered which emerging events could not render somewhat irrelevant. And the same held for any systematic interpretation.

Intelligent community sociology now appeared to rest on complex meditation on earlier community forms, on recent social changes, and on the best available frameworks for interpreting these, but, as Park had so cogently insisted, the student of community life must deeply involve himself in the life of a particular community whose problems he takes over and makes his own. His success at making them his own, while still viewing them in larger perspectives, depends very much on his capacity for real attachment as well as for real detachment, the same problem with which I began in my study of the gypsum miners.

The epilogue also registered my discontent with any vision of sociology that did not have room for the substantive ethnographic findings of studies of earlier years. To reject a comprehensive set of theories such as Park offered simply because he never quite settled on a single set of structural-functional propositions was to miss the nature of his contribution. And to reject the Lynd's research because they never offered explicit generalizations about industrialization was to miss the innovations that they made when they constructed literary forms for showing how this vital process affected everyone by tracing its detailed impact in a particular setting. In other words I was here arguing that the current versions of systematic theory and research, which excluded Park, the Lynds, and the other community sociologists from serious attention, were blinding themselves to central strands of American sociology. In addition, I was convinced that these community sociologists, in their own way, had picked up themes that lay at the heart of the classical tradition in European social theory. In fact, I felt that they may have advanced the thinking of this tradition at least as much as did the neat systematic formulations offered by Merton or Parsons or the neat empirical generalizations coming out of survey studies.

VI

So my argument returns to its starting point. I found it as necessary to detach myself from the standards of professional sociology with which I had become deeply involved in graduate school as I had found it necessary to detach myself from the standards of the gypsum miners in order to study their life or to participate in it on my own terms. Writing *The Eclipse of Community* and reflecting on it made me sharply aware of the necessity for choosing which kinds of systematization one will adopt, how much history one will consider, and what kinds of dramatization one will allow when pursuing sociological inquiry.[2] It was absolutely clear that these issues could not be avoided by presenting oneself as a systematic, and therefore scientific, sociologist. The classical sociologists are distinguished by their evolving incorporation of multiple dimensions of history, system, and drama, just as are successful community sociologists. In fact, good sociological work seems to stem from commitment to a peculiar, almost personal, combination of the three which carries forward the kind of inquiry that the sociologist wishes to pursue. And there are as many workable combinations as there are good sociologists.

[2] Further discussion of these choices can be found in my contribution to *Sociology on Trial*, New York: Prentice Hall, 1963 and in a forthcoming book, *The Root Metaphors of Sociology: History System and Drama.*

7

Surrender and Community Study:
The Study of Loma

Kurt H. Wolff

"Loma"

I was in "Loma" in 1940, 1942, 1944, 1948, and 1960. Located in northern New Mexico, Loma is a community—that is, a group of people whose lives are bounded in significant ways by that habitat. For a long time my question has been: what does this mean? More particularly, following my longest and most important stay in Loma, my questions have come to be: what did it mean to study these people? What was the nature of my research, my contact with Loma? What did it mean to collect "field notes"? What was their meaning? Who was I to have gone to Loma, what had I done there, what was I to have done? What had I inquired into? How had I gone about it, how was I to have gone about it?

These are not questions particularly characteristic of the social scientist. The social scientist usually has a definition, if only an operational one, of "community." Typically, what it means to *him* to study a community is scientifically irrelevant although privately it may be relevant; but this does not enter his study. The nature of his study is formulated by the problems, scientific or practical, that he brings to it; so formulated, it defines his contact with the "field"; and to collect "field" notes means to collect material relevant to his research, which is their only meaning.

In the field my own questions only *began* to trouble, fascinate,

Author's note: I wish to record my sincere gratitude to those friends—Jack Behar, Joseph Bensman, Fred H. Blum, Josephine L. Burroughs, Yonina Talmon, and Arthur J. Vidich, colleagues; and Nancy Hahn, Laura Harris, Nancy Howell, Deborah Rothenberg, and Joan Zwebèn, students and former students—who read an earlier draft of this paper and made pertinent comments that encouraged me and helped me much in revising it.

exhilarate, and prod me; there is nothing explicit about them in my notes. The "field," as soon as I saw it, struck me as a landscape such as I had not known before. It was high, calm, yet exciting, with sagebrush rolling wide, rolling up the hills, mesas razed flat, shaking their green brown hues into nothingness buzzing with flowers: purple, blue, lemon tufts in the gray circled by rocky tables. The clear, blue-seamed plain receded in a constant quiver toward the glassy ranges of mountains under the darker blue sky, where shy smoke rose from earthen houses. Life here seemed different and splendid. And I was drawn to the people. The Spanish-speaking ones: the young, alive, beautiful, ugly, endangered; the old, ripe, sad, and slow; those not young, not old, drifting, confused. I was impressed by the two or three Anglo pioneers left, by their sparse looks, their generosity, by the parents of one of them who were in their nineties, by the respect between these old people and the Spanish old people, by the wisdom, I thought, of those everywhere who stayed on the land.

These were the impressions of my first stay. On my second, although I was impressed by the landscape and the people, I invaded the people (or defended myself against them) as a social scientist. I made a house-to-house canvass and presented its results with hardly more than the dead-pan face of a research tradition at its most tepid: location and physical aspects; history; population (marital status, children, origin, mobility, property and income, occupation; education, language, cultural diffusion, housing, health, religion, recreation); outside agencies and institutions operative in Loma; community problems, community consciousness, community stratification.

The aim of my third, longest visit was to develop a method by which "culture patterns" could be established so as to allow another student to go back and check point by point.[1] I found this interesting, though not all-absorbing. What did absorb me, even though I did not so understand it till later, were questions of the nature I mentioned at the beginning of this paper; what I did, at any rate, was to obey my strong need for holding on to all I could possibly keep up with.

. . . I had at once begun to observe and to record my observations, and without any attempt at order or selection. My field notes thus resembled a diary, expanding page by page, immediately typed from short notes, memory, or dictation. As writing accumulated, however, some sort of structuring became imperative: I proceeded to break down my notes by

[1] I formulated my tentative solution as "A Methodological Note on the Empirical Establishment of Culture Patterns," *American Sociological Review*, 10 (1945), pp. 176–184.

topics. I started with this only after having produced about 80 single-spaced pages of typescript; but once I had completed the classification (at a point when the pages had increased to approximately 140–I had continued to write down notes even while going on with the breakdown), I kept it up to date.[2]

It was years before I understood what had happened to me: I had fallen through the web of "culture patterns" and assorted conceptual meshes into the chaos of *love;* I was looking everywhere, famished, with a "ruthless glance."[3] Despite admonitions to be selective and form hypotheses that would tell me what to select, I was not and did not. Another thing I sensed was that I was not content with the probable but wanted to *know;* and I thought I might *know* if, instead of looking for culture patterns, for instance, I looked directly–not through the lens of *any* received notion but the adequate lens that would come out of my being in Loma. "Culture pattern," indeed any conceptual scheme, had come to strike me as something learned *outside* Loma that I would import, impose, and that had been imposed on me. Instead, I was busy, even panicky at times, observing, ruminating, and recording as best I could. Everything, I felt, was important, although the ways in which it was important would yet have to become clear. But then there also was the fear that I should be overwhelmed by the mass of my notes; I could not possibly keep in mind all the veins, lodes, and outcroppings of that growing mountain of typescript.

I came to write three versions of "my study of Loma." The first two were entitled "Loma Culture Change," the second subheaded "A Contribution to the Study of Man"; the third I tentatively called "The Story of Loma." In all three I made use of only part of my field notes, as well as of life histories and compositions by school children,[4] all of which only covered the first two of the seven categories into which I had classified my data. These were "Background Materials" and "Culture Change." By "background materials," I referred to

[2] From a report on how I wrote and ordered my field notes: "The Collection and Organization of Field Materials: A Research Report," *Ohio Journal of Science,* 52 (1952), pp. 49–61 (50); reprinted, slightly altered, in Richard N. Adams and Jack J. Preiss, Eds., *Human Organization Research: Field Relations and Techniques,* Homewood, Ill.: Irwin, 1960, pp. 240–254 (241).

[3] José Ortega y Gasset, *The Revolt of the Masses,* New York: Mentor Books, 1930, p. 115.

[4] The latter two sets of materials are published as "Life Histories of a Spanish-American Man and Two Women," *Microcard Publications of Primary Records in Culture and Personality,* 1:18, 1956, Madison, Wis.; and "School Compositions of 25 Spanish-American Children," *ibid.,* 2:15, 1957.

aspects of a culture that can be grasped as readily understood by the same means as they would be in the study of a culture very similar to that of the student; [that is] those materials which strike the student as not presenting methodological problems;

by "culture change," I referred to

change in culture; [which] presupposes, for its apperception, a conception of the culture under study as different, or as methodologically assumed to be different, from that of the student.[5]

The big break in my preoccupation with Loma came between the first and second versions, for in the meantime I had found a way, which has not let me go, of talking about what had happened in the field—or more accurately, about what reflection on me in the field showed me to have had its beginning there: "surrender." For a long time, I thought that I had "surrendered" to Loma, and my effort in the second and third versions was to accomplish two things in one: to present "surrender" and attendant ideas, and to present the study of Loma, which was entailed by that first presentation—or, rather, which *was* to be, which at all costs *had* to be, so entailed. For I finally realized after my last attempt at the enterprise that I could not possibly succeed; it dawned on me, or I marshaled the courage to admit, that I had *not* surrendered to Loma, nor, of course, had I studied Loma with the idea of surrender in mind. The study, therefore, could be neither an exemplification of surrender nor a test of its idea; it *could* not be entailed by the presentation of this idea. Nevertheless, adumbrations of the idea did go back to the field, as I have tried to indicate and as will become clearer by a discussion of what "surrender" means.

"Surrender" [6]

Its seminal meaning is cognitive love, in the sense in which this is redundant for love. "Surrender" has a military connotation, as well

[5] Both quotations are from "The Collection and Organization of Field Materials," *loc. cit.*, Table 3 (53; reprint, p. 246).
[6] For some descriptions of surrender, see my "Surrender and Religion," *Journal for the Scientific Study of Religion*, 2 (1962), pp. 36–50; or "Surrender as a Response to Our Crisis," *Journal of Humanistic Psychology*, 2 (1962), pp. 16–30; for many more, though under the name of "ecstasy," see Marghanita Laski, *Ecstasy: A Study of Some Secular and Religious Experiences*, London, 1961, esp. Appendix A.

as the sound of passivity, of "giving up." I have therefore thought of other words, such as "abandonment," but this suggests a dissoluteness alien to it; "exposure," but this has a gratuitous ring of exhibitionism; "devotion" or "dedication," but these envisage only an attitude and inappropriately introduce a moral note; "laying oneself open" or "laying the cards on the table," but these, too, convey only part of the meaning—unconditionality or honesty. Thus I have stuck to "surrender." Its meaning of "cognitive love" is seminal because all the other meanings follow from it.[7]   Major among them are: total involvement, suspension of received notions, pertinence of everything, identification, and risk of being hurt.

I can give no excerpts from my field notes that would exemplify or analyze these meanings.   The reason is, as I have said, that I had not surrendered to Loma beyond the low degree of being most tensely alert to what was going on around me; what was going on in myself had not yet begun to announce itself as relevant to my enterprise. Hence there is no record—or at least none that I could present in a brief excerpt—of self-observation which would show involvement, identification, or hurt.   The other two meanings of "surrender"— suspension of received notions and "pertinence of everything"—are illustrated, to an extent, by the effort to have the conceptualization arise from the data and the frenzy of observing whatever came to my attention.   Both characterize all three versions of my study, and both of them I have mentioned already.   Short descriptions of surrender by others—descriptions exemplifying all five of the meanings that I have listed—may be found in the materials cited in note 6; but here I may add a short passage from a manuscript (1950) in the writing of which the very term "surrender" (and the complementary one of "catch," of which more presently) occurred to me for the first time, and which I, indeed, entitled "Surrender and Catch":

When I drove out of the city, I was slowly becoming surprised and frightened. . . . I felt that I was no longer on streets, . . . but in what was the untouched—rocks, creeks, bushes, things unmastered, things staring me in the face . . . I . . . had no scheme at all; . . . I wanted to know. But what? Something of the sort that had been adumbrated to me: that my fear outside the city was the fear of the undefined which I had to learn how to define . . . I thus was in the process of surrender to the other . . . what had guided me while all along I had not been able to say it: the new, the undefined . . . there is no literature that reports what happens when we see a street for the first time, when we meet a new

[7] In articulating them, I have been much helped by David Bakan's (unpublished) "Some Elaborations of the Meaning of the Concept of Surrender" (August 1951).

person, . . . when we travel, when time, or a "point" in time, sinks us, when space, or a place, assaults us, screaming, riddle. I do not mean smells and speculations—there are the noses, brains of poets, writers, philosophers: I mean the surrender which is the catch.

What follows, then, is the result of further reflection.

Total Involvement

In surrender, an individual becomes involved, undifferentiatedly and indistinguishably, with himself, with his act or state, and with his object or partner—just as the lover's "involvement" refers to all three of these: in both cases, differentiation between subject, act, and object disappears. Such involvement does not drive the person who would know into error; for surrender is not fanaticism, dogmatism, giving in to the "need for closure." Love (in contrast to infatuation, which makes one blind) makes one see. Both surrender and love are states of high tension and concentration, undifferentiated states in which "anything can happen"; the outcome or "catch" or yield of surrender (and of love) is unforeseeable.

But from what I said surrender is *not,* it follows that the undifferentiation characteristic of it must be qualified. For surrender also is the state in which one's self is most whole—the state which Hofmannsthal must have had in mind when he wrote: "Where is your Self to be found? Always in the deepest enchantment that you have experienced. The whole soul is never one, save in ecstasy." [8] Perhaps in surrender it is the ego that is suspended, scattered, undifferentiated, while the self is gathered: if there were *only* undifferentiation, there could be no cognitive catch (or the realization of miscarriage) but only blind identification with the moment, only abandon, *not* surrender.

Suspension of Received Notions

In surrender, a person's received notions are suspended, including those that he feels in any way bear on his exploration—for instance, his belief in the plausibility of theories, the appropriateness of concepts, the validity of assumptions and generalizations. In respect to Loma, I have referred to a premonition of this when I mentioned my setting "culture patterns" aside in favor of advocating the emergence of concepts out of the situation or experience, that is, without as yet

[8] Hugo von Hofmannsthal, *Buch der Freunde: Tagebuch-Aufzeichnungen* (1922), in *Selected Prose,* trans. Mary Hottinger and James Stern, intr. Hermann Broch, New York, 1952, p. 356.

seeing it in relation to surrender, of advocating the very idea of suspending received notions. In surrendering, man does not know, and finds it wholly irrelevant to ask, whether whatever it may be he is exploring is something to which received notions are adequate—only his "catch," if anything, will tell him. He is in an "extreme situation"; he cannot distinguish between doubt and certainty, truth and falsehood, fact and theory, hypothesis, metaphor, image, poetry, and other things he ordinarily distinguishes. Above all, he does not know whether he knows, whether he is compelled by forces alien to his concern or whether his necessity is also his freedom; whether, it might be put, he is under duress or under necessity—and this is another way of saying that surrender is a (relatively) undifferentiated state. When some sort of order reappears, he knows that he is emerging from surrender, and as he emerges he tries to recognize the differentiations in the new structure that is his catch.

Pertinence of Everything

Since notions are selective, that is, since they select, to say that in surrender "everything is pertinent" is another way of pointing to the suspension of received notions. All that comes to the surrenderer's attention is pertinent, as everything about his beloved is pertinent to the lover. Again, the great difficulty is to keep pace with "everything" (for instance, all that came to my attention in Loma amounted to almost five hundred single-spaced pages of field notes that I typed in the four and a half months I was there in 1944).

In this exclusive concentration at the moment of surrender, "everything" is pertinent but "all else" disappears. The world, in one process of shrinking and growing, becomes experience in its infinity. The immeasurable quantity of matters that in this supreme concentration vanish for the surrenderer is irrelevant, both for him and for the person who would understand his experience.[9]

Identification

Surrender also means identification with the moment of surrender. "Identification" must be understood (analytically, not psychologically) as the aim of surrender, not as the aim of its "catch." It cannot be the aim of the catch, because if it were, surrender would indeed be *completely* undifferentiated; the surrenderer would not want to know but to identify, become assimilated, go native, or otherwise change.

[9] For to "open up" is too extraordinary beside it. On the self-therapeutic significance of something closely related to surrender, see Joanna Field (pseud.), *A Life of One's Own*, London, Pelican Books, rev. ed., 1952.

Since he wants to know, he must examine his catch so that he can tell others about it; if identification itself were the catch, he could not. The lover must lose himself to find himself, not to lose himself.

Risk of Being Hurt

This last meaning is distinguished from the previous ones in two respects: it characterizes not only surrender but also acting on the insight gained, acting on the catch. And, of course, this risk also attends experiences and activities other than surrender and catch. Still, it *is* a meaning of surrender. Since the surrenderer can and wants to know and change as a result of knowing, he is prepared to sustain injury; and in both surrendering and acting on his catch, he may be hurt in various ways. For instance, my writing and talking about surrender (part of a catch I have been exploring) have alienated some persons from me, and my professional prestige has suffered in their eyes—undoubtedly of more than I know. Yet injury sustained in surrender itself is seen by the surrenderer in its bearing on insight and involvement, for it does not come or threaten to come from any desire to hurt or be hurt. Surrender has nothing to do with sadism or masochism, even though the passive ring of the term might suggest the latter. Here, again, we do well to recall the lover: he, too, is bound to take risks of being hurt in many ways.

Surrender, Community Study, and Social Science

It probably is obvious that the meaning of surrender has come for me to extend far beyond Loma: surrender is a pervasive orientation toward a great many phenomena.[10] Even its brief exposition may suggest its bearing on conceptions of knowledge, love, therapy and other areas of psychology, including sadism, masochism, and identification—hence this interpretation may apply more generally to control; relations among men, and thus social organization; politics; a diagnosis of our time, and thus of history; of social criticism; of other problems of social science and philosophy, including "philosophical anthropology." There are many more—I have hardly begun to inspect the catch, which is the catch of "Loma." The catch *is* unforeseeable; I had thought it would be a "community study."

[10] At the time of this writing I have worked out preliminary articulations in regard to three of them: religion, our crisis, and esthetic experience; for the first two, see the papers cited in note 6; for the last, "Surrender and Aesthetic Experience," *Review of Existential Psychology and Psychiatry*, 3 (1963), pp. 209–226.

Instead, among the contents of the catch are the implications of "surrender" for social science. Let us touch on them on the way to inspecting what they mean for "community study."

The conception of the essential nature of man that corresponds to the idea of surrender is precisely that of his capacity to surrender and catch. On such a view, in order to justify their claim to study man, the social sciences must include this essential nature. Can they do so properly and remain sciences? Must they give up or revise their scientific procedure? Suspending these questions for the moment, it should be clear that on the view here submitted, man, in contrast to all other phenomena in the universe, can be done justice to only by surrender and catch—or "invention" (I shall clarify this term later) —rather than by the customary varieties of describing, defining, or reducing to instances of generalizations. For such modes do not allow man fully to relate to man in his inventiveness as well as inventedness; they do not allow any one of us fully to relate to man, including ourselves. Nor can I in these ordinary modes optimally relate to phenomena attendant on man's, and hence my own, essense: efforts to surrender and catch, the record of such efforts, their occasions, ideas born out of surrender. Thus man in his essence and that which is characteristic of man in his essence are the phenomena we can expect to do justice to only by surrender and catch, by "invention."

Yet surrender, of course, cannot be commanded; it may or may not occur on any occasion. However, if it does not occur on the occasion, say, of a landscape, the landscape is not injured; whereas if it does not occur on the occasion of a person, both that person and the non-surrenderer are hurt, if only in comparison with whom they might have become had it happened. Thus there is continual hurt among human beings, and the desire to reduce it infuses reverence, charity, and faith regarding man and men, and the search for what, at my most honest, I can truly hold about man and men.

This consideration leads from surrender as an individual phenomenon—its only aspect here touched on—to the light surrender may throw on social organization. There are other avenues that also point in this direction. For instance, must I hold that I can accept somebody's ideas as true only if the catch of my surrender to these ideas confirms them—if they are *my* catch? If so, then how is society possible? Or how must social science (and social philosophy) be considered, or reconsidered, in the light of the idea of surrender?

The present paper, we see again, falls into the vast area of the last question. But as I must also say again, it can do no more by way of answering this question—which is little, indeed—than to begin an inquiry into the relevance of surrender for community study. Nevertheless, this inquiry will also throw into relief other aspects of social science.[11]

The view that the capacity to surrender is man's essence implies no neglect of the fact that man has innumerable other characteristics which he shares with animals, organisms, or objects. Indeed, if he did not have such characteristics he would have nothing that he could in any way suspend, overcome, transcend in surrender; surrender takes him beyond only a small part of his vast share, as it were, of his pervasive embeddedness, his deep anchorage. An overwhelming number of the characteristics man shares with other contents of the cosmos by virtue of his also being an object among objects, an organism among organisms, an animal among animals, a social animal among social animals—an overwhelming number of these characteristics enter his social life and thus can become legitimate topics of social-scientific study. Relatively recently, human communities have become such a topic. On the view here submitted, they clearly are, whether as particular communities like Loma, or as types, in whatever sense of this term.

Reflection on my experience with Loma has made me aware of how important it is to relate the assessment of this experience to a far-reaching distinction that I have quite casually used but must now make explicit: the distinction between "surrender" and "surrender to."[12] Surrender is unforeseeable, unpredictable, happens, befalls, whereas surrender-to is concentration, dedication, devotion, attention.

[11] Among contemporary practices of social science familiar to me I am drawn and influenced by Dorothy Lee's (*Freedom and Culture*, Englewood Cliffs, N. J.: Prentice-Hall Spectrum Book, 1959); certain aspects of "action anthropology" (cf. my brief discussions in *Human Organization*, 17 [1958], pp. 23–24, and 18 [1959], pp. 10–12); the phenomenology of Alfred Schutz (*Collected Papers, I, The Problem of Social Reality*, ed. and intr. Maurice Natanson, The Hague: Nijhoff, 1962); and the critical social theory of Herbert Marcuse (*Reason and Revolution* [1941], Boston, 1960; *Eros and Civilization*, Boston: Beacon, 1955; and *One-Dimensional Man: Studies in Advanced Industrial Society*, Boston: Beacon, 1964). It is probably symptomatic of certain aspects of the state of contemporary sociology and of its relation to the society in which we live that Franco Ferrarotti, both in his teaching (University of Rome) and in his writing— see especially "La sociologia come partecipazione" (1960), in his *La sociologia come partecipazione e altri saggi*, Torino, 1961—has come to take and defend a position significantly similar to that of "surrender," even though his and mine have developed quite independently.

[12] This distinction turned out to be essential for a clarification of "esthetic experience" and "esthetic object." Cf. "Surrender and Aesthetic Experience," *op. cit.*, esp. p. 215, and see below.

With surrender it shares involvement, the suspension of received notions, the "pertinence of everything," identification, and the risk of being hurt, but only to the extent that these can be willed or consciously risked. If surrender to unexpectedly grows into the "infinity" of its experience, it becomes surrender (and in retrospect, the occasion of surrender), which has the other meanings mentioned *beyond the degrees anticipated*. That this unforeseeable transformation may occur corroborates the unforeseeableness of surrender itself and the indeterminability of its occasions; at the same time it serves to bring out its distinction from surrender to.

Like everything else a community may of course be the occasion of surrender; its catch, however, being unforeseeable, is foreseeably not a "community study" either. On the other hand, I can *will* to "surrender *to*" a community, wishing to study it as intimately as is compatible with my plan for the result of my experience and exploration to be a study (rather than, say, a novel, philosophical treatise, symphony, painting, feeling). I repeat that it took me a long time to understand that in my own case I had *not* surrendered to Loma. Rather, "Loma" was the occasion of a surrender whose catch, as I suggested a few paragraphs ago, has been the very idea of surrender and its implications.[13]

What is involved in "surrendering to" a community? A person comes to a community with received notions and spontaneously makes use of them for whatever purpose he may wish. If he is a social scientist, he has more or less explicit theories that structure his study. In fact, he may have too many to apply on the occasion; and this occasion may also force him to revise some of them; here arises the danger of revising so much in the direction of the community's own conceptions that he ceases to be a student and "goes native."[14] This is to say that though he may have more notions than he can apply to the study, the community may yet be more of an experience for

[13] With this knowledge, I may yet surrender to my Loma materials and memories and write a book, though it will not be a community study; I may also attempt a community study based on the ideas clarified in the subsequent pages.

[14] On this point, in regard to surrender itself, see pp. 239–240; on "going native" as a problem for anthropologists and students of communities, see Benjamin D. Paul, "Interview Techniques and Field Relationships," in A. L. Kroeber et al., Eds., *Anthropology Today: An Encyclopedic Inventory*, Chicago: University of Chicago Press, 1953, p. 435, and Arthur J. Vidich, "Participant Observation and the Collection and Interpretation of Data," *American Journal of Sociology*, 60 (1955), pp. 356, 357, 358; also Colin M. Turnbull, *The Forest People*, London: Methuen, 1961, p. 209.

him than he can do justice to, no matter how much theory is at his command; he must select.[15]

Communities, like societies or like individuals, institutions, customs, and other social phenomena, are mixed phenomena, reflecting both features attesting to the essence of man and features shared by man with nonhuman contents of the world.[16] Even as a social scientist, however, I may focus only on the latter, undertaking, for instance, a study of transportation, demography, mobility, hygiene, and many other community aspects in their social relevance. In fact, no matter what I study—ecological processes, demographic regularities, conflict, power, in most actual cases social-scientific uniformities of any kind—provided I treat it as an *object,* it is not something exclusive of man but shared by him (or it becomes such by virtue of being studied as an object). For if I relate to phenomena as objects, I am not involved with uniquely human affairs but with candidates for generalizations; I do not suspend received notions on principle and as best I can, but at most selectively, to my intents and purposes. I do not find "everything" pertinent, but only those matters that relate to my more or less

[15] In these formulations, I gratefully acknowledge the stimulation I have received from Joseph Bensman's reflections (in a letter of May 8, 1962) on his experience with "Springdale" (cf. Arthur J. Vidich and Joseph Bensman, *Small Town in Mass Society,* Garden City, N. Y.: Doubleday Anchor Book, 1960). Cf. Vidich, *op. cit.,* p. 359.

[16] In the related Weberian frame of reference, social phenomena involve both "meaningful" and "nonsensical" (*sinnfremde*) factors; in Scheler's likewise, but even more distantly, related terms, both "ideal" and "real" factors. (Max Weber, "The Fundamental Concepts of Sociology" [1911–1913], in *The Theory of Social and Economic Organization,* trans. A. M. Henderson and Talcott Parsons, ed. with an intr. Talcott Parsons, New York: Oxford University Press, 1947, esp. pp. 93–94 [Parsons translates *"sinnfremd"* as "devoid of subjective meaning" (*ibid.,* p. 93 and n. 8)]; Max Scheler, "Probleme einer Soziologie des Wissens," in *Die Wissensformen und die Gesellschaft* [1926], 2nd ed., Bern, 1960, pp. 18–23, 39–51.) The distinction is also related to that between the "unique" and the "general" that I made in "The Unique and the General: Toward a Philosophy of Sociology," *Philosophy of Science,* 15 (1948), pp. 192–210. There even goes a connecting line to Durkheim's dichotomy between the sacred and the profane in his *"homo duplex";* cf. particularly his "The Dualism of Human Nature and Its Social Conditions" (1914), trans. Charles Blend, in Kurt H. Wolff, Ed., *Émile Durkheim, 1858–1917: A Collection of Essays, with Translations and a Bibliography,* Columbus: University of Ohio State Press, 1960, pp. 325–340, esp. 326–330; but there also are profound differences, which, fundamentally, derive from the fact that for Durkheim the central contrast is that between individual and society. (Cf. Edward A. Tiryakian, *Sociologism and Existentialism: Two Perspectives on the Individual and Society,* Englewood Cliffs, N. J.: Prentice-Hall Insight Book, 1962, esp. Chap. 8.)

clearly defined problem, which is largely imported from the outside, rather than emerging from the occasion of the study. I do not "identify" with human affairs in all their height and depth but with subject matter; and I risk being hurt, not in what is essential of man and thus of me, but in my scientific achievement or, if there is physical danger, quite possibly in my very life. In short, I am not fully man who is studying, and it is not fully man I am studying.

What is essential, unique, exclusive of man is that which is universally human. "Man, whoever he may be, when thrown back on what he really is, is thrown back on what he shares with mankind."[17] The essentially or uniquely or transcendingly human (that by which man transcends all other contents of the cosmos) thus is also the universally human, but can be humanly approached only in experience, which is short for the redundant "in experience as unique." This is the sense of suggesting that we can do justice to man in his essence and to that which is characteristic of man in his essence only by surrender and catch, by "invention." It implies that we can do justice to what he shares with other phenomena of the universe only by description, definition, reduction to instances of generalizations, and the like.[18] I have now added that we can do justice to mixed phenomena, social and other, only by "surrendering to" them.[19] Since communities

[17] Wolff, "Surrender and Religion," op. cit., p. 40.
[18] Cf. also Joseph Campbell's interpretation of Paul Radin's use of William James's two types of man, the tough-minded and the tender-minded: "It appears to me that any science that takes into consideration only or even primarily the vulgar, tough-minded interpretation of symbols will inevitably be committed to a study largely of local differentiations, while, on the other hand, one addressed to the views of thinkers will find that the ultimate references of their cogitations are few and of universal distribution": Joseph Campbell, "Primitive Man as Metaphysician," in Stanley Diamond, Ed., Culture in History: Essays in Honor of Paul Radin, New York: Columbia University Press, 1960, p. 381 ff.; also cf. William Earle's conception of philosophy in his "Notes on the Death of Culture" (1958), in Maurice R. Stein, Arthur J. Vidich, and David Manning White, Eds., Identity and Anxiety: Survival of the Person in Mass Society, Glencoe, Ill.: Free Press, 1960, pp. 367–383, esp. 375.
[19] This threefold division of human phenomena—essential, shared, mixed—is relative or subject to, that is, can be superseded by, at least three circumstances. (1) Like the idea of surrender itself, it is relative to history. I have argued the historical relevance of surrender at this time more explicitly in "Surrender as a Response to Our Crisis"; at another time, a different taxonomy may be more urgent or cogent, as it has been in the past. (2) It is relative to surrender (and "surrender to"), whose catch may change it (see below). (3) It is relative to the outcome of an analysis of the relations between surrender and knowledge (see footnote 32), which will have to clarify, among other things, the appropriateness and the relativity of the trichotomy in regard to all possible candidates for cog-

are such mixed phenomena, it follows that both the study and the student of a community must do justice to features essentially human *and* features shared with nonhuman phenomena, because only then is the student true to his task as a student of the phenomenon "community." If, instead of a study, he were to write a novel, poem, or musical composition about the community or paint a picture of it, his obligations would be different, in part because he would focus more on essential human features, on exclusively human meanings, but he would miss part of the community itself. Analogously, if he were to investigate the road system or the age, income, occupational, educational distribution of the resident population, again he would not make a study of all of the community, and, obviously, his obligations would be different yet, in part because he would focus more on the manifestations of features man shares with nonhuman phenomena.[20]

What I have said makes it necessary to clarify the relation between the impossibility of studying something exclusively human as an *object*, and the concept "esthetic *object*": "object," used in the two contexts, has different implications.

In exploring the relation between surrender and esthetic experience, I have come to conceive of "esthetic experience" as "surrender to an esthetic object," such that both experience and object emerge in one process. To experience esthetically is to look at an object directly, to see how in all its individuality, *objectively*, it *is*. The capacity to do so is characteristically human; but, once more, this does not mean that man or a given person is an esthetic object (or an object in any other sense). To put it in the extreme, in the esthetic mode, we may "watch the consummation of some impending catastrophe with the

nition and classes or types of them. Here also belongs the distinction between theoretical (scientific, stipulative, hypothetical, propositional) and practical (existential, experiential, philosophical) knowledge and truth, the occasions on which they are sought and are adequate, and the relations between them (cf. my "The Sociology of Knowledge and Sociological Theory," in Llewellyn Gross, Ed., *Symposium on Sociological Theory*, Evanston, Ill., and White Plains, N. Y., 1959, pp. 579–580; and "On the Significance of Hannah Arendt's *The Human Condition* for Sociology," *Inquiry*, 4 [1961], pp. 77–106).

[20] To avoid possible misunderstandings, what I have said has nothing to do with any distinctions between "unique" and "typical" communities; or between characteristics of all communities as against those of some of them; or between characteristics methodologically construed as shared as against those otherwise found to be shared. Finally, there is nothing in my statements that bears on the proposition that since each community has a unique pattern (whatever its analyst may mean by this), it is this "uniqueness" that all communities share.

marveling unconcern of a mere spectator," [21] but as human beings we come to the rescue, if we can, or suffer; for man, in addition to being capable of surrender and catch, also lives in this world, which, on the occasion just suggested, threatens him—and, thus, us.[22]

"Surrender" is cognitive love, and so is "surrender to," the difference, again, being between cognitive love unexpected and willed. If I surrender to a community or any other social phenomenon, I must as a man and a student eschew two dangers. On the one hand, I must not reduce the community to a case in point, an item more or less exhaustively subsumable under a generalization, an element in a theory; if I do, it means that I have treated it exclusively as an object, have neglected the essentially human features at work in it and in myself. On the other hand, I must not forget that I am a student who wants to find out and report as objectively as he can; if I do forget this, it means either that I was not in control of my private needs or wishes (in a fashion that ranges all the way from simple distortion to "getting lost," in various senses of this term, including the "going native" mentioned before) or that I have neglected features at work in it that man shares with nonhuman phenomena, including nature, other communities, society at large, the economy, the political situation, the historical moment—and, once more, in myself.[23]

It will be noted that I have just used the word "object" in a third sense: I said that as a student I want to find out and report as objectively as I can. This is "objective" in the sense predicated of science and the scientist, which means procedure that is both as specifically and as fully adequate to the object studied as possible; [24] the clear grasp of the object must not be interfered with by what can only be

[21] Edward Bullough, quoted in Wolff, "Surrender and Aesthetic Experience," op. cit., p. 11.

[22] In other words, the idea of surrender is not an otherworldly, but a this-worldly, idea.

[23] This paragraph, it seems to me, translates the several problems of the community student mentioned in the passage to which footnote 15 is attached into two basic ones.

[24] The following observation by Hannah Arendt (The Human Condition, Chicago: University of Chicago Press, 1958, p. 271, n. 26) may suggest the need for efforts toward a more objective understanding of objectivity in this sense than is customarily considered: "When it [the Royal Society] was founded, members had to agree to take no part in matters outside the terms of reference given it by the King, especially to take no part in political or religious strife. One is tempted to conclude that the modern scientific ideal of 'objectivity' was born here, which would suggest that its origin is political and not scientific."

shortcomings on the student's part (biases, ignorance, etc.).[25] To
attain such objectivity requires detachment from both subject matter
and self; involvement with either makes attainment difficult or impossible.[26]

I seem to have fallen into two contradictions which I must try to
resolve. One contradiction is between the advocacy, in the study of
mixed phenomena, of objective procedure, and surrender to them,
which sounds incompatible with objectivity. The second contradiction is between my characterization of a community as a mixed phenomenon, as a certain kind of object, and my claim that in surrender
notions such as the classifications of objects are, or should be, suspended.

The first apparent contradiction (between the simultaneous insistence on the objective study of mixed phenomena and surrender to
them) is resolved by recognizing that, for their optimal cognition,
mixed phenomena objectively require—are the kinds of objects that
require—surrender to them. The very act of surrendering to them
will determine which of their elements or aspects is done justice to
by the usual procedures of science (such as describing, defining, reducing to instances of generalizations), and which, instead, by procedures that will emerge from the encounter with them.[27]

[25] The question whether such objectivity is possible is, of course, an old one.
Within social science, one of its most important recent expressions occurs in
the so-called sociology of knowledge. Is the scheme of knowledge, in Werner
Stark's formulation, "*adequatio* [sic] *intellectus et rei*, the correspondence between
thought and thing [object] . . . [or] *adequatio* [sic] *intellectus et situs*, a correspondence between thought and thinker, or rather, thought and location in social
space and time": Werner Stark, *The Sociology of Knowledge: An Essay in Aid
of a Deeper Understanding of the History of Ideas*, Glencoe, Ill.: Free Press,
1958, p. 180.

[26] In the discussion of objectivity in social science, "understanding" (*Verstehen*),
which at least does not wholly eschew involvement, has, very broadly speaking,
remained problematical as a road to objectivity. The considerable literature on
it and attendant topics and problems goes back, above all, to Wilhelm Dilthey
and Max Weber. Among the most important discussions are those by Alexander
von Schelting (*Max Webers Wissenschaftslehre*, Tübingen, 1934, esp. pp. 325–
329) and Talcott Parsons (*The Structure of Social Action*, New York, McGraw-
Hill, 1937, esp. pp. 588–589, 635–637).

[27] Approximate names for the former are "background materials" (cf. the passage
to which note 5 refers) or "the general"; an approximate name for the latter
is "the unique" (cf. "The Unique and the General" cited in note 16). For
excellent instructions on how to go about studying what I would call "background
materials" of a community, see Robert K. Lamb, "Suggestions for a Study of
Your Hometown" (1952), in Adams and Preiss, Eds., *op. cit.*, Chap. XXXI,
pp. 422–430.

The second apparent contradiction (between the simultaneous insistence on a definition of "community" and on the suspension of
definitions) is resolved by recognizing that the definition of "community" as a mixed phenomenon requiring surrender to it is, like all
definitions, heuristic.   That is, it is modifiable by acting on it, by
"surrendering to" the "mixed phenomenon": [28] it is a notion received
in order to be suspended,[29] which it could not be if it were not available as a received notion.[30]   It follows that the richer the arsenal of
received notions available for testing in surrendering to an object of
study or in examining the catch, the more closely is truth approximated and the more pervasive and "relatively absolute" [31] is that

[28] This propositional skeleton is fleshed by Maurice R. Stein (*The Eclipse of
Community: An Interpretation of American Studies,* Princeton, N. J.: Princeton
University Press, 1960, p. 319).   The community sociologist, Stein writers,
"literally creates the picture of the community while he writes his book. Naturally, this creative process involves exploring the irrational self-images and
community images held by his subjects, along with the objective structures that
his scientific framework and observational stance enable him to discern. Finally,
what he finds and what he reports is determined as much by his sympathetic
and experiential limits as by anything else. The quality of the study hinges
largely upon his capacity to broaden these limits so as to comprehend human
behavior which expresses meanings that he ordinarily would not entertain in his
personal world. In doing and synthesizing the study, he dissolves the boundaries of his old self and recreates new boundaries simultaneously with his creation
of a new and more accurate image of the community." (The last two sentences
are italicized in the original.)

[29] This suggests another reminder of Max Weber: this time, his characterization
of science, where "each of us knows that what he has accomplished will be anti-
quated. . . . That is the fate to which science is subjected; it is the very *meaning*
of scientific work, to which it is devoted in a quite specific sense. . . . Every
scientific 'fulfilment' raises new 'questions'; it *asks* to be 'surpassed' and out-
dated. . . . Scientific works . . . will be surpassed scientifically—let that be repeated—for it is our common fate and, more, our common goal. We cannot
work without hoping that others will advance further than we have. In principle,
this progress goes on ad infinitum." "Science as a Vocation" (1918), in *From
Max Weber: Essays in Sociology,* trans., ed., and with an introduction by H. H.
Gerth and C. Wright Mills, New York: Oxford University Press, 1946, p. 138.

[30] Of course, it could be a notion contained in the catch, as has been true in my
own case, where the idea of social phenomena, including communities, as mixed
phenomena is part of the catch of surrender on the occasion of Loma (cf. the
end of the first paragraph of this section and the passage to which note 13 is
attached).

[31] Cf. my "A Preliminary Inquiry into the Sociology of Knowledge from the
Standpoint of the Study of Man," *Scritti di sociologia e politica in onore di Luigi
Sturzo,* Vol. III, pp. 615–616.

truth.[32] Furthermore, unlike surrender, which, we must recall, is un-foreseeable and "amethodical" in its essence, "surrender to" can be a method—and, of course, I here advocate it as a method. As a method it is characterized by openness toward its origin, that is, toward questioning, doubting, suspending, and abandoning itself in favor of such other cognitive modes as may emerge in its practice; hence it "is self-correcting and, therefore, in the spirit, of the essence, of knowledge." [33]

I may put my advocacy in a different frame of reference: I can say that the result of the study of "mixed phenomena," including com-munities, should be true not only scientifically, factually, theoretically, but also existentially. This implies the assumption of two kinds, or two meanings, of truth. The first, scientific truth, is theoretical, rela-tive; the second, existential truth, is absolute—also philosophical, artis-tic, poetic, if you will. The first

has nothing to do with the things of the world as they exist in themselves. According to the other definition, "truth" is first and foremost an attribute of *existence*, and only secondarily of *discourse*. One *is* or *is not* in the Truth; and one's possession of Truth depends on being in communion with a reality which "is" or embodies truth.[34]

[32] But there is the important proviso that this proposition holds subject to the nature of the received notions (their cognitive appropriateness and power, their psychological suspendability, etc.). The analysis of the relation between kinds of received notions and truth attained on their suspension, however, belongs in an inquiry into the relations between surrender and knowledge, the relevance of surrender for knowledge, including scientific knowledge generally and social-scientific knowledge in particular. This analysis may also be phrased as that of the relation between kinds of received notions ("knowledge," error, belief, superstition, etc.) and chances of new knowledge. (An important source for such an inquiry because, among other reasons, of its conception of scientific knowledge, is Michael Polanyi, *Personal Knowledge: Towards a Post-Critical Philosophy*, Chicago: University of Chicago Press, 1958. Cf. [p. 64]: "personal knowledge in science . . . commits us, passionately and far beyond our compre-hension, to a vision of reality. . . . Like love, to which it is akin, this commit-ment is a 'shirt of flame,' blazing with passion and, also like love, consumed by devotion to a universal demand. Such is the true sense of objectivity in science. . . ." Also cf. John R. Seeley, "Psychoanalysis: Model for Social Science," in Hendrik M. Ruitenbeek, Ed., *Psychoanalysis and Social Science*, New York: Dutton Paperback, 1962, pp. 102–111.)
[33] "Surrender and Religion," *op. cit.*, p. 43.
[34] Paul Kecskemeti, Chapter I: Introduction, in Karl Mannheim, *Essays on the Sociology of Knowledge*, ed. by Paul Kecskemeti, London: Rutledge and Kegan Paul, 1952, p. 15; quoted in my "The Sociology of Knowledge and Sociological Theory," p. 580; cf. the end of note 19.

No matter how elliptic and preliminary this is, it is all that I can say here on the question whether, on the view submitted, the social sciences can remain sciences while being concerned with man. It is a large question that needs separate treatment (see note 32). The point of view that I advocate as proper in respect to mixed phenomena is itself mixed, scientific *and* existential; and at this juncture, the question of its articulation must remain the task of each study that adopts it.[85]

Probing Some Community Studies

I shall now examine some community studies with regard to the extent to which and the sense in which they do right by man in his essence, what he shares with nonhuman phenomena, and the mixture of these two features that characterize communities, as I have argued. I can, of course, only submit some impressions and examples.

(1) My most general impression is that the majority of at least American community studies I directly or indirectly know fall in the second category. That is, they focus on features man shares with nonhuman phenomena, in the sense of either not questioning or only refining the author's received approach to his undertaking, or being interested in generalizable aspects of his subject matter at the expense of the effort to understand the community under study in its uniqueness (including even the uniqueness resulting from the unique configuration of generalizable features).[36] If this impression is correct, it is not difficult to account for it, although accounting, of course, does not demonstrate that the accounting is correct. Above all, there is the pervasive tendency of American sociology to be a generalizing enterprise, detached, "value-free," thus to prove its scientific character; and this tendency, in turn, partly reflects even more widely diffused, defensive Western tendencies such as the near-monopoly of control as the relation to the world (which I shall point to in discussing the "irony of 'surrender'") and the near-reduction of the

[85] One illustration of this task, specifically in reference to communities, is the delineation of the community under study.

[36] Such aspects range all the way from those chosen for their "newsworthiness" or "human interest" to those of theoretical significance. One of the more solid bases of my impression is work in the early 1940's on a community bibliography for 1930–1941, resulting in a collection of 2670 titles by 1999 authors dealing with 804 different places and classified, in addition, under 627 topical headings (cf. Kurt H. Wolff and Walter T. Watson, "Practicability of a Community Bibliography," ms.).

meaning of "total" to that of terror (which I shall mention in connection with "total experience"—for both, see the section entitled "The Critical Import of 'Surrender'").[37]

(2) My second impression is that there is a very much smaller number of studies, almost all of them stemming from anthropologists rather than sociologists, that are stronger in their insistence on man's essential features than on those he shares with other phenomena of the cosmos, including the fact that the community studied is embedded in the world. They exhibit this characteristic either (a) in their attention to what happens to the author himself in the field, or (b) in their effort to present as palpably as possible individuals encountered in the communities explored. Some examples may help clarify this impression.

(a) I point to the following books: [38] Cornelius Osgood, *Winter;* Colin M. Turnbull, *The Forest People;* Elenore Smith Bowen, *Return to Laughter;* Claude Lévi-Strauss, *World on the Wane;* and Gregory Bateson, *Naven.*[39]

Osgood's volume is a description of the author's stay during a winter almost twenty-five years previously at Great Bear Lake, Northwest Territories, "one of the coldest places on earth" (p. 8). *Winter* is not a community study by the author's intent, but the people with whom he was in contact do form a community, especially while they are almost marooned in the long cold months. The foreword to the book promises far more self-analysis and attendant analyses of the author's relations with these people than the book contains; the situation, however, in which he found himself and with which he came to terms raises important questions about man's adaptability and strength and about ranges of relations to other men.

Turnbull achieves his aim, "to convey something of the lives and feelings of a people who live in a forest world [Pygmies in the northeast corner of the Congo], something of their intense love for that world, and their trust in it" (p. vii). The author is more nearly

---

[37] For an illuminating interpretation of major community studies in this country in various perspectives based on a historical-diagnostic approach and moving toward a "dramatic" conception of community study (and sociology more generally), see Stein, *The Eclipse of Community, op. cit.* The quotation in note 28 will suggest something of its nature.

[38] In choosing the sequence in which I comment on them, I venture to indicate my assessment of the order of the increasing relevance of their more or less explicit contributions to our understanding of various aspects of "community."

[39] Osgood: New York, Norton, 1953; Turnbull, *op. cit.* (in note 14); Bowen: New York, 1954; Lévi-Strauss (1955): trans. John Russell, London, Hutchinson, 1961; Bateson: Cambridge, 1936 (2nd ed., Stanford, 1958).

emerging from his straightforward, lively, accurate narrative than engaging in self-analysis (as is more characteristic of Bowen and Lévi-Strauss); and the nature of his report does not appear problematic to him (as it does to Bowen). There are occasional reflections of the sort illustrated by the passage referred to in note 14.

Bowen's work is best characterized by what she writes in the "Authors' Note," placed at the beginning:

All the characters in this book, except myself, are fictitious in the fullest meaning of that word. I know people of the type I have described here; the incidents of the book are of the genre I myself experienced in Africa. Nevertheless, so much is fiction. I am an anthropologist. The tribe I have described here does exist. This book is the story of the way I did field work among them. The ethnographic background given here is accurate, but it is neither complete nor technical. When I write as a social anthropologist and within the canons of that discipline, I write under another name. Here I have written simply as a human being, and the truth I have tried to tell concerns the sea change in oneself that comes from immersion in another and savage culture.

There are two points of interest. One is the author's statement that she has written fiction, although she does not explain why; and the book, for that matter, reads like a description of what happened to her and to the people she associated with, to some of whom she came quite close. The second point is the contrast she makes between herself as an anthropologist and "simply as a human being"; writing as a human being, she took a fictitious name, reserving her real one for her identity as an anthropologist. The book contains many observations on how her experiences in the field changed her; one example (p. 270) must do:

I had held that knowledge is worth the acquisition. I had willingly accepted the supposition that one cannot learn save by suppressing one's prejudices, or, at the very least, holding them morally in abeyance [that is, suspending received notions]. The trouble lay in my careless assumption that it would be only my "prejudices" that were to be involved, and never my "principles" [an additional part, perhaps a deeper layer, of the received notions were questioned]—it had never occurred to me that the distinction between "prejudice" and "principle" is itself a matter of prejudice [that is, is received also and calls for suspension in certain situations].

But such observations were apparently relevant to the pseudonymous author of fiction, an anonymous human being, not to the anthropologist; she drew no consequences, or at least does not report them, from the fact that she had to question the received distinction between the two.[40]

Lévi-Strauss's book is a mixture of intellectual autobiography, travelogue, ethnography (of the Caduveo, the Bororo, the Nambi-kwara, and the Tupi-Kawahib in the interior of Brazil), and reflection arising from these and going beyond them into very broad questions. These reflections are scattered throughout the book but are concentrated in the last three chapters (Part IX). An earlier section, in which Lévi-Strauss recalls a sea voyage, contains this passage (p. 66):

Many years have passed, and I don't know if I could recapture that early state of grace. Could I re-live those moments of fever when, note-book in hand, I would jot down, second by second, phrases evocative of the evanescent and constantly renewed forms before me? It's a gamble that still fascinates, and I'm often tempted to begin it all over again.

This is one of many passages attesting to his readiness to look afresh, to suspend received notions, for, he writes elsewhere in the book, the "darkness in which we grope our way is too intense for us to hazard any comment on it"—yet: "we cannot even say that it will last forever" (p. 248). "What lay behind those confused appearances," Lévi-Strauss asks, "which are everything and nothing at one and the same time? . . ."

I turned a prosecutor's eye upon the enormous landscape, narrowing it down to a strip of clayey river-marge and a handful of grasses: nothing, there, to prove that when I next raised my eyes to the world about me I should not find the Bois de Boulogne stretched out all around that insig-nificant patch of ground. Yet that same ground was trodden daily by the most authentic of savages, though Man Friday's print had yet to be found there. (p. 327)

---

[40] The contrast between professional and human being is often noted, more or less explicitly, in the literature on field work, and, particularly, participant ob-servation. See several papers in Adams and Preiss, *op. cit.*, esp. those by Rosalie Hankey Wax (Chaps. VIII and XIV) and Arthur Vidich and Joseph Bensman (Chap. XVI). The contrast is made explicit as between two roles, both of which can and should be used in the service of research, by Morris S. Schwartz and Charlotte Green Schwartz in their "Problems in Participant Observation," *American Journal of Sociology*, 60 (1955), pp. 343–353, esp. pp. 347, 349, and by Morris S. Schwartz in his "On Being a Social Scientist in a Mental Hos-pital" (chapter in a forthcoming book on social science and medicine, Robert Rapoport and Robert Wilson, Eds.).

For the anthropologist, time in the field is indeed

a time, above all, of self-interrogation. Why did he come to such a place? With what hopes? And to what end? What *is*, in point of fact, an anthropological investigation? Is it the exercise of a profession like any other, differentiated only by the fact that home and office-laboratory are several thousand miles apart? Or does it follow upon some more radical decision—one that calls in question the system within which one was born and has come to manhood? (p. 374)

Those questions are similar to those that arose for me, too, as I reported in the very beginning of this paper. Nevertheless, for Lévi-Strauss they seem to have been much less significant in revising his conception and practice of anthropology than they have come to be for my relation to the world and some of its parts, such as social science and the study of communities.

Less also, I suspect, than for Bateson,[41] who has turned to quite other preoccupations since he published *Naven* in 1936, a book in which the author himself, along with his subject matter, one might almost say, is transformed into theory. Although such a theory[42] arose from Bateson's puzzlement over a highly circumscribed phenomenon—the ceremony that gives the book its title, taking place between the *wau* (mother's brother) and his *laua* (sister's child) among the Iatmul in New Guinea—it is comprehensive enough to be applicable to a wide range of social phenomena.[43] The basic aim of this theory—the effort to grasp a culture as comprehensively and intimately as is compatible with communicability and generalizability—

[41] Also cf. Bateson's subsequent paper, "Experiments in Thinking about Observed Ethnological Material," *Philosophy of Science,* 8 (1941), pp. 53–69.
[42] On which see my "A Critique of Bateson's *Naven,*" *Journal of the Royal Anthropological Institute,* 74 (1944), pp. 59–74.
[43] In this respect (though hardly otherwise), *Naven* resembles Godfrey and Monica Wilson's *The Analysis of Social Change: Based on Observations in Central Africa* (Cambridge, 1945). As the title suggests, the analysis of change in a particular area and specifically of three groups (the Nyakyusa [South Tanganyika], the people of Ngonde [Nyasaland], and a "semi-detribalized urban group" [p. 2] in Northern Rhodesia) gives rise to a generalized theory of social change. As the title also indicates, however, this is not a community study, and furthermore, we learn hardly anything about the authors' involvement and change except in their theorizing, detached from its experiential ground; in Bateson's case, this process goes considerably further to the point where the author is "transformed" into his theory (and in this sense, perhaps, can be said to re-emerge); also note the subtitle of *Naven: A Survey of the Problems suggested by a Composite Picture of a New Guinea Tribe drawn from Three Points of View.*

is served by the considerable inventory of concepts and their inter-relations that the author finds it necessary to develop.

A clue to what I mean by "transformation into theory" is furnished by Bateson's insistence that his problem was how to come to terms with "anthropological material." "The writing of this book"—so begins the "Epilogue," [44] that is, the "Narrative of the writer's analysis of methods" (p. xvii)—"has been an experiment, or rather a series of experiments, in methods of thinking about anthropological material" (p. 257); and five years after *Naven* appeared, he wrote a paper (cited in note 41), "Experiments in Thinking about Observed Ethnological Material." That is to say, the relevance of what is observed is transformed into theoretical relevance, and the relevance of the observer into theoretical interest. Even the field worker's confusion has a purely theoretical meaning; when he writes, "I did not clearly see any reason why I should enquire into one matter rather than another" (p. 257), there is no affective or interactive component in his meaning: interaction and affect are limited for him to interaction with and affect for cognitive problems, although they are more purely limited and more passionate, more unconditional within these limits than anywhere else in a community study that I know of. It is as if Bateson's humanity was absent from relations with the people he lived with and studied and had been wholly absorbed in his burning theoretical concern. But why this "zoning" of humanity? Bateson parallels those methodologists of science who advocate the replacement of causal analysis by mathematical functions, but in so doing, as Robert M. MacIver has suggested,[45] far from eliminating the principle of causality, they unwittingly vindicate it, for they display it at work in their own mind, causally arguing as they do that it should be banned from the world outside.

I commented on these five books only, of course, as examples of community studies which "are stronger in their insistence on man's essential features than on those he shares . . . , including the fact that the community studied is embedded in the world" and which "exhibit this characteristic . . . in their attention to what happens to the author himself in the field." I tried to show something of the degrees and modes of this attention; I can only add, for the reader to check, that in general they focus on *culture* and hardly touch on the im-

---

[44] It would be highly instructive to compare this with William Foote Whyte's "On the Evolution of Street Corner Society," Chap. 1 in this book; also cf. Whyte's "Interviewing in Field Research," Chap. XXVII, pp. 352–374, in Adams and Preiss, *op. cit.*

[45] Cf. Robert M. MacIver, *Social Causation*, Boston, Ginn, 1942, pp. 48–56.

SURRENDER AND COMMUNITY STUDY 257

pingement of technological, economic, political, historical circumstances on that culture, on those communities, on their inhabitants.
This feature will stand out more clearly if the reader thinks for a
moment of such studies, so contrasting in this respect, as Godfrey and
Monica Wilson's (see note 43) or, in the United States, Vidich and
Bensman's *Small Town in Mass Society* (see note 15)—to cite only
two out of a much larger number.[46]

(*b*) A similar strength and a similar weakness are shown by those
inquiries that excel "in their effort to present as palpably as possible
individuals encountered in the communities explored." Here two
books will have to do for several others; both are by Oscar Lewis—
again an anthropologist: *Five Families* and *The Children of Sanchez*.[47]

Five Families, Oscar Lewis writes,

has grown out of my conviction that anthropologists have a new function
in the modern world: to serve as students and reporters of the great mass
of peasants and urban dwellers of the underdeveloped countries who constitute almost eighty per cent of the world's population (p. 1).

Thus, Lewis's enterprise (as well as that of *The Children of Sanchez*
—Sanchez's is one of the families presented in the first volume) seems
to be the outcome of a historical diagnosis; but I place it in the
second category of this brief survey (works that focus on "man's
essential features") rather than in the first (works that "focus on
features man shares with nonhuman phenomena") for two reasons.
One reason is that the author must have gone far toward surrendering
to the families he describes and to the people he lets describe themselves. The other is that *Five Families* is the study of these families
"as a whole . . . through detailed observation of a typical day" (p. 4)
in their lives. Neither fiction, like Bowen's book, nor "conventional
anthropology," it is "ethnographic realism, in contrast to literary
realism" (p. 5): the days are real and the people are real, but Lewis

---

[46] Or Laurence Wylie's *Village in the Vaucluse*, Cambridge, Mass.: Harvard
University Press, 1957, and more generally, his "Social Change at the Grass
Roots," in Stanley Hoffmann, Charles P. Kindleberger, Laurence Wylie, Jesse R.
Pitts, Jean-Baptiste Duroselle, Francois Goguel, Eds., *In Search of France*, Cambridge, Mass.: Harvard University Press, 1963, pp. 159–234, 418–422. Also cf.,
e.g., Bert E. Swanson, Ed., *Current Trends in Comparative Community Studies*,
Kansas City, Community Studies, Inc., 1962.
[47] Oscar Lewis, *Five Families: Mexican Case Studies in the Culture of Poverty*
(1959), New York: Science Editions, 1962 (I am using this latter, paperback,
edition); *The Children of Sanchez: Autobiography of a Mexican Family*, New
York: Basic Books, 1961.

himself is wholly absent, far more even than Bateson is in *Naven*, by which its author is absorbed, as I have tried to argue. This absence obscures Lewis's procedure, despite his seemingly explicit account of it:

Although the controlled laboratory procedures of small-group studies . . . were not possible, these case studies give a camera-like view of the movements, conversations, and interactions that occurred in each family during one day. Of necessity this meant the reporting of some pedestrian details as well as severe restraint in manipulating the data to sharpen interest or to reveal the "essence" of the lives. Some selection of data had to be made to avoid repetition and insignificant events, but approximately ninety per cent of all the recorded data has been retained. To give more depth and meaning to the studies, descriptions of the characters and of their homes and autobiographical material, in flashbacks, have been added (p. 6).

Lewis thus tells us what he has and has not done with the data, but we are left in the dark, as we are in the novelist's work, because we do not see him dealing with the "data," as we see Osgood, Bowen, Turnbull, Lévi-Strauss, and Bateson (all of whom write in the first person). Yet Lewis's book is not fiction; "ethnographic realism," as I understand it, is somewhere between the novelist's comparatively pure *making* and either the interaction with subject matter of the scientist or theorist such as Bateson (to stick with our limited collection only) [48] or the interaction with self and people met that we found in Bowen and Lévi-Strauss. Substantively, "ethnographic realism" strikes me as the effort to restrict fiction to the imagery suggested by the actual data, which means, of course, that it is neither art nor science (as Lewis himself says) and, although plausible and palpable, impossible to locate precisely between the two.

Similarly for *The Children of Sanchez*: "In preparing the interviews for publication," Lewis writes (p. xxi), "I have eliminated my questions and have selected, arranged, and organized their [the interviewees'] materials into coherent life stories." Again the author is absent, which here means in particular that we do not know how much of what the children of Sanchez say was stimulated by his questions.[49]

[48] Cf. Lewis's own, pre-"ethnographic-realist," more "conventional-anthropological" "Controls and Experiments in Field Work," in Kroeber et al., Eds., *op. cit.*, pp. 452–475.

[49] It is only fair to say that Lewis invites colleagues interested "in the raw materials" to consult his taped interviews (p. xxi); I am talking about the book alone.

The first group of books focused on culture, whereas Lewis's focuses on families and individuals, and in all of them we learn a great deal about the subject focused on. As to our way to community, it is simple description of community in Osgood and Turnbull; in addition to this, self-reflection and description of persons in Bowen and Lévi-Strauss; analysis of culture in Bateson; in Lewis (except for his own introductions—"The Setting," pp. 1–19, in *Five Families*, and "Introduction," pp. xi–xxxi, in *The Children of Sanchez*—some pages of which overlap in the two books), it is entirely the actions and statements of the protagonists. And despite the first sentence of *Five Families*, which I have quoted, Lewis's studies, too, fall short on an analysis of the embeddedness of the community in the world: he himself would have had to supply it since the people portrayed are far less capable of it; but he is not there. Once more, comparison with either the Wilsons or Vidich and Bensman will make my point.

(3) My third and last impression is the deepest of all, but it comes from only one book: *Let Us Now Praise Famous Men*, by James Agee and Walker Evans.[50] It is the closest I know of surrender to a community, although not even this book quite follows my model, as I shall try to show. It is written in surrender and it is the catch of surrender which unexpectedly occurred on the occasion of "field work" consequent on a magazine assignment to do a report on white share-croppers. And indeed one thing that can be said about the book, although it is a wholly inadequate characterization, is that it is a study of three "poor white" tenant families, the Rickettses, the Woodses, and the Gudgers. The way Agee felt about his enterprise is far more telling:

Beethoven said a thing as rash and noble as the best of his work. By my memory, he said: "He who understands my music can never know unhappiness again." I believe it. And I would be a liar and a coward and one of your safe world if I should fear to say the same words of my best perception, and of my best intention.

And he adds: "Performance, in which the whole fate and terror rests, is another matter" (p. 16).

His business, he finds, "is beyond my human power to do" (p. 110);

I shall not be able so to sustain it, so to sustain its intensity toward this center of human life, so to yield it out that it all strikes inward upon this center at once and in all its intersections and in the meanings of its inter-relations and interenhancements: it is this which so paralyzes me: yet one can write only one word at a time, and if these seem lists and inventories merely, things dead unto themselves, devoid of mutual magnetisms, and if they sink, lose impetus, meter, intension, then bear in mind at least my wish, and perceive in them and restore them what strength you can of yourself: for I must say to you, this is not a work of art or of entertainment, nor will I assume the obligations of the artist or entertainer, but is a human effort which must require human co-operation (p. 111).

The parts of the book dealing with matters that community studies also deal with—"Money," "Shelter," "Clothing," "Education," "Work" —here are the catch of surrender, the capture of the describable world; Agee calls them "Some Findings and Comments" (pp. 115–348). Compare one of his many inventories of objects, for example, those on "The Mantel" (pp. 172–173), with very similar ones to be found in Lewis's *Five Families* ("The Gomez Family," p. 91; "The Gutierrez Family," pp. 132–134), and Lewis's passages, despite their formal similarity, appear so different from Agee's as skill is from invention or appropriateness from necessity.

These matters, and what we learn about the people Agee describes, longs for, and falls in love with, qualify the book as a community study, although it also is one of mankind as a community, with this spot in Alabama its locale, for Agee and his people are more than anything else exemplifications of man; their lives, exemplifications of human life. But to say this is to disqualify the book as an optimal community study: features man shares with nonhuman phenomena are defined out of Agee's approach. A second objection is Agee's obtrusiveness, which is as inappropriate to his book as is Lewis's absence to Lewis's. In Agee there is something of guilt and the craving for redemption, which romanticizes his sharecroppers, dehumanizing them into angels living in shacks of beauty (pp. 202–204), and which makes him despair of the word to capture and convey the world, seducing him into sheer celebration and worship (the poem, p. 74; Matthew 5: 1–12, pp. 81–82; Psalms 43: 1–5, p. 360; The Lord's Prayer, p. 439; and as if to legitimate his attitude of worship, "Let Us Now Praise Famous Men" [Ecclesiasticus, XLIV], p. 445).

The whole book is dominated by its author's extraordinary experience.[51] At the end, Agee feels, perhaps, ready to begin (p. 471),

---

[51] The only other piece of writing I know of that comes anywhere near Agee's in rendering such an experience of "cognitive love" for other people is a piece of "library research": the unpublished paper for the B.A. with honors in social relations by Paul Riesman, *Freedom, Being, and Necessity: A Study of the Eskimos in Their World* (Harvard University, 1960); see particularly Part I, "I Try to Be an Eskimo."

and there are at least three previous beginnings beyond the fact that the volume starts on page i:

[1] But there must be an end to this: a sharp and clean silence: a steep and most serious withdrawal: a new and more succinct beginning. ("Colon," p. 99)

[2] To come devotedly into the depths of a subject . . . : Let me hope in any case that it is something to have begun to learn. . . . By what kind of foreword I can make clear some essential coherence in it, which I know is there, balanced of its chaos, I do not yet know. But the time is come when it is necessary for me to say at least this much: and now, having said it, to go on, and to try to make an entrance into this chapter, which should be an image of the very essence of their lives: that is, of the work they do ("Work," p. 319). [And after two pages:] But I must make a new beginning (p. 321).

[3] Finally, "Inductions" (that is to say, leadings-into, beginnings):

I remember so well, the first night I spent under one of these roofs: We know you already, a little, some of you, most of you . . .
Down in front of the courthouse Walker [Evans] had picked up talk with you, Fred, Fred Ricketts (it was easy enough to do, you talk so much; you are so insecure, before the eyes of any human being); and there you were, when I came out of the courthouse, the two of you sitting at the base of that pedestal wherefrom a brave stone soldier, frowning, blows the silence of a stone bugle searching into the North. . . . (p. 361).

Thus Agee had to let his book stand as a series of beginnings followed by fragments: this is the extent of his emergence from surrender, of his achieving his catch. Its greatness is its failure as a community study: a community is a *mixed* phenomenon.

My impressions and brief glances at examples have made it clear to me—and I naturally hope to the reader—what I mean by a community study, and that I know of none to which I could point, saying: this is it. I am less surprised by this than confirmed—and eager to attempt one, now that I have learned from Loma and my notions attendant on it, in order to find out what surrendering to a community may be like and what it may lead to.

The Critical Import of "Surrender"

I conclude taking a different and vaster perspective. I have discussed surrender in this paper looking from the inside out. Now I move outside: I place myself into our time and look at surrender from there, pointing to its irony and to the meanings of "invention" and "total experience."

The Irony of "Surrender"

This is the opposition of the idea of surrender to our official contemporary Western, and potentially worldwide, consciousness, in which the relation to the world is *not* surrender but mastery, control, efficiency, manipulation. Such a relation, furthermore, is "virile" rather than womanly. A nonvirile, and in this sense womanly, relation is another polemical connotation of "surrender," for we tend to think of woman, not of man, as surrendering, as giving; and of man, if he does surrender, as forfeiting his virility. Among other implications, "surrender" thus has both a political and a sexual one, and much of the thrust of either lies in its combination with the other.

"Invention"

"Invention" is synonymous with "catch." But as "surrender" has a feminine ring, "invention" has a masculine one. Yet to "invent," that is, "to come into," most poignantly in the tabooed word "come," has a bisexual flavor; it is the same that "surrender" intends, even though it does not have the meaning in linguistic custom.

This suggests a comparison of the term with a related one, "breakthrough," and two connotations of "break-through." The first connotation is that of triumph or conquest, namely, of what, in the environment or in the person himself, would obstruct surrender. The second is that of victory over restrictions, of the breaking down of the wall, of this or that prohibition, claim, requirement, demand; of saying yes where the nonself, the other-than-self, says no, and no where it says yes; of the experience of "Lift up your heads, O ye gates; even lift them up, ye everlasting doors; and the King of glory shall come in."[52]

"Invention," nevertheless, *has* a masculine bias, as compared to the bisexuality of "surrender" or "break-through," the love that precedes it. A clue to a reason for this lies in the very synonymity of "invention" and "catch," the *result* of surrender, surrender transformed, love transformed, into the *object* "catch" or "invention." If surrender is being, its transformation into a result, into an object, partakes of *making*. If it is *thinking* (to use a distinction made and made much of by Hannah Arendt[53])—and we must recall the affective component of thinking—then to catch or invent also and necessarily partakes of

---

[52] Psalms 24: 7.
[53] In *The Human Condition*.

communicating. But to make, communicate, and engage in such closely related activities as organizing (if only "organizing my thoughts"), presenting, clarifying, fashioning, polishing, and the like, are, as Arendt points out, essentially the activities of *homo faber*—who in Western history has above all been a man. "Invention" and "catch" do indeed belong to the same image of man against whose mastering, controlling, manipulatory aspects surrender and its name argue. They do not, however, and probably cannot, argue against the universally human source of the phenomenon to which they refer: making; whatever else men and women have always and everywhere done, they have *made* things (and each other).

"Total Experience"

We have seen that the military connotation of "surrender" implies a polemic against the contemporary consciousness of control. Similarly, in "total experience," a synonym of "surrender," the association of "total" with "totalitarianism" is directed *against* totalitarianism, which is so intimately related to that consciousness. Nor do such other predicates of "experience" as "crucial," "germinal," or "peak" [54] convey either this polemic or one of the salient characteristics of total experiences, their undifferentiatedness, their suspension of all previous classification. Hence the name.

Just as our official consciousness is opposed to surrender as the relation to the world, so it also has all but lost any meaning of "total" or "absolute" except as terror [55]—first in our memories as the terror of totalitarianism, then as that of the thermonuclear bomb. Total experiences, and their name which proclaims them, oppose to such terror, to such nightmares of totality, an image of man for whom the absolute is not only terror but also home, for whom "extreme situation" calls forth not only his death but also his greatness.

[54] Abraham H. Maslow, *Toward a Psychology of Being*, New York: Van Nostrand Insight Book, 1962, esp. Chaps. 6 and 7.
[55] Cf. my "Sociology and History; Theory and Practice," *American Journal of Sociology*, **65** (1959), p. 38.

Part Three

Public Responses
to the Community Study

8

Problems in the Publication
of Field Studies

Howard S. Becker

The Problem

Publication of field research findings often poses ethical problems. The social scientist learns things about the people he studies that may harm them, if made public, either in fact or in their belief. In what form and under what conditions can he properly publish his findings? What can he do about the possible harm his report may do?

Although many social scientists have faced the problem, it seldom receives any public discussion. We find warnings that one must not violate confidences or bring harm to the people one studies, but seldom a detailed consideration of the circumstances under which harm may be done or of the norms that might guide publication practices.

Let us make our discussion more concrete by referring to a few cases that have been discussed publicly. Most thoroughly discussed, perhaps, is the "Springdale" case, which was the subject of controversy in several successive issues of *Human Organization.*[1] Arthur Vidich and Joseph Bensman published a book—*Small Town in Mass*

[1] The discussion of the Springdale case began with an editorial, "Freedom and Responsibility in Research: The 'Springdale' Case," in *Human Organization,* **17** (Summer 1958), pp. 1–2. This editorial provoked comments by Arthur Vidich and Joseph Bensman, Robert Risley, Raymond E. Ries, and Howard S. Becker, *ibid.,* **17** (Winter 1958–1959), pp. 2–7, and by Earl H. Bell and Ure Bronfenbrenner, *ibid.,* **18** (Summer 1959), pp. 49–52. A final statement by Vidich appeared in *ibid.,* **19** (Spring 1960), pp. 3–4. The book whose effects are discussed is Arthur Vidich and Joseph Bensman, *Small Town in Mass Society,* Princeton, N. J.: Princeton University Press, 1958.

Author's note: I am indebted to Blanche Geer, William Kornhauser, and Arthur Vidich for their comments on an earlier version of this paper.

Society—based on Vidich's observations and interviews in a small, upstate New York village. The findings reported in that book were said to be offensive to some of the residents of Springdale; for instance, there were references to individuals who, though their names were disguised, were recognizable by virtue of their positions in the town's social structure. Some townspeople, it is alleged, also found the "tone" of the book offensive. For instance, the authors used the phrase "invisible government" to refer to people who held no official position in the town government but influenced the decisions made by elected officials. The implication of illegitimate usurpation of power may have offended those involved.

Some social scientists felt the authors had gone too far, and had damaged the town's image of itself and betrayed the research bargain other social scientists had made with the townspeople. The authors, on the other hand, felt they were dealing with problems that required discussing the facts they did discuss. They made every effort to disguise people but, when that was impossible to do effectively, felt it necessary to present the material as they did.

In another case John F. Lofland and Robert A. Lejeune [2] had students attend open meetings of Alcoholics Anonymous, posing as alcoholic newcomers to the group. The "agents" dressed in different social-class styles and made various measurements designed to assess the effect of the relation between the social class of the group and that of the newcomer on his initial acceptance in the group. Fred Davis [3] criticized the authors for, among other things, failing to take into account the effect of publication of the article on the attitudes of A. A. toward social science in view of its possible consequences on the A. A. program. (A. A. groups might have refused to cooperate in further studies had the authors reported, for instance, that A. A. groups discriminate on the basis of social class. That their finding led to no such conclusion does not negate Davis' criticism.)

Lofland [4] suggested in reply that the results of the study were in fact not unfavorable to A. A., that it was published in a place where A. A. members would be unlikely to see it, and, therefore, that no harm was actually done. Julius Roth,[5] commenting on this exchange,

[2] John F. Lofland and Robert A. Lejeune, "Initial Interaction of Newcomers in Alcoholics Anonymous: A Field Experiment in Class Symbols and Socialization," *Social Problems*, 8 (Fall 1960), pp. 102–111.

[3] Fred Davis, "Comment," *Social Problems*, 8 (Spring 1961), pp. 364–365.

[4] John F. Lofland, "Reply to Davis," *ibid.*, pp. 365–367.

[5] Julius A. Roth, "Comments on Secret Observation," *Social Problems*, 9 (Winter 1962), pp. 283–284.

noted that the problem is not unique. In a certain sense all social science research is secret, just as the fact that observers were present at A. A. meetings was kept secret from the members. He argued that we decide to study some things only after we have been in the field a while and after the initial agreements with people involved have already been negotiated. Thus, even though it is known that the scientist is making a study, the people under observation do not know what he is studying and would perhaps (in many cases certainly would) object and refuse to countenance the research if they knew what it was about.

When one is doing research on a well-defined organization such as a factory, a hospital, or a school, as opposed to some looser organization such as a community or a voluntary association, the problem may arise in slightly different form. The "top management" of the organization will often be given the right to review the social scientist's manuscript prior to publication. William Foote Whyte describes the kinds of difficulties that may arise.

I encountered such a situation in my research project which led finally to the publication of *Human Relations in the Restaurant Industry*. When members of the sponsoring committee of the National Restaurant Association read the first draft of the proposed book, some of them had strong reservations. In fact, one member wrote that he had understood that one of the purposes of establishing an educational and research program at the University of Chicago was to raise the status of the restaurant industry. This book, he claimed, would have the opposite effect, and therefore he recommended that it should not be published. In this case, the Committee on Human Relations in Industry of that university had a contract guaranteeing the right to publish, and I, as author, was to have the final say in the matter. However, I hoped to make the study useful to the industry, and I undertook to see what changes I could make while at the same time retaining what seemed to me, from a scientific standpoint, the heart of the study. . . . The chief problem seemed to be that I had found the workers not having as high a regard for the industry as the sponsoring committee would have liked. Since this seemed to me an important part of the human relations problem, I could hardly cut it out of the book. I was, however, prepared to go as far as I thought possible to change offensive words and phrases in my own text without altering what seemed to me the essential meaning.[6]

It should be kept in mind that these few published accounts must stand for a considerably larger number of incidents in which the

[6] William Foote Whyte, *Man and Organization: Three Problems in Human Relations in Industry*, Homewood, Ill.: Irwin, 1959, pp. 96–97.

rights of the people studied, from some points of view, have been infringed. The vast majority of such incidents are never reported in print, but are circulated in private conversations and documents. In discussing the problem of publication I am, somewhat ironically, often prevented from being as concrete as I would like to be because I am bound by the fact that many of the cases I know about have been told me in confidence.

Not much is lost by this omission, however. Whether the institution studied is a school for retarded children, an upper-class preparatory school, a college, a mental hospital, or a business establishment, the story is much the same. The scientist does a study with the cooperation of the people he studies and writes a report that angers at least some of them. He has then to face the problem of whether to change the report or, if he decides not to, whether to ignore or somehow attempt to deal with their anger.

Conditions Affecting Publication

Fichter and Kolb have presented the most systematic consideration of ethical problems in reporting.[7] They begin by suggesting that several conditions, which vary from situation to situation, will affect the problem of reporting. First, the social scientist has multiple loyalties: to those who have allowed or sponsored the study, to the source from which research funds were obtained, to the publisher of the research report, to other social scientists, to the society itself, and to the community or group studied and its individual members. These loyalties and obligations often conflict. Second, the group under study may or may not be in a position to be affected by the published report. A historical study, describing the way of life of a people who never will have access to the research report, poses few problems, whereas the description of a contemporary community or institution poses many. Third, problems arise when the report analyzes behavior related to traditional and sacred values, such as religion and sex, and also when the report deals with private rather than public facts. Fourth, when data are presented in a statistical form, the problem of identifying an individual does not arise as it does when the mode of analysis is more anthropological.

Fichter and Kolb distinguish three kinds of harm that can be done

[7] Joseph H. Fichter and William L. Kolb, "Ethical Limitations on Sociological Reporting," *American Sociological Review*, 18 (October 1953), pp. 96–97.

by a sociological research report. It may reveal secrets, violate privacy, or destroy or harm someone's reputation.

Finally, Fichter and Kolb discuss four variables that will affect the social scientist's decision to publish or not to publish. First, his conception of science will affect his action. If he regards social science simply as a game, he must protect the people he has studied at any cost, for his conception of science gives him no warrant or justification for doing anything that might harm them. He will feel a greater urgency if he believes that science can be used to create a better life for people.

The social scientist's decision to publish will also be affected by his determination of the degree of harm that will actually be done to a person or group by the publication of data about them. Fichter and Kolb note that there is a difference between imaginary and real harm and that the subjects of studies may fear harm where none is likely. On the other hand, it may be necessary to cause some harm. People, even those studied by social scientists, must take responsibility for their actions; a false sentimentality must not cause the scientist to cover up that responsibility in his report.

Fichter and Kolb further argue that the scientist's decision to publish will be conditioned by the degree to which he regards the people he has studied as fellow members of his own moral community. If a group (they use the examples of Hitler, Stalin, Murder Incorporated, and the Ku Klux Klan) has placed itself outside the moral community, the social scientist can feel free to publish whatever he wants about them without worrying about the harm that may be done. They caution, however, that one should not be too quick to judge another group as being outside the moral community; it is too easy to make the judgment when the group is a disreputable one: homosexuals, drug addicts, unpopular political groups, and so on.

Fichter and Kolb conclude by suggesting that the urgency of society's need for the research will also condition the scientist's decision to publish. Where he believes the information absolutely necessary for the determination of public policy, he may decide that it is a lesser evil to harm some of the people he has studied.

Although the statement of Fichter and Kolb is an admirable attempt to deal with the problem of publication, it does not do justice to the complexities involved. In the remainder of this paper I will first consider the possibility that the relationship between the social scientist and those he studies contains elements of irreducible conflict. I will then discuss the reasons why some reports of social science research do not contain conflict-provoking findings. Finally, I will suggest some possible ways of dealing with the problem.

Before embarking on the main line of my argument, I would like to make clear the limits of the area to which my discussion is meant to apply. I assume that the scientist is not engaged in willful and malicious defamation of character, that his published report has some reasonable scientific purpose, and therefore do not consider those cases in which a scientist might attempt, out of malice, ideological or personal, to destroy the reputation of persons or institutions. I further assume that the scientist is subject to no external constraint, other than that imposed by his relationship to those he has studied, which would hinder him in reporting his results fully and freely. In many cases this assumption is not tenable. Vidich and Bensman argue [8] that a researcher who does his work in the setting of a bureaucratic research organization of necessity must be unable to report his results freely; he will have too many obligations to the organization to do anything that would harm its interests in the research situation and thus cannot make the kind of report required by the ethic of scientific inquiry. Although I do not share their belief that bureaucratic research organizations necessarily and inevitably restrict scientific freedom, this result certainly occurs frequently. (One should remember, however, that the implied corollary of their proposition—that the individual researcher will be bound only by the ethic of scientific inquiry—is also often untrue. Individual researchers on many occasions have shown themselves to be so bound by organizational or ideological commitments as to be unable to report their results freely.) In any case my argument deals with the researcher who is encumbered only by his own conscience.

The Irreducible Conflict

Fichter and Kolb seem to assume that, except for Hitler, Stalin, and others who are not members of our moral community, there is no irreconcilable conflict between the researcher and those he studies. In some cases he will clearly harm people and will refrain from publication; in others no harm will be done and publication is not problematic. The vast majority of cases will fall between and, as men of good will, the researcher and those he studies will be able to find some common ground for decision.

[8] Arthur Vidich and Joseph Bensman, "The Springdale Case: Academic Bureaucrats and Sensitive Townspeople," in this book, pp. 345–348.

But this analysis can be true only when there is some consensus about norms and some community of interest between the two parties. In my view that consensus and community of interest do not exist for the sociologist and those he studies.

The impossibility of achieving consensus, and hence the necessity of conflict, stems in part from the difference between the character- istic approach of the social scientist and that of the layman to the analysis of social life. Everett Hughes has often pointed out that the sociological view of the world—abstract, relativistic, generalizing— necessarily deflates people's view of themselves and their organiza- tions. Sociological analysis has this effect whether it consists of a detailed description of informal behavior or an abstract discussion of theoretical categories. The members of a church, for instance, may be no happier to learn that their behavior exhibits the influence of "pattern variables" than to read a description of their everyday be- havior which shows that it differs radically from what they profess on Sunday morning in church. In either case something precious to them is treated as merely an instance of a class.

Consensus cannot be achieved also because organizations and com- munities are internally differentiated and the interests of subgroups differ. The scientific report that pleases one faction and serves its interests will offend another faction by attacking its interests. Even to say that factions exist may upset the faction in control. What upsets management may be welcomed by the lower ranks, who hope the report will improve their position. Since one cannot achieve consensus with all factions simultaneously, the problem is not to avoid harming people but rather to decide which people to harm.

Trouble occurs primarily, however, because what the social scien- tist reports is what the people studied would prefer not to know, no matter how obvious or easy it is to discover. Typically, the social scientist offends those he studies by describing deviations, either from some formal or informal rule, or from a strongly held ideal. The deviations reported are things that, according to the ideals of the people under study, should be punished and corrected, but about which, for various reasons that seem compelling to them, nothing can be done. In other words the research report reveals that things are not as they ought to be and that nothing is being done about it. By making his report the social scientist makes the deviation public and may thereby force people to enforce a rule they have allowed to lapse. He blows the whistle both on those who are deviating but not being punished for it and on those who are allowing the deviation to go unpunished.[9] Just as the federal government, by making public the list of persons to whom it has sold a gambling-tax stamp, forces local law-enforcement officials to take action against gamblers whose existence they have always known of, so the social scientist, by calling attention to deviations, forces those in power to take action about things they know to exist but about which they do not want to do anything.

Certain typical forms of blowing the whistle recur in many studies. A study of a therapeutic organization—a mental hospital, a general hospital, a rehabilitation center—may show that many institutional practices are essentially custodial and may in fact be antitherapeutic. A study of a school reveals that the curriculum does not have the intended effect on students, and that many students turn out to be quite different from what the members of the faculty would like them to be. A study of a factory or office discloses that many customary practices are, far from being rational and businesslike, irrational and wasteful. Another typical situation has already been mentioned: a study reveals that members of the lower ranks of an organization dislike their subordinate position.

Nor is this phenomenon peculiar to studies that depend largely on the techniques of anthropological field work, though it is probably most common among them. Any kind of social science research may evoke a hostile reaction when it is published. Official statistics put out by communities or organizations can do this. For example, remember the indignation when the 1960 Census revealed that many major cities had lost population, the demands for recounts by Chambers of Commerce, and so on. By simply enumerating the number of inhabitants in a city, and reporting that number publicly, the Bureau of the Census deflated many public-relations dreams and caused a hostile reaction. The statistics on admissions and discharges to hospitals, on salaries and similar matters kept by hospitals and other institutions can similarly be analyzed to reveal great discrepancies, and the revelation can cause much hostile criticism. The results of survey research similarly can cause trouble as, for instance, when a survey of students reveals that they have reactionary political or cultural attitudes. A program of testing can produce the same result by showing that an organization does not recruit people of as high a caliber as it claims, or that a school does not have the effect

[9] I have discussed the role of the person who makes deviation public, the rule enforcer, at some length in *Outsiders: Studies in the Sociology of Deviance*, New York: Free Press of Glencoe, 1963, pp. 155–163.

on its students it supposes it has. Any kind of research, in short, can expose a disparity between reality and some rule or ideal and cause trouble.

That the sociologist, by publishing his findings, blows the whistle on deviance whose existence is not publicly acknowledged may explain why the poor, powerless, and disreputable seldom complain about the studies published about them. They seldom complain, of course, because they are seldom organized enough to do so. Yet I think further reasons for their silence can be found. The deviance of homosexuals or drug addicts is no secret. They have nothing to lose by a further exposure and may believe that an honest account of their lives will counter the stereotypes that have grown up about them. My own studies of dance musicians and marihuana users bear this out.[10] Marihuana users, particularly, urged me to finish my study quickly and publish it so that people could "know the truth" about them.

It may be thought that social science research exposes deviations only when the scientist has an ax to grind, when he is particularly interested in exposing evil. This is not the case. As Vidich and Bensman note:

One of the principal ideas of our book is that the public atmosphere of an organization or a community tends to be optimistic, positive, and geared to the public relations image of the community or the organization. The public mentality veils the dynamics and functional determinants of the group being studied. Any attempt in social analysis at presenting other than public relations rends the veil and must necessarily cause resentment. Moreover, any organization tends to represent a balance of divergent interests held in some kind of equilibrium by the power status of the parties involved. A simple description of these factors, no matter how stated, will offend some of the groups in question.[11]

Unless the scientist deliberately restricts himself to research on the ideologies and beliefs of the people studied and does not touch on the behavior of the members of the community or organization, he must in some way deal with the disparity between reality and ideal, with the discrepancy between the number of crimes committed and the number of criminals apprehended. A study that purports to deal with social structure thus inevitably will reveal that the organization

---

[10] The studies are reported in Becker, Outsiders, op. cit., pp. 41–119.
[11] Vidich and Bensman, "Comment," op. cit.

or community is not all it claims to be, not all it would like to be able to feel itself to be. A good study, therefore, will make somebody angry.

Self-censorship: A Danger

I have just argued that a good study of a community or organization must reflect the irreconcilable conflict between the interests of science and the interests of those studied, and thereby provoke a hostile reaction. Yet many studies conducted by competent scientists do not have this consequence. Under what circumstances will the report of a study fail to provoke conflict? Can such a failure be justified?

In the simplest case, the social scientist may be taken in by those he studies and be kept from seeing the things that would cause conflict were he to report them. Melville Dalton states the problem for studies of industry.

In no case did I make a formal approach to the top management of any of the firms to get approval or support for the research. Several times I have seen other researchers do this and have watched higher managers set the scene and limit the inquiry to specific areas—outside management proper—as though the problem existed in a vacuum. The findings in some cases were then regarded as "controlled experiments," which in final form made impressive reading. But the smiles and delighted manipulation of researchers by guarded personnel, the assessments made of researchers and their findings, and the frequently trivial areas to which alerted and fearful officers guided the inquiry—all raised questions about who controlled the experiments.[12]

This is probably an uncommon occurrence. Few people social scientists study are sophisticated enough to anticipate or control what the researcher will see. More frequently, the social scientist takes himself in, "goes native," becomes identified with the ideology of the dominant faction in the organization or community and frames the questions to which his research provides answers so that no one will be hurt. He does not do this deliberately or with the intent to suppress scientific knowledge. Rather, he unwittingly chooses problems that are not likely to cause trouble or inconvenience to those he has found to be such pleasant associates. Herbert Butterfield, the

[12] Melville Dalton, *Men Who Manage: Fusions of Feeling and Theory in Administration*, New York: Wiley, 1959, p. 275.

British historian, puts the point well in his discussion of the dangers of "official history." He talks of the problems that arise when a government allows historians access to secret documents.

A Foreign Secretary once complained that, while he, for his part, was only trying to be helpful, Professor Temperley (as one of the editors of the British Documents [On the Origins of the War of 1914]) persisted in treating him as though he were a hostile Power. Certainly it is possible for the historian to be unnecessarily militant, and even a little ungracious in his militancy; but what a satisfaction it is to the student if he can be sure that his interests have been guarded with unremitting jealousy! And if we employ a watchdog (which is the function the independent historian would be expected to perform on our behalf), what an assurance it is to be able to feel that we are served by one whom we know to be vigilant and unsleeping! The ideal, in this respect, would certainly not be represented by the picture of a Professor Temperley and a Foreign Secretary as thick as thieves, each merely thinking the other a jolly good fellow; for the historian who is collecting evidence—and particularly the historian who pretends as an independent authority to certify the documents or verify the claims of the government department—must be as jealous and importunate as the cad of a detective who has to find the murderer amongst a party of his friends. One of the widest of the general causes of historical error has been the disposition of a Macaulay to recognize in the case of Tory witnesses a need for historical criticism which it did not occur to him to have in the same way for the witnesses on his own side. Nothing in the whole of historiography is more subtly dangerous than the natural disposition to withhold criticism because John Smith belongs to one's own circle or because he is a nice man, so that it seems ungracious to try to press him on a point too far, or because it does not occur to one that something more could be extracted from him by importunate endeavor. In this sense all is not lost if our historian-detective even makes himself locally unpopular; for (to take an imaginary case) if he communicates to us his judgment that the Foreign Office does not burn important papers, the point is not without its interest; but we could only attach weight to the judgment if he had gone into the matter with all the alertness of an hostile enquirer and with the keenly critical view concerning the kind of evidence which could possibly authorise a detective to come to such a conclusion. And if an historian were to say: "This particular group of documents ought not to be published, because it would expose the officials concerned to serious misunderstandings," then we must answer that he has already thrown in his lot with officialdom—already he is thinking of their interests rather than ours; for since these documents, by definition, carry us outside the framework of stories somebody wants to impose on us, they are the very ones that the independent historian must most desire. To be sure, no documents can be published without laying many people open to grievous misunderstanding. In this connection an uncommon significance must attach therefore to the choice of the people who are to be spared. The only way to reduce misunderstanding is to keep up the clamour for more and more of the strategic kinds of evidence. . . .[13]

It is essential for everybody to be aware that the whole problem of "censorship" to-day has been transformed into the phenomenon of "auto-censorship"—a matter to be borne in mind even when the people involved are only indirectly the servants of government, or are attached by no further tie than the enjoyment of privileges that might be taken away. It is even true that where all are "pals" there is no need for censorship, no point where it is necessary to imagine that one man is being overruled by another. And in any case it is possible to conceive of a State in which members of different organizations could control or prevent a revelation with nothing more than a hint or a wink as they casually pass one another amidst the crowd at some tea-party.[14]

Although Butterfield is speaking of the relations of the social scientist to a national government, it takes no great leap of imagination to see the relevance of his discussion to the problem of the sociologist who has studied a community or organization.

Finally, even if he is not deceived in either of the ways so far suggested, the social scientist may deliberately decide to suppress conflict-provoking findings. He may suppress his findings because publication will violate a bargain he has made with those studied. If, for example, he has given the subjects of his study the right to excise offensive portions of his manuscript prior to publication in return for the privilege of making the study, he will feel bound to honor that agreement. Because of the far-reaching consequences such an agreement could have, most social scientists take care to specify, when reaching an agreement with an organization they want to study, that they have the final say as to what will be published, though they often grant representatives of the organization the right to review the manuscript and suggest changes.

The social scientist may also suppress his findings because of an ideological commitment to the maintenance of society as it is now constituted. Shils makes the following case.

Good arguments can be made against continuous publicity about public institutions. It could be claimed that extreme publicity not only breaks the confidentiality which enhances the imaginativeness and reflectiveness

[13] Herbert Butterfield, "Official History: Its Pitfalls and Criteria," in his *History and Human Relations*, London: Collins, 1951, pp. 194–195.
[14] *Ibid.*, pp. 197–198.

necessary for the effective working of institutions but also destroys the respect in which they should, at least tentatively, be held by the citizenry.[15]

He believes that the first of these considerations is probably correct and thus constitutes a legitimate restriction on scientific inquiry, whereas the second, although not entirely groundless ethically, is so unlikely to occur as not to constitute a clear danger.

It is only in the case of deliberate suppression that an argument can be made, for in the other two cases the scientist presumably reports all his findings, the difficulty arising from his failure to make them in the first place. I will discuss the problem of the research bargain in the next section, in the context of possible solutions to the problem of publication. It remains only to consider Shils' argument before concluding that there is no reasonable basis for avoiding conflict over publication by failing to include the items that will provoke conflict.

Shils rests his case on the possibility that the publicity generated by research may interfere with the "effective working of institutions." When this occurs the scientist should restrict his inquiry. We can accept this argument only if we agree that the effective working of institutions as they are presently constituted is an overriding good. Shils, in his disdain for the "populistic" frame of mind that has informed much of American sociology (his way of characterizing the "easy-going irreverence toward authority" and the consequent tendency to social criticism among social scientists), is probably more ready to accept such a proposition than the majority of working social scientists. Furthermore, and I do not know that he would carry his argument so far, the right of public institutions to delude themselves about the character of their actions and the consequences of those actions does not seem to me easily defended.

Possible Solutions

An apparently easy solution to the dilemma of publishing findings and interpretations that may harm those studied is to decide that if a proper bargain has been struck at the beginning of a research relationship no one has any right to complain. If the researcher has

[15] Edward A. Shils, "Social Inquiry and the Autonomy of the Individual," in Danier Lerner, Ed., *Meaning of the Social Sciences*, New York: Meridian Books, 1959, p. 137. I am indebted to William Kornhauser for calling this article to my attention.

agreed to allow those studied to censor his report, he cannot complain when they do. If the people studied have been properly warned, in sufficient and graphic detail, of the consequences of a report about them and have still agreed to have a study done, then they cannot complain if the report is not what they would prefer. But the solution, from the point of view of either party, ignores the real problems.

From the scientist's point of view, the problem is only pushed back a step. Instead of asking what findings he should be prepared to publish, we ask what bargain he should be prepared to strike. Considering only his own scientific interests, he should clearly drive the hardest bargain, demanding complete freedom, and should settle for less only when he must in order to gain access to a theoretically important class of institutions that would otherwise be closed to him.

When we look at the problem from the side of those studied, reaching a firm bargain is also only an apparent solution. As Roth pointed out,[16] the people who agree to have a social scientist study them have not had the experience before and do not know what to expect; nor are they aware of the experience of others social scientists have studied. Even if the social scientist has pointed out the possible consequences of a report, the person whose organization or community is to be studied is unlikely to think it will happen to him; he cannot believe this fine fellow, the social scientist with whom he now sees eye to eye, would actually do something to harm him. He thinks the social scientist, being a fine fellow, will abide by the ethics of the group under study, not realizing the force and scope of the scientist's impersonal ethic and, particularly, of the scientific obligation to report findings fully and frankly. He may feel easy, having been assured that no specific item of behavior will be attributed to any particular person, but will he think of the "tone" of the report, said to be offensive to the inhabitants of Springdale?

Making a proper research bargain, then, is no solution to the problem of publication. Indeed, with respect to the question of *what to publish,* I think there is no general solution except as one may be dictated by the individual's conscience. But there are other questions and it is possible to take constructive action on them without prejudicing one's right to publish. The social scientist can warn those studied of the effect of publication and help them prepare for it. When his report is written he can help those concerned to assimilate what it says and adjust to the consequences of being reported on publicly.

It is probably true that the first sociological report on a given kind

[16] Roth, *op. cit.*

of institution sits least well, and that succeeding studies are less of a shock to those studied, creating fewer problems both for the researcher and those he studies. The personnel of the first mental hospital or prison studied by sociologists probably took it harder than those of similar institutions studied later. Once the deviations characteristic of a whole class of institutions have been exposed they are no longer secrets peculiar to one. Subsequent reports have less impact. They only affirm that the deviations found in one place also exist elsewhere. Those whose institutions are the subject of later reports can only suffer from having it shown that they have the same faults, a lesser crime than being the only place where such deviations occur. The difference between "In this mental hospital attendants beat patients" and "In this mental hospital *also*, attendants beat patients" may seem small, but the consequences of the difference are large and important.

By having those he studies read earlier reports on their kind of institution or community, the social scientist can lead them to understand that what he reports about them is not unique. By making available to them other studies, which describe similar deviations in other kinds of institutions and communities, he can teach them that the deviations whose exposure they fear are in fact characteristic features of all human organizations and societies. Thus a carefully thought out educational program may help those reported on come to terms with what the scientist reports, and spare both parties unnecessary difficulties.

The program might take the form of a series of seminars or conversations, in which the discussion would move from a consideration of social science in general to studies of similar institutions, culminating in a close analysis of the about-to-be-published report. In analyzing the report the social scientist can point out the two contexts in which publication will have meaning for those it describes.

First, it can affect their relations with other groups outside the institution: the press, the public, national professional organizations, members of other professions, clients, citizens' watchdog groups, and so on. By describing facts about the organization that may be interpreted as deviations by outside groups, the social scientist may endanger the institution's position with them. Second, the publication of descriptions of deviation may add fuel to internal political fires.[17] The social scientist, by discussing the report with those it describes,

---

[17] The danger of exposure to external publics is most salient in studies of institutions; the danger of exposure of deviation within the group studied is most important in studies of communities.

can help them to face these problems openly and warn them against one-sided interpretations of his data and analyses. For instance, he can help them to see the kinds of interpretations that may be made of his report by outside groups, aid them in assessing the possibility of serious damage (which they are likely to overestimate), and let them test on him possible answers they might make to adverse reaction.

If he confers with institutional personnel, he will no doubt be present when various people attempt to make use of his work in a selective or distorted way for internal political advantage, when they cite fragments of his conclusions in support of a position they have taken on some institutional or community issue. He can then, at the moment it takes place, correct the distortion or selective citation and force those involved to see the issue in more complete perspective.

In conferring with representatives of the institution or community, the social scientist should keep two things in mind. First, although he should be sensitive to the damage his report might do, he should not simply take complaints and make revisions so that the complaints will cease. Even with his best efforts, the complaints may remain, because an integral part of his analysis has touched on some chronic sore point in the organization; if this is the case, he must publish his report without changing the offending portions. Second, his conferences with representatives of the organization should not simply be attempts to softsoap them into believing that no damage will occur when, in fact, it may. He must keep this possibility alive for them and make them take it seriously; unless he does, he is only postponing the complaints and difficulties to a later time when reactions to the report, within and outside the organization, will bring them out in full strength. In this connection it is useful to make clear to those studied that the preliminary report, if that is what they are given, is slated for publication in some form, even though it may be substantially revised; this fact is sometimes forgotten and many criticisms that would be made if it were clear that the document was intended for publication are not made, with the result that the process must be gone through again when the final version is prepared.

People whose organizations have been studied by social scientists often complain that the report made about them is "pessimistic" or "impractical," and their complaint points to another reason for their anger. Insofar as the report gives the impression that the facts and situations it describes are irremediable, it puts them in the position of being chronic offenders for whom there is no hope. Although some social science reports have such a pessimistic tone, it is more often the case that the report makes clear that there are no easy solutions to the organization's problems. There are solutions, but they are solutions that call for major changes in organizational practice, and for this reason they are likely to be considered impractical. The social scientist can explain that there are no panaceas, no small shifts in practice that will do away with the "evils" his report describes without in any way upsetting existing arrangements, and thus educate those he has studied to the unpleasant truth that they cannot change the things they want to change without causing repercussions in other parts of the organization.[18] By the same token, however, he can point to the directions in which change is possible, even though difficult, and thus relieve them of the oppressive feeling that they have no way out.

A regime of conferring with and educating those studied may seem like an additional and unwelcome job for the social scientist to take on. Is it not difficult enough to do the field work, analyze the data, and prepare a report, without taking on further obligations? Why not finish the work and leave, letting someone else bear the burden of educating the subjects of the study? Although flight may often seem the most attractive alternative, the social scientist should remember that, in the course of working over his report with those it describes, he may get some extremely useful data. For instance, in the course of discussions about the possible effect of the report on various audiences, it is possible to discover new sources of constraint on the actors involved that had not turned up in the original study. One may be told about sources on inhibition of change that are so pervasive as to never have been mentioned until a discussion of change, occasioned by the report, brings them to light. The desire for further data, coupled with simple altruism and the desire to avoid trouble, may prove sufficiently strong motive for an educational effort.

Conclusion

In discussing the several facets of the problem, I have avoided stating any ethical canons. I have relied on those canons implicit in the scientific enterprise in suggesting that the scientist must strive for the freest possible conditions of reporting. Beyond that I have

---

[18] See the discussion of panaceas in Howard S. Becker and Blanche Geer, "Medical Education," in Howard E. Freeman, Leo G. Reeder, and Sol Levine, Eds., *Handbook of Medical Sociology*, Englewood Cliffs, N. J.: Prentice-Hall, 1963, pp. 180–184.

said only that it is a matter of individual conscience. In so restricting my remarks and in discussing the problem largely in technical terms, I have not meant to indicate that one need have no conscience at all, but only that it must remain a matter of individual judgment.

I ought properly, therefore, to express my own judgment. Briefly, it is that one should refrain from publishing items of fact or conclusions that are not necessary to one's argument or that would cause suffering out of proportion to the scientific gain of making them public. This judgment is of course ambiguous. When is something "necessary" to an argument? What is "suffering"? When is an amount of suffering "out of proportion"? Even though the statement as it stands cannot determine a clear line of action for any given situation, I think it does suggest a viable vantage point, an appropriate mood, from which decisions can be approached. In particular, it suggests on the one hand that the scientist must be able to give himself good reasons for including potentially harmful material, rather than including it simply because it is "interesting." On the other hand, it guards him against either an overly formal or an overly sentimental view of the harm those he studies may suffer, requiring that it be serious and substantial enough to warrant calling it "suffering." Finally, it insists that he know enough about the situation he has studied to know whether the suffering will in any sense be proportional to gains science may expect from publication of his findings.

The judgment I have expressed is clearly not very original. Nor is it likely that any judgment expressed by a working social scientist would be strikingly original. All the reasonable positions have been stated long ago. The intent of this paper has been to show that a sociological understanding of what we do when we publish potentially harmful materials may help us make the ethical decisions that we must, inevitably, make alone.

9

Plainville: The Twice-Studied Town

Art Gallaher, Jr.

A *community study* involves social interaction between researcher and subjects. It is a special form of interaction in that the researcher can define, or even perhaps innovate and have accepted, a role that permits him to collect data he thinks he is interested in. The role structure that the community researcher seeks to establish involves two factors: (1) the purpose of his research as it is understood by the community and by himself; and (2) behavior that the community comes to expect from one who is an anthropologist or sociologist. It is from these two factors that respondents derive their images of the field worker, which they in turn use as criteria for defining the kind of data they will make available to him, and the circumstances under which these data are collected.

In doing an independent follow-up study of Plainville,[1] my wife and I faced a novel situation which took us one stage beyond the ordinary role ambiguities of the community researcher. Plainville already held an image of the social researcher—an image that had been subject to significant modification by James West's book, *Plainville, U.S.A.*,[2] and its related publicity, and by other considerations which occurred in the intervening period since the original research. Our experience in restudying Plainville taught us that the initial energies in a restudy must be invested in learning this image and the variables by which it is defined, because these will affect the role structure that the restudy field worker hopes to establish.

[1] See my *Plainville Fifteen Years Later*, New York: Columbia University Press, 1961. My wife and I lived in Plainville from August 1954 through August 1955, during which time we collected data on the changes in Plainville culture during the preceding fifteen-year period, and the processes by which these changes had occurred. We used data from West's earlier work as the baseline against which to measure and evaluate change. All place names and personal names have been altered.

[2] James West, *Plainville, U.S.A.*, New York: Columbia University Press, 1945. James West is a pseudonym for Carl Withers.

From a methodological standpoint, a major advantage of the independent restudy is that one can enter the field apprised, to some extent, of the experiences of his predecessor. Of course, I did ask West for his suggestions and opinions regarding a restudy of Plainville. He thought the idea a good one, and volunteered that, to the best of his knowledge, with one outstanding exception most Plainvillers had taken his report "with relative composure." The exception was the mail carrier whose social rise West had described. Furthermore, while formulating a research design for the restudy, my wife and I read *Plainville, U.S.A.* many times, and thus felt we knew a lot about the community. Certainly, we knew something of West's rapport problems and how he had overcome these.[3] We were aware, then, that we could expect some problems, but as I remember the situation now we had no real anxieties deriving from these expectations. Rather, because of knowledge already gained of the community, we believed we could handle difficulties that might arise. We were psychologically at ease with the project.

Our first physical contact with Plainville came on a hot afternoon in July—the twentieth, to be exact—in 1954. However, before entering the community we stopped in Liberty, twenty-five miles south, and secured Missouri license plates for our 1948 model car. Upon entering Plainville we drove immediately to the square. There before us were the old hotel, the feed store, and other businesses, the apartment beside the post office where West had lived, elderly men sitting on loafer's benches, the bandstand in the middle of the square, all as West had described them in *Plainville, U.S.A.*, and the new highway, which was built even as West did his research. As I remember it now, there was so much that was familiar, because of West's description and my own efforts to absorb literally all that he included in his monograph, that my first contact seemed not that at all, but rather more as the return to a community left long ago. I felt something akin to surprise and, I suppose, relief to find so much about Plainville that was as West had depicted it.

Our first order of business on that particular afternoon was to find a place to live. We learned quickly that nothing was available immediately, but that an apartment would be vacated in about two weeks. We had no alternative but to rent the apartment and reluctantly withdraw from the community until it was available. In securing a place to live we spent three hours in Plainville and were in contact with a total of five people. We explained to each, in precisely the same way,

[3] See West, *ibid.*, pp. vii–xv for discussion of the problems he encountered and the techniques by which he overcame them.

that we were moving to Plainville to study changes in farming practices over the past fifteen to twenty years. This was combined with
talk of the current drought, farm prices, government farm programs,
fishing and hunting, high school basketball, and other topics which I
presumed to have general interest, based on my own experience of
growing up in an Oklahoma community about the size of Plainville.
Our initial contacts seemed interested in our project, expressed the
view that it made sense, and volunteered to help us with it. They
were friendly and very willing to help us find a place to live. *No one
mentioned that the community had been studied by West fifteen
years earlier.*

Two weeks later we were in Plainville to stay. Our plan was to
blanket immediately the entire community with the statuses we hoped
to establish—for me, that of anthropologist, for my wife, that of
teacher in a rural school in a neighboring district. For initial research
emphases we followed through with what we had told our initial
contacts, and what we assumed was a relatively low-affect interest
area, that is, changes in agricultural technology since 1940. By using
this as a device of entry we could expand gradually our emphasis to
other areas of the culture as the research progressed and our rapport
became more firmly established. We were in the community only a
few hours, however, before detecting certain anxieties regarding
West's work and the possible association of us with his book.

I received the first clue when I went into a general store, near our
apartment, to buy some groceries. I introduced myself to Dent Craig,
the elderly proprietor, explaining that I had just moved to town and
why, and that I was living in Joe Dyer's apartment. He said he had
heard that Joe had a renter coming who was going to write *another*
book about Plainville! I explained to Dent that what he had heard
was not exactly true, that I was there to do research and there might,
or might not, be a book developed from it, but that *my main concern
was research* since I was an anthropologist.

Our next clue came that evening as we sat on our front porch and
talked with Joe and Elma Dyer. The Dyers, though born and reared
in Plainville, had lived much of their lives in other states. They spent
only the summer months in the community, and felt themselves definitely marginal to Plainville life. They identified with us readily, and
were excellent advisers on the subtleties of the norms for acceptance
into the community. The most revealing information which they im-
parted during our first evening with them was something of the community's reaction to *Plainville, U.S.A.* They told of a fellow who had
come to Plainville years ago—"No one seemed to know for sure what

he was up to, but he wrote a book about the town"—and a great number of people were mightily upset. "Why, he had a map drew in the front of his book, so's anyone who read it would know it was Plainville." The Dyers made special reference to the intense hostility that the mailman expressed toward West, and they repeated a number of times his threats to do physical harm to him. The mailman, however, died a few months before we arrived, without ever gaining the chance to confront West directly. They told us that many other people were unhappy over the book, and indicated the belief that we should be cautious, that it would be very easy for our motives to be misunderstood. That first conversation with the Dyers lasted until early morning and triggered many anxieties, some of which we were not to rid ourselves of for some time.

In our first contacts with the Dyers we learned from them what seemed to be the main centers for disseminating information. These were the beauty shop, two grocery stores, a service station, and the post office. We early made individuals identified with each of these centers aware of our motives and kept them informed of what we were doing. In addition, we set out to meet personally as many people as possible. In our initial contacts we found that most Plainvillers were willing to let us talk to them. They were curious and our interest in changes in agricultural technology seemed not to be threatening. They assured us we would enjoy our stay in their village, wished us luck with our work, and maintained an attitude of *formal* friendliness. There were many, for example, who talked freely and at great lengths with us about our interests, but when we solicited their assistance explained that others could better help with our problems, or, as was frequently the case, said that when we got our research underway they would help. Since it was obvious that my research was underway, this was merely a nice way of putting me off. Practically everyone we saw posed the question "Are you here to write another book?" Some asked if I had come to "write the second book . . . the one about the 'Scandals of Plainville'?" In line with this, a number of people made negative reference to West's monograph, even though, in many cases, expressing agreement with it. Their criticisms seemed to focus more on his handling of the data. There were some who personally registered their disapproval that we were studying Plainville. Only a few of this number were obviously hostile, and I am convinced they initiated contact for the specific purpose of releasing aggressions deriving from the first study. Typical reactions from these people were: "I certainly hope you are not here to do the same thing that feller West did a few years ago.

. . . Folks here are mighty unhappy with him. . . . Some would like to lynch him. . . . Some here will want to ride you out of town on a rail." Though messages such as these were most often communicated in a joking manner, they were, nevertheless, disquieting. More upsetting were other kinds of messages, disturbing for the most part by the subtle way in which they were communicated. For instance, an elderly man, after questioning me in some detail about how I intended to go about my research, replied that he had known West—"used to talk with him. A nice guy, *but he asked a hell of a lot of questions.*" The negative implication of his message came not in what he said, but the way in which he said it.

A few people avoided any contact with us. Others, particularly those of obvious status advantage, were ambivalent. A merchant, for example, said that he liked me personally, but it made him uneasy to have me around. Another told me it was a shame I was a "research man," because otherwise I was an "all right guy." And there were a few who early—that is, in the first three or four weeks—indicated willingness to cooperate.[4] Their number initially was so small, and by the time they were known to me my own anxieties were such a factor in establishing rapport, that I was somewhat suspicious of their motives. By this time I was bothered by our seeming inability to shake the book-writer tag. Furthermore, it was obvious that the role I had cast for myself was not holding up. We were getting very formal and reserved responses, and I knew that these would not allow me to respond in the direction of my research interest. There was some comfort in the fact that Plainvillers seemed to like both my wife and me, and certainly our landlord and others kept us adequately informed of that, as well as the fact that people were favorably impressed by our friendliness. But it was frustrating and, in terms of the research we intended, anxiety provoking that most of those willing to accept us were doing so only as friends—once we assumed the role of researchers and tried to define a social relationship with them as informants, they shied away.

[4] I am convinced, and personal communication from West indicates concurrence, that our initial acceptance into the community actually came faster than his. He did not secure informants willing to cooperate to the extent that he could devote full time to data gathering until around the fourth or fifth month. His acceptance followed mainly the article he published in the county paper (see West, *ibid.*, p. x), and the cooperation he obtained from a local political leader. West has hypothesized, and I can agree with him, that his book gave Plainvillers a different kind of rationalization of their resistance to intrusion, perhaps even a friendlier rationalization, than he encountered in the long initial "clamming up" with which they greeted him.

My wife and I often discussed all of these problems, and we frequently compared our reactions to personalities and made comparisons of our perceptions of how certain people were assessing us. These discussions were not planned and I do not imply any methodological sophistication in their structure. They derived logically from the kinds of problems we were encountering and, from a more personal standpoint, our own anxieties associated with those problems. The fact that I had someone to talk to was in itself a psychological advantage, but the discussions were useful for a number of other reasons. Still, as I assess them now their chief advantage was in fact that they gave me a chance to air my own anxieties. I wish now that we had recorded those talks or at least sketched them roughly in our notes, but there was no thought of it at the time.

We soon came to realize that the Plainvillers' question of "why" was turning more away from the nature of our own research—they seemed generally to accept our interest in a changing agricultural technology—and increasingly toward "why" a book had been written about them. Our coming there for research purposes had obviously reminded them again that their community had been studied before. West, too, had come there to do research, and he had written a book. There was no question but that we were caught up in their revival of interest in that book, and their reaction to it. Certainly we expected some of this but, as I remember the situation now, the community's aggressive denunciation of the West monograph threw us off badly. In this regard we were particularly troubled that some of West's bitterest critics were people who also agreed with his findings.

We also came to realize that we were getting involved with more than merely the book; we were becoming intensely involved with a mythical West. A small number of people were bothered by more than the fact that the community was being studied for a second time, and their concern, which we managed to learn from others, derived from my self-definition as an anthropologist. They, of course, identified West as an anthropologist, and since I defined myself as West had, they were responding to West as much as they were to me.[5]

We had decided before ever entering the community that ethically we should have to maintain a neutral position regarding both West and *Plainville, U.S.A.* However, Plainvillers let us know quickly that we could not ignore the book. In fact, they seemed bent upon talking about it. Thus whenever we encountered criticism of the book or

---

[5] The identification of West as an anthropologist came not so much from his own identification as such while he was in the community, but more after publication of *Plainville, U.S.A.*

of West, we invited elaboration, explaining that we were interested in the people's reactions to what had been written about them. At the same time we felt that we should explain to Plainvillers, as best we could, whenever the opportunity arose, something of what West had tried to do. And, since the book was an issue, I also encouraged a few people, whom I felt sure were friendly to West, to discreetly support him with their neighbors. This involved considerable discretion on our part because we were by now aware that expressions of agreement with *Plainville, U.S.A.* did not necessarily imply sympathy with either West or myself. In this regard the community's reaction to the first study and to West led us to believe that perhaps we had been too aggressive in trying to structure my research role. It was obvious that, through the Plainvillers' association of researcher, book writer, and anthropologist, I was somehow all tangled up with West. This awareness, combined with the feeling that we had been too aggressive in structuring the research role, plus, I am sure, our own anxieties, forced a reconsideration of our efforts to achieve the kind of rapport needed to obtain data. Our interview technique became more nondirective, we pushed less the formal role of anthropologist, and emphasized more our desire to be friends.

Simultaneously we became more concerned with understanding the Plainvillers' conception of the role structure of a field researcher. They had, after all, had prior contact with another anthropologist and, therefore, had some preconceived notions of what an anthropologist does. Presumably there was some connection between their definition of research and anthropologist and their reaction to the published monograph on their community.

With this task in mind, we discovered that criticism of the first research originated mainly with a very small number of people who had, over the years, aggressively kept their views before the community. A central figure was the mailman, a vehement, vociferous critic, who, as best I could tell, threatened physical harm to West at the mere mention of his name.[6] Lesser vocal critics were those who

[6] The following is quoted from personal correspondence from West, with his permission: "My account in *Plainville, U.S.A.* of the mail carrier was an unpardonable error of reporting which caused avoidable personal suffering. I should have constructed a hypothetical, unidentifiable case to illustrate the point I wanted to make. In my belief, no other Plainville individual suffered any deep hurt as a result of my study. I further believe that more than a few people benefited, in deeper perception and greater appreciation of their environment, through sharing my exploration of their way of life. A number of warm friendships with Plainvillers have continued nearly a quarter of a century to the present day, maintained by correspondence and by visits, in Plainville and elsewhere. I did not revisit Plainville after 1944 until 1955."

sympathized with the mailman ("West slurred him"), though perhaps agreeing with West's analysis of his social rise, and a few others who believed that West painted an incomplete picture of their community. The latter were upper-status people, some of whom were West's informants. Their prevalent judgment was that *Plainville, U.S.A.* was *largely* correct as far as it went, but that it stressed only the negative side of the community. The views of these people, especially, had been impressed upon those who had not read West's book, and I would estimate that most Plainvillers did not read it in its entirety, but could, on cue, criticize and talk of the work as though they had thoroughly digested it.

The more sophisticated critics stressed that the researcher came to do a history of Plainville, that he was sent by, and paid by, Columbia University. I was asked many times, in fact, if I had been sent to Plainville by Columbia. The published monograph, however, by their definition, was not history. Consequently, there was strong feeling that the book was not the real report of West's findings. They believed the *real report* was tucked away some place at Columbia—that in it there was included the positive side of the community. They believed that the book they know about was written only to make money, and in order to make it sell West exaggerated their poverty and their backwardness. They saw the book as an effort to single them out as a unique entity, and, in a more specific sense, they believed the author too closely identified too many people in it. As they say in Plainville, "He had to do that to make it interesting." In line with this, a well-thumbed copy of *Plainville, U.S.A.* in the local library has the real names carefully pencilled beside the pseudonyms invented by West. The really professional critics pointed especially to the introductory chapter of the book as an exposition by an anthropologist of how he gained their confidence and then violated it. He was, in their terms, an outsider whom they took to their bosom. As one woman explained to us: "Why, he came in here and everyone took him in, just like we've done you folks, and then he writes stuff like this." The theme expressed by this woman was strongly emphasized by most of West's critics—in essence they cooperated and because the finished product was not to their liking, West betrayed them. The fact that he "double-crossed" them was patently obvious to these critics—why else, they asked, would he use a pseudonym?

Those Plainvillers who were inclined to doubt the validity of the original monograph were given, over the years, additional ammunition in the form of a number of anthropology and sociology students who attempted mail-order culture-change studies. Requests for information from students doing term papers in college and university classes were received by superintendents of the Plainville schools, the county superintendent, vocational agriculture teachers, extension agents, other county officials, and one such request that came to my attention was addressed merely to the mayor. A number of these queries sought to establish rapport by indicating that their desire for information was prompted by doubts about West's material, especially his depiction of the community as so backward. The full significance of this kind of variable is difficult to assess, and I probably would have tended to minimize it except for the fact that three such requests for information were referred directly to me while I was in the community, and in each case I had an opportunity to witness the interest they generated. Consistent with this, a student casually dropped by Plainville one afternoon, took pictures, talked with people, informed them that *Plainville, U.S.A.* is a classic monograph on American rural life, and that they should feel flattered to have been a part of it. Granted that a few Plainvillers may have been flattered that their community was selected for study, there were many more who seemed not to share that view.

The same people who criticized most strongly the monograph succeeded also in creating a negative image of West. This image, largely fashioned after publication of the monograph, emphasized negatively many characteristics that *were acceptable to most people during the actual research,* and included other characteristics that were mythical. The main points of criticism were that West paid informants—"he bought his information" [7]—and he wrote down everything that people told him. Joe Dyer, for example, advised me early that I should not write down any notes while talking with people: "West did that, and

[7] The following is quoted from personal correspondence from West, with his permission, to indicate the extent to which he derived information from paid informants. "Following the historical practice by many anthropologists working in tribal groups I paid a very few Plainville informants for their *time.* That they were few, rather than many, does not comment either favorably or unfavorably on the merits of my book. Far less than ten per cent of my working time was spent with paid informants, and most of it during the earliest stages of fieldwork. Six adults spent some paid-for time talking with me, of whom three contributed vastly more gratis time, systematically spent in interview situations. These three were among my twelve or fifteen major informants, among the fifty or more individuals with whom I had formal interviews, and among the two hundred or so that I talked with and recorded data from. The bulk of my data came, of course, out of time given freely and generously, through friendship and interest in my study."

a lot of 'em didn't like it a bit. There's some that'll talk with you, but most would probably clam up." I later found this to be true. Most people did object to having notes taken in their presence, always with negative reference to West's "little black book." Other critics said that West spent too much time loafing, and gained too much data from loafers. In this regard, one man, now deceased, but still remembered as "a notorious loafer," was identified by most critics as West's main informant.[8] In fact, most people criticized as West's informants either were dead or no longer lived in Plainville; a number of people known to have worked with him still lived in the community, but they were not often mentioned, critically or otherwise, in association with West or his book. Other criticisms of West were: he was too aggressive in his interviewing—"he didn't care if you didn't want to answer questions, he just kept asking them anyway"; he did not inform people well enough of the true motives of his research; he was too secretive about himself; and he identified too closely with one of the political factions.

Thus the town, through selective memory and ex-post-facto distortion, developed a line on West that was consistent with their attitude of betrayal. This enabled many of the people to admit that West's analysis was essentially correct and at the same time strongly criticize him and his book because the latter "didn't go far enough," that is, it did not include their own self-image. The myths they created of West and his research, then, constituted a tightly organized defense, the capstone of which was their reasoning about West's use of a pseudonym.[9]

It was against this background of criticism—of the monograph and the researcher's role—that we were trying to structure our research role. That these characteristics and motives were attributed to me became apparent when I learned early in my tenure in Plainville that I had been given the nickname of James West, Jr. Not until somewhat later, though, did I learn that the nickname defined me as the scapegoat in a joking pattern. Some people who had not known West were told that I was he, and that because of my knowledge of the community the government had hired me to look into the background of local participants in the federal welfare and farm programs.

[8] Personal correspondence from West indicates that this man was not known as a "loafer," and that he was not a major informant.
[9] See West, op. cit., p. xv. "All place names and personal names, including my own, have been withheld or altered. This has been done out of no desire of mine for secrecy, but because every serious informant requested, and was promised, the protection of complete anonymity."

Unfortunately, I never dispelled the anxieties of a few older people, and in the two or three known cases of welfare difficulty, I am sure they felt I was to blame. In assigning West's name to me, and in making a scapegoat of me, many people thus managed early to find a slot for me in their social life. It also provided an acceptable way for them to express hostility, that is, not directly to my face.

As we came to understand better the image held by Plainvillers of the anthropologist, what he does, and of West and how he went about the business of being an anthropologist, we came to understand better the limits of our problem and the kinds of tensions in our role. We also felt we were learning something fundamental, almost intimate, about Plainvillers—their extreme sensitivity to real or assumed threats made on their self-image. We began, then, to emphasize the detailed, personal, private basis of our motivations. I made clear, for example, that I had not been sent to Plainville by any organization, but was there of my own accord and largely my own expense. We explained that my wife was teaching in a one-room country school in a nearby district so as to partly finance my research. I stressed my role as graduate student, and when possible elaborated the expectations of this role. I broke down the stereotyped image of anthropologists by talking about the variety of anthropologists and the many things they do. I emphasized the practical implications of my coming to Plainville, especially that I wanted a degree. At the same time contacts were made aware that I had grown up in an Oklahoma "town" about the size of Plainville. This kind of biographical data was appreciated—often used in introducing me—and I am convinced it conveyed to Plainvillers that my interest in them was not just academic.

We established informally structured family-visiting patterns, and though initially our visits were seldom returned, we found that we were developing more information than heretofore. My interviews with Plainville men at this stage were equally informal and unstructured, occurring usually on hunting or fishing trips. We "saturated" ourselves with topical information combed from county statistics and regional newspapers; we tried in this way to develop expert knowledge of Plainvillers' current interests, such as the drought in progress when we arrived. This information, then, we easily and comfortably introduced into our conversations—not as additional questions, but more that these interests were ours because we now lived in Plainville. We were seen frequently in all areas of the community—we conveyed the impression that we were busy and successfully developing data.

Playing this activist role altered us psychologically in several important ways that may not be wholly typical of the usual community study. Among other things it kept us from responding so much to our own anxieties, that is, from withdrawing psychologically and physically from Plainvillers. But more significantly it enabled us ultimately to achieve a depth of involvement beyond all stereotypes and roles to the point of intimate, private sharing and commitment. In short, we managed to grow close to the people of Plainville. We began to experience something of the community's problems and concerns, even though many people did not yet fully accept us. With the latter we did not push, nor were we aggressive with our friends. We were interested, uncritical, circumspect, and meticulously discreet. This they appreciated and they came to view our visits as wholly personal, and so far as we could tell did little comparing of notes among themselves. In fact, seldom did any Plainviller ask about our sources of information, mention that he may have seen our car parked in the yard of a neighbor, or in other ways express an interest in our "friends." Not until late in our stay did we reach certain people whom we knew by reputation to have been closely associated with West, and they, for obvious reasons, avoided us.

We confronted directly the lack of interest in assisting with our project by trying to convince our friends, especially those in key positions, that they should be interested in the kinds of changes occurring in Plainville. Using census materials, county and state records, we compiled data of all kinds having to do with changes since 1939–1940, the time of West's study. Armed with this information we engaged key people in what Madge in *The Tools of Social Science* [10] called "motivating interviews." These stressed general understanding and sympathy with our objectives, and how the latter were relevant to Plainville. This worked remarkably well, much better than we had anticipated. A number of people became genuinely interested, and in retrospect I view this as a real turning point in our rapport.

We did find dangers, though, in this approach. There is the possibility, for example, that one will manage the impression that he can determine the answers to all of a community's problems. Some Plainvillers, at least for a time, viewed me as such a resource person, and there was the uncomfortable problem of having to convince them to the contrary. We did this by shifting responsibility for innovation to formal agencies "who, if properly motivated, could make use of

[10] John Madge, *The Tools of Social Science*, 1953, p. 146.

our data." We also found that we were under pressure during the rest of the project to feed certain kinds of information back into the community. This pressure came partly from identification with our interests as communicated in our motivating interviews, partly from friends, who felt this their right (but still never asked of our sources), and partly from the fact that many people wanted to keep abreast of what was going on. In line with this, and because of the difficulties we had in structuring our role, we made a special effort to know what was happening among those people not directly involved with us as informants but who, nevertheless, could influence the people who were. We wanted especially to keep informed of their conceptions of our role. Therefore, we periodically interviewed a number of informants who were linked to this segment of the community. This permitted me, on a number of occasions, to scotch false roles before these were widely disseminated. However, if a false role was disseminated we tried systematically to trace the source. In this way we learned early something of the cliques, lines of communications, and derived some clues as to the informal or covert power structure of Plainville. As an example, I traced one rumor to Dent Craig who, until then, I was sure was accurately representing me to others. In this case, however, he had succumbed to the temptation to deliberately misrepresent the status I was trying to establish, not with malicious intent but to "get the community riled." Dent was proud of his knowledge of communicative channels, and he enjoyed fabricating rumors and introducing them to key clique members. When confronted he could not fully appreciate the seriousness of his sport from my standpoint, but since I was a friend he compromised by "tipping" me ahead of time of the kind of rumor he was starting and to whom he was telling it. He was amused that I had "caught" him, and since we were playing a similar game, that is, understanding the communications between cliques, our bond of rapport tightened. He was a good student of the clique system, had a number of hypotheses to explain why people cliqued, and detailed to me the structures, as he saw them, of a number of major cliques.

By the second and third months of our stay in Plainville we were aware of a number of positive indicators of acceptance. By this time a number of those who had been the severest critics of West shortly after our arrival had indicated signs of moderation. They were criticizing less, and, as we came to know some of them, we found that they too believed the monograph essentially correct, though one-sided. Their view, as was true of their more facile neighbors, was always coupled with the question: "Why would he want to write a book like that?"

Also, by now more of West's supporters had made themselves known to us, and one recognized community leader, the Baptist minister, and a close friend of West, had publicly defended him. The occasion was the annual 4-H Club achievement program, at which Brother Seth was the main speaker. His talk was of agricultural changes he had witnessed in Plainville during his lifetime, and the role of 4-H Clubs in securing these changes. In his talk Brother Seth pointedly referred to West's book, and followed this with an anecdote to the effect that West did not think Plainville "backward," but instead, defended the community against this view, stating on occasion that "people around here just had different ways of doing things." Informants agreed that this was the first time they had heard public support for West.

It was at about this time, too, that a number of couples began to return our visits, though some admitted trepidations about so doing. Also, we had by now managed to define a formal interview-informant relationship with a number of people—their main stipulations being no fees and keep their identity quiet. More important, though, were a number of clues that my wife and I had finally succeeded in creating a public opinion for our acceptance. In this regard the most dramatic and obvious public legitimation of our interests and our integration into the community structure came from the local Commercial Club, following its October dinner meeting. I had been absent from Plainville (my wife stayed in the community) for a few days, having gone to the University of Arizona to take various academic examinations, and had returned just in time for the dinner meeting. To emphasize my role as graduate student, we had widely disseminated where I was going and why. The main predinner topic at the club that evening concerned my success with the exams and some pleasant bantering about the fact that I had returned to Plainville only a few minutes before the meeting "and just couldn't stay away." After dinner the leader of the club told the men present that I had passed my exams, and then asked for my impressions of the community, and requested me to elaborate my interests in it. As he so aptly put it, "There are still some here who are a little confused and worried about what you are up to." I talked for a few minutes, emphasizing our satisfaction with the community and the cooperation extended us. The club president thanked me for my response, expressed pleasure at my satisfaction, and then announced that the club would be willing to help me with my "thesis" in any way that it could.

A number of others who were present verbally affirmed this stand. This, combined with the warm interest shown earlier in my success on the exam, made me, for a moment, feel very much like the home-town boy who had made good.

Shortly after this the club actively involved me by making me co-chairman of the March of Dimes Carnival Committee, a member of the community Christmas decorations committee, and formal assistant to the scoutmaster. These roles sanctioned a great number of con-tacts for me, and, in the case of the polio committee, meant that I spoke for the community in the county organization. This proved more of an honor than I realized at the time, because I discovered later that Plainvillers took the March of Dimes Carnival very seri-ously. They were accustomed to "winning" the contributions race in the county, and they did not intend to relax their efforts in 1954. Much to my relief, "we" won again.

Simultaneously, my wife and I were incorporated into the com-munity structure in a number of other participant roles. In lieu of an inventory of these roles, we can cite the following as examples: we were invited to participate in education meetings, local and county; I was asked to deliver a lay sermon in the Christian Church (I managed to avoid this by appealing privately to a leader in the congregation); we were invited to show slides and talk to neighbor-hood organizations of our travels in the Southwest (never about our research); my hunting and fishing obligations, especially with higher prestige men, were greatly extended; and later I was asked to deliver the high school commencement address.

We soon had a problem of major proportions, then, but of a nature different than heretofore. We suddenly were quite occupied with community business. Phrased another way, now that we were ac-cepted, Plainvillers seemed bent on emotionally consolidating us with the community.[11] Granted that this was good politics on their part, it was frustrating for us—we were involved in formal roles to the point that research time was curtailed.

[11] The role we hoped to establish is what Raymond L. Gold has codified as "participant-as-observer." See his "Roles in Sociological Field Observations," *Social Forces*, 36 (1958), 217–223. See also Nicholas Babchuk, "The Role of the Researcher as Participant Observer and Participant-as-Observer in the Field Situation," *Human Organization*, 21 (1962), 225–228. Though this was the role we mainly hoped to establish, we had no objection to engaging in conscious and systematic sharing of some phases of Plainville life, that is, to assuming the role of participant observer in the more conventional sense. Plainvillers, once they accepted us, insisted more upon the latter role for us than the "participant-as-observer" one that we were trying to structure.

The fact that Plainvillers finally embraced us so securely did not mean, of course, that *Plainville, U.S.A.* was forgotten. They could never wholly deny it into nonexistence, nor could we in our overt relations with them, so the book continued as a permanent variable in our dealing with Plainvillers. However, as our involvement increased we found our concern with the monograph taking new directions. Many people now suggested, again often in a joking manner, that we "straighten out" the original monograph. A few, in fact, wanted to make this a precondition for working with us. More difficult to deal with, though, were those who sought confirmation from us as a professional source in their criticism of West, his methods, motives, or his findings. We continued throughout the project, however, not to agree or disagree, but to observe a strict and meticulous neutrality, just as we had done earlier. Even late in our research, I felt that to publicly pass judgment on West would have opened the floodgates again, just as our first appearance in the town had done.

We ultimately had to deal directly with the attempts to emotionally consolidate us with the community. We did so by reiterating our research interests; we stressed that our identification with Plainville could only be temporary; we emphasized our need for objectivity and our rights and responsibilities as researchers to be honest. In this regard we often put our case on the line with key persons, asking them to nip, whenever they could, certain kinds of sensitive involvements. We did this especially in those situations in which I might be placed before a mass audience, such as giving a lay sermon, the commencement address, talking to a high school assembly, or before county school teachers. Our problem eased some, but our commitment to the community was so great that there were, right up to the end of our stay in Plainville, many areas of participation where we felt the option to decline was not legitimately ours.

When we left Plainville in August of 1955 I knew that we were close to the people and that they were close to us. For my part, I felt a strong personal ambivalence. I was impatient of course, to get on with my academic career, the real reason I had gone to Plainville in the first place, but at the same time I was sad that we were withdrawing from a large number of very close friends. The latter flattered us, and made our departure more difficult, by seeming genuinely surprised when we reminded them that the time was near for us to disengage from the community.

I felt then, and the feeling stuck through my dissertation and my book, a strong commitment to the community. As I see it now, this is the kind of commitment that one who does an independent restudy, especially of a literate community, can likely expect. The people, after all, have been studied before; this is their second time around. They may have read or heard of the published results; they may have been exposed to publicity attending the project, or to other variables, as in the case of the students who communicated with Plainvillers. Whatever their sources, and however they are combined, the people do have an image of the social researcher, and they will have defined as relevant certain kinds of experience deriving from their having been studied before. These are the conditions, then, with which the restudy researcher must come to terms quickly, because they set the technical limits within which he must structure his role. Neither of the conditions, image or experience, can ever be completely denied by researcher or community; rather, they are more likely to be omnipresent in the bargains that the community tries to exact and those that the researcher agrees to in order to permit his work.

Some of these bargains will involve data-gathering procedures, if nothing else, determining the connection that one's informants had with the first study. There will be others. In Plainville, for example, we found that we could not pay informants or record notes in their presence, that we had to take extra precautions to insure their anonymity. We found further that we obtained most of our data in social relationships defined as "friends," rather than in formal interviewer-informant relationships. This situation derived, in Plainville at least, from the major bargain which I believe one must make in the restudy situation. Remembering the experience of prior examination, the community will want to insure a similar experience if the first was positive, or a different experience if it was negative. They will, therefore, demand intimate, private, sharing of the researcher's motivations and interests; they will demand a lot more explanation; they will demand that he give more personally of himself. They will insist, as Plainvillers did, on *less professionalism* by the researcher. This, then, focuses certain tasks of research diplomacy. The researcher must get unusually close to the community to obtain the kind of data he needs; he must be extra cautious in making contacts; he must be alert to the kinds of demands that others will make of him, precisely because they are friends (in Plainville, to know constantly what was going on); and from an ethical standpoint, the researcher must be constantly alert to the community's desire to protect its self-image by emotionally consolidating him either for or against the earlier project. The community may well try to "smother" him, as I believe Plainvillers tried with us, and if he is experiencing personal anxieties, as we especially were shortly after our arrival, the tendency to identify with the community's self-image as a way of minimizing one's anxieties is great. One must guard against this tendency, even though it would cement rapport, which at the time may be desperately needed. Furthermore, such identification would tend to selectively channel the kinds of data the community is willing to make available to the researcher and raises the obvious ethical problem of the latter's responsibility to the discipline and his peers.

Since leaving Plainville we have corresponded with a great number of people and we have twice returned for short visits. Many friends have expressed a continued personal interest in us and in my career, and we have kept them informed as I have worked through the field materials. We have done this partly because they are friends, and partly because we have wanted to keep the community informed so as to minimize their concluding that we have tried to put something by them. I let them know, for example, when my dissertation was finished, and I was pleased to learn later that three Plainvillers, each unknown to the others, while on vacations or trips to the West Coast to visit relatives, made side trips to the University of Arizona Library to examine the dissertation. I informed a number of people that I was contemplating an elaboration of the dissertation into a book, later that the book was being written, and still later that it was going to be published. And in the front pages of my book I included a personal "Note to Plainvillers," to remind them once again of what I was about. What is contained in the note should have come as no surprise to many people, because they have heard that message many times before.

As soon as the book was published I sent a number of copies to friends in Plainville and encouraged them to circulate the books. I explained that I hoped the book would be read widely, and I wanted their honest reactions. From the comments that were written to me immediately, and judging from those communicated to me in a recent (December 1963) short visit there, our strategy thus far seems to have worked. The ultimate test, of course, will be the reaction of Plainvillers to the next anthropologist who hopes to study their community.

As nearly as I can tell at this point, there has been a lively and sustained interest in the work over the two years since publication. No one seems to have become personally involved as the mailman did with the original monograph, and thus far no one has expressed any sentiment of betrayal. If there is hostility—and I cannot help but feel there is, since there were some who at the time were not in favor of our doing the restudy—it must be confined to a small number, and so far has remained latent.

A number of people have indicated that they agree with my findings, that they feel I presented an honest picture, but "it still hurts to see things so carefully laid out." Others have talked frankly of the problem of "trying to be objective about your own hometown." I have the greatest sympathy for these reactions. There are some, too, who have written or told me, with some pride, of friends or relatives who have been "required to read" the book in their college or university classes. There are, of course, minor disagreements with various interpretations—these are to be expected—but thus far no one has implied that I deliberately distorted the data.[12]

Finally, there are a number of reactions and comments which I especially enjoy and appreciate, such as: "You should come study us again"; "You fellows (anthropologists) can see things in a community like ours that us people living here can't"; "We can't exactly figure out who the individual people are"; "The type that read it to try to identify all the characters and pick the scandal found it rather dull"; "You didn't build us up and you didn't tear us down"; and "You did the best you could." Some added to the last phrase "with what you had to work with." I am enough of a Plainviller to appreciate the humor in that qualifying phrase, and to know that it connotes nothing of an apology.

[12] Two other superficial impressions emerged clearly from my visit to Plainville two years after publication of the book: (1) The people I saw are quite sophisticated now about the business of being studied, and they may even be proud of having been studied twice. If so, we can hypothesize that the next person to study the community will have less trouble establishing rapport than either West or myself. (2) Those Plainvillers who have read the book carefully are very conscious of change. Most of my conversation with these people, by their direction, had to do with their analysis of changes that have occurred during the nine years that I have been away. Again, if this is true the logical hypothesis is that they will be more amenable to another research effort.

10

Black Bourgeoisie:

Public and Academic Reactions

E. Franklin Frazier

My book Black Bourgeiosie, first appeared in France as one of the studies in the collection known as *Recherches en Sciences Humaines.*[1] When the French edition was published I expected that like so many social science studies it would become lost on the shelves of university libraries. It came as a pleasant surprise, therefore, to learn that it attracted sufficient attention in the academic world for it to be made the basis of the MacIver Lectureship award by the American Sociological Society in 1956. When the English edition was published in the United States in 1957, I was even more surprised by the controversy which it aroused among Negroes and by the unfavorable reactions of many whites.

The reaction of the Negro community is understandable when one realizes the extent to which the book created the shock of self-revelation. In fact, if one should undertake to conceptualize the reaction of the Negro community, the initial reaction—at least on the part of its more articulate leaders—was one of shock. It appeared that middle-class Negroes were able to see themselves for the first time and, as they feared, in the way they appeared to outsiders. They did not challenge the truth of the picture which had been presented so much as they were shocked that a Negro would dare place on display their behavior and innermost thoughts. Their naive attitude toward their behavior and outlook on life was strikingly revealed in the remark of a journalist whose publication had been drawn on for much illustrative material in the book. When I met his criticism of quoting materials by asking him if his publication was not a reliable source of information, he replied that the facts in the book looked and

[1] *Bourgeoisie Noire,* Paris: Librairie Plon, 1955.

sounded different from what they did where they appeared in his magazine.

Following the initial shock of self-revelation was intense anger on the part of many leaders in the Negro community. This anger was based largely upon their feeling that I had betrayed Negroes by revealing their life to the white world. I was attacked by some Negroes as being bitter because I had not been accepted socially and by others as having been paid to defame the Negro. In one Negro newspaper there was a sly suggestion that Negroes should use violence to punish me for being a traitor to the Negro race. Some of the anger was undoubtedly due to the fact that I had revealed the real economic position of the Negro. They were particularly incensed by a mere statement of fact that the total assets of all Negro banks in the United States were less than those of a single small white bank in a small town in the State of New York.

The anger of the middle class over this statement showed how much they regarded the book as a threat to their economic interests. They had helped to create the myth of the vast purchasing power of Negroes which had become the justification for large corporations to employ Negro salesmen so as to exploit the Negro market.

It is interesting to note, however, that the anger on the part of the Negro community was not shared by all strata. From rumors and from what had appeared in book reviews in both white and Negro newspapers, some working-class Negroes got the impression that I had written a book attacking "upper-class, light-skinned" Negroes. As a consequence I was even stopped on the street by working-class Negroes who shook my hand for having performed this long overdue service.

As the book became more widely read and discussed, Negroes began to judge the book more soberly and in many cases not only to applaud my "courage" in writing the book but to say that it was an important contribution to an understanding of the Negro's plight in the United States. Numerous letters were sent directly to me and sometimes to the Negro newspapers defending the book or congratulating me on my courage. One minister wrote that the book should be read by every Negro preacher in the United States. Letters of this type continue to come to me and I am constantly invited to speak to forums and groups on the position and outlook of the new Negro middle class. This reaction of the Negro community presented a sharp contrast to what happened when the reaction of Negroes was characterized by anger. For example, I was invited by a Negro sorority to discuss the book but so much bitterness was aroused by the invitation that it had to be canceled. One leading member of the sorority accused me of having set the Negro race back fifty years. But such reactions are rare today and I am much more likely to receive copies of articles or speeches in which there are favorable references to the book, discussions of the book's implications or even documentation in support of its analysis.

The reaction of the white people outside the United States was different, on the whole, from that of white Americans. European and Latin American scholars praised the book, on the whole, as a contribution to social science and as a lucid analysis of what is happening to the American Negro. A liberal European scholar living in South Africa said that when she read the book her first reaction was, "My God, the American Negro has finally come of age; he is capable of self-analysis and self-criticism." Under the title, "Un Livre Explosif," a leading French newspaper, *Le Monde* (February 13, 1957), carried a perceptive summary review of the book. In fact, it was often European scholars who were most puzzled by the reactions of white Americans. A European told me two years ago that he could understand why middle-class Negroes might be angry about the book but that he could not understand the anger which it aroused among some white Americans. Let us turn to the reactions of some white Americans and undertake to explain them.

The critical reviews which appeared in American scholarly journals were concerned for the most part with questions involving methodology and the validity of my conclusions. In some of the more serious journals of opinion there also appeared critical reviews. But even in some of the scholarly reviews as well as in the serious journals of opinion there was either an implicit or explicit criticism that the book exhibited anger or lack of sympathy in its stark objectivity. A leading political analyst said that the book was cruel because if Negroes were happy in their world of make-believe, why should I feel it was my duty to let them know the truth about their real position in the United States? Although it appeared that many whites shared this opinion, there were others who welcomed the book as an explanation of the behavior of middle-class Negroes—behavior which had long puzzled them. Some of them came to me and stated frankly that they had been puzzled, for example, by the conspicuous consumption on the part of middle-class Negroes but that after reading the book they could understand it.

Perhaps the main reason for the bitter reaction on the part of some white Americans (some book stores refused to carry the book because it was "controversial") was that it destroyed or tended to destroy the image of Negroes which they wanted to present to the world at this time. The picture which white Americans wanted to present to the world was that although Negroes had been enslaved and had suffered many disabilities since Emancipation, on the whole they were well off economically, had gained civil rights, and had improved their social status. Therefore, what had happened to them during slavery, which was after all a mild paternalistic system, should be forgotten along with the other injustices which they have suffered since. Moreover, their economic position was superior to that of other peoples of the world, especially the colored peoples. One article published by a distinguished statesman even went so far as to state that Negroes were spending annually an amount equal to the annual national income of Canada.

Now, *Black Bourgeoisie* was a refutation of this image. It showed that slavery was a cruel and barbaric system that annihilated the Negro as a person, a fact which has been well documented and substantiated in a recent book.[2] Moreover, the book also showed how, since Emancipation, Negroes had been outsiders in American society. Finally, it demonstrated on the basis of factual knowledge that Negroes were not only at the bottom of the economic ladder but that all the pretended economic gains which Negroes were supposed to have made had not changed fundamentally their relative economic position in American life. It revealed also that the new Negro middle class was comprised almost entirely of wage earners and salaried professionals and that so-called Negro business enterprises amounted to practically nothing in the American economy. This was not, of course, the image of Negroes that white Americans wanted to present to the world, especially at a time when they were endeavoring to win the confidence and friendship of the colored world.

Very often the question is asked whether there is need for a revision of this book. Has not the economic position of the Negro middle classes changed? Have not middle-class Negroes become accustomed to their new prosperity and given up much of their conspicuous consumption? From the latest figures on the occupations and the incomes of middle-class Negroes there is no reason to revise what was written about the relative size of the middle class and their occupational status nor the source and amount of their incomes. The essential fact is that they still do not own any of the real wealth of America or play an important role in American business. And it

[2] Stanley M. Elkins, *Slavery, A Problem in American Institutional and Intellectual Life,* Chicago: University of Chicago Press, 1959.

is difficult to see how their economic position could change fundamentally within five years. In reply to the second question one would only need to read Negro newspapers and magazines to see to what extent conspicuous consumption is still the dominant pattern of this class. In the cities of the country middle-class Negro communities are expanding but they are characterized by the same conspicuous consumption the book describes. School teachers and college professors who earn less than $10,000 a year are building homes that cost $40,000 and $50,000 and entertaining lavishly. In this connection one is reminded of the article which appeared recently in a white publication on the Negro aristocracy and Negro millionaires.[3] It should be noted that many Negroes resented this article as a misrepresentation of the real economic position of Negro professional men and women. Since this article appeared I have received numerous letters and comments saying the article confirmed what I had said about the world of make-believe in which middle-class Negroes live.

There is, however, an important aspect of the development of the new Negro middle class that might have been included in this book and certainly could not be omitted from a more detailed study. It is strange that the omission was overlooked by American critics but suggested in a foreign review. I am referring to the most recent accessions to the Negro middle classes who are prominent in the sit-ins and in the other protest movements against racial segregation. They do not have the same social background as the black bourgeoisie in my study who represent a fusion of the peasant and the gentleman. Although they have been influenced to some extent by the genteel tradition, on the whole, their social background is essentially that of the Negro folk. Very seldom can they or their parents claim ancestors among the mixed-blood aristocracy which was free before the Civil War.

Some attention must be given to two more serious criticisms of the book as it now stands. The first concerns the materials upon which the analyses are based. Here I am not concerned with the question of adequate samplings of middle-class Negroes with respect to attributes that can be treated statistically. I am referring especially to the analyses of the patterns of behavior and values of this class. Let me begin by stating that it would be difficult to secure a more reliable validation of this study in regard to patterns of behavior and style of life and values of the Negro middle class than that which has been

[3] Bill Davidson, "Our Negro Aristocracy," *The Saturday Evening Post*, January 13, 1962.

provided in the letters and comments which have come to me from cities all over the country. These letters have stated first that they did not know that I had carried on researches in their community until they had read the book which provided such an authentic picture of the middle class in their city. In many cases they complained that the picture was so true to life that they could recognize the people by their behavior and verbal statements and their relation to the rest of the community. As a matter of fact, in most cases I had never made a study in their community. An amusing incident connected with this aspect of the study happened in one city where my junior colleagues had made a housing survey. After the English edition appeared, they were accused of having spied on the behavior of the middle classes and were threatened with a thrashing if they ever returned to that city. The majority of the materials upon which this study was based were materials on thousands of Negro families and many Negro communities which I had collected during studies over the years. For the purposes of this study, additional materials were collected from newspapers and magazines and from students from middle-class families. In many cases, as a participant-observer, I collected case materials in the same manner as an anthropologist gathers materials for studies.

Another criticism which deserves attention was that this study did not reveal anything peculiar to Negroes. This was a criticism offered not only by Negroes who are sensitive about being different from other people, but by white people as well. Some of them were the so-called liberal whites who, when any statement is made which might be considered derogatory concerning Negroes, are quick to say that the "same thing is found among whites." Other whites pointed out what is undoubtedly true: that this book dealt with behavior which is characteristic of middle-class people—white, black, or brown. Some of my Jewish friends, including some young sociologists, went so far as to say that the book was the best account that they had ever read concerning middle-class Jews. Here I might repeat what I stated in the book: that the behavior of middle-class Negroes was an American phenomenon, and that in writing I was constantly tempted to make comparisons with middle-class whites, but that the book was essentially a case study of the new Negro middle class. It was not my intention to make a comparative study. As a case study of middle-class Negroes, it does show the peculiar conditions under which a middle class emerged among the Negro minority and the peculiar social and cultural heritage of the Negro middle class which was responsible for its outlook on life.

In retrospect when I consider the reaction of the Negro community and the criticisms of both Negroes and whites of all intellectual levels, I am reminded of a review of the French edition which appeared on the front page of a French newspaper published in the United States.[4] The review concluded with the questions: Would this book arouse heated discussions in which each protagonist would hold stubbornly to his particular opinion? Would it contribute to modifying the mentality of this élite which is oblivious of its duties and responsibilities? A partial answer was given to these questions by some of the young leaders of the sit-ins who said they did not aspire to become the middle-class Negroes described in *Black Bourgeoisie*. Finally, in regard to the charge that the presentation was brutal or cruel, I will only quote the words of a Catholic sociological review concerning the book: "A sad truth is better than a merry lie."

[4] *Le Travailleur,* Worcester, Mass., April 12, 1956.

11

The Springdale Case: Academic Bureaucrats and Sensitive Townspeople

Arthur J. Vidich and Joseph Bensman

Since the advent of large-scale research and large-scale financing of research, the community study has come to be thought of as a "project" for which it is necessary to have a systematic statement of problem, a staff, legitimate sponsorship, and a budget. One of the first steps in setting up project research is making application for the research grant, a procedure requiring a formal statement of the problem, an explicit theory, and a specific methodology that will be used as the operational procedure in conducting the research. The dignity of scientific enterprise is attached to the whole of the project structure.

In this essay we report on the consequences of carrying out a community research study that ignored all the procedures of the scientific project research. The community study which we reported in *Small Town in Mass Society* [1] was unintentionally unplanned, had no budget, no a priori theory, no staff, no research stages or phases, and was not conceived as a study or a project until it was almost over.

Although the research and writing that resulted in *Small Town in Mass Society* were informal and unprogrammed, the work was actually carried out within the formal structure of an organized and programmed research project known as Cornell Studies in Social Growth, sponsored by the Department of Child Development and Family Relationships of the College of Home Economics, School of Agriculture, Cornell University. We must note that our study could

[1] Princeton University Press, 1958; Doubleday Anchor Book, 1960.

not have been done except as a byproduct of this formalized and organized research structure.

Our study of Springdale was related to the Cornell Studies in Social Growth project by the accident that one of the collaborators was hired as a resident field director to observe and participate in the life of the community, to maintain liaison between the community and the research organization, to administer and supervise mass surveys, and to provide background social structural data for the project's formal study of modes and qualities of community participation and leadership.[2]

The responsibility of the field director was to collect the data necessary to the formal study with a minimum of embarrassment to all parties concerned while not compromising the quality of the data. For this reason all research activities in the town were highly calculated and restricted to those areas of investigation and community personnel that had a direct bearing on the project design at the time each specific field operation was being carried out.

Administratively, the field director was a temporary employee of an annually renewable, long-range research project housed in and "supported" by Cornell University. The job requirement was that the field director live in Ithaca for several months until he could become familiar with the project and that he then move with his family to Springdale where he would live as if he were a resident of the town working for the university which was doing a study of the town. This was thought to be a reasonable approach to the town because other Cornell employees, including a professor, a graduate assistant and extension agents, already lived in the town, thus giving the role some legitimation. These administrative and residence arrangements had a number of implications pertinent to nonprogrammed research.

Simply by being present in the town and by being interested in the day-to-day nonresearch life of the community residents, a great deal of material which was not encompassed by the Cornell Studies in Social Growth study design inevitably came to the attention of the field director. In some instances highly personal information was acquired from personal friends in the town, and this information remains as part of the personal experience of the field director. In other instances the field director was advised or directed to join organizations and activities for purposes that were not directly related to the project design. For example, it was a joint staff decision that

---

[2] This study has been published as "Leadership and Participation in a Changing Rural Community," in *The Journal of Social Issues*, Vol. XVI, No. 4, 1960.

the field director should go to church, but be given a personal option on teaching Sunday school. Although the project was almost exclusively interested in the participational structure of church life, the field director, by participating in the church himself, became familiar with at least some dimensions of all aspects of church life.

Theoretically the project research design allowed for all levels of information, but only on the grounds that anything and everything that could be known might be relevant. This was why the field director was put into the town. Practically, however, there was a project tendency to regard as data only the information that found its way into a formal protocol or an interview schedule, so that even within the framework of the official research, the material that came to the attention of the field director exceeded the limits of the formal study. By being in the town it was difficult not to see more than could be contained in field reports. The general, informal experience resulting from continuous exposure left an image of the town that was never quite summed up in staff and field reports. As a result of these differences in the quality of information possessed by different researchers on the staff, different images of the town were held by researchers who occupied different positions in the research organization.

These differences in imagery were further complicated by the difference in intellectual starting points of the different members of the research staff. Data became relevant to the field director simply because he had previous theoretical interests and field experiences in "primitive" and other rural communities which were independent of the research design. For example, the field director's earlier field experiences left him with the impression that Springdale was as much a "colony" as Palau in the Western Carolines and as deeply penetrated by central bureaucracy as Kropa in Yugoslavia. So compelling were the similarities among Palau, Kropa, and Springdale that all points at which Springdale had a relationship to the rest of American society began to stand out as especially salient data. This orientation resulted in semisystematic observation and collection of data on a number of peripheral issues which seemingly had no relationship to any formal design or, least of all, to the project design. At this stage of the informal research, the continuity and structure of these observations was given by the personal life history of the field director.

Both of the authors had been interested in some of these peripheral issues from previous collaborative work, and out of this mutual interest and a continuing personal friendship came discussions of some of the implications of these early observations. The project had no interest in the ideas that evolved from these observations because it was from the project's point of view that the ideas were peripheral. As a result we explored the ideas as a personal project which we conducted informally in the form of conversation.

After we had explored what seemed to us to be all the implications of Springdale's relationship to the external world, we discovered that certain dimensions of the class and status structure of the town could not be explained by external factors. The social and economic position of prosperous farmers, for example, could only be explained partially by subsidy programs and price supports; part of their status in the community rested on the productive mystique of agriculture for other members of the community. This and other leads forced us to look into the internal dynamics of the community in a way which otherwise would not have been accessible to our consciousness. It was at this point that the field director secured permission from the project director to conduct twenty special interviews focusing on the social structure of the town. These interviews (conducted with Jones, Flint, Lee, Peabody, several merchants, ethnic leaders, religious leaders, and industrial workers) were specifically aimed at discovering some of the internal dimensions of community life as seen by the individuals interviewed.

Though it is apparent from the selection of informants that the interviews focused on special themes, at that time there was no notion of doing a study, a project, or a book independent of the formal project.

As the informal work progressed, a number of ad hoc memoranda, outlines, and analyses of specific problem areas were submitted to the project as relevant theoretical themes implicit in the situation of the small town. We had thought of these analyses as bearing a direct importance for the theoretical foundations of the project's research design and as offering a basis for its conceptual reformulation in a way that would account for the total situation of the small town in the modern world. The project was interested in these formulations but did not feel they were of crucial importance to its central study design. The authors continued to work on these problems simply because they were fascinating.

After two more years of continued informal work, a series of other areas had been explored on an ad hoc basis, and it was only then that it occurred to the authors that they were actually doing a community study which not only had a unified theoretical focus, but which could actually become the object of an extended and integrated monograph. At this point, which coincided with the field director's termination of his employment with the project, we asked for and received permission to do an independent study with the understanding that our work be submitted to the directors of the project as it was being written and revised so that it would be available to the project staff while its members were making their analysis of the formal survey data.

Programmed versus Unprogrammed Project Administration [3]

It was our experience that by and large the logic of a problem has its own internal dynamic which means that once one has embarked on the pursuit of the problem and is willing to follow its logics, he must *administer* in terms of where the problem leads and not in terms of prearranged schedules.

It is in the structure of project organization that termination points must be set, deadlines must be met, production schedules must be set, annual reports must be made, production functions must be distributed among staff members, and so on. Bureaucratic structure and staff organization in and of themselves impose on project research a flow whose direction is not easily redirected. Staff and organization become significant functions of research in programmed studies.

In the Springdale research we observed a variety of tensions arising from the conflict between research functions and bureaucratic functions.

1. Staff distribution of field functions leaves each staff functionary with a uniquely specialized view of individual informants and of the dimensions of community life. There are as many images of the community in circulation as there are staff functions in the research organization. This means that staff conferees are continuously involved in discussions whose major latent function is to reduce the community to a single bureaucratically acceptable image, so that for the project research purposes a major objective of the committee process is to reach a mutually acceptable fictional definition of the

[3] We have discussed two other dimensions of unprogrammed research, namely, undesigned field work and heuristic theorizing in essays otherwise available. See the authors' "The Validity of Field Data," *Human Organization*, 13, No. 1, pp. 20–27 (reprinted in *Human Organization Research*, Homewood, Ill.: Dorsey Press, 1960), and "Social Theory in Field Research," *The American Journal of Sociology*, 65, No. 6 (May 1960), pp. 577–584 (reprinted in M. Stein and A. Vidich, *Sociology on Trial*, Englewood Cliffs, N. J.: Prentice-Hall, Spectrum Series, 1963).

community which all staff members can work with while playing their project roles.

2. Since each interview is a source of standardized as well as subliminal information, all standardization of observational or interview procedures necessitated by quality control requirements arising from the uneven distribution of skills and interests among the staff has the effect of destroying all but formal information.

3. Staff execution of research, which must necessarily be guided in part by time and logistic factors relevant to other organizational and personal responsibilities (teaching, committee meetings, staff discussions, travel, vacations, family, etc.), prohibits continuity of contact between informant and researcher: the informant meets a variety of researchers and the researcher infrequently meets any informant in depth. Under this system the simple building up of personality profiles and sketches involves vast amounts of filing and collecting of information by clerks whose final product is always less than the cumulative impression that is acquired by the continuous observation by one person of another over a period of time.

4. Once the research machinery is committed to securing a certain type or level of information, it is difficult for the research organization to accept, absorb or acknowledge data which might threaten to undermine that commitment. In accepting a "fixed" statement of the project problem, it is both psychologically and bureaucratically risky to move in directions that might deviate from the last agreed-upon plan.

In the Springdale research the project was committed to finding solutions to what makes for constructive, positive, community functioning. The project thus directed itself to a study of creative activity and to the locating of leadership and participator types of local citizens who could exemplify constructive activity.

Because it was assumed that there was creative activity in the community, it was psychologically difficult for those committed to the research design to acknowledge the absence of creativity where it might have only appeared to be at first glance. Thus the case of the telephone company's expansion program which was to have been a major illustration of community creativity was simply abandoned as an illustration when it was found that the modernization program had nothing to do with the local town except insofar as the local town was a front for the state telephone company.[4]

[4] See Vidich and Bensman, "Social Theory in Field Research," *op. cit.*, pp. 578–579 for a discussion of the telephone company.

In the same manner the research organization made a major commitment to the local community club as a creative community activity. When it was found that the community club involved only a few hundred persons and that nine-tenths of the community was excluded from participation in spite of the club slogan that all were invited even if they did not pay dues, the research project continued its commitment for research reasons. Even after the practical limitations of the club's role in community affairs were acknowledged by all research personnel, it was not possible to ignore the club because ignoring it would have been a violation of the previous commitments to the club.

The community club represented a handful of activists and a shifting number of aspirants. It excluded all shack people, the marginal middle classes, and major portions of all other classes including the middle class. In short, the community club represented the minor segment of the middle class that was most attuned to social affairs and the outside world. The inspiration for the founding of the club was initially provided by community organizers and extension specialists hired by the same institution and the same college as those who were studying it as a creative community activity. Acknowledgment of these observations would have constituted a major embarrassment for the project since it would have meant in effect a reformulation of the study design. Instead a number of defenses were invoked which allowed prior commitments to be upheld. The defenses were:

1. A blindness to the existence of all community groups except the middle class, and an equating of creative activity with middle-class activities.

2. Failure to see any relationship between social club activity leaders and the community's economic and political structure.

3. The necessity to see the town only in terms of itself and without reference to anything located outside it, especially Cornell University and the research project itself.

4. The unwillingness to acknowledge all critical groups in the town and especially the refusal to listen to other outside experts who were the project's counterparts in the town. Thus the 4-H agent became the enemy of the project because he was a concrete counterimage of what the project "expected" of the town even though the original idea for a community club had come from the 4-H agent.

The foregoing illustrations indicate a fundamental tension between research as a bureaucratic enterprise and the perceptual freedom that nonbureaucratic research usually involves. As a bureaucratic employee the functionary has the responsibility of following those problems which are bureaucratically defined by authority as the purpose of the project. The project directors are obliged to stay with the problem for which they received money. The problems must be approached with the previously specified methods, and, moreover, official interpretations of what constitutes a finding come to pervade the entire project structure. Individual discoveries may be expressed so long as this is done with due caution and within the previously agreed-upon framework.

The research perspective of an individual who is independently pursuing knowledge is quite different from the one that prevails in bureaucratic settings. The perspective of independent investigation is based on whatever concatenation of theoretical background and experience the researcher brings to the field, and on his discovery of problems while he is in the midst of the field experience. He devises means to follow those insights that appear to him to be appropriate to the insight and the data, and he tends to push his explorations to their logical conclusion (whether they result in failure or success) to the point where he is satisfied he has made all efforts possible in examining the problems that stimulated inquiry.

The existence of external and formalized bureaucratic constraints may:

1. Deflect the worker from seeing the problem except perhaps as a minor deviation from a central plan since the preordained design acts to funnel his vision. Thus, there is always the possibility of a number of leads that were not followed up which then constitute the fund of anecdotes about the project.

2. Force the investigator to systematically avoid pursuit of such insights even if they are central to his own theoretical and perceptual apparatus. To accomplish this form of avoidance involves complicated intellectual self-manipulation.

3. May make it necessary to find ways of reporting findings which are not relevant to the agreed-upon research design even though such findings are actually acknowledged by the investigators to each other.

4. Force the investigator to find devices such as aesopian language to sneak in the point in the report.

The result of all of this for the bureaucratic researcher is that he must build up a complicated apparatus to justify the neglect of the perceived issue when he felt that bureaucratic loyalty was more important than the issues that he himself once felt were more important. The pressures "to play ball" are enormous, and ways are found.

Most of the issues that were developed in *Small Town in Mass Society* were issues that did not fit the formal design of the project study. The issues we saw were:

1. The relationship of the community to the society at large.
2. The analysis of social and economic class as central to the community.
3. The analysis of power and politics.
4. The inclusion of economic data as relevant to the design.
5. Reporting on the actions of individual institutional leaders in the exercise of their institutional roles.
6. Reporting on "negative" or not affirmative aspects of community life [5] as necessary to an examination of the social and psychological basis of community participation.

Our pursuit of these issues as issues that were personally interesting to us could be carried out without conflict or tension within project administration so long as our work was not made public. As we shall later note more fully, however, it is difficult for programmed project administration to tolerate public discussion or publication of nonprogrammed issues. Under ordinary circumstances, the structure of project administration with its hierarchy of control, committee meetings, and other forms of maintaining discipline prevents the individual from developing an independent perspective. This has a number of consequences for both the intellectual development of the individual and for the project bureaucracy.

In the extreme case the inability on the part of an individual to find a way of developing his theoretical perspective or of pursuing what he regards as valid insights results in double-think wherein language publicly sanctioned by research officials defines "research realities" as opposed to "normal" realities. In other instances it results in forms of research and nonresearch language, ironic detachment from one's own work, or compliant work as a "team man" who moves intellectually in phase with project policy changes. The net result of all this for the individual is various forms of conscious or subliminal self-hatred, so that all of the categories that are found in

[5] It was the project that introduced the idea of positive as opposed to negative ways of evaluating the facts: "We agree with most of what these authors (i.e., Vidich and Bensman) say about the facts of community life in Springdale, but our evaluation of these facts tends to be positive rather than negative." See "Leadership and Participation in a Changing Rural Community," *op. cit.*, p. 53, footnote.

Merton's description of bureaucratic self-hatred are found in bureaucratic research.

The failure of the foregoing techniques to function adequately leads to personnel crises, demoralization of staff, bickering, feuds, and stalemates. The measure of the failure of these techniques is the rate of labor turnover of project personnel. The unsuccessful project never quite succeeds in repressing intellectual individuality and thus is fraught with tensions and impasses, whereas the successful project succeeds in achieving organizational stability, regulated production schedules, and so on at the cost of repressing the individual idea.[6]

In the face of these dynamics, a large part of project research becomes the reconciling of differences of viewpoints and insights and arriving at formulas of consensus which are quite similar to those described for village politics in Springdale. This is to say issues disappear, problems lose their sharpness, and talking and memo writing define the dominant ethos of the research enterprise until no individual insight embarrasses the smooth functioning of the organization of the project. In terms of organizational operations, this means:

1. When there are differences of opinion between researchers, especially between subordinates and supervisors or project heads, endless meetings ensue.

2. If the differences are fundamental and irreconcilable, there may be a suppression and postponement of an accumulating pile of differences.

3. Self-imposed conscious and begrudging suppression of differences of opinion and hostility, especially on the part of subordinates, and the development of factions and private gossip groups build up around stylized forms of suppression.

4. The development of diplomatic styles of language and other linguistic formulas which allow different views to be expressed in the same sentences, paragraphs, or chapters.

5. The building up of long, drawn-out feuds, political factionalization of the research organization, all of which is usually covered over on public occasions and always concealed from the view of the financial backers of the research.

6. The factions and feuds embellish the research with various forms of bureaucratic chicanery.

7. There is a continuous possibility for the occurrence of shifts in the direction of the project problem and in the research design as

[6] The problem of repressing original ideas can be solved in advance by personnel recruitment policies: when only like-minded social scientists are hired, agreement is assured. It is for this reason that recruitment policies in bureaucratic research may be a decisive factor in determining the success or failure of the project.

different individuals become predominant in the organizational structure over the course of the history of the project. As a result a project can have dozens of false starts, none of which is pursued because no one individual or faction ever achieves a clear victory.

8. There is always the chance for publication of multiple reports, a solution which in our opinion is the best method of resolving differences.

Retrospectively, it appears to us that only two things can be concluded from all this. First, it seems that the best bureaucratic research is achieved when one man is able to set himself up as an absolute dictator, almost no matter on what basis he gains his power. Then at least *his* point of view comes through in the work, thus giving the project a focus, even if this denies "democracy" to the other participating academicians. Second, it appears that the primary qualities necessary to doing bureaucratic research lie in the fields of statecraft, diplomacy, and group work techniques by which consensus can be engineered.

From the perspective of the individual researcher, all group and bureaucratic research is a form of torture.

Project Foreign Affairs and Their Effect on Research

Just as a community exists in a social matrix larger than itself, so any formal research project operates in an institutional context that encompasses more than itself. This fact may or may not determine the direction of research. The individual researcher who lacks plan and design and who has no staff or budget can ignore almost all problems of "foreign affairs" if he has the time and resources to pursue his demons as and where they may emerge. Programmed research finds itself in a much more complicated situation. The programmed project always faces outside publics and, moreover, must come to terms with them, make agreements with them, and reach an understanding on problems and issues defined by the publics. In university-connected community research these publics include the sponsor, the community, and the university. Each of these publics is a reference group, and each poses his own problems for scientific research investigation.

The Sponsor as Reference Group

The first problem facing the prospective researcher is to find a project for which a potential sponsor exists. Since it is only in extreme cases that a researcher will completely phrase his problem to meet sponsorship requirements, the usual tactic is to find a sponsor who will be interested and willing to provide funds to support a study that is still in some way related to the researcher's interests.[7]

The sponsoring agency, as is clearly understandable to everyone, wishes to support research within an area or within a range of problems related to its fundamental purposes as specified in its brochure. For a sponsoring agency to do otherwise is a breach of trust and is sometimes illegal as well. The researcher, then, begins his research by conducting research on sponsoring agencies which are likely to support his research.

Although basic research on sponsors has itself progressed to the point where directories of sponsors and synopses of their interests are published, the existence of these research tools does not solve the researchers' problems. Sponsors are suspicious of claimants, first, because there are so many of them and, second, because some of them from the sponsor's viewpoint are quacks whose ideas are inadmissible. This then leads to the necessity for finding "respectable, clean-cut, stable, responsible" directors and negotiators to meet with their foundation counterparts. The requirements for creative research are only accidentally related to the talent for negotiating with foundations. If and when the smooth, pleasant negotiator gains actual authority in the project (on the basis of his access to funds), any value of the research findings is also likely to be accidental.

In spite of all basic research on sponsors, the project researcher is still faced with:

1. Making contacts with the potential sponsor either through third parties or by hiring personnel because they bring the contact with them, or by directly hiring the sponsor's personnel. The choice of technique depends on stage of research, level of organiaztion, and quality of connections.

[7] The problem is more complicated than this. We have seen researchers whose interests have changed in phase with changes in sources of available funds. When a large number of individuals in a scientific community do this, we witness the phenomenon of research fads, for example, the mental health and organizational research which are popular at the present time. Available pools of money determine the dominant emphasis of the over-all research enterprise. More recently the directors of the philanthropic foundations and bureaus have come to conceive of themselves as possessing an explicit managerial function in choosing the direction of research investments. That is, a decision is made to invest in a given area, problem, or place, and proposals that fit the predefinition are supported. It is perfectly understandable that fund dispensers should try in this way to make their work interesting and creative.

2. Defining the project in terms of language, theories, and hypotheses that will be congenial to sponsor views as indicated in their statement of purposes and as expressed by specific administrative agents of the sponsor. A higher level of complexity is introduced where multiple sponsors are involved, for this means finding linguistic and theoretical compromises that will breach the differences between sponsors and that will yet appear to leave no contradictions in the statement of the problem. A field of expertise has grown up around this function.[8]

It is part of the rhythm of the total research cycle that the sponsor recedes as an important reference group after the grant has been received and is only again reasserted as a significant other when findings are to be discovered, written, and reported. No matter what happens between the time the money is given and the research operations are completed, at the time of writing and reporting the analyst must address himself to the original problem statement because the sponsor is still thinking in its terms in spite of the passage of time and the new experiences gained by the researcher from carrying out the research.[9] As a result the researcher is obliged to come up with findings that in some way relate to the original problem statements as worked out with and for the sponsor. Maintaining trust with the sponsor is as important for this kind of research as the research itself because, apart from other considerations, specific projects are always part of a larger career pattern which requires future sponsors.

Faithfulness to the original statement of the problem is only one of a number of problems that arise in the later stages of project research.

1. A report discharging, at least at formal levels, the obligation to the grant must be delivered. The pressures at this point make the successful project director a virtuoso at putting something between two covers.

---

[8] In a fund-raising experience recently encountered by one of the authors, a team of two incompatible applicants agreed not to disagree with each other until funds could be secured from two incompatible agencies, each of which had "other" reasons for desiring to give research funds. Almost all of the negotiators to this transaction were experts who understood the fundamental contradictions between the participants but who also realized that it was necessary not to mention these differences during the monetary negotiations.

[9] Researchers who attempt to keep sponsors informed of every change in direction of the research find themselves involved in endless negotiations with sponsors and with little time for research.

2. The production of the report may not be as simple as it appears to an outsider or even to the sponsor. Since the project's inception there have been many changes in project personnel: people who carried out crucial research operations have moved to other positions and universities, and important project officers who may have had little contact with the actual research data remain. As if this were not enough, all of the data may not bear a relationship to the stated problem since some of them at least will reflect "hunches" that were followed but did not produce the desired results—during the heat of data collection the formally stated problem sometimes loses its saliency. As a consequence of factors such as these, there is the institution known as the "rescue operation" wherein no one on the staff is willing or able to write a report, so the last man hired is hired specifically to piece together all the bits, to create the appearance of a unified structure to the data, and to write all this in a form that can be bound, even if it is only a mimeographed, hectographed, or subsidized publication.

The salvage expert may be a junior project member who happens to have literary skills; he may be a specialized expert who moves from project to project because he can write, but lacks the organizational stature and competence to get his own grants; or he may be primarily a writer who has little specialized competence in the research field. The rescue operation has become so standardized in project research that (1) salvage skills are a recognized professional ability, (2) men may build reputations only on the fact that they have never failed to submit a report, and (3) at times the mimeographed and the heavily subsidized publication has more prestige in some circles than real books because it is understood that the hectographed report represents a large cash investment which a book may not.

3. In final form the report must eliminate all embarrassing findings and, more specifically, all mention of specific people and instances that might otherwise be necessary to illustrate a point. The definition of what is an embarrassing finding of course is always related to the ideology of the audience to which the report is directed, but at a minimum the report is written with at least one eye to the sponsor, and at a maximum an attempt is made to create a unified and pleasant image of the whole project. The major value conveyed by the report is academic and research respectability. Any "rocking the boat" becomes a major crime against the sponsor, his values, and those whose careers are identified with the project.

The Community as a Reference Group

From the inception of the first contacts with the community, the town wants to know what the research is about and how the town will be affected by it. The answers to these questions define the project and the research to the townspeople and add up to a set of future promises to the town.

As in most research, many people in the community are unenthusiastic if not suspicious about being investigated. Springdale, in upstate New York, was a Republican-dominated, conservative town which had previous experiences, not all of them happy, with researchers from Cornell University.[10] In order to secure acceptance by the community in the face of its suspiciousness, its past experiences with research, and a certain amount of hostility and resentment it had toward the University simply because it was a big and dominant institution in the area, the research project presented itself to the town as an upholder of rural values. Scientific investigators regularly attended meetings of the Community Club and told jokes and played games with its members in order to get in exchange their adherence to the research project.

By the terms of its own past the project was committed to studying socially creative activity, and at the time of the Springdale phase of the research it had elected to study this creativity in the form of socially constructive community activities. Springdale was selected for study because the directors of the project thought it was more "constructive" than other towns surveyed as possible choices. Even after the selection of the town and the hiring of a field director it was not entirely clear what was constructive activity. This was natural enough, of course, because if it had been known in advance the research would have been unnecessary.

Nevertheless, without knowing exactly what we would be studying, we were pressed by the community to tell what the study was about, who it included, what its purpose was, and what kind of book would be written. In response to these inquiries, the project developed a line that included:

"We are not interested in the negative features of the town because too much fruitless work on that has been done already."

---

[10] Several years prior to our research, a division of the agricultural school had made a land classification survey which rated all land from bad to excellent depending on various criteria of soil content. Farmers in low-rated areas remembered and resented this survey because it had tended to set relative real-estate values on land so that prospective buyers could point to Cornell's survey and argue land prices on the basis of its authority.

"A positive approach is needed."

"We are interested in constructive activities because from this we feel we can help other people in other communities to live better lives. Springdale is a laboratory which may help us find important solutions."

"We are especially interested in the Community Club because it is a democratic organization that brings *all the people* together and there are no restrictions on membership and no entrance fees."

"We have to get back to the older values of the individual, neighboring and the neighborhood, and Springdale seems to provide an opportune setting for this. We enlist your cooperation in helping us to solve this scientific problem."

All of these commitments were made as a way of selling the project to the townspeople at a time when no one knew what the project would be studying or where it would locate the community's constructive activities. In giving "nonexistent" answers to community inquiries when the project's methods and results are indefinite, the project, unfortunately, becomes committed to those answers.

The greatest concern of some townspeople was with how they personally would be portrayed in the "book." In some instances this concern bordered on anxiety and in other instances an exhibitionism, with a desire only to appear in a favorable light. In the field work the statement, "I hope you're not going to quote me on this," seemed to demand a reassuring answer, and again the issue of community relations played a role in shaping policy. Let us illustrate this with an example presented in another paper.

As the research progressed, the "assurance" of anonymity came to be equated with "doing an entirely statistical report." This happened in a curiously inadvertent way: on various occasions when the project was asked to explain its purposes in greater detail or when community suspicions had been aroused, the standard practice of some staff members was to assure members of the community that there was nothing to worry about because all individuals and specific events would get lost in the statistical analysis. At the time, these assurances were very successful in allaying the fears and anxieties of the key members of the community, and so some members of the project, particularly those who were less trained and more prone to panic, began to give such assurances whenever resistances developed. Unfortunately, some key members of the community were left with the impression that the entire report would be statistical. As this impression became more prevalent in the community, it also became more prevalent in the research project until it was understood by many persons in both groups that no other than a statistical presentation of the data was to be made.[11]

This was not an explicit policy of the project. It was an implied promise always accepted more by the town than by the project. Among the project members it tended to receive more acceptance when they were in the town than in the central offices, but as time progressed it became difficult for project members themselves to think of any kind of report other than a statistical one, even though it was always also assumed that there would be an analysis of the social structure of the town.

The idea of doing only a statistical report grew out of the project's promise to the community not to identify any of its members in a recognizable way. When people asked how identities would be concealed, the easiest answer was, "It'll be all statistical." In the writing and analysis, however, the problem of identity concealment could not be handled so easily. In the writing of *Small Town in Mass Society,* we decided we would use the solution used by community sociologists in the past, namely, the use of pseudonyms.[12] When we published our book we were criticized in *Human Organization* and by Cornell University for following that policy. However, when the staff of Cornell Studies in Social Growth later came to write its report, it discovered the same dilemma.

. . . We were all very much disturbed by the reaction of our major Springdale informants to your book. The essential problem was that they had been promised in their initial contacts with us that in any report out of the research they would not be personally identifiable. This was true of the kind of report which we foresaw at the time, and I think it will be true of the *Journal of Social Issues* number. However, it is certainly not true of your book, so we were naturally asked the question, "What about this?" The line we took with the support of the college administration and the Social Science Research Center was that we had expected you to be bound by the same promises which were made to the Springdale people before you appeared on the scene, that we were very much disappointed by the amount and kind of information about clearly recognizable Springdale individuals, which was included in your book, but that we did not have any control over what was finally published. However, we made it clear that we disapproved of this type of publication and

[11] A. Vidich, "Freedom and Responsibility in Research: A Rejoinder," *Human Organization,* 19, No. 1 (Spring 1960), pp. 3–4.

[12] Our reasons for doing this have been stated more fully in *Human Organization,* "Freedom and Responsibility in Research," 17, No. 4, and "Freedom and Responsibility in Research: A Rejoinder," *ibid.*

wished to dissociate ourselves from it as much as possible. We are now faced with the problem of producing a report which will meet the criteria which was laid down in the original contacts with the Springdale residents. I do not know how well we will be able to do this . . .[13]

In the final official project report[14] on the town the following solution to the problem of identification was reached.

The main problem which publication presented was, of course, the one of identifying the individual participants in the community. We became convinced that you were right in thinking that it is not possible to provide a meaningful discussion of community action without describing at least some of the principal leaders in a way that makes them readily identifiable to others in the community. Consequently, we decided to use your (Vidich and Bensman) code names in our account, at least the code names Jones, Hilton, Lee, and Flint. The other main participants centering around the repair of the mill dam were people who did not seem to us to require accurate placement in the community power structure; consequently, we used pseudonyms for these people which, I think, would not allow them to be identified by their friends and neighbors—except, of course, those who were themselves involved in the dam project. My present interpretation of the basic reason for the difficulty between you and the project over the write-up of your material is that the project made promises to the people in Springdale which were compatible with the kind of report which was originally planned . . . , but which was not compatible with a report which would deal in any realistic fashion with the social structure of the community.[15]

It is in the nature of the social structure of a community that a project can never have a relationship with it as a totality. It is necessary from the beginning to deal selectively with specific persons in order to secure and sustain some acceptance. The Springdale project worked on the theory that admission to the community would be best secured by working through the important social and organizational leaders. The logic of this action was that since leadership and social organization were the important dimensions of the study, gaining support and acceptance from these sources would both secure legitimacy quickly and efficiently and give access to a strata of important respondents. In practical field terms this strategy was effective—the doors to the community members and organizations were opened— but in scientific terms the implications of this identification with the town fathers and social respectability had far-reaching implications.

[13] Personal communication from project official, January 1958.
[14] "Leadership and Participation in a Changing Rural Community," *op. cit.*
[15] Personal communication from project official, July 1961.

1. Because of the organizational importance of particular individuals, these individuals came to be regarded as more valid sources of information than others. As the work progressed it was assumed that, before starting field-work plans for new research, activities would be presented to the executive officers of the Community Club and then to the entire club. The club became a major sounding board for the project and some of its members were used as "consultants" on matters concerning project-town relations. The more the project began to depend on selected informants, the more it became committed to and dependent on their perspective of the town. An operating structure of images of the town was built up which would be violated if other informants were to be used. In practice critics of the Community Club and community leaders were dismissed as "bad citizens."

2. The project's image of the town thus came to coincide with the image held by the town's leadership strata. This created its own problems. Since the official, dominant image of the town was not held by all members of the community, the problem arose of disposing of the unacceptable counterimages in circulation in the community. Two methods of disposition were found. (a) Minority images could be dismissed as being irrelevant to the project because they did not fall within its purview. This was the case with the world view of the shack people as a whole who were not regarded as instrumental in promoting community mindedness. (b) They could be dismissed as representing a deviant or ridiculous viewpoint. The project's attitude to West, the potato and gladiola farmer, became the same as Lee's; West was laughed off the stage. Though West almost became a major innovator by his near successful political campaign to oust the town powers from office, it never occurred to anyone in the central research offices to consider this as creative activity or even leadership.

After three years of contact with the community, the members of the project and "The Project" as an official organization had established many personal and official contacts, commitments, friendships, and confidences. This was inevitable simply because of the duration and closeness of the contact. The problem was how these personal and official relations relate to scientific reporting. In the Springdale case the project director took the position that certain materials were questionable from the point of view of ethics and possible injury to persons.

I have just finished reading the manuscript of you and Bensman and, in response to your request, am giving concrete examples of material which, though it may represent public knowledge, is, in our judgment, highly questionable from the point of view of professional ethics and possible injury to the persons involved.   Since there are many instances of this kind, I shall confine myself to a few outstanding examples.

1. There are many references to the enmity between Flint and Lee . . . Since, as you yourself have emphasized, these two persons will be immediately recognizable to anyone familiar with the community, assertions that Flint "has been excluded from town politics by Lee" who harbors "resentment" against him are fairly strong accusations.   Moreover, the discussion of their personal antagonism is not really central to your analysis of the way in which the community operates and hence you would not lose much by omitting mention of the matter.

2. The whole discussion of Peabody, the school principal, and his relation to the community could, if it remained in its present form, do a good deal of harm and arouse justifiable resentment.   For example, consider the possible impact on him and others of reading the following direct quotation attributed "to a prominent member of invisible government": "He's a little too inhuman—has never gone into anything in the town. He's good for Springdale until he gets things straightened out.   Then we will have to get rid of him."   Potentially equally damaging are the statements quoted from the observers' report, but these, along with all excerpts from the project files, would of course no longer appear in the manuscript.

3. In pointing out that the Polish community is controlled by political leaders through intermediaries who are willing to do their bidding in exchange for acceptance, is it necessary to point the finger so visibly at Kinserna?   You do this very pointedly . . . where you go so far as to assert that the upshot of his activities is "to get the Poles to accept measures and policies which are disadvantageous to them."

4. Personality descriptions of the ministers . . . are likewise conspicuously on the *ad hominem* side.   For example, you refer to one as "awkward, condescending, and not of the people" and to another as a "cantankerous trouble-maker."   Also, I wonder whether the description of the Episcopalian minister as trained in "one of the 'radical' Eastern seminaries" is not subject to misinterpretation by Springdale readers despite your use of quotations around the word radical.   Given upstate New York's climate of opinion, such a statement may have some unfortunate consequences for the man concerned.

5. The clearly uncomplimentary remarks about Grainger . . . have especial importance for not only is he likely to read them himself, even though he is no longer living in the community, but they are also likely to be read by his colleagues and superiors in the Extension Service.   It would be particularly unfair and unfortunate, especially in view of Grainger's wholehearted cooperation with the project, if any statement made by you jeopardized Grainger's professional future.   As the manuscript now stands, such a possibility is by no means out of the question. . . .[16]

[16] Personal communication from project director, July 1956.

The issue here is not the specific items of censorship, but rather the assumption of protective attitudes toward specific community members on the basis of personal attractiveness, entangling commitments, respondent's earlier cooperativeness, and other nonresearch consider-ations. As a result of personal, social, and organizational commit-ments, the project finds itself in the position of writing its findings with an eye to other than research or theoretical interests and issues.

As a final step in viewing the community as a reference group, the project decided that:

. . . Before any manuscripts are shown to outside representatives, such as publishers or their agents, we will ask one or two persons within the college and possibly in Springdale to read the manuscripts from the point of view of public relations. Although the final responsibility for deciding what we publish will rest with the project staff, the reactions of such readers would receive serious consideration and we would probably rewrite and omit in accordance with their recommendations. . . .[17]

In this instance, to avoid personal responsibility for the project's research reporting, selected nonresearch respondents would be in-vited to pass on manuscripts purely as a way of avoiding bad public relations, so that aspects of community life that may be theoretically relevant can be censored by local individuals on nonresearch grounds. Moreover, the local individuals to be selected would be specifically those who constituted the project's dominant reference group in the town, namely, the town's official leaders and spokesmen who repre-sented most forcefully the stereotyped image of the positive-minded community which the project has absorbed as its own image of the town.

The identification of the project and its personnel with the town's interests and with the feelings and sentiments of individuals and groups being studied leads to a subtle adaptation of the research to the problems of the community even though those problems are not the problems of the research. In an extreme instance this policy would lead to no point of view except the point of view of the com-munity. Acting Dean Grisely [18] of Cornell University seems to take this position as the only viable one for social science.

The first thing that happened with a book like this has to be taken in the context that people are not very happy to be studied. I don't know to

[17] Personal letter from project director, January 1956.
[18] Since the Dean is a resident of the Springdale community, we have, in accord-ance with past practice, invented this name in order to maintain the anonymity of our informants.

what extent you may find yourselves, those of you who are becoming involved in the social science field, are likely to find that one of the most difficult things that you will have to do is to sell a project to a group, an organization, by getting them to permit you to come in and ask questions, observe them, write them up, interfere with their time, and in most cases for uses that they don't know or understand, and they are somewhat suspicious and concerned with this whole process. This particular project (Cornell Studies in Social Growth) was introduced to the community through the Extension Service system of the College of Agriculture. People in the community who had confidence in the university for a variety of reasons accepted and sponsored the project and the individuals connected with it. Now Mr. Vidich, as he points out, lived in the community and was accepted in a real sense as one of the people in the community, with people making an effort to see that he was introduced to various groups and so on. Now when this book came out with some of the characterizations and implications, I think there were several kinds of reactions.

In the first place it made people mad. It made those people mad who had brought the study in, who had been responsible and had participated in it. It was in total violation of the understandings which they felt existed between the university and themselves and the community. Second, it made other people feel very badly and hurt them, some of them I'm afraid considerably because they felt that the friendships and confidences they had extended to Mr. Vidich and his family had been violated. Further, I think the distortion of the characterization of these people, many of whom were friends of his and some of whom were very good friends during the time he was in the community, created a self-consciousness of these individuals which they found very discomforting, which lasted for a time, but from which they recovered. Fourth, I think that the community itself could not particularly welcome the outside attention that it received, especially those people who were in a variety of ways related to outside activities and they found that they were being examined and cross-examined about the community by outsiders with whom they came in contact.

There was a problem of some loss of faith and disruption of university relationships, and I suspect there is an increase in suspicion of outsiders, particularly inquisitive outsiders.[19]

At certain stages the community may become a more important reference group for the project than is the scientific community to which the research is ostensibly addressed. In Springdale, for example, the study of constructive activities in the community gradually came to include the ideology that the project and its members assume constructive attitudes toward Springdale in all phases of work includ-

---

[19] From a tape-recorded address delivered to a group of sociology students at Harpur College, 1962.

ing community relations, field work, participation, analysis of data, and reporting of scientific results.

The highest form of project identification with the town is when the research organization attempts to take responsibility for the actions of all its agents who act in and on the town. The Springdale field work was carried out by more than one hundred people who at a variety of organizational levels participated in the work at different times over a period of three years. Simply by sending large numbers of people into a town, a large amount of public relations is required; new field operations have to be announced, results of preceding surveys must be tentatively reported, newspaper stories have to be written, apologies must be made for field workers' errors, the project's local landlord must be placated when the field director fails to cut the grass, and so on. In order to avoid public-relations errors, field personnel begin to be selected on public-relations grounds. Can you send a foreign student into an upstate New York community? In what positions is it advisable not to have a Jew? What about the Negro who is the husband of a staff member? Some members of the project are excluded from the town completely because they are too "argumentative," too "controversial," or too "unreliable" in some way as defined by the project.

When research workers in their field work provoke a complaint from a community member or a local official, the complaint is sent to research headquarters, and, by the act of accepting the complaint, the project assumes responsibility for rectification either to the individual in question or to the "community as a whole." This means the project is placed in the position of apologizing for its research workers and on occasion publicly reprimanding and punishing its research staff. Punishment of staff usually takes the form of revoking privileges to enter the field; complaints from community members can jeopardize sociological careers.

Standard practice is for the project to make a scapegoat of the last man who left the project, so that all the project's ills in the community will be attributed to him; the man who is no longer there to defend himself serves the purpose of absorbing all of the free-floating resentment the town has against the project. In the same measure as the departee acts as a scapegoat, so his ideas, insights, and knowledge of the community can be safely ignored and forgotten. The project's offering of scapegoats to the town is always a concession to the ideology of the town.

As already indicated the officials of the Springdale project were placed in the position of taking a policy stand before the opinion of the community on the existence of our book. There could be no question to anyone who had any familiarity with the town that *Small Town in Mass Society* would be a provocative experience for Springdale. So far had the project commitment to the community and its values become entrenched that, almost as a reflex response, the publication of *Small Town in Mass Society* evoked a public project apology [20] published on page one of the Springdale *Courier*.

February 6, 1958

The Editor
Springdale *Courier*
Springdale, New York

Dear Sir:

We at Cornell have read the book by Vidich and Bensman entitled *Small Town in Mass Society* and wish to make clear that this work in no sense reflects the intentions or views of the Cornell Project. The book was written after Dr. Vidich had left our employ. Mr. Bensman, of course, never had any connection with the Cornell Project. The general orientation of the work, as well as the material with which it deals, stands in direct contradiction to our policies regarding confidentiality of data and the publication of identifiable information.

Upon learning of Dr. Vidich's plans, we requested him to eliminate or, at least, modify the materials in the manuscript which we felt to be most objectionable, and received his assurances that he would do so. Accordingly, we were doubly shocked to find that much of the objectionable material had been retained.

Since Dr. Vidich entered and lived in the community as a member of our staff, we must accept some indirect responsibility for what has happened. Unfortunately, we know of no way to undo what has been done but can only express our sincere regrets.

Sincerely yours,

Project Director
Cornell Studies in Social Growth

This project apology, addressed though it is to the community at large, is clearly meant to placate those particular individuals and groups in the community who might have taken offense. First and foremost, these are the official leaders and the middle class. It must be recalled that the community is composed of individuals and groups

[20] Letter to the editor of the Springdale *Courier* published as a lead article shortly after the publication of *Small Town in Mass Society*.

who do not see eye to eye on all issues, and that not all community members would be equally offended or even offended at all by the publication of this book. However, it was in the logic of the project's commitment to the community, namely, that it was tied to certain individuals and groups, that it must necessarily condemn, disavow, and dissociate from the study of *Small Town in Mass Society*. The scientific enterprise had come to fully reflect the ideology of the rural community.

Insofar as the ideology of the community grew in salience and became the basis of project reactions, all project actions more and more came to be addressed to it. In due course any offense against the community ideology became a risk to the project and a major crime for the project members.

Once the point was reached that an offense against the town was a crime, the project began to spend more and more time attempting to avert both the crime and the risk of the crime. This could be done only by making a major effort to control the town, the movements of research workers within it, and, finally, by controlling the town's image of the project by organized public relations. Because of this a large part of the field director's activities were devoted to maintaining project-community harmony. This same process apparently was carried out in just as intensive a form at the time of the publication of the book.

At this point I found myself [Dean Grisely] in the interesting position of becoming a liaison between the director of the study who was greatly concerned with this thing being published over which he could not exercise any control really, and the community. I transmitted messages back and forth and so on. I thought you might be interested to know that I received during the process of this a lot of notes from people in the community, and one from an elderly lady who was a retired teacher. I just want to give you a sampling of this. She wrote the note to my wife and said, "I'm so glad your husband gave that Cornell report at the Community Club because now I feel better towards Cornell." I attempted to explain that this was not a Cornell study, it was not an official study, but it was a violation of the study itself.[21]

Once the cycle has reached this stage, there is little left of research except diplomacy and public relations. When project diplomacy and public relations win out, it means converting the town into a rat lab, that is, the project converts the community into so many actors for

[21] From Dean Grisely's address to the sociology group at Harpur College, 1962.

the research project, and the research investigators respond like actors to the roles they have created.

The reactions of both the town and the University to the book's publication reflected their accumulated public-relations expectations. A number of people, particularly those officials who had collaborated most closely with the project, felt that their trust had been betrayed, and they lodged complaints with the project staff and Cornell University. Since we were not participants to that scene, others will have to report that aspect of the problem. The official position of Cornell as already noted was to dissociate from the book and its authors and to identify with the town. At the time of publication, Vidich was privately reprimanded as follows:

Having read your book, we, no less than the people of Springdale, are surprised and shocked. Despite your assurances that, wherever possible, you would delete material that we considered objectionable, you have made little more than a token effort in this direction. . . .

It is yet too early to judge how serious the effects of your book will be on Springdale and Cornell. We already have indications, however, that a number of people have been badly hurt, and at least one of Cornell's programs in the area has encountered resistance and resentment directly attributable to your publication.[22]

We find it difficult to believe that, in choosing to retain objectionable material, you were not well aware of what you were doing. In any event, we wish to make it absolutely clear that we regard your actions in this matter as a breach of faith and professional ethics both with ourselves, and, what is much more important, with the many people of Springdale who granted us the privilege of their hospitality and confidence.[23]

The town itself came to its own defense in reviews of the book which appeared in Springdale and neighboring towns. For example, the *Times* in the county seat: [24]

[22] So far as we know this was one of Dean Grisely's projects on small business-men. If true, we refuse to take full responsibility for the resentment because, in terms of our analysis, the small businessman will seize on any easily available object of resentment so long as the object in question absolutely lacks defenses.
[23] Personal communication from project director, February 1958.
[24] We were not able to secure a copy of the issue of the Springdale *Courier* which carried the review of the book. Though we wrote to the publishers asking for copies and enclosed funds to cover costs, no one ever replied to our request. Our relations with Cornell have been so strained that we have not asked to see their files on the matter. Reviews appeared in other regional papers like the Ithaca *Journal*, but we have made no effort to collect these.

THE SMALL TOWN IN MASS SOCIETY—[SPRINGDALE] SAYS IT ISN'T SO

Small Town in Mass Society, by Arthur J. Vidich
and Joseph Bensman (Princeton University Press,
$6.00)

An accurate review of this book should be from the viewpoint of a professional sociologist since it is intended as a textbook for the social sciences.

Lacking that point of view, our interest in the book stems from the fact that it is written by a former resident of [Springdale] and concerns itself with "class, power and religion" in [Springdale], called Springdale in the book.

Mr. Vidich is currently about as popular in [Springdale] as the author of *Peyton Place* is in her small town and for the same reason—both authors violate what Vidich calls the etiquette of gossip.

During the three years he lived here, Vidich was engaged in a research project. "Cornell Studies in Social Growth" sponsored by the New York State College of Home Economics and with the aid of funds from the National Institute of Mental Health, United Public Health Service and the Social Science Research Council.

He then proceeded to use portions of the survey material, making Cornell very unhappy, added a considerable amount of misinformation and gossip and drew certain conclusions based on the three sources.

The Cornell survey material is fairly accurate and pertains to economics and population trends. The misinformation indicates that Vidich is something less than a scientist and has either deliberately distorted facts to prove his personal conclusions or has failed to inquire into basic facts. For example, he states that the railroad running through the village has not made a stop there in years: this misstatement seems immaterial except that he uses it to bolster his conclusion that local business is at a standstill.

He discusses the failure of ecumenicalism in [Springdale], stating that Episcopal and Congregational churches failed to merge because of the opposition of powerful members of the older generation who were fearful of losing the traditions of their churches. Actually, no merger was ever contemplated and the temporary arrangement of sharing one minister ceased when his superior decided he was being overworked.

The inference is that [Springdale] is living in the past, unable to accept new ideas of mass society, and, further, that it is run by certain individuals.

The theme of control runs throughout the book. [Springdale] citizens will be amazed to discover that practically every phase of daily living is subject to the whims of one man and his cohorts. They run local government, including the school, decide church policies and influence the economic life of the community.

No attempt is made to disguise the individuals who may be readily identified by anyone having any knowledge of [Springdale]. In this field, Vidich seems to have resorted to pure gossip as his source of material.

The author is shocked by the fact people settle their differences in private rather than resorting to public argument; economy in government becomes "the psychology of scarcity"; he arrives at the conclusion people work fantastically hard to avoid coming to terms with themselves.

He finally sums up the whole picture by proclaiming that the entire population is disenchanted, has surrendered all aspirations and illusions. But, says he, Springdalers are too stupid to realize they are frustrated. To a certain extent (they) live a full and not wholly unenjoyable life. "Because they do not recognize their defeat, they are not defeated."

"Life consists in making an adjustment that is as satisfactory as possible within a world which is not often tractable to basic wishes and desires."

It should not have taken 314 pages of repetition and technical language to discover that life, as so defined, is not a problem peculiar to a small town.—CC [25]

The reactions of some of the people in the community were recorded in one part of a three-part feature story about the book which was carried by the Ithaca *Journal*. The varied reactions indicate that the town's response was not monolithic, and, moreover, that not all persons had equally absorbed the public relations.

BOOK'S SALES SPIRAL IN SUBJECT VILLAGE

Here is the last of three articles about a book and its effect on the town about which it was written.

By Donald Greet

For a book that costs $6 and is "slow" to read, "Small Town" proved to be a best-seller in [Springdale].

Elmer G. Kilpatric, proprietor of a main street store, sold more than two dozen copies. He says only "Peyton Place" in a half-dollar paperback did better.

Mrs. Mary Lou Van Scoy, librarian at the village library (which does not have "Peyton Place"), says two copies "have been on the move since we got it."

One copy, she says, "got bitten up by a dog."

There is evidence, then, that a good many people in [Springdale] have read the book and a good many more have been treated to certain salient passages by their friends.

Ask a waitress in the local restaurant if she is acquainted with "Small Town" and she will say, "Oh, yes, that book."

The three persons who felt the chief impact of the book are called in its pages Sam Lee, Howard Jones and John Flint.

Villagers know these men respectively as C. Arthur Beebe, C. Paul Ward and Winston S. Ives. Beebe is the retired head of the [Springdale] *Courier*,

Ward is a partner in Ward & Van Scoy Feed Mill and Ives is an attorney.

All three have been and are active in local politics. The book refers to the threesome as the "invisible government," a term that has provoked both merriment and anger in [Springdale].

All three proved real enough to give their impressions of "Small Town." Says Beebe: "People have talked over every situation in the book. They have not felt generally that the book was fair.

"It was not as objective as it was supposed to have been. It was only one man's opinion. He (author Vidich) was judging a small community by big city standards. We felt it was sneaky."

Ward comments: "The whole thing is based on gossip and is not a true study. He (Vidich) didn't find it out by any bona fide investigation.

"The book could just as well have been written from New York (City). It was not a scientific study, which is what it purports to be."

Attorney Ives is somewhat more generous:

"Two-thirds of the book is probably alright but he (Vidich) got into his biggest difficulty with personalities and in dealing with certain recent events.

"My principal objection to the book is that there are unfortunately a number of factual inaccuracies which in some cases create a distinctly misleading impression.

"Another objection is that the book suggests 'invisible government' had no motive but control. In my experience and to my knowledge leaders have been motivated to do what they thought best for the community."

Others in town added their comments. The Rev. V. F. Cline, minister of the Baptist Church for 14 years, said: "It (the book) has caused a suspicion between individuals and groups."

Funeral director Myron Miller puts it succinctly: "Much ado about nothing."

Off-the-cuff statements, not intended for quoted publication, indicate that some portions of the book struck pretty close to home and gave [Springdalers] the chance to see themselves as others see them.

Said one observer: "The book did more to allay apathy in [Springdale] than anything in a long time."

Perhaps it is just coincidence, but interest in a village election this spring shot up from the usual two dozen votes to 178.

The village's two fire companies, needled in the book for pursuing their separate ways over the years, recently joined forces.

One thing is certain: Walk into [Springdale] and mention "Small Town" and you won't get away without a reaction. Those reactions range from horse-laughs, to polite smiles to the angry bristle of a porcupine.[26]

Later when the town held its annual Fourth of July parade, several floats were addressed to the book. It is clear from the following

[26] Ithaca *Journal*, June 13, 1958.

account of the event that the community had managed to reassert its image of itself.

[SPRINGDALE] CALLS IT EVEN

The people of the village of [Springdale] waited quite a while to get even with Art Vidich who wrote a "Peyton Place" type book about their town recently.

The featured float of the annual Fourth of July parade today followed an authentic copy of the jacket of the book *Small Town in Mass Society*, done large scale by Mrs. Beverly Robinson. Following the book cover came residents of [Springdale], riding masked in cars labeled with the fictitious names given them in the book.

But the pay-off was the final scene, a manure-spreader filled with very rich barnyard fertilizer, over which was bending an effigy of "The Author."

Vidich, who lived in the town and won confidence of the local citizenry over a period of two years, worked under the auspices of Cornell University to complete a survey of typical village life. The survey was made available to village planners.

However, Vidich in collaboration with Joseph Bensman decided to capitalize on the material in a way that would benefit themselves financially.[27]

With this final defeat of the book in terms consistent with the psychology of the town's residents, the community was able to continue as if the book had never been published or, more exactly, that it had now been consigned to its proper place in the town's imagery. The community could return to its former self-image and to the project's definition of rural life.

Public relations is a form of promise to a public. All the public-relations attitudes and postures of the town will focus the report to the point of view that the town holds on the project in response to the project's prior public relations. Even if research administrators are quite conscious that they are using public relations to get the work done, they are forced into reporting their findings on the basis of past promises. At this point all of the accumulated public relations stand as a barrier to reporting anything but the *bon homie* which the project projected onto the town beforehand. The project leaders then have the choice of either making a bland, pleasant report, or of violating a trust relationship which they have purposely created to further the carrying out of the research. Since it is difficult for the researcher to see beforehand all of the ramifications of a public-

---

[27] Springdale *Courier* press release, July 4, 1958.

relations program at the time it is instituted, he may find himself paralyzed by the task of writing a report consistent with public-relations commitments. Due to these dynamics many reports are never written.

The University as a Project Reference Group and Pressure Group

The relationship between the university and the project rests on the consideration that each has some value for the other.

The university is interested in the research project because it helps in the financing of the institution. Project budgets contain standard overhead items, help to cover staff salaries, and help with the purchasing of equipment. Frequently the project will bring to the university additional staff members who otherwise could not be brought because of lack of funds, because the number of departmental positions is limited, or because salary rates are too low to attract the research stars. As a rule research projects allow universities to grow, if not painlessly, at least easily.

Also, the project brings prestige to the university in its competition for prestige with other universities. A university without projects is regarded as not doing any research, and without projects it is not possible to get other projects. In addition to all this, there is at least the ideology that there should be a coincidence of interest between research and the idea of the university; that is, teaching, research, and knowledge are thought of as related to each other positively and as being necessary to the idea of the university.

For their parts the individual project members and the project director receive status in the university because they bring money to it in the form of overhead write-offs, because the staff underwrites its own costs and because the project brings additional staff to the university at little or no cost. If looked at only in the form of statistical aggregates, the student-teacher ratio is improved and the standing of the university, with the accrediting agencies and other interested publics, is given a more solid foundation by project research.

In addition, the project brings a promise of prestige in the form of a future publication which will be linked to the name of the university. Not only is there the promise of publication as such, but the research may receive rewards from professional associations, and individual project members may be cited for the importance of their work by relevant reference groups. In its early stages, at least, almost any project is full of hoped-for gains to the university.

Personnel connected with the project receive short-range esteem within the university for different reasons. If the project is heavily financed by "respectable" money and staffed by prestigious "leaders of the field," almost all personnel connected with the project may absorb some of the surplus prestige as their own. At times researchers may elect to be or not to be associated with a project accordingly as it possesses surpluses of prestige. Up to a point, at least within the world of projects, project reputation is personal and institutional prestige. For this reason projects address themselves to project prestige competition within the university.

To the university community at large, project personnel receive esteem because they are busy, because they publish, because they possess a whole range of anecdotes which enliven the life of the university with something different (especially something that appears to have some relevance to the "real" world), and because they can talk knowingly about research designs and the other apparatus of scientific research. An occasional trip to Washington or upper Fifth Avenue can be an added embellishment.

In the research project there is a general evidence of activity which appears to be in the pursuit of knowledge, and this knowledge is different from the general run of routine teaching or "unreal" knowledge that otherwise appears to inhabit the university. Project members can hold their own in campus conversations and, the face they present to the campus world is that they are getting things done, not just teaching the standard stock of knowledge, but actually expanding its frontiers and producing what will later appear in the textbooks. The research project lends a certain excitement and importance to campus life.

Whosoever brings a research project to the university enhances his department's prestige in relation to other departments in the university, and helps to advertise his department to the outside world, especially in relation to the competition between departments in different universities. Gaining a competitive edge over competitive departments is important to the university administration not only because it helps the recruiting of students but more importantly it creates a generalized image that important research is taking place which can then become a basis for recruiting other research funds. Economically speaking, the total corpus that is the university can reach the point where, if it has *enough* research, it can ideally live off itself.

Research projects tie in with the expansion of graduate training programs since they bring in funds to support graduate students who otherwise would not come to the university if it did not provide them with a livelihood while they are studying. The graduate student who is being subsidized by the research project considers himself fortunate to be able to continue his education without monetary cost to himself. At the same time as he is being subsidized, he is available to the administration as an item of display to potential sponsors of other research projects. The university must have projects, staff, and graduate students in order to get more projects, staff, and graduate students.

In exchange for allowing projects to settle in its territory, the university expects in return to place certain constraints on the way projects conduct their business. At a minimum the project sponsor must be respectable within the terms of respectability adhered to by the administration of the university. Sometimes size of grant helps to establish the donor's respectability.

Since the university has an obligation to the community and to prestigious sponsors, there are a number of political obligations that must be met. Nowadays these political obligations are organized under the university Social Science Research Center, an institution which seems to be based on the model of the historic Agricultural Extension Services: the Social Science Research Center is to the bureaucratic age what the Extension Service was to the agricultural age. This is not to mention that the university president himself as well as second level officials in the university bureaucracy have personal communication with the foundations, government, segments of the business world, and with the alumni who are themselves connected to these agencies and foundations.

Because of whatever complex network of interconnections exists between the university and the outside benefactors and supporters, the university places certain requirements on research. The major requirement is that specific findings should not alienate any group of benefactors or sponsors, including political figures in the town or the state. At the political level there is a great deal of variability between the social and physical sciences and within the social sciences. Different schools may be connected to different reference groups with different ideologies and positions. The only point being made is that for any specific school there will usually be some correspondence between research lines and the line of the higher administrative officials of the school as a whole, which means that for the research project:

1. Specific findings should not alienate any groups of sponsors or benefactors or the general line of political commitment.

2. Pressure will always be placed by the school to see that the

project is at least in a minimal way fulfilled. The report must be written in a way and in terms that are acceptable to the sponsoring foundation.

There is always a point at which the report is unacceptable, and this point is discovered only when a project overreaches the prevailing line of the institution in which it is located. At other stages there are always points at which people who might cause embarrassment are either not hired or are fired. At every stage it is embarrassing for the project to embarrass the administration.

3. At all points the university administration maintains a public-relations-type supervision over the operation of its projects and this supervision in the fully bureaucratic university is embodied in the University Research Center.

4. Apart from all this, even under ideal conditions, the project director must be aware of the consequences of research for the public-relations position of the university. One might go so far as to say that in the pure case he enacts public-relations functions without knowing it, and that to the extent that the pure case prevails all research is a function of public relations.

When one adds up all of the pressures, conflicts, tensions, and contradictions which are functions of bureaucratic research, one can only ask how all of this effects the quality of the "official" research report. What does it mean in concrete terms when an analyst-writer responds to the public-relations requirements of the town, the politics of the university, and the internal contradictions of the bureaucratic research organization?

The official Springdale report, "Leadership and Participation in a Changing Rural Community," [28] is available to us as a case illustration. This is to be criticized less for its viewpoint than for its lack of a focus or an organizing idea. When one has read this booklet, one is aware of having read six essays, each reflecting the interests of the given author or combination of authors. The lack of a central problem or, rather, the succession of different problems and theories introduced on an ad hoc basis mirrors the failure of any one project point of view to develop or prevail.

For lack of a consistent point of view or a problem, the report cannot present a consistent or integrated portrait of the community along several or even any single dimension of its institutional organization. From reading "Leadership and Participation" one is left with the impression that neither leadership nor participation has any rela-

---

[28] *Op. cit.* (see footnote 2 in this chapter).

tionship to the economic and political life of Springdale. The Community Club emerges as a central institution which exists largely outside the framework of other social realities as if it were conditioned only by itself and by the project's conception of the neighborhood structure of the township. When specific roles and their incumbents are mentioned, they are mentioned not to describe their structural position in the town, but only to clarify their participation in an important Community Club project, the repair of the dam. This is not the place to provide an analysis for why the project did not develop a consistent theory for leadership and participation. For present purposes it is only necessary to note that the substantive limits set by the project for itself stay well within the limits of what the community and the university administrative officials expected. No one need be offended because everyone's feelings have been taken into account in advance. In short the report achieves such a level of blandness and neutrality that after reading it any reader can go on as if nothing had happened to him. Nothing is said sharply enough to give anyone in the community a pretext for complaining to the university administration, and those who are dissatisfied because the report does not make any points do not complain because there is nothing to complain against.

One might speculate that the absence of a central problem, the absence of a central theory, and even the absence of the sense of the social structure of the community may be due to the inability of the project leaders to see and pose issues sharply in order to avoid offending significant members of the community.

The Ethos of Research

From the foregoing discussion it is apparent that there are at least three different criteria by which the fundamental values in research can be evaluated:

1. By the ethic of scientific inquiry—the pursuit of knowledge for the sake of knowledge regardless of its consequences.
2. By the ethic of bureaucratic inquiry which we have already outlined.
3. And by the ethic of Christian human relations—for the sake of helping or at least not hurting others.

Every organizational structure imposes its own set of ethics on the individuals who work in it. This is largely because ethics have largely come to be work rules. Knowing that bureaucratic research is here to stay means also that bureaucratic ethics are here to stay, and that, furthermore, they will be elaborated in formal codes as part of the bureaucratic rules. All current trends in bureaucratic research point in the direction of ethical and professional codes which try to specify codes of research conduct that will be consistent with the exigencies of the bureaucratic method of research.

Much of the current concern with ethics in the social sciences is simply a working out of an attempt to resolve some of the contradictions between individual responsibility and corporate group responsibility. The general trend is toward statements of viable rules for specifying the canons of individuals working in a bureaucratic setting. Actually this is not a new problem. It is the same problem that has been confronted by business and industry and government for the past two hundred years, since the beginning of the bureaucratic trend in all phases of life. These trends are only now beginning to emerge in the research process itself because research itself has come to occupy a unique position with a halo of its own, no matter how far behind the times it may actually be.

However, the ethic of independent and disinterested research with regard only for the creation of new theories and the discovery of new facts is much older than the modern bureaucratic ethic. At some point almost everyone is willing to accept the ancient Greek ideal of personal integrity, especially after an individual scholar produces valuable and useful results.

Even in modern times the advocates of bureaucratic research ethics are themselves at some point perfectly willing to accept the findings of individuals whose work was conducted in violation of the bureaucratic ethics, so that we assume that some value is still placed on independent research.

It is our opinion that the basic conflict in research ethics is not only a conflict of values but also a conflict in the very structure of the research enterprise. Therefore, if bureaucratically organized research is necessary and if it is the esteemed form for carrying out research activity, it appears that the conflict between the two ethics is a permanent part of the research scene which will never be resolved by any further explication of ethics. It would be dangerous for the freedom of inquiry if the formalized ethics of bureaucracy prevailed or predominated in all research. At the same time it does not seem likely that bureaucratic research will disappear just because a few individual scholars dislike its methods and results. Therefore, pluralistic, conflicting research ethics are likely to exist so long as adherents to both types of research exist and so long as individuals have the spontaneity and the insight to see an unanticipated problem, to pursue a new insight or hypothesis that contravenes the formal design and expectations of whole series of administrators, sponsors, officials, respondents, politicians, and seekers for prospects for grants from foundations who are presold in another direction.

Fundamentally, then, the problem is not one of ethics, but of what type or method of social research is most likely to be productive.

Large-scale bureaucratic research has the advantage of being able to mobilize vast funds and large numbers of researchers in relatively narrow problem areas. It is weak in allowing the unplanned, unplannable, unanticipated, and unpredictable operation of insight, curiosity, creative hypothesis formulation, pursuit of incongruous and inconvenient facts—all of which may challenge the validity of received theory or evoke the possibility of a new theory.

Only the individual scholar working alone—even in the midst of a bureaucratic setting—has the possibility to raise himself above the routine and mechanics of research. If, when, and under what circumstances this happens is not predictable in advance.

Bureaucratic constraints make it all but impossible for the individual to follow the insights he otherwise would because such constraints are central to the plans and obligations that are the heart of large-scale organization.

As a result large-scale research organizations are most effective at gathering and processing data along the lines of sharply defined hypotheses which have standardized variables, dimensions, and methods of analysis.

The work of the individual scholar, no matter where he is located, and no matter how he is financed, organized, constrained, or aided, is perhaps the sole source of creativity. The successful placing of limitations on individual scholarship under the guise of "ethics," work rules, institutional responsibility, or higher considerations forces a society to live off the intellectual capital of its independent thinkers.

Notes on Contributors

Howard S. Becker is research associate at the Institute for the Study of Human Problems, Stanford University. He is the author of *Outsiders: Studies in the Sociology of Deviance* and co-author of *Boys in White: Student Culture in Medical School.*

Joseph Bensman is associate professor of sociology at the City College of New York, and co-author of *Mass, Class and Bureaucracy* and *Small Town in Mass Society.*

Stanley Diamond is associate professor of anthropology and associate in the East African Program at the Maxwell Graduate School of Syracuse University. He is author of *The Search for the Primitive,* editor of *Culture and History: Essays in Honor of Paul Radin,* and a frequent contributor to *Africa To-Day.*

E. Franklin Frazier was professor of sociology at Howard University. Among his works are *The Negro Family in the United States, The Negro in the United States,* and *Race and Culture Contacts in the Modern World.*

Art Gallaher, Jr., is associate professor in the Department of Anthropology and in the Center for the Study of Developmental Change, University of Kentucky. He is author of *Plainville Fifteen Years Later.*

Everett C. Hughes is now professor of sociology at Brandeis University. Among his works are *Men and Their Work, Boys in White* (co-author), and *French Canada in Transition.*

Morris S. Schwartz is professor and chairman in the Department of Sociology at Brandeis University. He has conducted extensive research in mental health and illness. Among his other studies in this field is his latest, *Social Approaches to Mental Patient Care.*

John R. Seeley is now a professor of sociology at Brandeis University. He is the co-author of *Community Chest* and *Crestwood Heights.*

Maurice R. Stein is associate professor of sociology at Brandeis University, author of *The Eclipse of Community,* and co-editor of *Sociology on Trial* and *Identity and Anxiety.*

351

Arthur J. Vidich is associate professor of sociology and anthropology at the Graduate Faculty, New School for Social Research, co-editor of *Sociology on Trial* and *Identity and Anxiety,* and co-author of *Small Town in Mass Society.*

William F. Whyte is professor of sociology at the School of Industrial and Labor Relations, Cornell University. Among his many studies are *Human Relations in the Restaurant, Money and Motivation,* and *Street Corner Society.*

Kurt H. Wolff, professor of sociology at Brandeis University, studied in Germany, Italy, and the United States. He has published extensively in the fields of sociology of knowledge and the philosophy of sociology. He has edited and translated Simmel and Durkheim.

Index

353

Revised January, 1970

hARpER ⚡ τORChbOOKS

American Studies: General

HENRY ADAMS Degradation of the Democratic Dogma. ‡ *Introduction by Charles Hirschfeld.* TB/1450

LOUIS D. BRANDEIS: Other People's Money, *and How the Bankers Use It. Ed. with Intro, by Richard M. Abrams* TB/3081

HENRY STEELE COMMAGER, Ed.: The Struggle for Racial Equality TB/1300

CARL N. DEGLER: Out of Our Past: *The Forces that Shaped Modern America* CN/2

CARL N. DEGLER, Ed.: Pivotal Interpretations of American History
Vol. I TB/1240; Vol. II TB/1241

LAWRENCE H. FUCHS, Ed.: American Ethnic Politics TB/1368

ROBERT L. HEILBRONER: The Limits of American Capitalism TB/1305

JOHN HIGHAM, Ed.: The Reconstruction of American History TB/1068

ROBERT H. JACKSON: The Supreme Court in the American System of Government TB/1106

JOHN F. KENNEDY: A Nation of Immigrants. *Illus. Revised and Enlarged. Introduction by Robert F. Kennedy* TB/1118

RICHARD B. MORRIS: Fair Trial: *Fourteen Who Stood Accused, from Anne Hutchinson to Alger Hiss* TB/1335

GUNNAR MYRDAL: An American Dilemma: *The Negro Problem and Modern Democracy. Introduction by the Author.*
Vol. I TB/1443; Vol. II TB/1444

GILBERT OSOFSKY, Ed.: The Burden of Race: *A Documentary History of Negro-White Relations in America* TB/1405

ARNOLD ROSE: The Negro in America: *The Condensed Version of Gunnar Myrdal's* An American Dilemma. Second Edition TB/3048

JOHN E. SMITH: Themes in American Philosophy: *Purpose, Experience and Community* TB/1466

WILLIAM R. TAYLOR: Cavalier and Yankee: *The Old South and American National Character* TB/1474

American Studies: Colonial

BERNARD BAILYN: The New England Merchants in the Seventeenth Century TB/1149

ROBERT E. BROWN: Middle-Class Democracy and Revolution in Massachusetts, 1691–1780. *New Introduction by Author* TB/1413

JOSEPH CHARLES: The Origins of the American Party System TB/1049

WESLEY FRANK CRAVEN: The Colonies in Transition: 1660-1712† TB/3084

CHARLES GIBSON: Spain in America † TB/3077

CHARLES GIBSON, Ed.: The Spanish Tradition in America + HR/1351

LAWRENCE HENRY GIPSON: The Coming of the Revolution: 1763-1775. † *Illus.* TB/3007

JACK P. GREENE, Ed.: Great Britain and the American Colonies: 1606-1763. + *Introduction by the Author* HR/1477

AUBREY C. LAND, Ed.: Bases of the Plantation Society + HR/1429

PERRY MILLER: Errand Into the Wilderness TB/1139

PERRY MILLER & T. H. JOHNSON, Ed.: The Puritans: *A Sourcebook of Their Writings*
Vol. I TB/1093; Vol. II TB/1094

EDMUND S. MORGAN: The Puritan Family: *Religion and Domestic Relations in Seventeenth Century New England* TB/1227

WALLACE NOTESTEIN: The English People on the Eve of Colonization: 1603-1630. † *Illus.* TB/3006

LOUIS B. WRIGHT: The Cultural Life of the American Colonies: 1607-1763. † *Illus.* TB/3005

YVES F. ZOLTVANY, Ed.: The French Tradition in America + HR/1425

American Studies: The Revolution to 1860

JOHN R. ALDEN: The American Revolution: 1775-1783. † *Illus.* TB/3011

RAY A. BILLINGTON: The Far Western Frontier: 1830-1860. † *Illus.* TB/3012

STUART BRUCHEY: The Roots of American Economic Growth, 1607-1861: *An Essay in Social Causation. New Introduction by the Author.* TB/1350

NOBLE E. CUNNINGHAM, JR., Ed.: The Early Republic, 1789-1828 + HR/1394

GEORGE DANGERFIELD: The Awakening of American Nationalism, 1815-1828. † *Illus.* TB/3061

† The New American Nation Series, edited by Henry Steele Commager and Richard B. Morris.
‡ American Perspectives series, edited by Bernard Wishy and William E. Leuchtenburg.
α History of Europe series, edited by J. H. Plumb.
§ The Library of Religion and Culture, edited by Benjamin Nelson.
∥ Researches in the Social, Cultural, and Behavioral Sciences, edited by Benjamin Nelson.
Σ Harper Modern Science Series, edited by James A. Newman.
° Not for sale in Canada.
+ Documentary History of the United States series, edited by Richard B. Morris.
# Documentary History of Western Civilization series, edited by Eugene C. Black and Leonard W. Levy.
Λ The Economic History of the United States series, edited by Henry David et al.
¶ European Perspectives series, edited by Eugene C. Black.
** Contemporary Essays series, edited by Leonard W. Levy.
* The Stratum Series, edited by John Hale.

CLEMENT EATON: The Freedom-of-Thought Struggle in the Old South. *Revised and Enlarged. Illus.* TB/1150

CLEMENT EATON: The Growth of Southern Civilization, 1790-1860. † *Illus.* TB/3040

ROBERT H. FERRELL, Ed.: Foundations of American Diplomacy, 1775-1872 + HR/1393

LOUIS FILLER: The Crusade against Slavery: 1830-1860. † *Illus.* TB/3029

WILLIM W. FREEHLING: Prelude to Civil War: *The Nullification Controversy in South Carolina, 1816-1836* TB/1359

PAUL W. GATES: The Farmer's Age: *Agriculture, 1815-1860* ∆ TB/1398

THOMAS JEFFERSON: Notes on the State of Virginia. ‡ *Edited by Thomas P. Abernethy* TB/3052

FORREST MCDONALD, Ed.: Confederation and Constitution, 1781-1789 + HR/1396

JOHN C. MILLER: The Federalist Era: 1789-1801. † *Illus.* TB/3027

RICHARD B. MORRIS: The American Revolution Reconsidered TB/1363

CURTIS P. NETTELS: The Emergence of a National Economy, 1775-1815 ∆ TB/1438

DOUGLASS C. NORTH & ROBERT PAUL THOMAS, Eds.: *The Growth of the American Economy ot 1860* + HR/1352

R. B. NYE: The Cultural Life of the New Nation: 1776-1830. † *Illus.* TB/3026

GILBERT OSOFSKY, Ed.: Puttin' On Ole Massa: *The Slave Narratives of Henry Bibb, William Wells Brown, and Solomon Northup* ‡ TB/1432

JAMES PARTON: The Presidency of Andrew Jackson. *From Volume III of the Life of Andrew Jackson. Ed. with Intro. by Robert V. Remini* TB/3080

FRANCIS S. PHILBRICK: The Rise of the West, 1754-1830. † *Illus.* TB/3067

MARSHALL SMELSER: The Democratic Republic, 1801-1815 † TB/1406

JACK M. SOSIN, Ed.: The Opening of the West + HR/1424

GEORGE ROGERS TAYLOR: The Transportation Revolution, 1815-1860 ∆ TB/1347

A. F. TYLER: Freedom's Ferment: *Phases of American Social History from the Revolution to the Outbreak of the Civil War. Illus.* TB/1074

GLYNDON G. VAN DEUSEN: The Jacksonian Era: 1828-1848. † *Illus.* TB/3028

LOUIS B. WRIGHT: Culture on the Moving Frontier TB/1053

American Studies: The Civil War to 1900

W. R. BROCK: An American Crisis: *Congress and Reconstruction, 1865-67* ° TB/1283

T. C. COCHRAN & WILLIAM MILLER: The Age of Enterprise: *A Social History of Industrial America* TB/1054

W. A. DUNNING: Reconstruction, Political and Economic: 1865-1877 TB/1073

HAROLD U. FAULKNER: Politics, Reform and Expansion: 1890-1900. † *Illus.* TB/3020

GEORGE M. FREDRICKSON: The Inner Civil War: *Northern Intellectuals and the Crisis of the Union* TB/1358

JOHN A. GARRATY: The New Commonwealth, 1877-1890 † TB/1410

JOHN A. GARRATY, Ed.: The Transformation of American Society, 1870-1890 + HR/1395

HELEN HUNT JACKSON: A Century of Dishonor: *The Early Crusade for Indian Reform.* † *Edited by Andrew F. Rolle* TB/3063

WILLIAM G. MCLOUGHLIN, Ed.: The American Evangelicals, 1800-1900: An Anthology ‡ TB/1382

JAMES S. PIKE: The Prostrate State: *South Carolina under Negro Government.* ‡ *Intro. by Robert F. Durden* TB/3085

FRED A. SHANNON: The Farmer's Last Frontier: *Agriculture, 1860-1897* TB/1348

VERNON LANE WHARTON: The Negro in Mississippi, 1865-1890 TB/1178

American Studies: The Twentieth Century

RICHARD M. ABRAMS, Ed.: The Issues of the Populist and Progressive Eras, 1892-1912 + HR/1428

RAY STANNARD BAKER: Following the Color Line: *American Negro Citizenship in Progressive Era.* ‡ *Edited by Dewey W. Grantham, Jr. Illus.* TB/3053

RANDOLPH S. BOURNE: War and the Intellectuals: *Collected Essays, 1915-1919.* ‡ *Edited by Carl Resek* TB/3043

A. RUSSELL BUCHANAN: The United States and World War II. † *Illus.*
Vol. I TB/3044; Vol. II TB/3045

THOMAS C. COCHRAN: The American Business System: *A Historical Perspective, 1900-1955* TB/1080

FOSTER RHEA DULLES: America's Rise to World Power: 1898-1954. † *Illus.* TB/3021

HAROLD U. FAULKNER: The Decline of Laissez Faire, 1897-1917 TB/1397

JOHN D. HICKS: Republican Ascendancy: 1921-1933. † *Illus.* TB/3041

WILLIAM E. LEUCHTENBURG: Franklin D. Roosevelt and the New Deal: 1932-1940. † *Illus.* TB/3025

WILLIAM E. LEUCHTENBURG, Ed.: The New Deal: *A Documentary History* + HR/1354

ARTHUR S. LINK: Woodrow Wilson and the Progressive Era: 1910-1917. † *Illus.* TB/3023

BROADUS MITCHELL: Depression Decade: *From New Era through New Deal, 1929-1941* ∆ TB/1439

GEORGE E. MOWRY: The Era of Theodore Roosevelt and the Birth of Modern America: 1900-1912. † *Illus.* TB/3022

GEORGE SOULE: Prosperity Decade: *From War to Depression, 1917-1929* ∆ TB/1349

TWELVE SOUTHERNERS: I'll Take My Stand: *The South and the Agrarian Tradition. Intro. by Louis D. Rubin, Jr.; Biographical Essays by Virginia Rock* TB/1072

Art, Art History, Aesthetics

ERWIN PANOFSKY: Renaissance and Renascences in Western Art. *Illus.* TB/1447

ERWIN PANOFSKY: Studies in Iconology: *Humanistic Themes in the Art of the Renaissance. 180 illus.* TB/1077

OTTO VON SIMSON: The Gothic Cathedral: *Origins of Gothic Architecture and the Medieval Concept of Order. 58 illus.* TB/2018

HEINRICH ZIMMER: Myths and Symbols in Indian Art and Civilization. *70 illus.* TB/2005

Asian Studies

WOLFGANG FRANKE: China and the West: *The Cultural Encounter, 13th to 20th Centuries. Trans. by R. A. Wilson* TB/1326

L. CARRINGTON GOODRICH: A Short History of the Chinese People. *Illus.* TB/3015

2

Economics & Economic History

C. E. BLACK: The Dynamics of Modernization: *A Study in Comparative History*   TB/1321
GILBERT BURCK & EDITOR OF *Fortune:* The Computer Age: *And its Potential for Management*   TB/1179
SHEPARD B. CLOUGH, THOMAS MOODIE & CAROL MOODIE, Eds.: Economic History of Europe: *Twentieth Century* #   HR/1388
THOMAS C. COCHRAN: The American Business System: *A Historical Perspective, 1900-1955*   TB/1180
HAROLD U. FAULKNER: The Decline of Laissez Faire, 1897-1917 △   TB/1397
PAUL W. GATES: The Farmer's Age: *Agriculture, 1815-1860* △   TB/1398
WILLIAM GREENLEAF, Ed.: American Economic Development Since 1860 +   HR/1353
ROBERT L. HEILBRONER: The Future as History: *The Historic Currents of Our Time and the Direction in Which They Are Taking America*   TB/1386
ROBERT L. HEILBRONER: The Great Ascent: *The Struggle for Economic Development in Our Time*   TB/3030
DAVID S. LANDES: Bankers and Pashas: *International Finance and Economic Imperialism in Egypt. New Preface by the Author*   TB/1412
ROBERT LATOUCHE: The Birth of Western Economy: *Economic Aspects of the Dark Ages*   TB/1290
W. ARTHUR LEWIS: The Principles of Economic Planning. *New Introduction by the Author°*   TB/1436
ROBERT GREEN MC CLOSKEY: American Conservatism in the Age of Enterprise   TB/1137
WILLIAM MILLER, Ed.: Men in Business: *Essays on the Historical Role of the Entrepreneur*   TB/1081
HERBERT A. SIMON: The Shape of Automation: *For Men and Management*   TB/1245

Historiography and History of Ideas

J. BRONOWSKI & BRUCE MAZLISH: The Western Intellectual Tradition: *From Leonardo to Hegel*   TB/3001
WILHELM DILTHEY: Pattern and Meaning in History: *Thoughts on History and Society.° Edited with an Intro. by H. P. Rickman*   TB/1075
J. H. HEXTER: More's Utopia: *The Biography of an Idea. Epilogue by the Author*   TB/1195
H. STUART HUGHES: History as Art and as Science: *Twin Vistas on the Past*   TB/1207
ARTHUR O. LOVEJOY: The Great Chain of Being: *A Study of the History of an Idea*   TB/1009
RICHARD H. POPKIN: The History of Scepticism from Erasmus to Descartes. *Revised Edition*   TB/1391
MASSIMO SALVADORI, Ed.: Modern Socialism #   HR/1374
BRUNO SNELL: The Discovery of the Mind: *The Greek Origins of European Thought*   TB/1018

History: General

HANS KOHN: The Age of Nationalism: *The First Era of Global History*   TB/1380
BERNARD LEWIS: The Arabs in History   TB/1029
BERNARD LEWIS: The Middle East and the West °   TB/1274

History: Ancient

A. ANDREWS: The Greek Tyrants   TB/1103

THEODOR H. GASTER: Thespis: *Ritual Myth and Drama in the Ancient Near East*   TB/1281
MICHAEL GRANT: Ancient History °   TB/1190

History: Medieval

NORMAN COHN: The Pursuit of the Millennium: *Revolutionary Messianism in Medieval and Reformation Europe*   TB/1037
F. L. GANSHOF: Feudalism   TB/1058
F. L. GANSHOF: The Middle Ages: *A History of International Relations. Translated by Rémy Hall*   TB/1411
ROBERT LATOUCHE: The Birth of Western Economy: *Economic Aspects of the Dark Ages* °   TB/1290
HENRY CHARLES LEA: The Inquisition of the Middle Ages. || *Introduction by Walter Ullmann*   TB/1456

History: Renaissance & Reformation

JACOB BURCKHARDT: The Civilization of the Renaissance in Italy. *Introduction by Benjamin Nelson and Charles Trinkaus. Illus.*   Vol. I TB/40; Vol. II TB/41
JOHN CALVIN & JACOPO SADOLETO: A Reformation Debate. *Edited by John C. Olin*   TB/1239
FEDERICO CHABOD: Machiavelli and the Renaissance   TB/1193
THOMAS CROMWELL: Thomas Cromwell: *Selected Letters on Church and Commonwealth, 1523-1540. ¶ Ed. with an Intro. by Arthur J. Slavin*   TB/1462
FRANCESCO GUICCIARDINI: History of Florence. *Translated with an Introduction and Notes by Mario Domandi*   TB/1470
WERNER L. GUNDERSHEIMER, Ed.: French Humanism, 1470-1600. * Illus.   TB/1473
HANS J. HILLERBRAND, Ed., The Protestant Reformation #   HR/1342
JOHAN HUIZINGA: Erasmus and the Age of Reformation. *Illus.*   TB/19
JOEL HURSTFIELD: The Elizabethan Nation   TB/1312
JOEL HURSTFIELD, Ed.: The Reformation Crisis   TB/1267
PAUL OSKAR KRISTELLER: Renaissance Thought: *The Classic, Scholastic, and Humanist Strains*   TB/1048
PAUL OSKAR KRISTELLER: Renaissance Thought II: *Papers on Humanism and the Arts*   TB/1163
PAUL O. KRISTELLER & PHILIP P. WIENER, Eds.: Renaissance Essays   TB/1392
DAVID LITTLE: Religion, Order and Law: *A Study in Pre-Revolutionary England. § Preface by R. Bellah*   TB/1418
NICCOLO MACHIAVELLI: History of Florence and of the Affairs of Italy: *From the Earliest Times to the Death of Lorenzo the Magnificent. Introduction by Felix Gilbert*   TB/1027
ALFRED VON MARTIN: Sociology of the Renaissance. ° *Introduction by W. K. Ferguson*   TB/1099
GARRETT MATTINGLY et al.: Renaissance Profiles. *Edited by J. H. Plumb*   TB/1162
J. H. PARRY: The Establishment of the European Hegemony: 1415-1715: *Trade and Exploration in the Age of the Renaissance*   TB/1045
PAOLO ROSSI: Philosophy, Technology, and the Arts, in the Early Modern Era 1400-1700. || *Edited by Benjamin Nelson. Translated by Salvator Attanasio*   TB/1458
R. H. TAWNEY: The Agrarian Problem in the Sixteenth Century. *Intro. by Lawrence Stone*   TB/1315

H. R. TREVOR-ROPER: The European Witch-craze of the Sixteenth and Seventeenth Centuries and Other Essays ° TB/1416
VESPASIANO: Rennaissance Princes, Popes, and XVth Century: The Vespasiano Memoirs. Introduction by Myron P. Gilmore. Illus. TB/1111

History: Modern European

MAX BELOFF: The Age of Absolutism, 1660-1815 TB/1062
D. W. BROGAN: The Development of Modern France ° Vol. I: From the Fall of the Empire to the Dreyfus Affair TB/1184 Vol. II: The Shadow of War, World War I, Between the Two Wars TB/1185
ALAN BULLOCK: Hitler, A Study in Tyranny. ° Revised Edition. Illus. TB/1123
JOHANN GOTTLIEB FICHTE: Addresses to the German Nation. Ed. with Intro. by George A. Kelly ¶ TB/1366
ALBERT GOODWIN: The French Revolution TB/1064
H. STUART HUGHES: The Obstructed Path: French Social Thought in the Years of Desperation TB/1451
JOHAN HUIZINGA: Dutch Civilization in the 17th Century and Other Essays TB/1453
JOHN MCMANNERS: European History, 1789-1914: Men, Machines and Freedom TB/1419
FRANZ NEUMANN: Behemoth: The Structure and Practice of National Socialism, 1933-1944 TB/1289
DAVID OGG: Europe of the Ancien Régime, 1715-1783 ° a TB/1271
ALBERT SOREL: Europe Under the Old Regime. Translated by Francis H. Herrick TB/1121
A. J. P. TAYLOR: From Napoleon to Lenin: Historical Essays ° TB/1268
A. J. P. TAYLOR: The Habsburg Monarchy, 1809-1918: A History of the Austrian Empire and Austria-Hungary ° TB/1187
J. M. THOMPSON: European History, 1494-1789 TB/1431
H. R. TREVOR-ROPER: Historical Essays TB/1269

Literature & Literary Criticism

JACQUES BARZUN: The House of Intellect TB/1051
W. J. BATE: From Classic to Romantic: Premises of Taste in Eighteenth Century England TB/1036
VAN WYCK BROOKS: Van Wyck Brooks: The Early Years: A Selection from his Works, 1908-1921 Ed. with Intro. by Claire Sprague TB/3082
RICHMOND LATTIMORE, Translator: The Odyssey of Homer TB/1389

Philosophy

HENRI BERGSON: Time and Free Will: An Essay on the Immediate Data of Consciousness ° TB/1021
H. J. BLACKHAM: Six Existentialist Thinkers: Kierkegaard, Nietzsche, Jaspers, Marcel, Heidegger, Sartre ° TB/1002
J. M. BOCHENSKI: The Methods of Contemporary Thought. Trans by Peter Caws TB/1377
CRANE BRINTON: Nietzsche. Preface, Bibliography, and Epilogue by the Author TB/1197
ERNST CASSIRER: Rousseau, Kant and Goethe. Intro by Peter Gay TB/1092
WILFRID DESAN: The Tragic Finale: An Essay on the Philosophy of Jean-Paul Sartre TB/1030

MARVIN FARBER: The Aims of Phenomenology: The Motives, Methods, and Impact of Husserl's Thought TB/1291
PAUL FRIEDLANDER: Plato: An Introduction TB/2017
MICHAEL GELVEN: A Commentary on Heidegger's "Being and Time" TB/1464
G. W. F. HEGEL: On Art, Religion Philosophy: Introductory Lectures to the Realm of Absolute Spirit. || Edited with an Introduction by J. Glenn Gray TB/1463
G. W. F. HEGEL: Phenomenology of Mind. ° || Introduction by eGorge Lichtheim TB/1303
MARTIN HEIDEGGER: Discourse on Thinking. Translated with a Preface by John M. Anderson and E. Hans Freund. Introduction by John M. Anderson TB/1459
F. H. HEINEMANN: Existentialism and the Modern Predicament TB/28
WERER HEISENBERG: Physics and Philosophy: The Revolution in Modern Science. Intro. by F. S. C. Northrop TB/549
EDMUND HUSSERL: Phenomenology and the Crisis of Philosophy. § Translated with an Introduction by Quentin Lauer TB/1170
IMMANUEL KANT: Groundwork of the Metaphysic of Morals. Translated and Analyzed by H. J. Paton TB/1159
IMMANUEL KANT: Lectures on Ethics. § Introduction by Lewis White Beck TB/105
QUENTIN LAUER: Phenomenology: Its Genesis and Prospect. Preface by Aron Gurwitsch TB/1169
GEORGE A. MORGAN: What Nietzsche Means TB/1198
H. J. PATON: The Categorical Imperative: A Study in Kant's Moral Philosophy TB/1325
MICHAEL POLANYI: Personal Knowledge: Towards a Post-Critical Philosophy TB/1158
WILLARD VAN ORMAN QUINE: Elementary Logic Revised Edition TB/577
JOHN E. SMITH: Themes in American Philosophy: Purpose, Experience and Community TB/1466
MORTON WHITE: Foundations of Historical Knowledge TB/1440
WILHELM WINDELBAND: A History of Philosophy Vol. I: Greek, Roman, Medieval TB/38 Vol. II: Renaissance, Enlightenment, Modern TB/39
LUDWIG WITTGENSTEIN: The Blue and Brown Books ° TB/1211
LUDWIG WITTGENSTEIN: Notebooks, 1914-1916 TB/1441

Political Science & Government

C. E. BLACK: The Dynamics of Modernization: A Study in Comparative History TB/1321
KENNETH E. BOULDING: Conflict and Defense: A General Theory of Action TB/3024
DENIS W. BROGAN: Politics in America. New Introduction by the Author TB/1469
LEWIS COSER, Ed.: Political Sociology TB/1293
ROBERT A. DAHL & CHARLES E. LINDBLOM: Politics, Economics, and Welfare: Planning and Politico-Economic Systems Resolved into Basic Social Processes TB/3037
ROY C. MACRIDIS, Ed.: Political Parties: Contemporary Trends and Ideas ** TB/1322
ROBERT GREEN MC CLOSKEY: American Conservatism in the Age of Enterprise, 1865-1910 TB/1137
JOHN B. MORRALL: Political Thought in Medieval Times TB/1076

KARL R. POPPER: The Open Society and Its
Enemies *Vol. I: The Spell of Plato* TB/1101
*Vol. II: The High Tide of Prophecy: Hegel,
Marx, and the Aftermath* TB/1102
HENRI DE SAINT-SIMON: Social Organization, The
Science of Man, and Other Writings. ||
*Edited and Translated with an Introduction
by Felix Markham* TB/1152
JOSEPH A. SCHUMPETER: Capitalism, Socialism
and Democracy TB/3008

Psychology

LUDWIG BINSWANGER: Being-in-the-World: *Se-
lected Papers. || Trans. with Intro. by Jacob
Needleman* TB/1365
HADLEY CANTRIL: The Invasion from Mars: *A
Study in the Psychology of Panic* || TB/1282
MIRCEA ELIADE: Cosmos and History: *The Myth
of the Eternal Return* § TB/2050
MIRCEA ELIADE: Myth and Reality TB/1369
MIRCEA ELIADE: Myths, Dreams and Mysteries:
*The Encounter Between Contemporary Faiths
and Archaic Realities* § TB/1320
MIRCEA ELIADE: Rites and Symbols of Initiation:
The Mysteries of Birth and Rebirth §
TB/1236
SIGMUND FREUD: On Creativity and the Uncon-
scious: *Papers on the Psychology of Art,
Literature, Love, Religion.* § *Intro. by Ben-
jamin Nelson* TB/45
J. GLENN GRAY: The Warriors: *Reflections on
Men in Battle. Introduction by Hannah
Arendt* TB/1294
WILLIAM JAMES: Psychology: *The Briefer
Course. Edited with an Intro. by Gordon
Allport* TB/1034
KARL MENNINGER, M.D.: Theory of Psychoan-
alytic Technique TB/1144

Religion: Ancient and Classical, Biblical and
Judaic Traditions

MARTIN BUBER: Eclipse of God: *Studies in the
Relation Between Religion and Philosophy*
TB/12
MARTIN BUBER: Hasidism and Modern Man.
Edited and Translated by Maurice Friedman
TB/839
MARTIN BUBER: The Knowledge of Man. *Edited
with an Introduction by Maurice Friedman.
Translated by Maurice Friedman and Ronald
Gregor Smith* TB/135
MARTIN BUBER: Moses. *The Revelation and the
Covenant* TB/837
MARTIN BUBER: The Origin and Meaning of
Hasidism. *Edited and Translated by Maurice
Friedman* TB/835
MARTIN BUBER: The Prophetic Faith TB/73
MARTIN BUBER: Two Types of Faith: *Interpene-
tration of Judaism and Christianity* ° TB/75
MALCOLM L. DIAMOND: Martin Buber: *Jewish
Existentialist* TB/840
M. S. ENSLIN: Christian Beginnings TB/5
M. S. ENSLIN: The Literature of the Christian
Movement TB/6
HENRI FRANKFORT: Ancient Egyptian Religion:
An Interpretation TB/77
ABRAHAM HESCHEL: God in Search of Man: *A
Philosophy of Judaism* TB/807
ABRAHAM HESCHEL: Man Is not Alone: *A Phil-
osophy of Religion* TB/838
T. J. MEEK: Hebrew Origins TB/69
H. J. ROSE: Religion in Greece and Rome
TB/55

Religion: Early Christianity Through
Reformation

ANSELM OF CANTERBURY: Truth, Freedom, and
Evil: *Three Philosophical Dialogues. Edited
and Translated by Jasper Hopkins and Her-
bert Richardson* TB/317
JOHANNES ECKHART: Meister Eckhart: *A Mod-
ern Translation by R. Blakney* TB/8
EDGAR J. GOODSPEED: A Life of Jesus TB/1
ROBERT M. GRANT: Gnosticism and Early Christi-
anity TB/136
ARTHUR DARBY NOCK: St. Paul ° TB/104
GORDON RUPP: Luther's Progress to the Diet of
Worms ° TB/120

Religion: The Protestant Tradition

KARL BARTH: Church Dogmatics: *A Selection.
Intro. by H. Gollwitzer. Ed. by G. W. Bro-
miley* TB/95
KARL BARTH: Dogmatics in Outline TB/56
KARL BARTH: The Word of God and the Word
of Man TB/13
WILLIAM R. HUTCHISON, Ed.: American Prot-
estant Thought: *The Liberal Era* ‡ TB/1385
SOREN KIERKEGAARD: Edifying Discourses. *Edited
with an Intro. by Paul Holmer* TB/32
SOREN KIERKEGAARD: The Journals of Kierke-
gaard. ° *Edited with an Intro. by Alexander
Dru* TB/52
SOREN KIERKEGAARD: The Point of View for My
Work as an Author: *A Report to History.* §
Preface by Benjamin Nelson TB/88
SOREN KIERKEGAARD: The Present Age. § *Trans-
lated and edited by Alexander Dru. Intro-
duction by Walter Kaufmann* TB/94
SOREN KIERKEGAARD: Purity of Heart. *Trans. by
Douglas Steere* TB/4
SOREN KIERKEGAARD: Repetition: *An Essay in
Experimental Psychology* § TB/117
WOLFHART PANNENBERG, et al.: History and Her-
meneutic. *Volume 4 of* Journal for Theol-
ogy and the Church, *edited by Robert W.
Funk and Gerhard Ebeling* TB/254
F. SCHLEIERMACHER: The Christian Faith. *Intro-
duction by Richard R. Niebuhr.*
Vol. I TB/108; Vol. II TB/109
F. SCHLEIERMACHER: On Religion: *Speeches to
Its Cultured Despisers. Intro. by Rudolf
Otto* TB/36
PAUL TILLICH: Dynamics of Faith TB/42
PAUL TILLICH: Morality and Beyond TB/142

Religion: The Roman & Eastern Christian
Traditions

A. ROBERT CAPONIGRI, Ed.: Modern Catholic
Thinkers II: *The Church and the Political
Order* TB/307
G. P. FEDOTOV: The Russian Religious Mind:
*Kievan Christianity, the tenth to the thir-
teenth Centuries* TB/370
GABRIEL MARCEL: Being and Having: *An Ex-
istential Diary. Introduction by James Col-
lins* TB/310
GABRIEL MARCEL: Homo Viator: *Introduction to
a Metaphysic of Hope* TB/397

Religion: Oriental Religions

TOR ANDRAE: Mohammed: *The Man and His
Faith* § TB/62
EDWARD CONZE: Buddhism: *Its Essence and De-
velopment.* ° *Foreword by Arthur Waley*
TB/58

EDWARD CONZE et al, Editors: Buddhist Texts through the Ages TB/113
H. G. CREEL: Confucius and the Chinese Way TB/63
FRANKLIN EDGERTON, Trans. & Ed.: The Bhagavad Gita TB/115
SWAMI NIKHILANANDA, Trans. & Ed.: The Upanishads TB/114

Religion: Philosophy, Culture, and Society

NICOLAS BERDYAEV: The Destiny of Man TB/61
RUDOLF BULTMANN: History and Eschatology: The Presence of Eternity ° TB/91
LUDWIG FEUERBACH: The Essence of Christianity. § Introduction by Karl Barth. Foreword by H. Richard Niebuhr TB/11
ADOLF HARNACK: What Is Christianity? § Introduction by Rudolf Bultmann TB/17
KYLE HASELDEN: The Racial Problem in Christian Perspective TB/116
IMMANUEL KANT: Religion Within the Limits of Reason Alone. § Introduction by Theodore M. Greene and John Silber TB/67
H. RICHARD NIERUHR: Christ and Culture TB/3
H. RICHARD NIEBUHR: The Kingdom of God in America TB/49

Science and Mathematics

W. E. LE GROS CLARK: The Antecedents of Man: An Introduction to the Evolution of the Primates. ° Illus. TB/559
ROBERT E. COKER: Streams, Lakes, Ponds. Illus. TB/586
ROBERT E. COKER: This Great and Wide Sea: An Introduction to Oceanography and Marine Biology. Illus. TB/551
F. K. HARE: The Restless Atmosphere TB/560
WILLARD VAN ORMAN QUINE: Mathematical Logic TB/558

Science: Philosophy

J. M. BOCHENSKI: The Methods of Contemporary Thought. Tr. by Peter Caws TB/1377
J. BRONOWSKI: Science and Human Values. Revised and Enlarged. Illus. TB/505
WERNER HEISENBERG: Physics and Philosophy: The Revolution in Modern Science. Introduction by F. S. C. Northrop TB/549
KARL R. POPPER: Conjectures and Refutations: The Growth of Scientific Knowledge TB/1376
KARL R. POPPER: The Logic of Scientific Discovery TB/576

Sociology and Anthropology

REINHARD BENDIX: Work and Authority in Industry: Ideologies of Management in the Course of Industrialization TB/3035
BERNARD BERELSON, Ed., The Behavioral Sciences Today TB/1127
KENNETH B. CLARK: Dark Ghetto: Dilemmas of Social Power. Foreword by Gunnar Myrdal TB/1317

KENNETH CLARK & JEANNETTE HOPKINS: A Relevant War Against Poverty: A Study of Community Action Programs and Observable Social Change TB/1480
LEWIS COSER, Ed.: Political Sociology TB/1293
ALLISON DAVIS & JOHN DOLLARD: Children of Bondage: The Personality Development of Negro Youih in the Urban South || TB/3049
ST. CLAIR DRAKE & HORACE R. CAYTON: Black Metropolis: A Study of Negro Life in a Northern City. Introduction by Everett C. Hughes. Tables, maps, charts, and graphs Vol. I TB/1086; Vol. II TB/1087
PETER F. DRUCKER: The New Society: The Anatomy of Industrial Order TB/1082
CHARLES Y. GLOCK & RODNEY STARK: Christian Beliefs and Anti-Semitism. Introduction by the Authors TB/1454
ALVIN W. GOULDNER: The Hellenic World TB/1479
R. M. MACIVER: Social Causation TB/1153
GARY T. MARX: Protest and Prejudice: A Study of Belief in the Black Community TB/1435
ROBERT K. MERTON, LEONARD BROOM, LEONARD S. COTTRELL, JR., Editors: Sociology Today: Problems and Prospects || Vol. I TB/1173; Vol. II TB/1174
GILBERT OSOFSKY, Ed.: The Burden of Race: A Documentary History of Negro-White Relations in America TB/1405
GILBERT OSOFSKY: Harlem: The Making of a Ghetto: Negro New York 1890-1930 TB/1381
TALCOTT PARSONS & EDWARD A. SHILS, Editors: Toward a General Theory of Action: Theoretical Foundations for the Social Sciences TB/1083
PHILIP RIEFF: The Triumph of the Therapeutic: Uses of Faith After Freud TB/1360
JOHN H. ROHRER & MUNRO S. EDMONSON, Eds.: The Eighth Generation Grows Up: Cultures and Personalities of New Orleans Negroes || TB/3050
ARNOLD ROSE: The Negro in America: The Condensed Version of Gunnar Myrdal's An American Dilemma. Second Edition TB/3048
GEORGE ROSEN: Madness in Society: Chapters in the Historical Sociology of Mental Illness. || Preface by Benjamin Nelson TB/1337
PHILIP SELZNICK: TVA and the Grass Roots: A Study in the Sociology of Formal Organization TB/1230
PITIRIM A. SOROKIN: Contemporary Sociological Theories: Through the First Quarter of the Twentieth Century TB/3046
MAURICE R. STEIN: The Eclipse of Community: An Interpretation of American Studies TB/1128
FERDINAND TONNIES: Community and Society: Gemeinschaft und Gesellschaft. Translated and Edited by Charles P. Loomis TB/1116
W. LLOYD WARNER and Associates: Democracy in Jonesville: A Study in Quality and Inequality || TB/1129
W. LLOYD WARNER: Social Class in America: The Evaluation of Status TB/1013
FLORIAN ZNANIECKI: The Social Role of the Man of Knowledge. Introduction by Lewis A. Coser TB/1372